CHANGING PERSPECTIVES

CHANGING PERSPECTIVES

Black-Jewish Relations in Houston during the Civil Rights Era

by
Allison E. Schottenstein

Number 5 in the Texas Local Series

University of North Texas Press
Denton, Texas

10 9 8 7 6 5 4 3 2 1

Permissions:
University of North Texas Press
1155 Union Circle #311336
Denton, TX 76203-5017

The paper used in this book meets the minimum requirements of the
American National Standard for Permanence of Paper for Printed
Library Materials, z39.48.1984. Binding materials have been chosen
for durability.

Library of Congress Cataloging-in-Publication Data

Schottenstein, Allison E., 1986– author.
  Changing perspectives : Black-Jewish relations in Houston during the
civil rights era / Allison E. Schottenstein. | "Book is a history of the rela-
tions between the Jewish and Black communities in Houston starting in
the 1920s and leading up to the present"—Provided by publisher.
  Denton, Texas : University of North Texas Press, [2021]
      pages cm
  Includes bibliographical references and index.
  ISBN-13 978-1-57441-829-3 (hardback)
  ISBN-13 978-1-57441-837-8 (ebook)
  1. LCSH: African Americans—Texas—Houston—Relations with
Jews—History. 2. Antisemitism—Texas—Houston—History.
3. Blacks—Segregation—Texas—Houston—History. 4 Segregation—
Texas—Houston—Religious aspects—Judaism. 5. African Americans—
Civil rights—Texas—Houston—History. 6. Houston (Tex.)—Ethnic relations.

  E184.36.A34 S36 2021
  305.8009764/1411–dc23
                  2020048226

*Changing Perspectives: Black-Jewish Relations in Houston during the Civil
Rights Era* is Number 5 in the Texas Local Series

The electronic edition of this book was made possible by the support of the
Vick Family Foundation. Typeset by vPrompt eServices.

Dedicated to:

**The Three G's
(Gary, Gail, and Garland)**

Contents

Conclusion: "Together or Apart?"   283

List of Abbreviations

ACLU	American Civil Liberties Union
ADL	Anti-Defamation League
AJA	American Jewish Archives, Cincinnati, Ohio
AJC	American Jewish Committee
AJCongress	American Jewish Congress
AJHS	American Jewish Historical Society, New York, New York
AVC	American Veterans Committee
CBI	Congregation Beth Israel, Houston, Texas
CCAR	Central Conference of American Rabbis
CGS	Citizens for Good Schools
CIO	Congress of Industrial Organizations
DBCAH	Dolph Briscoe Center for American Jewish History
GHMA	Greater Houston Ministerial Association
HHA	Houston Housing Authority
HISD	Houston Independent School District
HMRC	Houston Metropolitan Research Center
HPL	Houston Public Library
HUC	Hebrew Union College, Cincinnati, Ohio
JCC	Jewish Community Center
JCRC	Jewish Community Relations Council, Houston, Texas
JH-V	*Jewish Herald-Voice*
NAACP	National Association for the Advancement of Colored People
NASA	National Aeronautics and Space Administration
NCJW	National Council of Jewish Women
NYPL	New York Public Library
PLO	Palestine Liberation Organization
PUSH	People for the Upgrading of Schools in Houston
SC	Special Collections
SCRBC	Schomburg Center for Research in Black Culture
SNCC	Student Nonviolent Coordinating Committee
TSU	Texas Southern University, Houston, Texas
UHL	University of Houston Libraries

Acknowledgments

T his journey has taught me that no one is an island, and it does take a village to create a book. Undoubtedly, this book would not have been attainable without the help of my parents. If I could split up the letters of Ph.D., I would give them each a letter to place beside their names. My parents relocated to Austin to live and support me through my Ph.D. My mom listened to me endlessly, gave me advice, and was my valued sounding board. My dad who helped me sift through the mounds of historical documents I accumulated. I would also like to acknowledge Garland Pohl; without her unfailing help, this book would lack the soul of Houston. She opened doors, arranged interviews, and always added her two cents. Though he will never know, I would like to thank my dog, Yuri, who sat with me for hours and always barked at me when he thought I needed to go to bed. To my dearest siblings, Sam and Dr. Melinda Schottenstein, for always loving me.

I want to extend my special appreciation to the Department of History at the University of Texas at Austin for their numerous fellowships as well as to my graduate advisors, Dr. Robert Abzug, Dr. Jacqueline Jones, Dr. Tatjana Lichtenstein, Dr. Bryan Stone, as well as scholars Dr. Leonard Moore, Dr. John Mckiernan-González, Dr. Gila Naveh, and Dr. Leonard Rogoff. Additionally, my mentor, Dr. Meredith Singelton, served as my light at the end of the tunnel.

I would like to offer my appreciation for the following generous fellowships: Texas State Historical Association's John H. Jenkins Research Fellowship in Texas History, The Briscoe Center for American History's Graduate Fellowship, Tulane's New Orleans Center for the Gulf South Global South Fellowship, The Schusterman Center Grant, the American Jewish Historical Society's Ruth B. Fein Prize, The American Jewish Archives' Rabbi Theodore S. Levy Tribute Fellowship and The Bernard

and Audre Rapport Fellowship, the Southern Jewish Historical
Society Grant, and the East Texas Historical Association Ottis
Lock Research Grant. I would also like to thank Phi Kappa Phi
for the Love of Learning Award. Lastly, I appreciate the Texas
Jewish Historical Society for their support.

There have been many archives that have been instrumental in my work. The *Jewish Herald-Voice* staff was an
invaluable resource. I cannot even imagine writing this book
without the bound copies of their newspapers. Vicki and
Jeanne Samuels, you were terrific! I also thank the American
Jewish Archives, especially my mentors Dr. Gary Zola and
Dr. Dana Herman, as well as Kevin Proffitt, Elisa Ho, Nathan
Tallman, and Joe Webber. Dr. Zola and Dr. Herman have both
watched me become a scholar from college through graduate
school and truly motivated me to get my Ph.D. My appreciation goes to the Briscoe Center for American History for their
great support through my entire graduate career especially:
Dr. Don Carleton, Margaret Schlankey, Brenda Gunn, Roy
Hinojosa, John Wheat, Sarah Clearly, Catherine Best, Katherine Kenfick, and Stephanie Malmros. I offer a special thanks
to my friend, Pattricus Fortiori, at the Mickey Leland Center
on Hunger, Poverty, and World Peace at Texas Southern
University, whose passion for Mickey Leland was genuinely
infectious. I want to thank Dr. Tomkin-Walsh, Nelda, Ryder,
Stacey, and Greg, who were extremely helpful and kind at
the University of Houston. Also, the Oral History of Houston
Project staff, Natalie Garza, Aimee L. Bachari, and Dr. Pratt
and Gary Chaffee and Joyce Thomas at Texas Southern
University helped me find information in the Texas Southern
University Archives and the Barbara Jordan collection. I am
grateful to the Houston synagogue archivists: Judy Weidman
Maxine Reingold, Jean Lerner, Hillary Kamin, and Monica
Woolf. I would also like to thank Rivka Schiller and Ralph
Elder for their research assistance. I am very much appre-
ciative of the individuals who helped me connect with the
Houston Holocaust community: Monica Rose, Carol Manley,

Ellen Trachtenberg, Mary Lee Weebeck, and Tobi Cooper. I am appreciative of the Evelyn Rubenstein Jewish Community Center of Houston, especially Morgan Steinberg and Marilyn Hassid.

I would also like to thank the following places for providing me access to their archives: Houston Metropolitan Research Center, Fondren Library and the Woodson Research Center at Rice University, the LBJ archives at the University of Texas at Austin, the Menil Collection, Rothko Chapel Archives, Houston Hillel, Museum of Fine Arts Archives, The Institute of Texas Cultures, University of Texas at San Antonio Archives, Harris County Archives, Center for Jewish History including the American Jewish Historical Society and Yivo, the Goldring/Woldenberg Institute, the African American Library at the Gregory School, the Wisconsin Historical Society, ADL Archives in New York, the library at the Jewish Theological Seminary, the King Center, the MARBL at Emory University, Robert D. Farber Archives at Brandeis University, Klau Library at Hebrew Union College, the Tarlton Law Library of Special Collections, New York Public Library's Dorot Division, Harvard University's Judaica Division at Widener Library, AJC Archives, Publication Information Office Legal Services of the Houston Independent School District, BBYO Lonestar region for Houston, Archdiocese of Galveston-Houston, Rosenberg Library, Texas Woman's University, and Texas Collection at Baylor. I am also thankful for the patience of archivist Joyce Lee of *Houston Chronicle*. Most importantly, I want to thank the Houston Jewish Community in general, but most especially all those individuals who allowed me to interview them. I am also indebted to the University of North Texas Press, especially Director Ron Chrisman, who believed in my book, and my editor Karen DeVinney. My friend Dr. Valerie Martinez was my partner in crime all throughout graduate school. "Lastly, the love of my life, Jonathan Levey, for always supporting me and loving me through thick and thin." Thank you all for your inspiration, which binds this work together.

Introduction

Two images—both in black and white, one in Germany and one in the United States—exemplify the passing of time. These two images were featured in the Houston Holocaust Museum exhibit the *Importance of Racist Ideologies: Jim Crow and the Nuremberg Laws*, which opened on August 11, 2011. Both demonstrate, that while time and location may have changed, the prejudiced mentality had not. The first image, as seen through the eyes of a faceless woman, reflects the simplicity of terror and the enforced discrimination Jews encountered at the hands of the government. This Nazi-imposed boycott of all Jewish-owned businesses was a precursor to the enforcement of anti-Jewish legislation. The second image, almost thirty years later in Houston, features a group of TSU students sitting at Weingarten's lunch counter. The young woman stares into the distance, full of hope, patiently waiting for a simple cup of coffee, a sign of equality. She is powerless, forced to follow a dictated set of government-sanctioned rules based solely on the color of her skin. The viewer who walks through the exhibit would see such images and begin to contemplate the parallels between these two systems of injustice. Both women are deprived of their rights

Image from the exhibition *Racist Ideologies: Jim Crow and the Nuremberg Laws*. LEFT: A woman reads a boycott sign posted in the window of a Jewish-owned department store, April 1, 1933. Holocaust Museum Houston, Houston, Texas. Courtesy of The United States Holocaust Memorial Museum. RIGHT: "Sit-in Weingarten cafeteria," March 5, 1960. Students at a sit-in at Weingarten counter, Houston, Texas. Photo by Dan Hardy. RGD0006-0131, Houston Post Photographs, Houston Metropolitan Research Center, Houston Public Library. Owen Johnson_HP/©Houston Chronicle. Used with permission.

because of their identity. By using these photographic images, the exhibition weaved together a story to show the dangers of racist ideologies.

The museum asks the viewer what were the parallels between southern Blacks under Jim Crow laws and German Jews under the Nuremberg Laws? The Houston Holocaust Museum makes the statement that there were "remarkable similarities" between both sets of laws. The Houston exhibition displayed how Nazi Germany and the American South marginalized and disenfranchised both groups and subjected them to violence. Visitors see the correlations between the two experiences and how prejudice disrupted and controlled the daily lives of both groups. What the exhibit does not explain is an uneasy fact that remains silenced which is that Weingarten's lunch counter was Jewish owned and there were Jewish owned segregated stores. Instead, of coming to terms with this complexity, the viewer unbeknownst to their city's Civil Rights history is left with an incomplete picture. As a result, the viewer is left wondering what happened in Houston? This missing piece is a result of a public narrative that has grown in the American Jewish community of the duality between Black and Jewish histories of persecution.[1]

Historian Peter Novick's *The Holocaust in American Life* claimed that the Holocaust did not figure centrally in the Jewish mindset until the latter half of the twentieth century. The Holocaust was not a universal experience that shaped every action of all American Jews. The comparison between the two groups diminishes the struggle that each group faced and the decisions they made. This marginalizes the African American experience, as it conflates it with Nazism. One cannot make assumptions of the experiences of Blacks and Jews, as each community has a different story to tell. History is not about broad generalities but about specific times and events and how it shapes a particular group and their interactions with one another.[2]

What was the nature of the relationship between Houston Jews and African Americans during segregation, and was the Holocaust an impetus for action, as the museum leads one to believe? Houston's Jewish leaders were well aware of the Nuremberg Laws that placed Jews under similar restrictions and degradation, yet Jewish memories of European anti-Jewish legislation were not enough to compel local Jews to engage actively and publicly in promoting African American rights in the 1950s and 1960s. It did not mean the Holocaust did not occasionally inspire this call, such as with European Jews who understood discrimination. In modern Jewish spaces, one sees this theme of shared experience emerge among both the northern and southern Jewish outlook on reflections of civil rights and how this connection influenced the Jewish response to the civil rights movement. The Holocaust did have a profound impact on northern Jews, like German-born Joachim Prinz, as well as on Martin Luther King Jr., who saw segregation as history repeating itself. King was disappointed that Jews in Montgomery did not publicly acknowledge the similarities between what was happening to Blacks in America and what had happened to Jews under the Third Reich.

Despite King's criticism, scholars have shown that southern Jews who did support the cause did so in more subtle ways, including sympathetic treatment of the African American plight in the sermons of southern rabbis or the involvement of southern business leaders in the desegregation process. But the reality was that Houston Jews feared making bold statements for the cause of civil rights and did not become automatically active as a result of the Holocaust; instead, Houston Jewish leadership was more concerned with what was going on inside and outside their community at any given time. They were interested in making the best decision for the community as a unit.[3]

This modern appropriation of the past pushes us to learn about what actually happened during this time and not make grand brushstrokes. How did Houston Jewish leaders react toward segregation in their city during the civil rights movement? How much were Jewish communal leaders inspired by their past and their own religious values to help their Black counterparts who also faced oppression? Did Black leaders see a connection between the groups, or did Blacks see Jews as a safer white ally because they understood the concept of discrimination rather than because their histories were paralleled?

The story of segregated Houston from a Jewish perspective reveals the decisions and actions Houston Jewish leaders took over a time that extended beyond the traditional civil rights timeline. It provides a glimpse into the nuances, thinking processes, and challenges Houston Jewish leaders and, later, African American politicians faced in contemplating their roles in the civil rights movement. The city is central not only for providing another perspective of Houston Jewish leadership during the civil rights period but also for deepening our understanding of southern Jews, who historians have often portrayed as ambivalent to the plight of African Americans. Houston provides a key snapshot of how the relationship between Blacks and Jews evolved through the civil rights period. Segregation may have forced the Houston Jews and African Americans to live in separate spheres, but their experiences remained inter-twined in both positive and negative ways.

The Houston Jewish leadership's perception and treatment of African Americans shaped this Jewish community's responses to the Black community. In particular, Jewish leaders led the Jewish community and guided them on civil rights issues. Beginning in the 1940s and continuing into the early 1960s, Houston Jewish leaders at times were conflicted between their liberalism and support of Black communities' fight for equality and the pressure to conform to segregation. After the passage of the Civil Rights Act of 1964, Houston Jewish leaders became more sympathetic to the problems African Americans faced. They began to see similar-ities between the African American struggle and their own battle against the conservative school board of the Houston Independent School District (HISD) in the mid-1960s through 1970. As the city became more international and multicultural in the 1970s, iden-tity politics began to concern both Jews and African Americans. The divide, between Black and white, Christian and Jewish, was beginning to crumble as more diverse religious, cultural, and ethnic groups arrived and made Houston their home.

At the same time, the Houston Jewish leadership had concerns over the rising anti-Zionism in the city as a direct result of the Arab oil embargo and the Arab-Israeli conflict. While the city and white middle-class residents were prospering, the African American population continued to suffer economic and political disadvantages. Jews and Blacks formed coalitions from the late 1960s through the 1980s in the South and particularly in Houston as a direct result of redistricting. This paved the way for minorities to support minority political candidates, garner-ing power they never had before. In the 1970s and 1980s, the South experienced a rise in Jewish political leaders as well as Jews voting for Black candidates. As a result, coalitions formed between both groups. One example was the Atlanta Black-Jewish Coalition founded in 1982, which originally centered on voting rights and then evolved into a dialogue group.[4]

At first, the Jewish leadership of Houston was insular, discussing matters of civil rights mostly within a Jewish context and, at times, in intergroup events. In the 1970s, however, Jewish and civil rights issues shifted from an internal leadership focus to an external one. The relationship between the two groups did not emerge from one particular moment—such a notion would be unrealistic. Prior to the 1970s and 1980s, Jewish interest in civil rights centered on moral, religious, and, most of all, liberal causes, such as interfaith dialogues, multiethnic events like Brotherhood Week, synagogue and organizational activities, and political participation in the Harris County Democrats, the liberal branch of the local Democratic Party. For the most part, these activities created only a surface-level connection and did not promote or sustain formal relations between the two communities. When rabbis preached the need for civil rights, African Americans were absent from the discussions—an almost silent partner. African Americans, even in Houston, were aware of Jewish interest in the cause, but it was not yet a mutual cause between both groups.

Houston Jewish leadership grappled with their liberal principles and their desire to acculturate in a closed society in which African Americans endured the confinement of segregation. It was not until the 1980s and the political rise of Mickey Leland and his support of the State of Israel through the creation of the Mickey Leland Kibbutzim Internship Foundation that an equitable relationship between Black and Jewish leaders evolved. The creation of the internship went beyond the monthly interfaith meetings or the occasional community Passover Seder. It also went beyond politically liberal Jews voting for a Black political leader. The Mickey Leland Kibbutzim Internship became an ongoing relationship between Houston's Jewish and African American communities.

This book was created using archival materials, personal oral histories, documentaries, and other historical materials to shed light on Houston during the civil rights period. What emerged was a more enriched picture of Houston formed from the varied perspectives of individuals, including Jews, Christians, and African Americans. In Houston, as in other southern cities, the term "leader" expanded to mean more than just the rabbi and included an extensive range of Jews and corporate Jewish bodies. At one time or another, synagogue leaders, communal organizations, activists, school board members, businesspeople, and the *JH-V* spoke on behalf of Houston's Jews. In the 1970s, additional voices advocated for the Jews, including Black politicians like Leland and state senator Barbara Jordan. Their involvement illustrated for the first time that leadership was not limited to the insular Jewish community but could expand to include unexpected voices. The willingness of Black politicians to speak on behalf of Houston Jewry showed how the political atmosphere had changed Houston for the better.

Because the influence of African American and Jewish political leaders in Houston did not exist in a vacuum, this book also includes, but is not restricted to, the voices of business leaders, activists, Christian clergy, and politicians. While these other voices are important to understanding the nuanced relationship between Houston Jews and the broader community, this narrative recognizes that the rabbis were a significant presence in Houston because religious affiliation was at the center of Jewish life. Being Jewish in Houston was not as simple as it was in the Northeast, where the Jewish population was larger. As one native Houstonian expressed: "[In New York], people do not have to belong to synagogues to be Jewish because their whole neighborhood is Jewish. In Houston, by contrast, there are only certain clearly delineated places where Jews are not afraid to 'stick out' and be Jewish ... in the synagogue or temple."[5]

Houston residents in the 1970s declared the synagogue "the central institution of Jewish life next to the home, and 'you should belong, whether or not you belong to anything else.'"[6] In Houston, synagogue affiliation was very high. According to a study by Alfred Hero, in the early 1960s, 90 percent of southern Jews belonged to a synagogue. Houston Jews participated in synagogue-sponsored activities—like intergroup relations during Brotherhood Week—and looked to the rabbi as their leader. The rabbis were the voice of their congregations, and collectively Houston rabbis were the voice of the Houston Jews. What the city's rabbis said in public, good or bad, affected the entire community, in large part because religion had a greater presence than it did in the North. In the South, religion dictated the cultural landscape and enabled clergy to have tremendous influence over their communities. In the case of the Jews, the community valued their rabbi more if he could transcend the boundaries between Jews and Christians.[7]

Additionally, the newspaper the *JH-V* became the mouthpiece of Houston's Jews over the course of the twentieth century.

LEFT to RIGHT: Rabbi Robert Kahn, Rabbi Moshe Cahana, Rabbi H. Silver, Rabbi Hyman Schachtel, Rabbi William Malev, and Rabbi Raphael Schwartzman at Westwood Country Club for Israel Bonds. Houston, Texas. November 12, 1960. RGD0006N-1960-5472-2, Houston Post Photographs, Houston Metropolitan Research Center, Houston Public Library. Ed Valdez_HP/©Houston Chronicle. Used with permission.

Gary Tobin and Sharon Sassler have explored the relationship between the editors and reporters of local Jewish newspapers and Jewish organizational life. This connection was especially true in small Jewish communities where, even though the Jewish newspaper may have been a separate entity, it still functioned as a reflection and voice of the community. In the case of the *JH-V*, editor David White was an active synagogue member. He reported not only on Jewish matters throughout the country and the world, but he directed Houston's Jews on how they could participate in civil rights. White became the moral compass for the community when he wrote editorials informing them, in the same manner as a rabbi, to consider their ethical obligation as Jews and Americans. In many ways, the *JH-V* became the community's diary.[8]

This history also highlights the pivotal role of Houston Jewish shop owners and tradesmen who, like southern Jews in general, relied on the white consumer for their livelihood. A focus on commerce is especially important not only because the bulk of local Jews made their living through commerce, both in Black neighborhoods and downtown, but also because Houston's economy guided the decisions of the white Gentile power structure. Their position in the business world and their interactions with white business leaders made their voices particularly important to the Jewish community. What is more, their financial influence positioned them to serve as representatives to both white and Black Gentiles.[9]

This book also focuses on the Jewish members of the Houston public school board who became educational activists and reflected the central role of public school education in the lives of Jewish children. Houston Jewish school board members, rabbis, school activists, and organizations sought to remove prayer and religious assemblies from the public schools, as well as the policy of segregation. Up until the 1970s, the majority of Jewish adolescents in Houston went to public school for middle and high school. A Jewish day school existed at Congregation Beth Yeshurun in Riverside Terrace that covered kindergarten through fifth grade, but it was not well attended. There were, at times, only seven children in a grade.[10]

Some wealthy Jews sent their children to private Episcopal schools, but for the most part, most Jews opted for the public schools. When the Jews primarily lived in Riverside Terrace, they went to San Jacinto High School, commonly known as "San Jewcinto." After the move to Meyerland in the early 1960s, they attended Bellaire High School, known as the "Jew Jungle."[11] Because Houston's Jews were highly integrated into the public school system, the voice of the Jews on public school boards influenced the everyday lives of the city's Jews.

Jewish organizations also represented and responded for the collective community because a substantial number of Jews belonged to Jewish organizations. Those who did not join still attended the events the organizations sponsored. In a 1976 demographic survey, the Jewish Community Council of Metropolitan Houston went so far as to define a member of the Houston Jewish community as someone who is part of Jewish organizations. As sociologist Harold Weisberg claimed, "To be a Jew is to belong to a [Jewish] organization." The organizations brought structure to the community, and Houston Jews left it to organizational leaders to be the voice of the community.[12]

Historically, southern Jews did not speak out as a collective on the cause of African American rights, and Houston's Jews were no different. Historian Hasia Diner, in reference to the pattern of southern passivity, asks the rhetorical question: "What would have happened if a majority of southern Jews—not just a handful of rabbis and women activists—had applied the words of Isaiah and Micah to the racial situation in which they lived and from which they benefited?"[13] During the civil rights movement, northern and southern Reform rabbis invoked prophets Micah and Isaiah to promote Judaism as a religion of ethics and social responsibility. The Jews could fulfill the message of the prophets and their biblical obligation to create a more ethical society by promoting fairness for African Americans. Yet despite their greater affiliation with synagogues, southern Jews did not often heed the call of the prophets.[14]

In her analysis of the South, Diner ponders: "Would violence against Jews really have escalated had more Southern Jews been outspoken?"[15] While Diner does not answer this question, my research on Houston suggests that there would have been repercussions to the Jews in Houston and elsewhere in the South, whether they were outspoken or remained silent. Being outspoken would have disturbed the structure of segregation and caused Jews to be seen as agitators. After all, segregation was an ideology ingrained within the minds of generations of southerners. African Americans first endured enslavement, and even though the Thirteenth Amendment of 1865 guaranteed them freedom from their servitude and the Fourteenth Amendment of 1868 solidified their rights as citizens, they did not gain freedom from oppression. Reconstruction did not end African American disenfranchisement but only acted as a Band-Aid over an open wound. Indeed, as historian Eric Foner says, it was an "era of noble dreams."[16] In 1896, *Plessy v. Ferguson* would demolish any chances African Americans would have to gain true citizenship.

The Jews of Houston, like their southern counterparts, followed the Jewish legal precept *dina d'malkhuta dina* ("the law of the state decides"), which pushed them to accept segregation laws.[17] Because of the rigidity of segregation, the small number of Jews in Houston chose not to fight back in the name of Micah and Isaiah. This was not surprising considering that the Jews living in Houston only accounted for 1.8 percent of the city's total population in the 1960s, as opposed to African Americans, who accounted for 22.9 percent.[18]

Houston's Jewish leaders, especially the rabbis, became the community's voice of ethical responsibility in white Gentile society, though they too had their own limitations and need for self-preservation. Whether the Jews always approved of who represented them was not as important to them as maintaining the status quo. As Rabbi Charles Martinband of Hattiesburg claimed, southern Jews held the belief, "Come weal, come woe, my status is quo."[19] In fact, the individual opinions and sentiments of Houston Jews remained unclear, like many of their southern counterparts, because they knew that publicly discussing controversial issues—like civil rights—opened them up to discrimination and violence. Unfortunately, after the rise of anti-Semitism, the temple bombings between 1957 and 1958 sparked legitimate fear.

Elaine Maas has observed that Houston's Jews tended to be "timid" and "afraid to be Jews." They did not want to be "'vocal' exponents of 'social justice.'" Rather, they tended "to meld with the community at large" instead of standing out.[20] For this reason, the discussion of the Houston civil rights movement is primarily through the perspective of Houston Jewish leaders and, later, Black politicians. We should not, however, assume that, even though the Jews of Houston were not outspoken individually, the civil rights movement was inconsequential to them. While relying on Jewish leaders to speak for the collective was customary in the South where Jews were a small minority, in the case of Houston, a few individuals became de facto leaders, regardless of their intentions, because they bravely took a stand. In the case of the president of the B'nai B'rith Women District #7, Mallory Robinson remembered feeling like a "freak" for her desire to make a difference through her civil rights work in Houston and throughout the South. Part of the problem, Robinson argued, was that Jews, like other minorities, were conscious of public opinion: "We don't wash our dirty linen in public."[21] When a person aired their metaphorical laundry in public, it became a reflection of all Houston's Jews.

Through the voices of Jewish leadership and others, this story reveals the way Houston Jewish leaders adapted a philosophy that was both liberal and focused on acculturation, one that coincided with the trend of American Jews after World War II. Liberalism enabled Jews to express their interest in inclusivity, pluralism, and equal rights without having to sacrifice their position in white Gentile society. Acculturation meant Jews could adapt to the environment of the majority culture while still retaining their own culture.

But sometimes the latter meant they sacrificed their liberal values to garner acceptance from white Gentiles. Mark Dollinger has argued that American Jews straddled the line between liberalism and acculturation, often having to choose between the two. Many times, the need for acculturation took precedent. Houston Jewish leaders made the community aware of the African American plight while also encouraging them to acculturate. This strategy revealed a degree of flexibility the Jews of Houston had in the 1950s and 1960s. If they continued to conform to the mores of white Gentile society, they could preserve their economic access and first-class citizenship, a privilege not as easily afforded to Black residents. And while Houston Jews may have adapted to their segregated city, they did not forsake their religion by fully assimilating. Because they still wanted to maintain both their American identity and their religion, they knew that full acceptance, especially in 1950s and 1960s, was not attainable.[22]

This story reveals the way, early on, the Jews aligned themselves with white non-Jews by creating the public perception that they accepted segregation laws. Jews knew the consequences of rejecting segregation not only precluded them from advancement in white society but also opened them to possible threats of violence. Therefore, the perception of their acceptance helped them to keep peace between themselves and white society. Still, this particular alignment with the white majority did not equalize them in all ways. They still were not Christian. Thus, Jews had to determine who they were and where they belonged. Were they a subgroup of the white majority? Or were they full members of the white majority who just happened to be of a different faith? The direction they chose determined the treatment they received from their white Gentile peers.[23]

In a 1955 sermon at the Emanu El synagogue, Rabbi Robert Kahn asked his congregants the following questions: "Who are we? What are we? Are Jews a race? A nationality? A religion? The answer to this question is not a simple one."[24] This challenge was a central problem for Houston Jews because they knew white Gentiles tolerated them as a group if they presented themselves as white Americans of Jewish faith. When Jews associated themselves as Americans first, they were proving that they were not much different from their white Gentile peers;

they simply belonged to a different place of worship. Ultimately, Jewish history reminded them of the travesty of persecution, but it also warned them of the need to adapt.[25]

Southern Jewish historian Eli Evans explained that southern Jews defined themselves as white to avoid comparison with African Americans, who they saw as "the lightning rod for prejudice."[26] Some have called African Americans the quintessential "American Jews" because they occupied the same position as the Jews in Eastern Europe.[27] Having shared such an experience, Houston Jewish leaders pondered whether to help African Americans, who they knew needed help, or to protect the status and progress of their own community. This book reveals the way this conflict continued throughout the history of Houston Jewry from the 1930s through the mid-1960s until politician Mickey Leland showed the advantage of cultivating a relationship between the two communities.

In the end, Houston's Jews and African Americans may have shared similarities in the discrimination they faced from white Gentile society, which ought to have inextricably linked them, but the stifling nature of segregation separated them and prevented them from presenting a coordinated front. Publicly, out of concern for their already tenuous position in the city, Houston Jewish leaders created a protectionist strategy to save them and the local community from the same social position as African Americans. This created a distance between the two groups, particularly from the 1930s through the mid-1960s. During this time, Jews interacted with African Americans only at intergroup and business events. Black newspapers such as *The Informer* discussed interactions between Blacks and Jews, but not to the extent of the *JH-V*. As Norton Shaw, a teen editor for the *JH-V*, wrote in 1963, "We boast of our liberal views ... Yet as the negro race struggles to free itself of chains wrought from universal ignorance, we Jews claim that we are righteous because we believe in the negro cause. But we do not act."[28]

Examining Jewish interactions with African Americans in Houston on the local level provides a more dynamic understanding of what happened between these two groups in the South during the long civil rights period. From a Jewish perspective, American Jewish historian Jonathan Sarna argued that Jewish history was not uniform and that local Jewish histories throughout the United States, with all their similarities and differences, made up the larger American Jewish experience. Historian Carol Kammen revealed that the merit of focusing on local history was not to write a national history on a smaller scale but to consider what she called "the special rhythms and themes" found when examining a specific place. In the case of looking at both communities, scholars have written its history from a limited perspective—when they came together and when they fell apart throughout different periods of time. This narrow national lens has caused a disparity in our understanding of the dynamics between these two populations: Black and Jewish.[29]

The lack of scholarship on Houston Jews has led historians to overlook the importance of Houston for the development of a coalition between Blacks and Jews. In his anthology of the Jews in America, Marc Lee Raphael claimed there has yet to be a published history of the Jews of Houston.[30] This means their role in the long civil rights movement is absent from southern Jewish history. Without knowing Houston's history, Congressman Mickey Leland's creation of the Mickey Leland Kibbutzim Internship, which initiated an alliance between these two communities, remains in obscurity. This Houston story challenges the notion that an alliance did not exist as well as shows the importance that African American leaders have played within Jewish history during the long civil rights era. It demonstrates how the Houston alliance was initiated on African American terms, not singularly Jewish terms. Such an example from local history provides a more complex view of this iconic American pair, African Americans and Jews.

Focusing on the southern perspective also allows historians to expand the purview of Black and Jewish encounters. Historians have largely structured the historical understanding of these interactions from a northern point of view. The African American and northern Jewish bond *supposedly* first emerged out of a shared struggle against racial discrimination, economic hardship, and social restriction. Out of this desire to combat prejudice, African Americans and Jews joined together to create such organizations as the NAACP (1909) and the National Urban League (1910). Outside of these organizations, Jews and African Americans associated themselves politically with Communist and Socialist parties as well as with early civil rights activism. In the 1930s, many Jews supported the persecuted young African American men unfairly accused of rape in the Scottsboro Boys case. For their part, at the height of the Holocaust, African Americans created the Double V Campaign of 1943, which advocated "victory against Nazism abroad and racism at home."[31]

Historians have discussed these events and historical moments to prove an alliance did exist, even if temporary. For example, in the summer of 1961, two-thirds of the white Freedom Riders were Jewish, and one-third to one-half of the whites who participated in the Mississippi Freedom Summer of 1964 were young Jewish men and women from the North who traveled south. The North also housed the headquarters of Jewish organizations like the Anti-Defamation League, the American Jewish Congress, the American Jewish Committee (AJC), the National Council of Jewish Women, Hadassah, and the National Community Relations Advisory Committee, as well as centers of Jewish movements (Reform, Conservative, and Orthodox). Affiliate organizations existed in the South, but the northern branches were more vocally committed to the Black freedom movement. The idea that the northern Jews were the great contributors to the civil rights movement created a rift with the southern Jews, whom they accused of lacking initiative in the fight for social justice.[32]

Another reason why scholars have focused on the relationship between northern Jews and African Americans is because Jewish immigrants from Eastern Europe mainly settled in urban areas in the North. Therefore, there were larger Jewish populations in that part of the country. As a result, historians perpetuated the notion that relations only existed when Jews lived in larger Jewish populations and where de jure segregation did not challenge both Jews and African Americans.[33]

While these northern Jews and African Americans did not always have smooth encounters, the American public saw them as allies who actively fought together on economic and social issues due to their common bonds of ancestral claims to enslavement, persecution, and the search for a homeland. Some historians have even depicted the civil rights movement as the golden age of Jewish and Black cooperation. One prominent Jewish leader involved in the movement was Rabbi Abraham Joshua Heschel, who had a close relationship with Dr. Martin Luther King Jr. The image of Rabbi Heschel and Dr. King linked arm in arm marching in 1965 from Selma to Montgomery embodied Jewish involvement in the cause of civil rights.[34]

Recently, scholars of Black-Jewish relations have also debated the "reality" of an "alliance" between northern Jews and African Americans.[35] Clayborne Carson downplayed the impact of northern Jews when he revealed that Jews and African Americans were more consistent in their voting interests than in their civil rights actions.[36] Other scholars have argued that northern Jews romanticized their involvement in the civil rights movement. The American press even perpetuated and sensationalized this iconic relationship. Cheryl Greenberg argued that this relationship "ha[d] a presence in American public culture that 'Black-Greek relations' or 'Jewish-Presbyterian' relations generally do not. Stories about the subject enjoy[ed] wide circulation even in the non-Black, non-Jewish press."[37] Dollinger further discredited the reality of this alliance and instead called Jewish participation in the civil rights movement "warm memories." In his perspective, a united Black-Jewish alliance exists within Jewish public history as opposed to African American history. Historians like Greenberg and Dollinger overfocus on northern Jewish history and neglect the intricacies of southern Jewish experience, especially specific southern cities where populations of Jews lived.[38]

Historians have focused on the surface level of relations between southern Jews and Black southerners and largely portrayed southern Jews as uninterested in the fight for Black equality. The fear of anti-Semitism shaped their decisions, particularly the trauma of the temple bombings and ongoing harassment from white supremacists like the Ku Klux Klan. The White Citizens' Council both recruited Jews, as seen in Montgomery, Alabama, to join their organizations and threatened those who seemed too supportive of African Americans. Where southern Jews lived affected their decision whether to protest, especially in the Deep South, where Jews most feared speaking out, both in their own communities and within their cities. Because southern Jews feared that support of African Americans threatened their identity as whites, Jewish leadership did not speak out openly against the injustices Black southerners endured or join with them politically until much later, during the rise of Black political power.[39]

More recently, scholars have challenged the traditional southern Jewish narrative, arguing the existence of multiple southern Jewish experiences. The most significant work to address the complexities between Blacks and Jews during the civil rights era is Clive Webb's revisionist interpretation in *Fight against Fear*, in which he attempts to prove that scholars have underestimated southern Jewish involvement. Webb has acknowledged the extent to which a fear of anti-Semitism prevented them from acting and underscored the lack of a unified southern Jewish response. In the South, there were Jews who protested the protesters as well as Jewish female activists. Ultimately, Webb labeled the southern Jewish response as ambivalent, a view that supports the scholarly consensus that southern Jews were not prominent in the civil rights movement.[40]

One glaring oversight in the body of scholarship on southern Jews is the failure to extend the collaboration between Jews and African Americans in terms of conflicts like the Black Power movement. There are some exceptions. Scholars like Dollinger and Seth Forman have extended the history of Jews and African American interactions by examining how this time period influenced American Jewry, but they do not acknowledge in detail the southern Jewish experience post-1960s. Most studies focus primarily on the height of the civil rights movement. For example, in their survey of 120 southern Reform rabbis, Micah D.

Greenstein and Howard Greenstein failed to present a nuanced picture, focusing mainly on relevant national trends like anti-Zionism and affirmative action without showing the specific interactions in the South. What is more, the scholars generalized that the South and the North were not much different from one another in contemporary America, arguing that the differences between the two regions visible during the classic civil rights movement had since ended. In addition, they only examined New Orleans and did not push for a more expansive analysis of the South or consider the possibility that the struggle for civil rights lasted beyond 1965.[41]

A significant gap exists in the scholarship on the interconnectedness between these two communities, in large part because Jewish historians have not tackled the Jewish and African American narrative simultaneously. The subnarrative of African American history within this book illuminates the significant role Blacks played within southern Jewish history. Often when scholars discuss the Jewish perspective only, it can create the illusion of Jewish exceptionalism. These relations did not develop because the leaders of both groups cultivated a strong bond throughout the civil rights movement; rather, the relationship between Jews and African Americans was the culmination of separate actions. Though Houston's Jewish leaders may have struggled to maintain their liberalism, they still consistently spoke of civil rights. As they acquired more political power, Black political leaders promoted interactions with the Jewish community. Both leaders may not have consistently worked together, but their complementary causes over time did create a space for a Black and Jewish alliance.

Many studies on northern Jews have emphasized individual Jewish activists, often secular Jews, who *appeared* more outspoken than southern Jews when they traveled to the South or joined national Jewish organizations. In contrast, southern Jewish scholars have failed to consider fully the presence of multiple Jewish leaders during the long civil rights movement, as in the case of Houston. To fill this gap in scholarship, it is essential to highlight how the visible presence of southern leaders—both Jewish and, later, African American—as representatives of their respective communities made space in Houston for an alliance.

The existing scholarship on Houston during the civil rights movement only provides a microscopic picture of the interactions between Jews and African Americans and instead focuses on other aspects of the movement. These include an in-depth look at the school board, the role of the NAACP, desegregation, the police, and economic disparities. Some scholars have overemphasized the extent to which the decisions of the Houston economic and political elite led the city to desegregate comparatively quietly and with no wide-scale riots. Other scholars have pointed out that Houston's strict hierarchy based on skin color caused desegregation to be a slow process.[42] Most accounts have relegated the Jewish experience to stories of Jewish shopkeepers who reluctantly practiced segregation and eventually embraced desegregation.

Though many mention the Jewish flight from Riverside Terrace—a once-thriving Jewish neighborhood, now a predominantly upper-mobile Black one—to Meyerland, scholars still have not comprehensively explored how Jews and African Americans in Houston related to one another. Of the two scholars who have focused exclusively on Houston Jews, only Elaine Maas surveys relations between Jews and white Gentiles, with only a few vague references to the city's African Americans.[43] Houston's Jewish histories mirrored Houston's African American histories in only allowing the other group to make guest appearances in the text. The closest thing to an in-depth analysis of Jewish involvement in the civil rights movement is one chapter in Bryan Stone's *The Chosen Folks: Jews on the Frontiers of Texas*, in which Stone discusses the Jewish businessmen and rabbis involved in the civil rights movement. Even then, he provides only a quick glimpse of the story of Houston Jewry.[44]

In this book, I seek to show the complexities of how Houston's Jewish leaders grappled with civil rights and the way local African American politicians eventually began to see the importance of their relations. This book is less about accomplishment—or lack thereof—and more about how these two groups developed simultaneously yet separately and eventually came to share a connection through leadership.

This multidecade story concentrates on the Jewish perspective of the Houston civil rights era, with African American voices intertwined to help create a fuller picture. In an attempt to provide a well-rounded history, I have also included interviews; however, as with everything in history, there are always voices left unheard.

There are three main reasons for focusing exclusively on Jews and African Americans as opposed to other groups. First, the American Jewish community has had a deep interest in the affairs of African Americans and in seeing themselves in comparison to this group even from early times, as we have seen in such scholarship as Eric Goldstein's *Price of Whiteness* or Hasia Diner's *Almost Promised Land*. Second, in American Jewish history, white Jews have negotiated between their minority status and conforming to the majority white Protestant community. Yet they are a minority. In contrast, African Americans do not have this privilege, which places them in deep contrast with this distinct white Jewish population. Lastly, in the period leading up to and during the civil rights movement, Texas had the largest African American population in the Southwest.

This book does not include a full discussion on Mexican Americans—despite Texas having one of the largest populations in the United States. Brian D. Behnken claimed in *Fighting Their Own Battles* that the Mexican and African American populations had separate civil rights movements. They may have shared similar goals, but their experiences were different. As a result, this causes a challenge in the narrative to introduce another civil rights movement. Max Krochmal's *Blue Texas* discusses the multiethnic political alliances in support of political activism for "Democratic Coalitions" in Texas; however, his book does not lead us to believe this united Jews with Mexican Americans and African Americans. In my research, the moments of interaction between Mexican Americans and Jews were not as visible as with African Americans. There are minor encounters in the mid- to late twentieth century, but not enough to balance the abundance of African American history; however, future research is vital to determine whether there were actual relations between Mexican Americans and Houston Jews during the long civil rights era.[45]

The historiography of southern Jews, overall, portrays them as uninterested in the fight for African American equality. Some of the reasons were fear, anti-Semitism, pressure from the outside white Gentile community, and a desire to fit into white society. Whiteness played a large role in the discussion because the South constructed race as a Black-and-white binary. Scholars emphasize the way southern Jews were unlike northern Jews in their fight against segregation, with the exception of people like Dollinger, who sees both the northern and southern Jews as being more similar than history remembers. Throughout the years, scholars have attempted to show that other groups besides rabbis were involved in the fight for civil rights. Overall, the scholarship demonstrates that southern Jews were not prominent in the movement.

Houston's story fits into this larger southern Jewish narrative. At various times, the Jewish community there was more willing to have a connection with the African American community beyond mere good relations. Demonstrating that these two communities could come together over time elucidates that change can happen, even in the South.

Changing Perspectives is divided into eight distinct events that influenced Houston Jewish history. The book begins with an early history of Houston's Black and Jewish populations but primarily focuses on the 1930s through the 1980s. It builds on each event to show how time changed the responses of many Houston Jewish leaders and how, in time, African American politicians could also become the face of leadership. These events led to the development of the Mickey Leland Kibbutzim Internship for inner-city youth that would inextricably link and forge a lasting alliance between Jews and Blacks in Houston for years to come.

Prologue

Early History of African American and Jewish Communities in Houston

B ecause of the strict boundaries of segregation that divided Jews and African Americans, the two populations developed simultaneously yet separately from the nineteenth century through the 1930s. Houston originally had mixed economic classes, which included a sizable poor population. By the 1850s, a small group of wealthy white Texans—who were Christians—politically controlled the town. Houston participated in the enslavement of Africans, both before and after Texas entered the Union in 1845. In 1850, enslaved African Americans accounted for 22 percent of the Houston population, which at that point totaled 2,396. While some free African Americans did live in Houston, most faced enslavement, a fact that was a major contributor to Houston becoming a business community. The large number of enslaved African Americans made them a substantially larger group than Jews.[1]

In the 1850s, there were approximately seventeen Jews living in Houston. They originated from other places, such as Ohio, Louisiana, Jamaica, Germany, England, and Holland. The most well-known Jew came to Houston in the 1840s from Jamaica. He was a Sephardic Jew named Jacob De Cardova, and he became a Harris County alderman. White Houstonians identified Jews as white, which spared them from enslavement; thus, Jews were in a much better social and economic position than African Americans.[2]

Jews created their own center in Houston. They established the first Jewish cemetery in 1844 and, a decade later, started their first synagogue in 1854. The first Jewish place of worship in Houston was Congregation Beth Israel, an Orthodox synagogue, chartered in 1859. The synagogue transitioned from Orthodox to Classical Reform Judaism in 1908. The early Houston Jews also created the Hebrew Benevolent Association in 1855 to act as a charitable society for any Jews who were poor, ill, elderly, or in need of assistance. In 1913, members of the Jewish community founded the Jewish Welfare Association (later known as Jewish Family Services) to provide financial aid to the poor, widows, and children. The Jewish population continued to grow in the 1860s when an influx of German Jews arrived in Houston and increased the Jewish population to sixty-eight.[3]

Jews also occupied the role of merchants as they did in other parts of the South. Jews involved in businesses were not able to achieve the same economic status as white Gentiles. However, the Houston Jews were well to do.[4] The Jewish newspaper *The Occident* reported that Jews were "in a prosperous pecuniary condition."[5] By the mid-nineteenth century, twenty-six Jewish families were living in Houston, and sixteen of those families owned real estate.[6]

The African American population in Houston grew to 3,691 in 1870, while the Jewish population was only 461 in 1877. By 1880, Houston's total population was 16,513. African Americans may have been there in great numbers; however, prior to the enforcement of legal segregation in Texas, they still faced severe economic inequality. During the 1870s, 82 percent of African Americans worked in low-status jobs. Only 9.54 percent of African Americans worked as skilled laborers, and even fewer—1.68 percent—worked in white-collar jobs. Because white labor unions did not permit African Americans to join, they formed their own in the 1870s and 1880s.[7]

Houston's white-dominated neighborhoods used restrictive covenants to prevent African Americans and Jews from coming into spaces deemed white and Gentile, and these inevitably caused housing to become a major factor for both groups. Since Houston did not have residential ordinances or zoning laws to legally separate whites from African Americans and other minorities, residents utilized these restrictive covenants. After the Civil War, African Americans predominantly lived in an area called Freedmen's Town, which activist Holly Hogrobrook described as a "city within itself." As Hogrobrook recalled, "Everything was here, your first African owning anything was here." Eventually, during the Great Depression, the African Americans of Freedmen's Town had to deed their land to Italians in the Fourth Ward, causing them to lose complete control of their area. In addition to Freedmen's Town, African Americans also lived in other segregated parts of the city, which put them into limited contact with Jews and other groups.[8]

In the 1870s, African Americans lived in the Third, Fourth, and Fifth Wards, and the Fourth Ward had the largest African American population until 1910, when the population moved in greater numbers into the Third Ward. Here, African Americans lived in shotgun houses, which were narrow in shape, inexpensive, not larger than twelve to fifteen feet wide, and with limited services compared to homes in some white neighborhoods. However, these homes were not exclusively for African Americans, as poor whites lived in them as well. Early on, the Third Ward was of sentimental importance to African Americans, as it housed Emancipation Park, which commemorated Juneteenth, the celebration of freedom from enslavement in Texas. This was the only park permissible to African Americans.[9]

While the Third Ward served as a Black sphere for African Americans, in the 1870s, there were also Jewish immigrants who lived there. German Jewish immigrants, who had few housing options, began to settle in Houston and lived either in or in close proximity to the Third Ward, where they established their second congregation, Beth Israel, in 1908. While they may

have lived near African Americans, these Houston Jews were
not truly their neighbors.[10]

There were additional instances in which Jews lived in close
proximity to African Americans but without full integration.
Between the 1880s and 1920s, the Fifth Ward experienced population growth because of the Southern Pacific Railroad. Additionally, in the early half of the twentieth century, between 1907
and 1914, around ten thousand Jews from Eastern Europe immigrated through Galveston, Texas, as part of what is now known
as the Galveston Movement. Some of these immigrants settled
in Houston. The city's Jewish population thus became a mix of
German and Eastern European Jews. Many Jews also came to
Houston after Galveston experienced a devastating hurricane in
1900 that destroyed many homes and businesses there.[11]

Homes were more affordable in the Fifth Ward, allowing
poor Jews, including Russian and Polish immigrants, to live
there among Mexicans and African Americans. From 1870 to
1920, more African Americans came to the Fifth Ward, many
of them from Louisiana. This migration resulted in the Eastern
European Jews and Irish Catholics leaving the Fifth Ward and
going to live in the Sixth Ward. In 1910, Russian Jews also lived
in the Second Ward alongside African Americans, Mexicans,
Irish, and Germans. However, Nagel Street separated the whites,
including Jews, from the Latino and African American areas.
By the 1920s, the neighborhood had changed to become mostly
Mexican, at which point both the Jews and African Americans
began to leave the area.[12]

There were small pockets of Jews who lived outside the
wards. By 1917, there were five thousand Jews in Houston.
Houston Jews moved to the areas of Montrose, Westheimer,
and Hyde Park and lived predominantly with other Jews rather
than scattered, but they were never the majority in any area
where they lived. However, sometime between 1917 and 1924,
Washington Terrace opened for Jews to live in, followed by the
rest of Riverside Terrace beginning in 1924. In 1927, the city
annexed Riverside Terrace, a new suburban residential space
that permitted Jewish residents without blatant discrimination.[13]

Between 1870 and 1915, Houston developed two societies, one white and one Black, as it enforced segregation. The earliest African American school that the Texas government created was the Third Ward School in 1870, later renamed the Frederick Douglass School. The first African American high school was the Fourth Ward's Colored High School, which the Houston public school system established in 1898 and later renamed for Booker T. Washington. While the populations became mixed in the wards as more Mexican, German, Russian, and other immigrants moved into the traditionally Black wards, they all remained separated in the classroom. Ernest Equia, a Mexican American, remembered going to school with Jews. He recalled that African Americans did not attend the same schools as he and white Europeans did because the Houston public school system forced African Americans to attend their own schools.[14]

Segregation extended into all of everyday life as early as 1891, when the railroads segregated the coaches. In the 1900s, a set of segregation laws barred African Americans from entering hotels, theaters, streetcars, restaurants, swimming pools, or public restrooms, and the city did not permit them to drink from the water fountains in front of city hall. There were even segregated prisons in the nineteenth century. Because white-owned hotels in Houston prohibited African Americans, the Houston Place, established in 1915, was a hotel just for the African American elite. Its guests included entertainers, educators, and dignitaries from other cities. In the Fourth Ward, territory where they did have some control, African Americans created their own library in 1907, as there was none available to them outside of the ward. The official "colored branch" of that library did not become available until 1913, when Andrew Carnegie donated funds for the project.[15]

As segregation developed in Houston, African American migration occurred from the 1900s to the 1930s. In 1900, African Americans were 12.4 percent of the population, but by 1910, that number had grown to 23,929—over 50 percent of a total population that was 44,633. The migration continued into the 1930s and brought in tens of thousands of African Americans from rural areas of the South, especially Louisiana. This population increase made Houston stand out as having the largest influx of African Americans in all of Texas.[16]

In addition to social life, the religious sphere was important to both African Americans and Jews. In 1913, Houston Jews supported the Hebrew Immigrant Aid Society, which financially assisted newcomers to the city. By 1915, the Jewish community had four places of worship, a Workmen's Circle, three Zionist organizations, groups for Jewish men and women, three B'nai B'rith lodges, and five fraternal lodges. The synagogues followed the residential movement of the Jewish community. Religious life began to grow in and around Riverside Terrace as well, even before it became a distinct Jewish subcommunity. Congregation Beth Israel saw a future in this area, so it built a new synagogue on Hollman Avenue between Austin and La Branch Streets near Riverside Terrace. Businessman Simon Sakowitz was chairman of the Building Committee, and Joseph Finger was the architect. Members of the congregation and visitors came to the grand opening for its dedication.[17] The *Houston Chronicle* reported that "a representative number of Jews and gentiles" were at the dedication of Beth Israel on December 12, 1925.[18]

In comparison, the African American community had 116 churches by the late 1920s. These churches stood at the center of their community and served as a source of strength, activism, support, and hope. Houston African Americans also had similar social organizations that assisted the poor, such as the Married Ladies Progressive Club. This organization helped pay off church debts and did charity work in the 1920s.[19]

Politically, Houston African Americans also faced disempowerment when they voted on both the state and local level. Poll taxes, instituted in Texas in 1902, excluded African Americans from the voting process; they also harmed Mexicans and less affluent whites. The Democratic Party ruled Texas, as it did other parts of the South. Houston's African Americans were originally by and large Republicans, but their allegiance to that party declined between the late nineteenth and early twentieth centuries because they were not welcome in the party as members. In 1920, for example, a white Houstonian, H. F. MacGregor, worked to remove African Americans from the Republican Party. However, the Democratic Party also banned African Americans from voting in primaries from 1923 until the 1940s.[20]

Because of Houston's extreme segregation, African Americans created their own insular society. While Houston Jews often owned businesses throughout the city, African Americans were restricted to owning businesses in their own neighborhoods. In 1929, Houston had the tenth-most Black-owned businesses in the United States, surpassing other southern cities and even places in the North like New York City. There were even African American insurance companies, like the American Mutual Benefit Association, which William Nickerson Jr. helped start in 1909. It hired only African Americans and was completely Black-owned. While most African American women worked as domestics, Houston was also a significant player in the African American beauty industry by the 1930s. The biggest beauty school in the South, Nobia A. Franklin Beauty, located in the Fourth Ward School, was so important that African Americans came from other parts of Texas to learn beauty techniques there. Grocery stores were the highest percentage of Black businesses.[21] There was also a professional class of African American teachers, lawyers, ministers, and doctors. Yet African American professionals did not receive the same salary as whites in the same profession. For example, African American policemen were not only subordinate to the white officers but received less pay.[22]

While African Americans were making strides in their own neighborhoods, blatant segregation and discriminatory practices continued. Houston promoted the image of the "Heavenly Houston" because it boasted about having better relations between whites and African Americans than cities in other parts of the South. This "Heavenly" image overlooked the Houston Riot of 1917, a rebellion among African American soldiers of the Twenty-Fourth Infantry Regiment who marched on Houston in retaliation against a white policeman who murdered an African American serviceman. However, the cause was a rumor. Prior to the riot, there had been mounting tensions between the African American soldiers and Houston whites, as white civilians had been harassing the soldiers. The riot was particularly noteworthy because it resulted in the largest court-martial in the history of the United States; 118 African American soldiers were court-martialed.[23]

Jewish and African American newspapers became an important source of insight into both communities. Edgar Goldberg founded the first Jewish newspaper in Houston, the *Texas Jewish Herald*, in 1909. Some of the more pertinent issues Goldberg reported on were an African American lynching, the rise of the Ku Klux Klan, and the rise of Nazism. David White, who had previously worked with Goldberg, bought Goldberg's paper upon his death in 1938 and created the *JH-V*. This newspaper united the Jewish community.[24]

The Ku Klux Klan used the media against Jews and African Americans. Houston became known as "Star Klan City" as it was

"Ku Klux Klan Initiation," 1921. Several klansmen gather for a Ku Klux Klan initiation, Houston, Texas, December 8, 1921. (Photo by Hulton Archive/Getty Images).

the first city in Texas to have a Klan chapter.[25] The Klan became prominent in 1920 and was initially not against the Jewish population. However, this view changed when Billy Mayfield became editor of *Colonel Mayfield's Weekly*, a Klan paper, which was one factor that turned the Klan against the Houston Jews. Mayfield perceived Jews as being an "unasimiliable [*sic*] race."[26] He saw Jews as unwilling to integrate, as they were more interested in self-segregation and protecting their community.

Colonel Mayfield's Weekly also went after African Americans, Mexicans, and Catholics. Mayfield was also interested in how they related to each other. The newspaper further insinuated that Jews and Catholics were the force behind Blacks gaining more equality. The KKK also saw African Americans and Mexicans as a threat to Americans and America.[27] On April 1, 1922, *Colonel Mayfield's Weekly* stated that "Jew peddlers, negro truck drivers, Mexicans ... have been taking away [jobs] from good old American boys."[28] The KKK thus portrayed Jews, African Americans, and Mexicans as an economic threat to white Christian Americans.

Many Jews in return boycotted any businesses that advertised in *Colonel Mayfield's Weekly*. Some of the Jewish merchants targeted were the Sakowitzes and Zindlers. The Zindlers did not back down from the Klan's intimidation, which caused them to lose sales and *Colonel Mayfield's Weekly* to publish anti-Semitic comments and cartoons about the Zindlers. The Klan was vicious in print and violent in its actions. The Klan also went after Jewish merchants for advertising in African American newspapers.[29]

African Americans also had numerous press outlets; the most famous was the *Houston Informer*, founded in 1919. At times, the African American community used the newspaper to talk about Jews and the African American situation.[30] For example, editor Clifton Richardson wrote an editorial titled "A Lesson from the Jewish Race" that praised Jews for their determination throughout history despite mistreatment. He classified Jews as both a "Jewish Race" and "Aryans" because he regarded them as white but also as a minority. Richardson encouraged

African Americans to heed the example of Jews, not because the Jews were perfect but because they had managed to rise above their oppression. His perspective on Jews was similar to that of Booker T. Washington, who had cited Jews as an example for African Americans to learn from to overcome their plight.[31] Richardson also spoke of Jews when he encouraged African Americans to "buy black" to oppose white merchant mistreatment and to embrace "race pride." Although Jews may have been some of these boycotted merchants, he did cite Jews as a model for African Americans to follow once again: "Jews stick together ... By pooling their money ... and combining their interests, they dominate the financial and commercial world."[32] Richardson's generalization of Jews was most likely a result of African American encounters with Jewish landlords and merchants.

Houston Jews were landlords in several of the wards. Most of the properties Jewish landlords owned were generational, as family members passed down ownership. There would always be one member of a family assigned to watch over rentals in the African American area. Cora Johnson, an African American born in 1928 who lived in the Fourth Ward in a shotgun house, remembered that her landlord was Jewish. She recalled that Jews lived where the "Caucasians" lived, but they owned the property where African Americans resided. Cora Johnson did not say anything disparaging about the Jews, but African Americans were certainly aware of Jewish landlords.[33] A Jewish reporter from the *Houston Chronicle*, Saul Friedman, further reported that "the boy learned the trade of the slum landlord: how to maintain patronizing control. How to cajole the tenants for their wrinkled rent dollars. How to soothe complaints." Jews were not the only ones who were landlords, however, as Italians also owned properties.[34]

African Americans at times had contentious interactions with immigrant-owned businesses in Houston throughout the 1920s and 1930s. Only 14 percent of all African Americans shopped in immigrant-owned grocery stores. Other immigrant groups that had businesses in predominantly African American neighborhoods were Chinese, Italians, and Mexicans. Sometimes these immigrant business owners would not adequately address their

African American customers.[35] For instance, in the 1930s, B.T. Brooks remembered that there were Chinese and Italians who would call all African American men "John" and all African American women "Mary," whereas they addressed their white customers as Mr., Mrs., and Miss. Domestic worker Manilla Lovelady recalled that Jewish store owners did not bother to learn her name even when she was a frequent customer, and she felt white customers received better treatment.[36]

African Americans felt financially exploited by the neighborhood immigrant stores in general. The principal of Booker T. Washington School, Ira Byrant, fervently disliked the Italian storekeepers because he saw firsthand the way they would cheat African Americans out of money. The Italian merchants kept ledgers of everything that African Americans bought on credit and would charge them inflated prices. While it was common for Chinese, Italians, and Jews to extend credit to African Americans, as in other parts of the South, at times they felt cheated and powerless to fight the injustices.[37]

However, they did find ways to fight for equal practices. African Americans at times boycotted immigrant-owned stores because of their unscrupulous dealings or unfair treatment. Newspapers like *The Informer* tried to instill into the community the value of having a Black-only economy by pushing African Americans not to buy from immigrant-owned stores, even if those stores hired African Americans as clerks. This sentiment continued into the 1950s.[38]

Most African Americans believed that immigrant businesses did not always treat them equally, but there were exceptions. William Johnson, an African American laborer, said that he could not always tell the difference between a Jewish or Italian grocer, but he remembered that they treated him well. There was one Jewish clothing store owner who he felt treated him "all right," but he also felt they would "do most anything that you ask them to do if you would just spend those little nickels and dimes with them." William Johnson felt that the Jewish and Italian merchants needed African Americans to buy from them to keep their stores afloat.[39]

However, Jews were the largest immigrant group in the Houston business sphere, and many small Jewish businesses hired African American employees. The family of Serra Gordon, who lived in the Fifth Ward, a predominantly African American neighborhood during the 1930s, owned a dry goods store. There were Jewish and Italian immigrants who were so poor they had to live in African American neighborhoods, and their families lived in the back of or above their stores. Gordon commented that Jews in the African American neighborhoods also owned liquor stores in addition to dry goods shops. In Gordon's experience, the African Americans she encountered were illiterate, although she also recalled that some of the African American employees who had worked with European Jews had learned Yiddish. African Americans in the neighborhood considered her father to be a reputable merchant. In fact, African Americans would stand in line to shop at her father's store and spend their weekly salaries to buy goods there because they knew he would not cheat them, even if they could only sign an x by their name.[40]

Jews of different economic means moved into the Riverside District starting in the 1930s and continuing through the 1940s, which encompassed three areas—Washington Terrace, Riverside Terrace, and Riverside. Houston Jews who were middle class lived in Washington Terrace, which was closest to the African American area of the Third Ward. This whole area would become known as Riverside Terrace. In contrast to the Third Ward, Washington Terrace was less crowded and lacked blighted areas. Riverside Terrace was middle to upper class, and Riverside was the wealthy area primarily composed of Reform Jews. The wealthy Jews gravitated to Riverside Terrace because of its undeveloped verdant land, where they could buy large tracts to build their mansions since the wealthy areas of Houston, like River Oaks, did not welcome them. Houses in Riverside Terrace were also architecturally significant because they were not uniform. Riverside Terrace was not the first "Jewish community," but it became identified as one because it had a prominent Jewish presence.[41]

In contrast to Riverside Terrace, the upscale River Oaks community excluded Jews and African Americans through its restrictive covenants. Malvena Weingarten, the wife of business-man Joe Weingarten, remembered that when she and her family tried to move to River Oaks, the Realtor, Hugh Potter Billy, told the Weingartens, "Well, let us let you know," but he never let them know. Unlike River Oaks, Riverside Terrace did not have any covenants that excluded Jewish residents.[42]

As in other parts of the United States, Houston banks and real estate agents practiced redlining. In the 1930s, the Home Owners' Loan Corporation created a redlined map that characterized areas in Houston as "best," "still desirable," "definite declining," and "hazardous."[43] Most African Americans living in Houston resided in wards considered "hazardous." To some extent, this description was true. Only 18.9 percent of African Americans had an indoor bathroom. Many homes had no functioning plumbing or access to drinking water; instead, African Americans often had to obtain their water from a spigot in an alleyway or street. However, real estate agents based their rating on location, the value of homes, mixed use of land, and type of population. Ultimately, African American neighborhoods rated the lowest in residential value, and as a result, African Americans were not eligible to secure loans to fix their homes or buy new homes because mortgages in those areas were considered high-risk investments.[44]

African Americans, unlike Jews, were not able to freely move out of their wards in Houston, and they faced tremendous housing discrimination. African Americans of all socioeconomic classes lived in the Third, Fourth, and Fifth Wards. Poverty existed in the community due to wage disparities and inadequate housing. On January 19, 1938, Congress passed the 1937 Wagner-Steagall Act, which implemented a nationwide public housing program. The Houston Housing Authority (HHA), affiliated with the national program, cleared out the blighted areas and developed new housing that provided families of low to moderate income with a place to live that was safe, clean, and respectable. At the time, there was a great need for public housing for African Americans, as 10,277 African American families were living in substandard residences. However, even when they found housing, African Americans paid higher monthly rents.[45]

The first housing authority program for African Americans in Houston was the Cuney Homes, located in the Third Ward. The project did not always run smoothly and took until 1940 to complete. The Cuney Homes were 360 brick apartments, to which the HHA added 204 more. Geraldine Pittman Wooten recalled living in one of these apartments with her family. They struggled to pay the rent even though the HHA promoted it as being affordable. African Americans had to make between $500 and $1,134 per year to qualify for public housing, but most only made between $700 and $800 per year. They also had to provide a character reference and proof that they held a secure job. Women whose husbands later went off to war had to move out of the Cuney Homes because they did not qualify as a family unit. The HHA made it difficult for the poorest African Americans. There was another set of public housing buildings called the A. K. Kelly Courts, which provided 333 more units for African Americans in the Fifth Ward.[46]

Despite the need for more African American housing, the city of Houston leveled condemned African American homes to make room for more white-only public housing. In the 1940 leveling, the HHA destroyed parts of the Fourth Ward, the oldest African American ward, to make way for two new housing projects: the San Felipe Courts and the Irvington Courts, which only allowed low-income whites. African Americans who lost their homes to slum clearance received only minimal reparations from the HHA. The HHA justified the low monetary compensation because the razed residences had little economic value.[47]

The HHA failed to see that the most reasonable solution was to improve living conditions for the African Americans of the Fourth Ward rather than force them to leave their homes to build new public housing for low-income whites. To fight for their own conditions, the Fourth Ward Club, an African American organization that raised funds for African American legal battles, tried to stop the HHA with the help of the NAACP, but the powerful HHA was still able to pursue its plan for slum clearance. Many African Americans of the Fourth Ward became homeless because of the development of the San Felipe and

Irvington Courts.[48] *The Informer* stated in 1940 that displaced African Americans now "wander about the city like lost sheep, flowing from one ward to the other in search of shelter."[49] Inevitably, this evacuation caused more African Americans to move into the crowded Third and Fifth Wards. While many of the homeless moved into the Cuney Homes and Kelly Courts, there were still those who could not meet the strict requirements to live in this housing, especially in the Cuney Homes.[50]

The Third Ward, which bordered Riverside Terrace, was the cultural center of African American life in Houston and became the center of its business and commerce, with African American–owned businesses in addition to those that were Jewish or Italian owned. Like the other wards, the Third Ward had a movie theater, Dowling Theater. There were also barbershops, beauty parlors, diners—including the Lunch Box Diner, which served cheap soul food—dives, and beer joints. One of the most famous restaurants was the East Texas Café, which was open twenty-four hours a day and had a pool hall. Some whites ventured into this African American ward to listen to the music of the new jazz bands; however, African Americans did not enjoy the same reciprocity with white clubs or eateries in other locations in Houston.[51]

The famous African American photographer Benny Joseph recalled living in the Third Ward, on the border of Riverside Terrace, as a young boy in the 1930s. He was playing with a group of friends when he glanced across the street and saw white children playing. He asked them to join him and his friends, and they agreed. He recalled that the game became intense: "We got it on. So we had a big game going." The white mothers suddenly saw their children playing with Joseph and his friends and immediately stopped the game. Joseph did not state whether these women were Christian or Jewish, but he remembered the incident vividly. He and his friends also often snuck over to Riverside Terrace to swim in the bayou because they did not have ready access to a swimming pool, except at the YMCA. The beauty of Riverside Terrace amazed Joseph, as it had "a lot of shrubbery, a lot of trees … a bunch of trees." Sometimes the police caught Joseph and his friends there and chased them away. Even though Riverside Terrace had been predominantly Gentile, he was still aware of its Jewish presence.[52]

The Cuney Homes, located in the African American Third Ward neighborhood of Truxillo, bordered Riverside Terrace. Although only a small distance divided the Cuney Homes from Riverside Terrace, the disparity in the housing between whites and African Americans in the two locations was remarkable. The Cuney Homes were two-story brick-and-mortar townhouses that were, as former resident Thurman W. Robins described, "adequate for the family." In contrast, the Riverside Terrace homes were single-family homes of various sizes and styles with backyards and greenery.[53] The Jews and white Gentiles of Riverside Terrace did not believe that African Americans in the Third Ward would ever attempt to disrupt the equilibrium of their neighborhood. However, the separation between the Jewish and white area and the African American area of Third Ward in Riverside Terrace did not last.[54]

Jewish and African American populations had limited contact with each other because of segregation. This imposed separation between whites and African Americans instilled in Houston Jews, especially the communal leaders, the need to prove they were similar to the white Gentiles and not a distinct group. In the first chapter, I will discuss how Congregation Beth Israel's Policy Formulation Committee made a drastic move when it instituted a "Caucasian clause" into its Basic Principles. This unorthodox move was to end the stigma that Jews were a distinct group and instead demonstrate that Jews were white Americans of Jewish faith and not much different from their white Gentile peers.

Chapter 1

The Implications
of the Basic Principles

Our Religion Is Judaism … Our Nationality Is American …
Our Race Is Caucasian
Congregation Beth Israel's Basic Principles

Houston's Jewish and African American populations developed simultaneously and yet separately over time. Each had their own distinct communities that did not intersect. From enslavement to the onset of segregation, most Jewish-Black interactions remained confined to economic exchanges. The two communities developed their own religious institutions and social organizations. Houston cultivated a segregated hierarchy that placed pressure on its Jews to become like white Gentiles. This acculturation process provided the city's Jews with certain privileges that African Americans lacked, such as access to proper medical care, housing, business opportunities, and social mobility. Forced to live separately, the Black community had to develop its own internal social structures.

The rise of Nazism and Jewish affiliation with Communism and Zionism forced Houston's Jews to redefine the public's perception of them lest they find themselves in a precarious position similar to African Americans. For this, they relied on their leaders to guide them. In 1943, the Policy Formulation Committee of Congregation Beth Israel created Basic Principles intended to preserve the image of Jews as white Americans of Jewish faith and secure their first-class citizenship in a city that divided people based on skin color. The congregation's Basic Principles created a definition of "Caucasian" that had far-reaching implications. The principles set specific events in motion that prompted the Houston Jewish community to eventually transition from being silent supporters of African Americans to political collaborators. Beth Israel's Basic Principles provide a starting point for unwrapping the complexities of that evolutionary relationship. The congregation's labeling of Houston's Jews as "Caucasian" brought about both internal and external struggles that challenged the understanding of who they really were.

This identity struggle began on November 23, 1943, when the Policy Formulation Committee at Congregation Beth Israel, under the leadership of former temple president Israel Friedlander, decided to feature seven Basic Principles on its membership application. One principle in particular caused controversy. The Union of American Hebrew Congregations, the governing body of Reform Judaism, objected to one part of Principle 2: "Our religion is Judaism. Our nation is the United States of America. Our nationality is American. Our flag is 'the Stars and Stripes.' Our race is Caucasian."[1] Principle 2 expanded the definition of a Jew to include race while the other six principles addressed common Jewish religious and cultural practices within the Classical Reform Judaism movement, including foundational principles from the Pittsburgh Platform of 1885. Some critics viewed this addition as being inconsistent with the Reform movement, which stressed religion over nation. The fifth principle of the Pittsburgh Platform declared Jews "no longer a nation, but a religious community."[2]

Many critics questioned the goal of this addition. Was it an expression of the committee's commitment to segregation? Or was the intent of the clause to deny the existence of Jews of color, or was it simply a demographic description of Congregation Beth Israel? Was the congregation concerned that Zionism had the potential to define Jews as a distinct group separate from white Gentiles, or was it an attempt to secure the place of Houston's Jews as white in a system that oppressed African Americans? Or did it have yet another purpose?

Scholars have given several explanations for this Caucasian clause. One speculates that Congregation Beth Israel had only white Jewish membership. Another posits that segregation and the positions of Houston's white Gentiles caused the congregants concern. Yet another scholar suggests it was meant to show Houston that Jews were no different from their white Gentile peers. These theories have merit, but they overlook the Policy Formulation Committee's concern over how Zionism could alter the non-Jewish perception of American Jewish identity.[3]

Conscious of their American identity, Houston's Jews also recognized the challenge of full acceptance in white society. They did not face the same level of inequality as African Americans did, but with the rise of Communism and Zionism, many of the city's Jews realized their status as Americans was becoming questionable. In 1936, with the assistance of prominent Jewish businessmen Simon Sakowitz and Joe Weingarten, the Houston Jewish community established the Jewish Community Relations Council with the purpose of promoting the well-being of the community and Jews abroad. Anti-Semitism posed enough concern that the council created a public relations committee to improve relations between Jews and Gentiles, monitor anti-Semitic publications, and work closely with Jewish defense groups. Many Jews felt pressure to assimilate and prove their commitment to America because they feared white Gentiles would see them as outsiders rather than loyal American patriots. Yet despite their efforts to appear as American as their white neighbors, certain invisible barriers prevented many of Houston's Jews from gaining complete acceptance.[4] One such barrier was the so-called "five o'clock curtain" that hung between Jews and non-Jews. They might have worked together, but Jews and non-Jews did not socialize after hours.[5]

The city's segregation laws created a hierarchy in Houston that placed white Gentiles on top, African Americans on the bottom, and Jews somewhere in between. Texas, like other parts of the South, imposed a poll tax to discourage African Americans from voting, a decision that also excluded poor whites from voting. In many cases, southern Democrats who wanted to disenfranchise all African Americans simply had to bar them from voting in Democratic primaries. Blacks could not gain any influence in local and state elections at that time because Texas and other southern states effectively had one-party rule.[6]

Such white primaries fueled Beth Israel's creation of Basic Principle 2. When a media frenzy occurred in response to the Caucasian clause, the congregation explained its actual intentions in two volumes: *The History of the Official Adoption of "The Basic Principles"* and *A Handbook of True Facts*. Congregation Beth Israel confirmed the American Council for Judaism's belief that Jews are not a distinct race. The congregation, concerned about the future of Houston Jewry, worried that growing Zionist sentiment made them seem disloyal to America. A stress on their Caucasian identity was an attempt to secure their position with their white Gentile peers. Moreover, Jewish involvement in Communism had already created suspicions that Jews were outsiders. The addition of Zionism compounded the possible perception of Jews as un-American and possibly even non-Caucasian. This was a real cause for concern in light of Texas's white primaries. In the end, a statement meant to protect Houston Jews from appearing disloyal instead caused internal tension within Houston and the greater Jewish world. Because of Principle 2, many American Jews portrayed Congregation Beth Israel as anti-Jewish when, in fact, their goal was to be pro-American.[7]

The Rise of Communism in Segregated Houston During the White Primaries

Politics in Houston defined how African Americans and Jews participated in the larger society. By the 1930s, the Communist Party in the United States had a significant number of Jewish members who were involved in labor unions alongside African Americans. Despite the decline in Jewish membership in the Communist Party after the Nazi-Soviet Pact in 1939, Americans still widely associated Jews with Communism. In Houston, public perceptions of Communism continued to be important politically for both Blacks and Jews. Even before concerns over Zionism arose for the Jews of Congregation Beth Israel, the emergence of Communism in Texas shone a spotlight on Jews and African Americans. In 1935, the Texas Communist Party in Houston had only two hundred members. It was not a significant organization; however, brewing tension between Communists and non-Communists laid the foundation for Houston's eventual Red Scare in 1950.[8]

Houston did not have any prominent Jewish Communists, primarily because Jews knew the label "Communist" in the South placed them in a precarious position vis-à-vis white Gentiles. Many white southerners, especially segregationists, viewed Communism as subversive because the Communist Party USA was at the forefront of the fight for civil rights. Especially in the South, most anti-Communist rhetoric focused its antipathy on African Americans because during the Great Depression many southern Blacks joined the Communist Party in search of economic relief due to higher rates of unemployment and discrimination. The party also appealed to Blacks because it called for their equal citizenship. Many southerners knew African Americans were already important members of the Communist Party in the North. Indeed, the Communist Party USA was the first political party to run an African American for vice president, James W. Ford, in the presidential election of 1932.[9]

In 1940, out of a total population of 384,314, approximately 86,000 African Americans lived in Houston. Thus, when local Democratic white primary elections deprived African Americans of the right to vote, this decision effectively denied voting rights to around one-fifth of its population. The Texas Legislature had a history of preventing Blacks from voting. In 1924, the refusal to allow Lawrence A. Nixon, a Black physician from El Paso, the right to vote resulted in two Supreme Court cases (*Nixon v.*

Herndon and *Nixon v. Condon*). Though the court ruled in favor of Nixon, affirming the violation of his Fourteenth Amendment rights, it did not rule that denying Nixon the right to vote in white primaries was unconstitutional. Had the court affirmed the violation of Nixon's Fifteenth Amendment rights, it could have prohibited the Texas white primaries from further disenfranchising African Americans.[10]

The Nixon case created a maelstrom in Houston. Local Black leaders, including the local NAACP president, prominent businessmen, and the editor of *The Informer*, Houston's Black newspaper, filed an injunction against the Harris County Democratic Executive Committee in order to allow Blacks to vote in the 1931 election. Because the city's Democrats had denied membership to African Americans, the group also created the Harris County Negro Democratic Club to oppose white primaries. Their efforts, however, were unsuccessful. In 1931, even those Blacks who had paid the poll tax were not allowed to vote in the white primaries.[11] The Texas Democrats went a step further in 1932 and proposed a new disenfranchisement plan that enabled discrimination against voters based on skin color. The Huggins Plan of 1932, presented at the state convention, gave the Democratic Party the ability to declare that "all white citizens of the State of Texas who are qualified to vote under the constitution and laws of the state shall be eligible to [have] membership in the Democratic Party."[12]

Such blatant exclusion led Houston's Black residents to more loudly voice their frustration about their second-class citizenship. B. T. Brooks, a local laborer, noted that when a Black grocer tried to vote in the 1930s, a group of whites threatened him with violence. R. R. Grovey, a political activist and barber in the city, saw having the vote fundamental for equality: "If we get it, there will be a decided change in the way that the Negro gets along here in Houston."[13] Grovey correctly surmised that whites wanted to withhold their right to vote for as long as possible to keep them powerless.

A 1938 editorial in *The Informer* by editor and lawyer Carter Wesley titled "The Primary and Hitlerism" explicitly compared the white primaries to Nazism. Wesley highlighted the Democratic Party's refusal to allow African Americans to vote: "[There is] absolutely no difference in the attitude of these demagogues and that of Hitler, who is now robbing the Jews."[14] Wesley's comparison was not unusual. During the 1930s, the Black press often drew such parallels.[15] This underscores the irony of Congregation Beth Israel's use of "Caucasian" in Basic Principle 2 to solidify their own first-class citizenship in Houston.

Unlike Houston's Black residents, Jews had the right to vote because they were white. Earning the distinction of "Caucasian" delineated their level of citizenship. Only white Americans had access to first-class citizenship. In the spring of 1943, the Texas Legislature passed the resolution "Caucasian Race— Equal Privileges," which not only defined Latinos as Caucasian but also proclaimed transnational unity between North and South America. It also solidified the idea that the patriotic fight against Nazism included Latinos. The resolution stated that "all persons of the Caucasian Race within the jurisdiction of this State are entitled to the full and equal accommodations, advantages, facilities, and privileges of all public places of business or amusement."[16] Even though Congregation Beth Israel and the Houston Jewish community did not acknowledge this resolution, they continued their efforts to ensure that Jews kept the identification of Caucasian. Since the local Jewish community did not include Black Jews, they did not see a conflict of interest in convincing white non-Jews that they, too, fit within the category of Caucasian.[17]

The Communist Party of Texas challenged American inequality and segregation. Its goals for African Americans included providing more opportunities to work, improving educational opportunities, and increasing Black political representation. In 1938 and 1940, the Communist Party introduced Black civil rights leader Cecil B. Robinett as its candidate for lieutenant governor.[18] The 1940 Communist Party platform described Robinett as "a militant young Houston leader of the fight for Negro rights."[19] This choice dovetailed with its focus on labor rights, equality for African Americans, and ending white primaries. On December 1, 1940, Robinett published an open letter in the *Houston Vanguard* addressed to Wesley of *The Informer*. Wesley had written an article titled "Crime Wave Among Negroes Great." In this undated article—which Robinett referred to—Wesley emphatically claimed that crime among Blacks was exponentially higher because of the police's racial bias and lack of "leniency" for arrested African Americans. Robinett felt Wesley's ideas were too narrowly focused and responded that the problem was much more nuanced. African Americans in Houston faced problems with the police because they "do not even treat our people as human beings." He further argued that African Americans lived in blighted and poverty-stricken areas where they suffered from unemployment, systemic discrimination, and lack of opportunities. This economic disparity caused crime to infiltrate the Black community.[20]

Around the same time as the founding of Houston's Communist Party, millionaire lumber baron and oilman John H. Kirby funded the creation of a counter-organization called the Christian Americans. The explicit goals of this organization were to save "Christian Americanism," root out Communism, and prevent Black equality. The conservative Kirby had been a friend and financial backer of US Representative Martin Dies, who chaired the House Committee on Un-American Activities that investigated the alleged Communist fronts in President Franklin Roosevelt's government from 1938 to 1944. In 1936, Vance Muse, the chairman of Kirby's company and a well-known anti-unionist, and former Indiana state legislator Lewis Ulrey created Christian Americans. Blacks in Houston referred to this group as the "Streamlined Klan, 1945 Model."[21] The group's weekly, *Christian American*, featured two symbols: a cross and an American flag. The weekly was anti-Communist, anti-liberal, anti-union, anti-Black, and anti-Semitic.[22] E. A. Piller's 1945 exposé of American fascism explored the dangers of this organization, concentrating on its anti-unionism and "race-baiting." From his perspective, the purpose of fascism was "to divide minorities; to weaken unions."[23] Ulrey, in particular, believed in "the coming Armageddon—the great struggle between Christianity and Jewish Marxism," a reality he even used to justify Hitler's actions against Jews.[24]

Other groups in Houston were even more forceful and vocal in their hatred of Jews and African Americans, such as the American Crusaders, a group that described itself as "vigilante" with a goal "to rid the country of the niggers and the Jews after the war."[25] The Order of American Patriots shared the same prejudice toward African Americans and Jews. It was likely that the local presence of these hate groups influenced the Jews of Beth Israel to reinforce their Caucasian identity in Basic Principle 2. After all, the Public Relations Committee of the Jewish Community Relations Council kept watch on all circulating anti-Semitic materials.

The public schools in Texas felt the effects of this fractious political climate. Teachers began to be cautious about expressing liberal views that conservatives had labeled anti-American. As early as 1935, the Texas Legislature required teachers to express their loyalty to their country. Beginning in the 1940s, the Houston Independent School District's (HISD) board became a locus for the association of Jews with Communism. Local anti-Communist attacks centered on two individuals who were associated with Communism but not Communists: Ray K. Daily and Arthur Mandell. Anti-Communists singled out Daily and Mandell for three reasons: they were publicly outspoken on Black issues, came from Eastern Europe, and were Jewish.[26]

Daily, a Jewish ophthalmologist and school board member, had been an earlier target of anti-Semitism and accusations of Communism. One major reason was her foreign birth. Daily was born in Vilna, Lithuania, and came to the United States when she was fourteen. However, it was her public support of Harold O. Rugg's textbook series that set the tone for the contempt directed at her. In the *Houston Post*, Daily defended Rugg as being "one of America's most progressive educators."[27] Both the Daughters of the American Revolution and the American Legion considered Rugg's textbooks to be un-American. Daily became a prime target because she was female, Jewish, and an immigrant. She first ran for the school board elections in 1928 and later became school board president. She devoted herself to being an advocate for minorities and even helped to establish the

Houston College for Negroes, which was in existence from 1934 to 1947. She decided to run for a position on the Houston School Board in 1943 with Ima Hogg, the daughter of former governor James Stephen Hogg. Conservative whites accused Daily, who openly supported Black equality in Houston, of affiliating with the Communist Party, a charge that would haunt her entire campaign and compromise her partnership with Hogg.[28]

Despite these accusations, Daily and Hogg won seats on the Houston School Board. Grand Duke Crawford, a businessperson from the Fifth Ward and former president of the Houston branch of the NAACP, put out an advertisement encouraging other African Americans to vote for Daily in the school board elections. The advertisement read: "Attention!! Colored Voters. The School Board Election Saturday is very important. If the right people are elected we can expect fair treatment."[29] Daily embodied hope for Houston's Black residents due to her unflagging support for their rights. Skeptical at first, even Carter Wesley eventually supported Daily and Hogg, who was also a supporter of Black rights. The white superintendent of the HISD, E. E. Oberholtzer, even told *The Informer* that he advised his principals to "have the Negroes vote for Mrs. Ray K. Daily and Miss Ima Hogg."[30] Oberholtzer's acknowledgment of Daily and Hogg as the candidates of the Black community further marginalized them from the white majority.

The second target of anti-Communist attacks in Houston—Arthur Mandell—was a well-known Romanian-born Jewish lawyer who was also involved in Daily and Hogg's school board election in 1943. Though not a Communist himself, he was affiliated with known Communists as well as unions like the Congress of Industrial Organizations (CIO). Mandell eventually focused exclusively on civil rights in his law practice, but he faced local obstacles because of his status as a left-leaning Jew. However, his efforts with Houston's marginalized populations helped Daily get votes, even as it reinforced her association with Communism.[31]

Mandell encouraged his union clients from the Oil Workers International Union, the United Steelworkers, and the National Maritime Union to vote for Daily and Hogg in the school board election. The unions also passed out leaflets in their work-ing-class neighborhoods to support the candidates. Mandell's law firm continued to voice its support well after the initial Communist accusation against Daily because the lawyer trusted that Daily had the capability to "raise the teachers' pay to a level where they can live with economic security, and provide for all Americans, regardless of race, creed, or color equal educational opportunities as befits our system of government."[32] The Oil Workers International Union, Local 227, promoted voting for Daily and Hogg as a patriotic duty to preserve "what our boys are fighting and dying for."[33]

Daily may have been the vice president of the Executive Committee of the Jewish Community Relations Council, but the HISD board and many white Houstonians branded her an enemy of the United States. Daily's support of Black equality increased public concern, so much so that in 1943 she felt the need to justify her devotion as an American. In a February letter to Hogg, a well-to-do Gentile, Daily reiterated her frustration about being branded a Communist: "Of course, I have never been a member of the Communist party or engaged in Communist activities. I do not even know who the local Communists are."[34]

Even though she was a naturalized citizen, Daily would have been cautious because in 1940 the United States passed the Alien Registration Act. With the overarching goal of preventing crime, the act not only forced noncitizens to register with the federal government, it also targeted alleged Communists. This act would not become unconstitutional until 1957.[35] Daily felt the need to emphasize her American values and justify America's relationship with Russia. Stressing the relationship between the two countries, she urged Hogg to remember that we were still at war, with "Russia [as] our ally." Daily also emphasized that she had lived in Houston for over thirty years. In order to mitigate against future accusations and to secure her voice on the school board, it was of paramount importance for Daily to stand on equal footing with a prominent public figure like Hogg.[36]

Accusations, however, would continue to bring trouble to the duo's relationship. On March 8, 1943, a woman named Milby

Porter wrote to Hogg about Daily's alleged Communist affiliation. Porter believed Hogg's alignment with Daily was a betrayal
to the American armed forces fighting overseas: "[Your relationship betrays] boys and men—and American women ... in
Jap prisons; and to those who are suffering all the other tortures
of a WAR."[37]

She reminded Hogg that she was a member of the political
elite, while Daily was a foreigner. In the letter, Porter clearly
spelled out her perspective of who was American and who was
not. Porter suggested that Daily had set out to trick Hogg in
order to gain control of the school board and implied that Daily
did not understand what it meant to be loyal to the United States.
Porter even went so far as to argue that Hogg's partnership with
Daily diminished Hogg's own work with American national
defense. Porter appeared to imply that Daily was suspect not
only because she was not a patriot but also because she was not
American born or Christian.[38]

In her response to Porter on March 11, 1943, Hogg defended
Daily and reinforced both their partnership and their mutual
patriotism. This letter of support was a significant step for
Hogg.[39] Years later in an interview, Daily recalled the harsh criticisms Hogg endured: "People were just using something against
these stories spread about you—you know—was that I was a
Jew and Ms. Ima was an old maid."[40] Even if Hogg faced gender
and age discrimination, the smear campaign labeled Daily a
"Russian born Red Jewess" allegedly under the FBI's watch.
In contrast, the campaign described Daily's opponent, Sam E.
Davis, as a "native born white Protestant ... mother of two children."[41] Despite these slur tactics, Daily and Hogg still won the
election. It took another nine years for the ongoing Communist
accusations against Daily to have an effect. In 1952, she lost her
school board reelection bid.

Daily and Hogg's 1943 election illustrates the extent to
which the rise of Communism in Houston hindered Jewish
involvement in Black affairs. Communism placed local Jews in
a precarious position in which the public questioned their American loyalty. Further, while Jews like Daily and Mandell may not

have been the only ones accused of being Communists because of their affiliation with the Black equality struggle, as members of a minority group, they had more to lose. Jews did not want white Gentiles to think they sympathized with Blacks. While anti-Communist sentiment caused friction within the Jewish community, the rise of Zionism was what solidified local Jewish concern about their place under segregation and what their relationship with Black residents could—or even should—be.

The Rise of Zionism and Anti-Zionism in Houston

Local backlash against Zionism spurred an internal communal conflict. Jews feared that this reaction made them appear as disloyal American citizens. After all, both Zionism and Communism were political movements that had the potential to threaten the stability of American Jewish life. Houston's Jews, much like most southern Jews, had a great concern that their white Gentile peers viewed their interest in Palestine as disloyalty to America. While Zionists only comprised 10 to 15 percent of the local Jewish community, their proportion increased during World War II.[42]

In 1937, the American Reform Movement had changed its stance on Palestine in its new Columbus Platform, thus signaling the end of the movement's strong anti-Zionist leanings evident in the Pittsburgh Platform of 1885. The platform stated: "We affirm the obligation of all Jewry to aid in its upbuilding as a Jewish homeland by endeavoring to make it not only a haven of refuge for the oppressed, but also a center of Jewish culture and spiritual life."[43]

This increased loyalty to Palestine could be felt regionally as well. The Southwest Jewish National Fund recognized in print the Texas Jewish organizations and individuals who had contributed monetarily toward the purchase of land in Palestine and even highlighted Governor James V. Allred's 1935 declaration of "Palestine Day." He proclaimed the celebration's purpose to be "to pay tribute to the ideals of justice that animated the nations of the earth, including our own, in approving the reestablishment of the Jewish homeland."[44]

Issued before the onset of World War II, the proclamation praised Palestine as a place for Christians and Jews because of its religious roots. With war looming on the horizon and the fate of European Jews hanging in the balance, the Southwest Jewish National Fund's reflection on prewar Zionist activities took on a different hue, leading American Jews to alter their views on Zionism yet again.

Disenchanted with the increasing support for Zionism within Reform Judaism, a group of rabbis and lay leaders established the American Council for Judaism in 1942, which clung to the earlier principles of the Pittsburgh Platform. Houston's Congregation Beth Israel embraced rabbis with ties to the American Council, including Harry Barnston and his successor, Hyman Judah Schachtel. Barnston's philosophy on Zionism was not fixed. Early in his career he spoke at Zionist events. However, by aligning himself later with the council, he stood in public opposition to the rise of Zionism and maintained Judaism as exclusively a religion rather than a political movement. The council and its leaders also opposed any national separation of Jews. In efforts to convince the American Jewish population of their viewpoint, they created pamphlets to oppose Jewish nationalism and reinforced the dangers of Jewish separatism. While they wanted Jews to immigrate freely to other countries, especially America, they promoted integration in the host countries over immigration to Palestine. However, no matter how popular the council was becoming, the Synagogue Council of America, the Central Conference of American Rabbis, the Rabbinical Assembly, and the Union of Orthodox Rabbis continued to oppose it.[45]

The anti-Zionist Houston Jews were at a loss. They wanted to save European Jews from Nazism and bring them to Houston. However, America's strict immigration laws placed quotas on immigration from Southern and Eastern Europe, which targeted Jews. The Johnson-Reed Act of 1924 enforced the eugenic ideology that certain groups of people, like foreign-born Jews, were racially unfit and would ultimately taint the purity of white Christian America. One congressman stated about the

Johnson-Reed Act that America was "the home ... [of] a white race with great ideals, the Christian religion, one race, one country, one destiny."[46]

The American Council for Judaism's main goal was to dismantle the anti-Semitic belief that Jews were a racially inferior group so Jews fleeing from Europe could immigrate freely and become American citizens. In August of 1943, the American Council for Judaism further complicated Jewish identity by presenting Jews in their platform as exclusively a religious group, not a nationality or distinct racial group. Southern Jews were "hostile to Zionism" because they rejected "Jewish nationalism" and believed "America was their Zion."[47]

Because Jews at large—and Houston's Jews specifically— worried that Zionism might confuse white Gentiles about the nature of being Jewish in America, they supported the anti-Zionist American Council of Judaism under the leadership of executive directors Elmer Berger and Lessing J. Rosenwald. On June 28, 1943, Rosenwald argued in *Life* magazine that American Jewry should oppose Zionism because "those of Jewish faith who oppose the creation of a national Jewish state ... [embrace] the very racist theories and nationalist philosophies that have become so prevalent in recent years, that have caused untold suffering to the world and particularly to the Jews."[48] Rosenwald implied that the council believed Zionist ideology perpetuated Nazi propaganda that Jews were a race with distinct physical and biological traits.[49] It was against the backdrop of the American Jewish Council and Rosenwald's campaign that Congregation Beth Israel created their Policy Formulation Committee. With the creation of the controversial Basic Principle 2, like Rosenwald, they had to explain and justify it publicly.

Defending Basic Principle 2

Beth Israel's senior rabbi, Hyman Judah Schachtel, commented on why the council needed to explicate this concept of race and have a Caucasian clause inserted in the Basic Principles. In an interview from 1975, Houston photographer Gay Block asked him, "Our race is Caucasian: was that in the original document?" Schachtel responded, "Our race is Caucasian was the answer to Hitler, who had said that the Jews belong to an inferior Semitic race. You know the antisemitism. And by using the word Caucasian ... this was the response to the Hitler who damned every Semite you see." In order to combat Nazi anti-Semitism, the committee merely wanted Jews to stop distinguishing themselves. From Schachtel's perspective, Communism, Zionism, and anti-Semitism drove the Policy Formulation Committee to create the Basic Principles—not his influence or the pressure from the American Council for Judaism. The committee created this principle of its own volition with the majority support of the congregation.[50]

In 1944, temple president Israel Friedlander compiled a history of the principles so that future readers would understand why Beth Israel's leaders took a bold step that put the congregation in a negative national light. Friedlander presented a chronology of events and included relevant materials like letters, news articles, timelines, photographic material, bulletins, and pamphlets.[51] Included is a personal letter from Friedlander to influential businessman and then president of the Houston congregation, Leopold Meyer, on May 30, 1944. Meyer did not oppose Zionism, even during the formation of the Basic Principles, but rather believed that "Judaism *was a religion and not a race.*" Reform Jews only followed the "*morality* and *prophetic* teaching" of Judaism.[52] In short, Meyer and the committee members believed that the Jewish *religion* fit better within modern-day American cultural surroundings rather than its antiquated past.

This letter, written after the formation of the Basic Principles, revealed Friedlander's perception of Zionism as the ultimate divide between Reform Jews. Friedlander reflected the complex sentiment that he and the congregants held about the changing climate and growing divides not only within Beth Israel but also within the Reform movement as a whole. Likening their situation to that of African Americans during enslavement, Friedlander wanted the temple to prevent traditional Judaism from "enslaving" Reform Judaism and permit them to practice according to

Reform principles. He compared the role of the Basic Principles to that of Lincoln: they were saving Reform Jews not only from Zionism but also from the practices of Orthodox and Conservative Judaism. Lincoln's "House Divided" speech stated that a nation cannot exist "half slave" and "half free." Likewise, Friedlander saw American Judaism as "half-traditional" and "half-reform" and stressed the devastation Zionism was having on the Reform movement. Considering that he lived in the South, it was ironic that Friedlander saw himself and his congregation on the side of the Union and in need of emancipation.[53]

Friedlander implied that the congregation needed to preserve its Reform identity to free itself metaphorically from the enslavement of Zionism. Ultimately, his comparison of the anti-Zionists to African Americans illustrated his lack of understanding of the historical plight of slaves. To him, they were merely a symbol of the need for redemption. Friedlander was poetic in his description of the impact that Zionism could have on the American Jewish population; however, his concept of Zionism imprisoning American Jews is not far off from how passionate Jewish anti-Zionists would have felt. Many saw the repercussions of Zionism as damaging to the Jewish people.[54]

At the end of the letter, Friedlander paralleled the passing of the Basic Principles on November 23, 1943, to the Battle of Gettysburg. Just as the Pennsylvania battle saved the "American Union," the only salvation for Reform Judaism was the Basic Principles. Although Texas was a part of the Confederacy during the Civil War, Friedlander associated the synagogue with the North. He did not want the Zionist question to lead to the division of the Union of American Hebrew Congregations and Hebrew Union College like slavery did to the Union and the Confederacy. Metaphorically, he wanted the Union to be whole.[55]

In particular, Friedlander's letter to Meyer urged the Union of American Hebrew Congregations and the Central Conference for American Rabbis to look closely at Kaufmann Kohler's 1911 speech titled "American Judaism." Friedlander considered the classic Reform leader's speech to be a "masterly address" that "should be read by the officers and trustees." In the speech,

Rabbi Kohler cited the founder of the American Reform Movement, Isaac Mayer Wise, who claimed that Judaism was not "a race nor a nation but a religious denomination." Expressing concern over the "backward" influence of Eastern European Jews, Kohler highlighted the role of American Judaism in preventing Judaism from transforming into a "Russianized, Hebraized or Orientalized" faith.[56] From Kohler's perspective, America was the Promised Land. While these may not have been Friedlander's words, the fact that he quoted this from Kohler exposes his own concerns about an increasing number of Jewish immigrants coming into Houston and his fear that white Gentiles would continue to see Jews as separate and distinct. Since Jewish migration to Houston had only begun in earnest after Hitler ascended to power in 1933, the community was still small and primarily composed of German refugees. Even after Kristallnacht in 1938, when the Jewish Community Relations Council created a coordinating committee for aid to refugees, the committee was forced to follow strict guidelines on who they helped. Each immigrant had to have an affidavit from someone in the Houston Jewish community who vouched for them, as well as job counseling.[57]

Friedlander and Congregation Beth Israel believed in only one type of Judaism in America, and that was a religious one. Judaism as a religion enabled the Jews to be counterparts of Caucasian Gentiles with only a different place of worship.

Friedlander's preoccupation with defining Jews as Caucasian, and with the rise of Zionism altering the identity of Jews in America, is only one factor that led the Caucasian clause to come into existence. Another was a February 1942 event at Congregation Beth Israel hosted by the Houston Commission of Interracial Cooperation. With over one thousand in attendance, the event unexpectedly put the congregation under the spotlight. Robert Kahn, an assistant rabbi and an officer of the commission, replaced Judge James G. Allred at the last minute as the keynote speaker. Kahn's speech on combating Black inequality made headlines in Houston and brought public attention to Congregation Beth Israel.

On February 9, 1942, the *Houston Chronicle* published an article titled "Negro Wants Normal Life, Meeting Told: Rabbi Compares Plight of Colored Race in U.S. to That of Persecuted Jews in Ancient Egypt." The article highlighted Kahn's mention of the disparities between Blacks and whites, including discrimination in health care, teacher wages, and job opportunities. He also criticized the Red Cross for separating Black and white blood for servicemen. At the time, this was an injustice that concerned many Black organizational leaders. Most significantly, Rabbi Kahn created an analogy between the ancient Egyptians and Americans, comparing the Egyptian biblical plagues as punishment for enslaving the Jews, just as America's punishment was the dearth of skilled defense workers due to America's restriction on Black employment. Rabbi Kahn argued that "the negro wants no more than he deserves ... the right to live normally."[58]

The *Houston Post* also reported on Kahn's speech in an article titled "Lack of Negro Training Called Defense Handicap: 1000 Hear Rabbi Kahn at Meeting Here." This article made a point of mentioning that more Blacks attended the event than whites, "four times as many." And African Americans and whites "sat together and listened."[59] On February 14, 1942, Carter Wesley at *The Informer* published "Interracial Meet Is Minus All Prejudice." According to Wesley, this event was unlike any other interracial meeting because Blacks and whites freely prayed, sang, and conversed together. The event at Beth Israel offered a glimpse into a nonsegregated world. Wesley further proclaimed, "The Lord gave us this ... meeting to prove to those who were saying that Negroes and whites could not sit together without the world coming to an end, or serious clashes."[60]

In Houston, segregation was a reality. Rabbi Kahn opposed this status quo in his speech, whereas his congregation perceived their assistant rabbi's speech as a threat to their status in the community. He had stepped out of turn in the white Gentile sphere by criticizing a system that white Houston fiercely wanted to preserve. In becoming an advocate for African Americans, he had placed his congregation in a difficult position. As a result, the leaders of the congregation told Rabbi Kahn in a private meeting that the African American issue was to remain publicly under the authority of the "Protestant denominations" rather than the Jews.[61]

Leaders felt that "less criticism would be directed at the Jews who being a minority themselves could lend but little effective assistance toward remedying the wrongs done other minority groups." They believed that Jews must stay away from "explosive" subjects, such as opposition to the Red Cross. While temple leaders knew Kahn's perspective on the Red Cross's discriminatory practices was in line with the Central Conference of American Rabbis (CCAR), they argued that it was foolish to state this view in public. The CCAR could more easily stand against the Red Cross because it was a larger group, while Houston's Jews were a small minority with little authority. In their response to Kahn, the leaders of Beth Israel quoted the poet Alexander Pope: "Truly, 'fools rush in where angels fear to tread.'"[62]

Kahn also faced a backlash from the US government, particularly District Attorney Douglas McGregor, who asked his friend Al Scharff, a US Customs official and Congregation Beth Israel member, about the interfaith event. McGregor wanted Scharff to investigate Kahn's controversial speech because the federal government suspected Nazi undercover agents of encouraging Black war industry workers to rally against their "imaginary injustices and discriminations."[63] As part of this investigation, Kahn had to release the names of officers on the Houston Interracial Commission. It was apparent that Kahn was not a good fit for Congregation Beth Israel, as he did not completely agree with the synagogue's values, especially the Basic Principles.

On the same date as Kahn's speech, the *Houston Chronicle* featured a story about how Rabbi A. M. Blumenthal of Congregation Beth El had attended a meeting at Trinity East Methodist Church, a Black church. The newspaper highlighted the absence of any "white preachers," even though Rabbi Blumenthal was there.

This and other descriptions of Jews as a group distinct from whites alarmed members of Beth Israel's Policy Formulation

Committee. They worried for the future fate of Jews, especially Jews in the South. Friedlander himself claimed that the presence of rabbis at this "inter-racial meeting and organizations may account for the acceptance by negro leaders of the Jews as a distinct 'race.'" Friedlander referenced another event at the African American New Hope Baptist Church at which a circular stated that the event had "representatives of the 'Chinese,' 'Mexican,' 'Negro,' 'White,' and 'Jewish' races." The Policy Formulation Committee underlined only "White" and "Jewish" to highlight the circular's differentiation between these two groups.[64]

An opinion piece in the *Tulsa Tribune* on February 27, 1943, titled "The American Flag for All of Us," caught Congregation Beth Israel's attention and led many to feel that they needed to retain the Pittsburgh Platform and the conservative ideology of the American Council for Judaism. The author of the Tulsa editorial portrayed Jews as a distinct group: "The habit of the Jew, wherever he goes, is always to remain Jew. He stays racial." He further wrote that "if the Jews must have an army they must first make a land theirs. They must build a national background and end their parasitic practices … But here, [the Jew must be] every inch an American. The American Army and the American Flag are good for us all."[65]

The message that the editorial sent to the committee at Beth Israel was loud and clear: Jews must decide between being loyal to America first or disloyal by choosing the Jewish people first. This dichotomy and the potential charge of dual loyalty propelled the committee to preserve Classical Reform Judaism's perception of the Jewish people as a religious group.

After the incident with the Houston Interracial Commission, the congregation's leaders considered Rabbi Kahn, who had been serving as an army chaplain overseas since 1942, "too young to cope with the more mature leadership of the churches of other denominations."[66] Although the synagogue had promoted him to associate rabbi in his absence, they did not deem him suitable for the position of head rabbi. After all, Kahn had openly advocated for Black rights and been outspoken in his support of a Jewish homeland. In July 1943, this prompted the temple to instead hire

Rabbi Schachtel, a charter member of the American Council for Judaism. Less than a month after Schachtel arrived, the Policy Formulation Committee came together on August 9, 1943, to formulate the Basic Principles and enforce Judaism exclusively as a religion.[67]

Before the Basic Principles passed, other synagogues across the country became aware of Beth Israel's Caucasian clause. On November 19, 1943, David Aronson, rabbi of Beth El Synagogue in Minneapolis, wrote "An Open Letter to Rabbi Schachtel" for the *American Jewish World*. Disputing the concept of "purity of any race," Aronson asked the Houston congregation how they planned to determine whether a person was Caucasian. Ironically, the American Council for Judaism, which had influenced Congregation Beth Israel, chose to describe its members as Caucasian as a reaction to Hitler, while Aronson saw this designation as simply preserving Hitler's plan. Aronson asked, "Will you apply Hitler's test of three generations?" What is more, the Minneapolis rabbi also subtly accused the southern synagogue of being discriminatory toward African Americans, proclaiming, "Has not one father created us all?"[68] To Aronson, proclaiming Jewishness as "Caucasian" bought into a false biological definition of what it meant to be a Jew. It was taking a cue from Hitler and placing Jews in the same position as Aryans. In doing so, Beth Israel was distorting the fundamental principle of Judaism of "B'tzelem Elohim," that each person was created in God's image.

Despite this and other accusations, Congregation Beth Israel passed the principles on November 23, 1943, with 632 in favor and 168 opposed. Those who wished to stay without acknowledging the Basic Principles lost their voting status, a move that created internal division and caused a public spectacle, both locally and nationally.[69]

In November and December 1943, Houston's *JH-V* published numerous critical responses to the Basic Principles. Its editor, David White, was a prominent member of the Jewish community with a keen understanding of the city. In order to inform all Houston's Jews of what had been passed at Congregation

Beth Israel, White published all seven principles as well as other national Jewish leaders' responses.[70]

The effect was swift and clear: Congregation Beth Israel's Basic Principles had become a national issue and thorn in the side of Reform Judaism. Israel Goldstein, president of the Zionist Organization of America, sent an editorial from his organization's newspaper, the *New Palestine*, titled "Pathological Jews" to Congregation Beth Israel on December 10, 1943. The editorial described the congregation as being almost mentally disturbed for creating the Basic Principles. Goldstein perceived them as self-hating Jews and mocked them for their naive beliefs: "These Jews defining themselves as 'Caucasians' seem to be straining to assure their Christian neighbors that

David H. White, Editor, *Jewish Herald Voice*. August 31, 1965. RGD0006N-1965-2839-1-2, Houston Post Photographs, Houston Metropolitan Research Center, Houston Public Library. HP staff/©Houston Chronicle. Used with permission.

they will merit special consideration 'in the day of trouble.'" Any fear he sensed was not a valid excuse for Goldstein, who sarcastically invoked the Jewish mystical concept of *gilgul*, or reincarnation: "Is it possible that the spirit of Ku Kluxism has found a gilgul in Beth Israel of Houston?"[71]

Rabbi Louis I. Newman's "Houston 'Reform Judaism': Folly in Masquerade," published on January 23, 1944, in the *Independent Jewish Press Service* and Rabbi James Heller's "Beth Israel Against Israel" less than a month later both stressed Houston's position as a southern city as the reason for the use of "Caucasian" and suggested that the city's Jews cared more about white perception of them than they did about being Jewish. Newman wrote, "How contemptuous must be Jews in the South who, in their fear lest they be associated with the Negro race, protest that they are 'Caucasian.'"[72]

Heller argued, "If Beth Israel is outraged by a racial interpretation of our Jewish heritage, then why glory in the possession of this racial title?" To Heller, the Caucasian clause excluded nonwhite Jews, similar to the way the South excluded African Americans. Both warned southern Jews that non-Jews would see through their foolish need to emphasize their whiteness and instead cast them aside like the African Americans.[73]

Most contentious toward the Caucasian clause was Rabbi Fred Isserman of Saint Louis. In the *Temple Israel Bulletin*, Isserman published an editorial titled "Jim Crowism—A Temple Creed?" to protest Beth Israel's new membership requirements. He argued that it inscribed segregation into their religious beliefs by denying Black Jews access to synagogue membership, a claim that Beth Israel later claimed was not its intent at all. Isserman asked: "Does its faith command it to exclude from membership all except Caucasians at a time when contempt for race is one of the great evils, and Jews have been its first and worst victims?" Rabbi Isserman agreed that Jews were not a distinct group but felt that Beth Israel's wording caused Jews to appear as a "religion of one race." He viewed the synagogue's "racial exclusion" as anti-Jewish because Judaism was an inclusive faith. In his opinion, the laymen who wrote the principles re-created Judaism "in the image of Jim Crow" and dismissed Judaism's tenet to "serve humanity."[74]

The first time non-Jews became aware of the Basic Principles was when *Time* magazine published "Storm Over Zion" in January 1944. The article acknowledged American Jewish fears surrounding the Zionist question. To the non-Jewish reader, the article presented American Jews as a fractured community at a time when they needed to demonstrate their utmost devotion to America. The article escalated the American Jewish fear of embracing Zionism and possible accusations of either dual loyalty or actual abandonment of America. Some Jews resented anti-Zionist Jews for contributing to Gentile perceptions of American Jews prioritizing Israel over America and even went so far as to blame them for contributing to the spread of anti-Semitism. The *Time* article included a statement from the pro-Zionist paper *Congress Weekly*, which accused Beth Israel of creating " 'Nuremberg laws' of their own."[75]

After nine years at Congregation Beth Israel, Associate Rabbi Kahn resigned publicly on March 27, 1944, in large part due to his speech at the Houston Commission of Interracial Cooperation event. In his letter of resignation, Kahn expressed his disapproval of the Basic Principles, especially their use of "Caucasian." He objected to situating Jews as "inferior stock"— i.e., in the "same racial stock as Hitler and Goebbels" and the perpetuation of a belief in "racial superiority at a time when it needed to be eradicated."[76] Kahn's reaction was not surprising, given his prior focus on Black inequality.

The Basic Principles became infamous throughout North America and eventually throughout the Jewish world. Interest was so widespread that it prompted the Policy Formulation Committee at Beth Israel to reconvene in 1944 to vote on publishing what would become known as *A Handbook of True Facts concerning the Basic Principles of Congregation Beth Israel*. They created the handbook not to define their principles but rather to dispel any misconceptions and turn the tide against negative public opinion. The pamphlet, thoroughly researched and written in a "readable" manner, was thirty-one pages long and structured around questions and answers that addressed those parts of the Basic Principles that had concerned the public.[77]

A Handbook of True Facts

The handbook was a restatement of their earlier words and "an exposition of the principles of Congregation Beth Israel *as a group*—a religious group." The committee's ultimate goal was to demonstrate that the original principles were a counterpoint to other streams of Judaism and that they reflected the *"views of a religious body upon religious matters."*[78] In many ways, the new handbook's intention was for the temple to take ownership of the Basic Principles and explain that they were not about enforcing the cultural system of segregation. The Policy Formulation Committee hoped to define their nationality as American and their faith as Judaism similar to post French emancipation in 1791 when the French Jews declared their nationality French and their religion Judaism to gain acceptance from the new French Republic under Napoleon.

The pamphlet asked: "Is non-voting membership un-Democratic?" The authors explained why they decided congregants who refused to accept the Basic Principles were ineligible to vote. Beth Israel's procedure mirrored America's democratic voting process, in which a nonvoting member became a "foreign born resident of this country, prior to his naturalization. He enjoyed all of the rights and privileges and protection of the country, but he *cannot* vote until he has lived here five years." At that point, the "foreign-born" must go through the process of citizenship. The handbook failed to mention how white primaries in the South denied Black citizens the right to vote.[79]

In the detailed section on "Our race is Caucasian," the committee drew on a mixture of linguistic, anthropological, and legal sources to explain the clause. Instead of focusing on the congregation's location in the South and the de jure segregation in Houston, the authors stressed their national identity as Americans.

The pamphlet asked questions about the Caucasian clause. The first asked why Beth Israel used the word "Caucasian" at all. The committee stressed their desire to distance themselves from the anti-Semitic notion that Jews were "a distinct 'Jewish' race." Emphasizing that they were "Americans of Jewish faith," the authors highlighted that a Jew in America was not any different than a *white* American. The committee also emphasized that, in their congregation, "all members ... are white."[80] They acknowledged other countries and regions had nonwhite Jews, but Houston lacked this diversity and likely would for some time. In light of the rise of anti-Semitism, Congregation Beth Israel encouraged American Jews to accept this principle.

The second question centered on how they should define Caucasian: "What is the *authority* for the statement that the Jews, or 'Semites,' are members of the general division of classes of the races of mankind known as the 'Caucasian' or 'White' race?"[81] The committee answered this question in five parts, first referring to the *Webster* dictionary's definition of Jews, which classified Jews and also Arabs as "Caucasian" based on their "Semitic" roots. The next part focused the anthropological view of Jewish distinctiveness as antiquated. To prevent any possible southern bias, the committee selected only anthropologists from the North. Apart from Carleton Coon, the featured scholars had all worked under Franz Boas (1858–1942), who believed the biological classification of human beings was not accurate to describe human differences. Boas stressed human populations as cultural constructs of their environment.[82]

The Beth Israel committee used these sources to prove three contradictory ideas. The first concept was that Jews were part of all *"three primary races"* ("Caucasian," "Mongoloid," and "Negroid"), in order to dismantle the idea that Jews were a distinct group.[83] This claim also served to validate the existence of Jews of color, even if they did not live in Houston. Second, the committee stressed that, even though Jews were a religion, a culture, and a community of people, they should not promote themselves as distinct because of anti-Semitism. Third, the committee reasserted that Jews were essentially

Caucasian. Though this idea did not necessarily align with their other points, it had the support not only of anthropologists but also Rabbi Julian Morgenstern, the president of Hebrew Union College, who was working to dismantle the idea of Jews as a "race."[84]

Though the Policy Formulation Committee utilized legal cases to justify their use of "Caucasian," they made no mention of the ways in which the laws they evoked discriminated against African Americans. In a telling absence, the handbook's authors did not mention the current white primaries in Houston. Instead, they focused on cases related to the difficulties nonwhite immigrants faced in obtaining citizenship. The unfair legal treatment of Black citizens was left out of their discussion even though a fear of similar treatment was arguably at the root of why the committee professed Jews to be "Caucasian." Whether intended or not, the Policy Formulation Committee had created a system parallel to Houston's discriminatory political system with a class similar to the white majority.

Citing the Naturalization Act of 1790, the committee discussed the legal implications of "Caucasian" for protecting Jewish immigrants: "The U.S. statute reads that 'the right to become a naturalized citizen ... shall extend only to *white* persons, etc. ... and the courts have been called upon to define and construe 'white' persons.'"[85] Until the Immigration and Nationality Act of 1952, whiteness secured citizenship for immigrants, including Jewish immigrants. The Policy Formulation Committee cited *Ozawa v. United States* (1922), which involved a Japanese immigrant's declaration of himself as white to obtain citizenship. The Supreme Court ruled that the color of one's skin did not designate a person "Caucasian" due to varying degrees of complexion within groups, but instead it was the individual's geographic origin—in this case, Asia.[86]

On the surface, the Supreme Court's ruling made it appear as though more flexibility existed in determining who was white; however, the ruling also enabled the government to discriminate against certain racial groups based on their national origin. In essence, the ruling was a facade. In the case of individuals from Asia, or Japan specifically, there was nothing they could do to prove their whiteness. America's history of favoring white immigrants concerned anti-Zionist American Jews, who wanted the option of bringing European Jewish refugees to the United States as opposed to Palestine. As early as 1939, Houston Jewish leadership, in conjunction with the Joint Distribution Committee and the National Palestine Fund, had raised over $100,000 to bring European Jews to the city.[87]

The Johnson-Reed Act was still intact when the congregation instituted the Basic Principles, giving further credence to their concerns about the future of refugees. The Jewish immigration quota also revealed the paradoxical stances of the American Jewish community when it came to immigration. It both advocated for increased immigration and opposed it because of the fear of escalating anti-Semitism. The Policy Formulation Committee at Beth Israel wanted to prove not only that they were Caucasian, thus allowing them access to first-class citizenship, but also that any newcomers who came to Houston were white as well.[88]

The Policy Formulation Committee also cited *In Re Ahmed Hassan*, 48 F. Supp. 843 (D.C. Mich. 1943). In this case, the Supreme Court decided that Hassan was not white and was therefore ineligible for citizenship based on his complexion and religion. Realizing the limits of American patriotism, especially when it came to race, the committee focused on this case because of the potential repercussions if Americans also started to perceive Jews as Middle Eastern.[89] They cited the 1921 petition of Easurk Emsen Charr, which denied citizenship to a World War I veteran because he was Korean. This case would concern the Jews of Houston, since the Nuremberg Laws of 1935 had stripped Jewish World War I veterans of their German citizenship. While Charr's case did not explicitly address African Americans, the result paralleled their experience. Blacks may have been citizens—unlike Easurk Emsen Charr—but like Charr, they had fought for the United States without receiving first-class citizenship. One had to be loyal to America *and* Caucasian to gain all its rights and privileges. In turn, the committee believed the malleability of American citizenship justified why they had to both denounce Zionism and assert that they were Caucasian.[90]

The heavy emphasis on immigration and naturalization in *A Handbook of True Facts* demonstrated the committee members' concerns for their own personal status and the potential status of European Jewish immigrants who might alter white Gentiles' perception of Jews. Congregation Beth Israel's actions mirrored those of its European peers of the past. Just as European Jews sought to define themselves as both compatriots and Jews during the quest for emancipation as they did in such places as France in 1791 and Germany in 1871, the congregation members also tried to convince Gentiles that they were like them—Americans—but of the Jewish faith. For Jews, whether in Europe or America, to feel secure as a minority, they had to gain white acceptance to secure citizenship.

Consequences of the Basic Principles

Neither all of Houston's Jews nor the local or national press ever fully accepted the Basic Principles, and in some respects *A Handbook of True Facts* compounded the problem. Because Congregation Beth Israel was a southern congregation, its critics assumed that its use of "Caucasian" adhered to the laws of segregation. Moreover, even though Rabbi Schachtel did not become head rabbi until after the committee created the Basic Principles, the public nonetheless considered him responsible. He even received anonymous calls at night threatening him and his family. Despite this hostility, Schachtel reiterated that Judaism was exclusively a religion.[91]

Initially, the Houston Rabbinical Association ostracized Schachtel, even as the rabbi tried to explain that the Basic Principles emerged out of a fear of local Jews becoming "ghettoized"— a self-segregating people. Eventually, in June of 1945, the Houston Rabbinical Association "adopted a resolution rebuking Rabbi Schachtel" for his continued attempt to defend his congregation's principles. The Jewish Community Relations

Council even created and passed a resolution that "censured" the American Council for Judaism's methods.[92]

Schachtel, however, weathered the controversy and continued to serve as Beth Israel's spiritual leader. He continued to be vocal about anti-Zionism and to deny the idea of the "Jewish race." It was only after Israel became a state in 1948 that he fully resigned from the American Council for Judaism.[93] The city's white Gentiles, even those in high society, never publicly reacted to the Basic Principles and embraced Rabbi Schachtel for years to come.

One of the most profound effects of the Basic Principles was the formation of Congregation Emanu El, the breakaway temple of Congregation Beth Israel. (This temple will become significant in my later discussion of Jewish involvement in civil rights.) In 1945, Rabbi Alan Green, the temple's interim rabbi, gave a sermon titled "Houston—Cross-Roads of Reform." He spoke of the ripple effect the Basic Principles had on other temples in Lincoln, Pontiac, and Baton Rouge that followed suit with their own anti-Zionist principles. Although Green did not include this in his sermon, these temples removed the Caucasian clause.[94]

In May 1945, the Basic Principles became part of Congregation Beth Israel's official bylaws and were not formally removed until 1968. Interestingly, David White, editor of the *JH-V* and a member of Congregation Emanu El, published an article that criticized the temple not long after Congregation Beth Israel's official affirmation of the Basic Principles. The paper readdressed the Caucasian clause on June 7, 1945. The headline read "Rabbi Tofield Takes Exception," and underneath it asked, "Who claims the Jews are a race? (Zionists do not call themselves 'Caucasian' Jews)."[95] This article denigrated the Basic Principles' use of the term "Caucasian."

A few months after this article appeared, Congregation Emanu El became the public voice of opposition against the Basic Principles when they installed Rabbi Kahn as head rabbi in November 1945. After fulfilling his role as a military chaplain, it was always the synagogue's intention to appoint Kahn; however, his new position marked the official schism between

the two synagogues. In his first sermon, Kahn stated that Emanu
El would stand out because it would be a temple "unfettered by
rigid dogma, uninhibited by fear of non-Jewish opinion, unstrati-
fied by the financial or social caste system, a Judaism that stands
for freedom of the pulpit and freedom of the pew."[96]

The Basic Principles marked the beginning of change
within the Houston Jewish community and showed that this
small population did not share the same views. These differences determined which temples took an interest in civil rights
issues and which ones prioritized other concerns. Despite these
differences, they shared a concern as to how as Jews they would
define themselves. Those local Jews who opposed the Caucasian clause did not want any label that publicly and permanently
defined them in a certain way, especially because the clause had
caused the city's Jews to appear as segregationists. Clear from
the reaction was that Congregation Beth Israel had overstepped
what American Jews and Houston Jews felt was permissible to
express publicly. In the future, they needed to consider carefully
what could be said outside the walls of the synagogue and what
belonged behind closed doors because what was said outside the
community represented all Houston's Jews.

When Reform Jewish leader Stephen S. Wise published the
article "The Shame of Houston" in 1944, he lambasted Beth
Israel for embarrassing American Jewry and making a public
spectacle of their "loathsome brand of cowardly anti-Jewish-
ness."[97] He wished the board had kept the principles to themselves rather than creating a media craze and a nationwide
Jewish scandal. Wise further rebuked the temple for publicizing
the issue even more with *A Handbook of True Facts*.

Prominent Houston Jewish businessman Joe Weingarten, along with more than two hundred congregants, resigned
from Congregation Beth Israel in protest of the principles' anti-
Zionist stance. Weingarten proclaimed that "we are Jews by
our glorious history as a nation, by our traditions, and culture,
by our common suffering, through our spirit of brotherhood."[98]
Weingarten believed he could be both Jewish and American and
that he did not have to compromise his love for his faith and

the Jewish people to be a good American. However, his role in the Houston business world precluded him from discussing this publicly. The above statement is from private correspondence. Indeed, despite having a large number of Black customers, Weingarten conformed to segregation laws to protect his wider business dealings and status in the Gentile community.[99]

While this public declaration of "Caucasian" created conflict both in the Houston and greater American Jewish communities, Beth Israel's Jews did so out of fear that not doing so would label them a minority and possibly subject them to the same discrimination African Americans in Houston experienced. Furthermore, while they may have privately disagreed with the segregationist systems in place in Houston, some of the city's Jews feared that any public dissent of segregation opened them up to Communist allegations, further threatening their status as loyal white Americans.

As this chapter clearly reveals, Basic Principle 2 was more about providing Jews security in a city that privileged white skin for first-class citizenship than it was a position on segregation. Moreover, we should not overlook the overriding concern with Zionism and its potential to alter American perceptions of Jewish identity. Although Schachtel would state on November 29, 1948, that "the name Jew is now associated with courage, stamina, heroism, fighting power—the anti-Semites have been confounded," Houston Jewish leaders would not truly become empowered by the State of Israel until the Six-Day War twenty years later. Ironically, in subsequent decades, the ideology of Zionism would become the impetus that would help to facilitate a political bond between Black and Jewish political leadership in Houston.[100]

For Houston's Jews, the topic of pro-Zionist and anti-Zionist sentiment remained in the foreground. However, the foremost question of Jewish identity in America, in regard to race and race relations, did not dissipate. Houston Jewish leaders, concerned with the way that non-Jews viewed them, wanted to be known as white Americans of Jewish faith simply because in Houston, as in other parts of the United States, a person's racial identity determined his or her privileges and rights. Communal leaders voiced their thoughts on racism cautiously, while they battled with the role Jews should play in the fight for civil rights.

In the next chapter, I explore how the Cold War continued to change the Houston Jewish community's perspective on their American identity. As a new Red Scare emerged in Houston, communal leaders declared tolerance an American value and promoted it for every citizen, including African Americans.

Chapter 2

Houston's Communist Scare and the Jewish Promotion of Tolerance

Let us be careful of labels.

David White
December 26, 1946

s the United States entrenched itself in a Cold War with the Soviet Union, Houston's Jews faced greater complexities in defining themselves as white Americans of Jewish faith. Fear of Communism loomed large over the city. As much as Houston's Jewish leaders wanted to support their own community and other minorities experiencing discrimination, they also understood the danger of Gentiles labeling them Communists. In response, communal leaders sought a delicate balance between pursuing a liberal strategy toward civil rights and attempting to acculturate into white society.

Growing anti-Semitism prompted Houston's Jewish leaders to encourage a communal focus on the United States as a nation that opposed intolerance. However, this assertion was in stark contrast to the ongoing treatment and marginalization of the city's African Americans. Under the premise that the

United States promoted equality for all, local rabbis and their congregants participated and sometimes organized interfaith and intergroup events to bring Jews, whites, and Black Christians together. Such events were not only a way to showcase the Jewish adherence to America and its values, they were also public displays against Communism.

Through sermons and published works, rabbis Robert Kahn and Hyman Judah Schachtel publicly promoted tolerance to secure their identity as loyal Americans. However, their inclusive message was a hard sell to many local whites who conflated the promotion of equal rights for African Americans with the spread of Communism. Their resistance created a two-sided battle between the white establishment and Houston Jewish leadership. In their quest to provide protection for their fellow Jews and secure white status, these so-called "Cold War liberals" felt the full weight of both anti-Semitism and anti-Communist scrutiny. This battle for tolerance did not improve the marginalized status of Houston's African Americans.

The postwar period witnessed the slow advent of tolerance as both an American and a Jewish value and eventually became a central tenet of Cold War liberalism. Also anti-Communists, Cold War Jewish liberals supported civil rights and equality for all in the name of American democracy.[1] Jews worked closely with non-Jewish organizations to promote tolerance of all Americans, but not in a way that celebrated differences as became common in the 1970s. Frank Sinatra's 1945 short film, *The House I Live In,* best encapsulated this mood when he sang, "All races and religion, that's America to me."[2] However, this new type of openness and the postwar liberal notion that everyone—despite their skin color, religion, or nationality—was American did not guarantee equal rights for all, especially not in segregated Houston.

It was important for Jews to assert their similarities to other Americans rather than their differences in a time when the threat of Communism caused Americans to turn against each other and accuse one another of being un-American. The founder of the National Conference of Christians and Jews, Everett R. Clinchy, stated in 1946 that "no group is making a greater sacrifice, a more earnest plea, or a more vigorous fight for the dignities and rights of all groups in this democracy than the Jews."[3] The recent horrors of Nazism emboldened American Jews to promote this liberal philosophy. In addition, the administration of President Harry Truman encouraged harmony between all Americans because of their concern that internal conflict, including the inability to resolve discrimination against African Americans, provided the Soviet Union with the fodder it needed to challenge the United States.

Taking a cue from national Jewish leadership, many Jewish leaders in Houston became outspoken proponents of tolerance of all minorities. In 1946, David White, the editor and owner of the *JH-V*, wrote an editorial titled "Let Us Be Careful of Labels" in which he warned local Jews not to let their personal fears cause them to make rash decisions about people. Instead, they should think before accusing an individual of being anti-Semitic, Communist, or Fascist. Cautioning against presuming the worst of anyone, White called for Jews to be a "bit more tolerant of the other man's point of view." After all, not all Europeans had cavorted with the Nazis, and Houston's Jews certainly did not want to repeat any of the same discrimination so recently perpetrated against European Jews. White argued that too many Jews were rallying against "antisemitism" and "fascism" in the name of American "patriotism" without knowing all the facts. He especially asked his coreligionists not to throw around Communist accusations without justification, since vehement anti-Communists were quick to label any Houston Jew who publicly supported tolerance as a Communist.[4]

Despite the ensuing social battle, postwar Houston was thriving economically because of a building boom and the growth of shipbuilding and the oil and gas industry. The construction of new businesses, including department stores, transformed downtown Houston into a cosmopolitan center. However, not all Houstonians shared in this prosperity. A small but powerful group of white Gentiles ruled the power structure of the city and perpetuated uneven economic growth for African Americans and poorer whites.[5] As the civil rights lawyer David Berg wrote in his memoir, "Houston appeared to be an open city, [but] it was run covertly by a tiny group of wealthy bankers, oilmen, and builders who ... made wise if self-interested decisions about the city's direction."[6]

Accompanying this economic boom was population growth. In fact, in the 1940s and 1950s, Houston's population grew faster than any other city in the country—from 384,514 to 596,163. Many feared this rapid growth, especially the increase of the Black population from 86,302 to 125,400. Though the city's Jewish population only rose from 13,500 to 14,000 in 1950, Houston still had the largest Jewish community in Texas.[7]

Houston's prosperity did not resolve the city's fear of Communism. Members of the Houston establishment became increasingly concerned with the growth of the federal government and its interference in certain local affairs, which they felt should be off limits to federal oversight. This included labor issues, taxes, education, and Black-white relations. Undergirding white conservative fear was the potential disruption of the city's social balance—and thereby their elite status—by federal enforcement of racial equality. This had been of local concern since President Franklin D. Roosevelt, but President Truman's creation of the President's Committee on Civil Rights in 1946 compounded their anxiety. Federal interference—especially in matters of intergroup relations—threatened to disrupt the city and sowed the seeds for later anti-Communist fears and organized action against suspected Communists, as well as a shift in voting allegiance.[8]

In the November 1952 election, the majority of the city's whites voted for Republicans, in large part out of a fear of Communism. The irony was that at the height of the Red Scare in Houston from 1952 to 1953, the city had no active Communist organizations.[9]

Anti-Semitism and Anti-Black Sentiment: Two Different Fights

Houston's Jews falsely envisioned that the postwar call for tolerance would protect them from anti-Semitism and also promote their status as good Americans. In particular, many still felt the presence of anti-Semitism in the housing restrictions they faced. After World War II, housing was in short supply in Houston, leaving some Jewish newcomers without residences. Fearing that publicly addressing such issues would highlight their differences, Jewish communal leaders handled their problems internally. Organizations like the Jewish Community Relations Council (JCRC), the National Council of Jewish Women (NCJW), and Jewish Family Service helped settle around one hundred new refugees in Houston. Leaders also established the Jewish Vocational Service to assist Jewish veterans, refugees, and young adults. To combat anti-Semitism and educational, housing, and work discrimination, Houston Jewish leaders created the Southwestern Jewish Community Council in sponsorship with the Anti-Defamation League (ADL), the American Jewish Committee (AJC), and the Jewish Community Relations Council.[10]

Despite efforts to form a united front against anti-Semitism, the city's Jews still faced internal conflict over Zionism. Colonel Albert A. Kaufman, who served as president of the JCRC from 1947 to 1949, described the ideological conflict "like a Civil War climate with brother pitted against brother and whole congregations splitting on the nation of Israel."[11] This sentiment echoed an earlier editorial by David White in the *JH-V* who, six months after World War II, asked the Jews to stop the infighting over Zionism and labeling each other un-American. White emphasized that Jews had enough enemies without having internal conflicts and stressed that it was time for Jews to unite as one community: "We are Americans! We are Jews." Further, he argued that such internal opposition made Jews vulnerable and that the fight against anti-Semitism was equally important to promoting Americanism. Jews needed to be "loyal to our nation and to our religion" without turning on each other.[12]

In the early 1950s, several local Zionist organizations and the American Council for Judaism published an article in several Houston newspapers debating Zionist loyalty to America. After local protest from the predominantly Zionist community, the groups met again and decided that, in order to protect Houston's Jews, they would no longer publish divisive articles on Zionism.

This included none in Jewish newspapers like the *JH-V.* Throughout the 1950s, however, a contingent of anti-Zionists still continued to exist, and in response, the wider community began to express even stronger pro-Israel sentiments, especially in the 1960s.[13]

In terms of burgeoning anti-Semitism, many local Jews in Houston criticized those leaders who recommended silence in the face of hate. After the *JH-V* published an article about Solomon A. Fineberg's 1943 work *Overcoming Anti-Semitism,* in which the director of the AJC argued that the most efficient way to oppose anti-Semites was to ignore their actions, Dr. Leon J. Taubenhaus wrote a strongly worded response to Fineberg in a letter to the editor on November 2, 1946. The doctor and public health expert argued that Fineberg's position was not only wrong, it was "dangerous to the Jewish people." American Jews, he stated, were falling into the same trap as the European Jews who ignored and did not fight Nazi oppressors. Taubenhaus fervently believed that Jews must "*lead* [an] aggressive fight against anti-Semitism." Even though he saw anti-Semitism as a Jewish problem, Taubenhaus believed Gentiles were more inclined to help if Jews publicly stood against prejudice. From his perspective, certain values united all Americans. One of those values was freedom of worship. Taubenhaus argued that the fear of Houston's Jews that their stance against religious discrimination might separate them from their American identity was unfounded. Their stance could unite them with those Gentiles most concerned with safeguarding freedom of religion.[14]

In response to numerous local lectures on the growth of anti-Semitism, David White wrote another editorial a few weeks after Taubenhaus's titled "Are We Selling 'Fear Judaism'?" White worried such speakers instilled unnecessary fear in the Jewish community. While he agreed that anti-Semitism was visible, like Dr. Taubenhaus he advised Jews to fight it without fear. He stressed that fear cannot exist in a democracy and that Jews must accept that some people might hate them. They must find a way to cope with their predicament—not just ignore their oppressors, as Fineberg encouraged.[15] When Thomas Friedman, the director of the Southwestern Jewish Community Relations

Council, spoke to the community on the ADL, he also urged those in attendance to take comfort that anti-Semitism was the antithesis of American democracy. Like other communal leaders, both locally and nationally, Friedman wanted to instill in his fellow Jews that the United States was a safe place. By being good Americans, Jews could become like their white Gentile counterparts and gain acceptance.[16]

Despite such pronouncements of hope, anti-Semitism hindered the lives of Jews in Houston. Certain companies, like oil corporations such as Texaco, would not interview or hire Jewish candidates. Because many middle-income neighborhoods in Houston had deed restrictions in the late 1940s and early 1950s, non-Jews had to act as third parties and buy houses for Jews. When in 1947 Fred Wiener of the Jewish Vocational Service spoke at the local Jewish Community Center (JCC) on employment discrimination, he acknowledged that statistically Jews still faced employment barriers, especially in training and working in the field of professional engineering. Weiner encouraged listeners not to allow such discrimination to defeat them or motivate them to "lie about their religion when applying for a position."[17]

To overcome prejudice, his solution was for Jews to become stronger candidates. This way, "any Jewish professional could meet the even higher standards set for him within his field." Weiner wanted Jewish job applicants to believe that the American dream was attainable as long as they worked hard. He presented recent employment figures to prove that Jews did work in Houston. Furthermore, the Jewish Vocational Service assessed that 80 percent of Houston's Jews worked in business, 7 percent in skilled labor, and 10 to 12 percent in Jewish organizations.[18]

In 1949, the Jews of Houston started responding to recent reports on American anti-Semitism published by the national ADL. The 1949 Passover edition of the *JH-V* mentioned an April 21 panel discussion at B'nai B'rith's Houston lodge. A panel of prominent Jewish leaders discussed the prepublication of the ADL's survey titled "How Secure These Rights."[19] Most likely inspired by Truman's Committee on Civil Rights, the survey focused on the main areas in which Jews still faced discrimination, such as in housing, hotels, employment, education, and social organizations. A year later, Congregation Emanu El's May 1950 discussion of Arnold Forster's *A Measure of Freedom: An Anti-Defamation League Report* once again suggested that the solution to anti-Semitism was to focus on the American value of tolerance. To prevent the destruction of American democracy, Forster strongly advocated for individuals to unite to oppose all forms of bigotry.[20]

While Forster's concept of unity might have protected Jews from additional discrimination, the concept was not as helpful for African Americans, for whom segregation continued unabated. After World War II, rural Blacks started to move to Houston in search of jobs and a better life. Contact between whites and African Americans only occurred in the Houston marketplace or through domestic service. Rarely, if ever, did they interact socially with whites, including Jews. For the Black residents of Houston, consciousness of their second-class status was unavoidable. In 1939, B. T. Brooks, a semiskilled worker for the Hughes Tool Company, expressed that "as long as a negro attends to his own business he gets along all right." Brooks confessed that when a white person came to his home, he made him sit on the porch regardless of the temperature because "when I have a white person in my power, I am tough on him. I try to be just as tough on him as they are on us."[21]

Ira B. Bryant, a former principal of Booker T. Washington High School, remembered the humiliation of having to go through the back door whenever he entered a public place. He was fortunate that the white people he encountered did not enforce it, but they were the exception. Bryant recalled how the older Black generations were "accustomed to going in back doors, taking off their hats, and bowing and scraping to white people."[22]

In Houston, as elsewhere in the South, African Americans did not share equally in postwar prosperity. They still worked menial jobs and lived in overcrowded neighborhoods with poor municipal services.[23] However, segregation presented a paradox in Houston. In 1940, the African American population was 86,302 compared to the miniscule population of Jews, which was

13,500. In some ways, the larger numbers of African Americans and the city's strict segregation made them less vulnerable to white confrontations than Jews who lived among whites.[24]

Even though its restrictions were all-encompassing, some leaders thought segregation protected Black residents from discriminatory whites and created a place where they could nurture their own culture and consciousness. For instance, Carter Wesley believed that African Americans needed identifiable Black spaces that portrayed Black identity, culture, and experiences, and he was against the idea of white spaces becoming inclusive spaces. Rather, Wesley thought that Black spaces needed to be on par with white spaces so that both communities would find each other's space worthy of racial intermingling.[25]

Regardless of the protections segregation *might* have afforded, the Black residents of Houston felt its weight. Dr. Ernie Attwell remembered feeling frustrated that even a hamburger shop had to be Black-owned for an African American to eat there. As Attwell explained, the problem with segregation was that it was "about power ... It's about, I have power over you."[26] In other words, segregation equaled control. Because African Americans did not interact with whites, their communities became self-supporting: they could go to school, attend church, go shopping, attend social institutions, and eat at Black-owned restaurants. The exception was retail, as there were foreign-born white merchants, including Jews, who had stores in Black parts of the city like the Third Ward. Even among African American wards, there was limited interaction. The main place the various communities interacted, if at all, was downtown.[27]

Despite ongoing segregation, African Americans made some political gains, including 1944's *Smith v. Allwright*, which declared prohibiting Blacks from voting to be unconstitutional. In addition, African Americans started to become precinct judges in Black neighborhoods. Reverend L. H. Simpson, leader of the NAACP, became the first African American to pursue political office in Houston when he ran for city council in 1946. Simpson lost, in large part because of the poll tax, which reduced the middle- and upper-class African American vote to a small number. A further sign of political advancement was the integration of the Democratic Harris County Convention in 1948. By the 1950s, local Black residents felt empowered enough to file several lawsuits that led to the desegregation of public golf courses and restrooms in city hall.[28]

These advancements, however, were small and not indicative of widespread ideological change. In 1948, a Texas poll demonstrated that 60 percent of whites saw Black Texans "as inferior and deserving of unequal treatment." This attitude translated into high levels of unemployment. When African Americans did have jobs, they remained, for the most part, unskilled. Only a small number of Blacks held government positions, and they continued to be underrepresented in professional fields like nursing, clerical work, and librarianships. In the 1940s, Houston had no Black firemen, even though city ordinances forced Black residents to pay taxes for public jobs inaccessible to them.[29]

Especially in the case of education, separate but equal was a facade. In 1946, the University of Texas at Austin denied Heman Sweatt, a former postal worker, entrance into its law school. In an attempt to gain public support, Sweatt approached the JCC in Houston. Explaining his plight, Sweatt spoke of two convergent histories: the wider Black struggle from enslavement through segregation and his personal fight to gain admittance to law school. Though the JCC made no effort to support Sweatt publicly, their publicist Jack Feinsilver wrote an article in the *JH-V* describing a recent Jewish discussion of tolerance in education at a Sunday night social: "The discussion that followed [after Sweatt spoke] showed considerable agreement on the objective of ending segregation in education." Reinforcing the liberal Cold War ideology of tolerance as an American value, he emphasized that "all minorities must be accorded dignity and status if Democracy is to flourish." Feinsilver and other communal members sided with Sweatt's argument that "the expense of maintaining two systems of education [was] very costly and [would] result in a lower standard of education to both White and Negro groups."[30]

Though Feinsilver's article revealed that the Jews of Houston supported Sweatt and sympathized with his unequal treatment, they did not publicly advocate on his behalf. Other national Jewish organizations took on this role, including the American Jewish Congress (AJCongress), the AJC, and the ADL.[31] Most likely, Houston Jews saw Sweatt's problem as an issue for the University of Texas at Austin, not Houston. With or without the support of Jewish communal leaders, Houston's African Americans, like Heman Sweatt, attempted to end segregation through judicial litigation. In 1948, the National Progressive Party formed a branch in Houston. One of the party's founding members was Black civil rights activist Moses Leroy. Sweatt and Lulu White were also members of the NAACP.[32]

In 1948, the Progressive Party presidential candidate, former vice president Henry A. Wallace, attended what Leroy proclaimed was "the first integrated political rally in the South." At this meeting, Wallace made a pivotal statement that impacted Black Houstonians: "I'm the candidate for the presidency of the United States of the third party ... Down with segregation. Down with racism." In a 1975 interview with the Houston Metropolitan Research Center, Leroy reflected on the noticeable Jewish interest in desegregation and the Progressive Party: "Oh, yeah, there were quite a few whites then, more especially, a lot of Jews."[33] When interviewer Florence Coleman asked Leroy to name party members, he refused in order to protect them from scrutiny.

The founding of the local Progressive Party marked the beginning of a concerted effort to end segregation, though it did not become the primary political vehicle of Black Houstonians moving forward. In 1949, local progressive leaders founded the Harris County Council of Organizations, a multifaceted group of churches, individuals, and organizations working to prevent economic discrimination, promote political progress, and advance educational opportunities. In particular, the council promoted the Black right to vote and helped to mobilize Black mayoral candidates. According to Eleanor Tinsley, who would be a future school board and city council member, "The Black community did very well for itself in getting behind candidates and then supporting them. It was not with money. It was actually with votes."[34] What is more, the Harris County Council of

Organizations enabled Black residents to report incidents of prejudice. The local NAACP fought to enforce fair employment rules and to gain Black employment in white businesses, further educational rights, and equal pay for Black teachers.[35]

In Houston, Jews and African Americans lived in two different worlds even though they both faced discrimination. Houston Jewish efforts to combat anti-Semitism under the umbrella of a democratic ideology failed to resonate with local Black residents who still lacked basic rights. With rising fears of Communism and anxiety toward the postwar promotion of tolerance as an American value, efforts to bridge the gap between these communities and the white Christian community only went so far.

The Challenges of Intergroup Relations

As early as the 1920s, intergroup events among Jews and white and Black Christians were part of efforts to promote tolerance. These events took place under the auspices of several different groups. The National Council of Churches hosted an event dubbed "Race Relations Sundays," which came into existence in February 1924 and occurred yearly until 1965 on the Sunday closest to Abraham Lincoln's birthday. In 1927, the National Conference of Christians and Jews (NCCJ) developed programming to promote positive relations between the two groups, and in the 1940s, the conference started to include African Americans. The NCCJ's National Brotherhood Week started in the 1940s as an annual meeting of Jews, whites, and African Americans. Held during the third week of February, corresponding with Washington's birthday, Brotherhood Week lasted until the 1980s.[36]

In Houston, the Council on Education in Race Relations was an umbrella group for the Houston Rabbinical Association, the YMCA and YWCA, the Greater Houston Ministerial Association (GHMA), the Interdenominational Ministerial Alliance, the Houston Council of Churchwomen, the Jewish Community Relations Council, the Council of Churches of Greater Houston, and the Houston Commission of Interracial Cooperation.[37] These programs all had different names, but they had the same premise—promoting tolerance by physically bringing Jews and Christians, both white and Black, together. In parts of the South, the problem was that "interracial" events often had no Blacks in attendance. Moreover, certain national civil rights organizations criticized Brotherhood events for being ineffective at creating long-lasting change.[38]

Despite these well-founded criticisms, these events did bring public attention to local and national efforts toward inclusion and tolerance. Gertrude Batiste, founder of the San Antonio chapter of the National Coalition of 100 Black Women, fondly remembered attending a Houston Brotherhood event as a young girl. To her, the event's significance was that it was one of the few times she interacted with people who were not African American. When whites came into her area, it was usually "when there was trouble." Batiste felt it "was a very brave thing" that her parents brought her to the event. Most poignantly, she remembered sitting next to Jews. If only briefly, these events enabled the Jews of Houston to interact with Blacks socially instead of in a business setting. Together, they spoke of their "heritages and even to recall that we have one God—one God for all people."[39]

By the late 1940s, Houston's Jewish community hosted several interracial events, including a February 1947 event called Race Relations Sunday, which included a Black choir from Booker T. Washington High School. Promoted in the *JH-V*, the newspaper asserted the pressing need for such events in the current political climate. Pointing to Cold War tensions, the paper expressed that "the benefits of democracy must be shared by all, regardless of color or creed, and it is necessary to rededicate ourselves to a greater appreciation of the true democratic ideals."[40]

In the same year, Rabbi William Malev of the Conservative synagogue Congregation Beth Yeshurun and the vice president of the Houston Inter-Racial Commission spoke at the First Presbyterian Church on November 23 at a Thanksgiving service. Even though it was at a church, Beth Yeshurun's monthly publication, *The Message*, urged the community to attend this service. That the event took place during the quintessential American holiday was significant because it reminded citizens of their country's founding. Moreover, Thanksgiving was a time to unite all groups despite differences.[41]

In the 1950s, efforts to promote tolerance as an American ideal through intergroup events continued with clergy at the helm. In the winter of 1952, the Council on Education in Race Relations hosted Dr. George D. Kelsey, a Black theologian who influenced Dr. King. He gave a speech on the "Religious Basis for Human Rights."[42] Sometimes the speakers at intergroup events were Christian clergy; other times the council invited rabbis.[43] In 1955, the council called for an intergroup program between whites and African Americans at Congregation Beth Yeshurun. Held at Beth Yeshurun on Thanksgiving, this open event used student ushers from the University of Houston, the Rice Institute, Baylor Medical School, and Texas Southern University. Congregation Beth Yeshurun encouraged its members to come because the event stressed "the equality of all American citizens, whatever their race, creed, or color."[44]

When he enrolled at the University of Houston for a doctorate in education, Rabbi Schachtel wrote his dissertation titled "Light of Liberty—A Guide to Better Human Relations," to encourage all students to promote intergroup relations. The University of Houston Press published the dissertation—a study and activity guide created for high school juniors and seniors to help them understand how to promote American ideals through positive relations with all people. Schachtel decided to address students because he felt that the school environment reflected "all of society in miniature."[45]

It is worth noting the irony of how Schachtel encouraged high school students to look past color not too long after Congregation Beth Israel chose to define Jews as "Caucasian." But in his push for new generations to embrace the new American ideal of tolerance, Schachtel was buoyed by the successful end to World War II, Israel's statehood, and the booming postwar economy of the United States. For a Cold War liberal, the future looked bright indeed.

Even though it did not bring them together into the same physical space, radio provided a means for Jews and Black and white Christians to interact and promote their unified message of tolerance. Still the main communication medium until television entered American households in the late 1950s, radio was a cultural equalizer. On the airways, there was no segregation or awareness of skin color.[46] In the late 1940s, the Council on Education in Race Relations sponsored a radio program in Houston with Congregation Beth Yeshurun's Rabbi Malev as host. Part of the *American Way* series, the program used entertainment to educate. During the broadcast, Rabbi Malev emphasized the need to promote relations between African Americans and whites as an American ideal for all ages.[47]

Also part of the *American Way* series, another program fostered the "ideal of brotherhood among races and creeds, which constituted the American ideal."[48] Geared toward adults and children, it centered on Houston's minority groups and was eventually picked up by both of the other radio stations in Houston. The program's goal was to engage all Houstonians to "[spread] the message of cooperation and brotherhood among the many racial and religious groups in our community."[49]

The radio programs, like other intergroup events, helped bridge the gap that segregation created. However, this break was only for discrete periods of time. Once listeners turned off the radio program, they simply returned to their segregated world.

Malev was not the only rabbi in Houston to host his own radio show. Beginning in the late 1940s, Rabbi Schachtel hosted his *Humanitarian Hour*, during which he urged his fellow listening Americans, particularly non-Jews, to advocate for a more inclusive vision of America. In a series of sermons, Schachtel voiced his Cold War liberal ideology of tolerance. At his pulpit at Congregation Emanu El and on his own radio program, Robert Kahn also waged war against Communism and included more explicit references to the local plight of African Americans in Houston.

Rabbi Schachtel and Rabbi Kahn's Sermons on Communism

On Sunday mornings, Schachtel's sermons spoke to a general audience on topics ranging from faith and Americanism to current political issues. The radio program aired on Houston's station KXYZ. On November 2, 1952, the rabbi gave a sermon titled "The 'Change' We Really Need," in which he reiterated the privileges of living in America, including the right to vote, the ability to own land, freedom of religious and civic expression, and access to a public education. He alluded to the victory in the Civil War, which brought about "freedom of mankind—the freedom of all the races of mankind. The colored man was given his freedom because democracy cannot be served when any of its people are kept underprivileged."[50]

Schachtel believed the end of slavery paved the way for dismantling child labor laws and for women's suffrage. Schachtel's history, however, failed to mention the ongoing plight of southern Blacks, especially in Houston. Instead, he promoted freedom for all—despite the fact that America did not live up to this ideal. His omission was likely because he did not want to openly appear on the radio as a Black rights activist, not because he did not actually believe in universal equality. Rather than focusing on the nation's shortcomings, Schachtel focused on the fear of Communism and how it disempowered America's rights and privileges.[51]

In February 1955, Rabbi Schachtel delivered another sermon titled "The Family of Mankind," in which he argued that Americans ought to engage in daily interactions with those from other races and creeds. If American citizens were to live up to the ideals of the Declaration of Independence, the Bill of Rights, and its historical legacy of immigration, then "bigotry, religious and racial prejudice would be the exception." Alluding to Black inequality, he argued that the soul of America was brotherhood: "No man claims to be a good American or a good Christian or a good Jew ... who hates his fellow man for no other reason but that he is of a different color or of a different religious affiliation."[52]

Schachtel's view of the United States was optimistic. He rejected the perception of widespread hatred, a view which overlooked the treatment of the Black residents of Houston. This blind spot meant that the rabbi offered only ideological and not concrete solutions for local Blacks. Instead, he advised patience.

Schachtel continued his arguments in print. In his 1956 book, *The Life You Want to Live*, he not only explained how to live a moral life, he also highlighted what it meant to be a good citizen in America as opposed to in the Soviet Union. Even though Schachtel argued against American exceptionalism, he nonetheless emphasized the dichotomy between America and the Soviet Union and the intersection between Communism and bigotry. Ideal Americans did not hold hatred in their hearts—that was the mainstay of the ignorant. "Goodness," according to Schachtel, was contextual. Under Communism, being "good" was being obedient to the state and willing to betray anyone for the nation. In contrast, Americans living in a "free society" were good citizens if they committed themselves to Judeo-Christian beliefs and the "just law" inherent in monotheism.[53]

Although Rabbi Schachtel did acknowledge that the United States still needed to work toward becoming a place for everyone, regardless of their religion or skin color, his juxtaposition of the United States with the Soviet Union downplayed American subjugation of its citizens. His Cold War liberalism overshadowed this discrepancy to glorify US democratic tolerance values. Additionally, it may appear that his underlying intent was to remind his Christian readers to see Jews as equals even though Jews went to a temple instead of a church. Schachtel contended that if any religion rejected people for their differences, then it was not a true religion. Ironically, Schachtel made this point in a southern city with widespread segregation. For the sake of peace, he called upon all Americans to view one another as created in "the image of God." Schachtel used anti-Zionism and anti-Communism to demonstrate to his white Gentile audience that not only was he a loyal American Jew, his congregation was as well.[54]

In contrast to Schachtel, Robert Kahn's anti-Communist stance included more explicit references to Black inequality. Kahn emphasized US progress toward Black rights as a way to underscore American exceptionalism. In his Rosh Hashanah sermon to Congregation Emanu El on October 1, 1951, he painted a rosy picture of Black-white relations in the United States. Titled "Promise of America," Kahn's sermon stressed how the

United States had not experienced the Holocaust or persecuted the Jews the way the Russians had for centuries. The nation was not in the middle of a religious war, like India and Pakistan. In his sermon, Kahn glossed over segregation, instead pointing to racial improvements and Black advancement in "the fields of education, housing, government, political rights, civil rights, and the army." Despite these advancements, Kahn urged the Jews of Houston to advocate for Black residents who still lived and learned separately and who had only recently gained the right to vote in local and state elections. Kahn also stressed the need to prevent Blacks from seeing Communism as a solution to their problems.[55]

The following year, Kahn expressed his anti-Communist views even more forcefully. In March 1952, the *JH-V* announced Kahn's new sermon series on Communism.[56] Congregation Emanu El compiled these sermons into a published work titled *An Affirmative Answer to Communism*. In particular, these sermons explored Black interest in the ideology. Kahn thought minorities found Communism alluring because American Communists had a history of providing political opportunities and labor rights to African Americans as well as promoting an antihierarchical view of the world. He provided the example of Mississippi-born novelist Richard Wright's first experience with Communism. Party members did not humiliate Wright and call him "Black boy" but instead treated him as an equal "comrade."[57] Kahn highlighted how, through Communism, Blacks found acceptance and equality. Additionally, he stressed the need for the South to reform its treatment of Blacks for foreign policy reasons. After all, the Soviet Union roundly criticized American treatment of African Americans.[58]

Kahn also had a radio program called *Emanu El On the Air* on which he argued that anti-Semitism was the primary reason to oppose Communism, since hatred of Jews permeated Soviet society. He openly mocked the hypocrisy of the Soviet Union, which tried "to pose as the friend of all minorities" by appealing to Jews and Blacks as their "friends." In reality, Kahn thought the country was committing "fraud" toward these minorities. This was in stark contrast to American democracy, which made the country an ideal place for minorities.[59]

Despite messages from their religious leaders not to be afraid, many of Houston's Jews were very concerned about being publicly accused of being a Communist. Pepi Nichols recalled her parents' fear of being labeled un-American or different simply because they were Holocaust survivors. They were extra cautious of voicing publicly their discontent with Houston. It was safer to fit in than to rebel. This same concern existed among Jews of all backgrounds, even prominent businessman Leopold Meyer.[60]

In December 1953, Meyer became concerned about how the Christian characterization of all Jews as Communists, despite their capitalistic role in American society, would incite anti-Semitism. Despite his financial success, he felt Jews were always under the microscope. In order to deflect suspicion, Meyer suggested creating a Jewish governmental subcommittee to root out Communists. Meyer's fear likely emerged from the trial and execution of Julius and Ethel Rosenberg for Communist espionage and treason.[61]

African Americans were also victims of Communist accusations. Lulu White, the executive secretary of the NAACP, became associated with Communism as early as the 1930s, in large part due to her work with labor unions and affiliation with the law firm of Arthur Mandell and Herman Wright. Originally lawyers for the CIO, Mandell and Wright helped to unionize Black workers. In 1947, major conflict erupted in Houston's Black community when Mandell and Wright, previously accused of being Communists, became the legal team for the local branch of the NAACP. Many association members did not want the NAACP to be affiliated with Communism in any way. White's affiliation with the law firm caused further tension between her and Carter Wesley. They had already been in a long-standing feud since 1945 over whether to integrate the University of Texas at Austin, which White favored, or to create a separate university for African Americans, which Wesley favored.[62]

In *The Informer*, Wesley wrote, "Our NAACP is taken over by the infiltration of the Communists through the stupidity and nearsightedness of our leaders."[63] While he did not name the leaders in question, the implication was obvious: Lulu White was leading the local NAACP astray. NAACP's 1950 national convention adopted a resolution that allowed the organization to expel anyone deemed a Communist, which made Lulu White's situation more precarious. After all, this resolution did not protect the southern NAACP from Communist accusations. Previously, in 1948, the Texas State University for Negroes was a target for anti-Communists, which threatened its very existence. However, intergroup events, for the most part, did continue in Houston without threatening the status quo, except for one event.[64]

On February 10, 1952, the Council on Education in Race Relations sponsored a controversial event at the white First Methodist Church in Houston. Three anti-Communist organizations—the Committee on Methodist Preservation, the Americanism Committee of the American Legion, and the Minute Women—were present. The Minute Women had opened chapters in the spring of 1951 in Dallas, Houston, San Antonio, and Wichita Falls, and Houston had the most active and best-known chapter. The Minute Women were against integration, any federal involvement in southern race relations, and what *Houston Post* journalist Ralph O'Leary called "social mingling" between whites and Blacks.[65] At this event, they accused the Black president of Atlanta University, Dr. Rufus Clement, of Communism before he had the chance to speak.[66]

In the end, Dr. Clement received the support of numerous individuals, including Rabbi Kahn, Brigadier General Elbert P. Tuttle, commander of the American Legion of Atlanta, and W. Kenneth Pope, pastor of First Methodist Church. The *Houston Post* expressed amazement at the "unusual" amount of support for Clement.[67]

The inability of anti-Communist groups like the Minute Women to stop these intergroup events revealed that, at some level, the city accepted these programs. During the Cold War, Houstonians, like many Americans, wanted to project a positive image to the Soviet Union. After all, the Soviet Union had responded to American critiques of its treatment of Russian citizens with a counter-critique of US segregation. As expressed by Methodist lawyer R. A. Childers, who came to the defense of Clement, not supporting him "cause[d] rejoicing in the Kremlin."[68] Support of Clement, however, did not mean most white Houstonians wanted to end segregation. When the anti-Communist school board accused Ray K. Daily of being a Communist for the second time, no one came to her defense, as had happened in the Clement affair. Most likely this was because Daily was a foreigner originally from Russia, while Clement was American.

The Daily and Ebey Affairs

In 1952, Congregation Beth Yeshurun's bulletin, *The Message*, featured Ray K. Daily as an American patriot. The congregation described her journey to America as a "saga of equality of opportunity and the blessings which our country reaps from granting to all the rights to an education and to achievements." The synagogue praised Daily's story as the epitome of the American dream. While the authors did not explicitly call attention to her working directly with African Americans, they highlighted that she was "a courageous fighter for justice for all."[69] Beth Yeshurun also supported her in the heated school board election when they invited Daily and Verna Rogers, a liberal Democrat, to speak about the "Problems Facing Houston Schools."[70] However, their support did not safeguard Daily from anti-Communist activists.

In 1952, nearly ten years after her election with Ima Hogg, Daily became entrenched in a second intense battle when she ran with Rogers. The anti-Communist Committee for Sound American Education blamed "creeping socialism" on the school board, claiming that it prevented children from having a "sound American education."[71] The committee spewed outright propaganda to prohibit liberals from taking control of the school system.

On the committee's board were Dallas Dyer and Bertie Maughmer, two Minute Women who were particularly critical of Daily's agenda. Maughmer declared that Daily "believed in … socialism and socialism was Communism. That was always the gist of whatever she was talking about." Daily was put in the spotlight because she advocated for federal support, which the anti-Communists believed would lead the federal government to impose its ideas on the school board—possibly even insisting that Blacks attend white schools. Daily advocated for both federal money for free lunches for children and for adult education. Daily commented on the unfairness of her support of the latter reform, "They always accused me of being a Communist because I supported adult education for which the state doesn't pay." Further, anti-Semitism became the companion to anti-Communist rhetoric. Although Daily did not confront virulent anti-Semitism, she did comment that her Jewish identity was "something to use against" her.[72]

To build further support for Daily, David White, the editor of the *JH-V*, warned local Jews of the potential danger of not electing her. In a 1952 editorial, "Our Schools—The Backbone of American Democracy," White endorsed Daily and depicted her as someone who worked toward preserving democracy within the school system as well as combating the evils of Communism. He saw anti-Communist opposition in the school board as a negative influence that would place a "fence around our children so that they will neither have the initiative nor the ability to think for themselves" and "close the eyes of our children to the realities of today."[73]

In Houston, and in America in general, White believed that people too easily threw "the term 'socialism' around. The terms 'pink and pinko' slip easily off the tongue."[74] Instead of throwing around accusations, Americans needed to preserve their democratic heritage and embrace freedom, not oppression. Younger generations needed to continue to live by the nation's founding principles, which included equality under the law and universal education.

Because White perceived the Communist scare as the potential death knell of American values, he wanted Houston's Jews to spend time promoting American ideals, not fighting or accusing others of Communism. He pressed his readers not to succumb to the fear of Communism since false charges of Communism disproportionately occurred against Blacks and Jews. To White, anti-Communist accusers were on a par with totalitarian accomplices in the "Germany of Hitler and the Russia of Stalin."[75] In the end, he argued that to prevent a bleak future, Daily must be elected to the school board.

Those who feared Daily's message of equality in the school system continued to work against her. Dyer spread rumors accusing Daily of infiltrating the school system with socialist ideas. Daily's opponents even went so far as to distribute fake Communist Party circulars throughout Houston, attempting to prove Daily and her co-runner, Verna Rogers, were Communists. Daily and Rogers fought against these attacks and offered a reward to assist detectives in finding the originator of the smear campaign. This effort ultimately backfired and led to backlash from the Houston School Board, which demanded that they prove they did not use public funds for the reward.[76]

However, not everyone was against Daily. Some supported her because they did not like the school board's anti-Communist propaganda. The Black community also remained steadfast in their support of her. Despite these supporters and despite clearing her name, Daily still lost the election. At the height of the so-called Red Scare, she had become a victim of "McCarthyite" scare tactics and anti-Semitism.[77]

Joseph Samuels, future editor of the *JH-V*, also ran for the school board in 1952.[78] He recalled that "because of the vicious attacks on Daily by her opponents and her 'Minute Women' followers, I felt the need to discredit the absurd McCarthy-type charges that were being whispered about the good Doctor." According to Samuels, Daily became an enemy of the state "for being too liberal."[79] Samuels had entered the race because two leaders at the University of Houston had asked him to run.[80] He made it far into the election process, but as his wife, Jeanne Samuels, stated, Houston's Jews "felt it unwise for another Jew to be on the school board, lest the Jewish community be blamed for integration."[81] In fact, Rabbi Schachtel urged him to withdraw from the race, most likely due to the Daily scandal. The Houston Jewish Federation even paid for Samuels to appear on television to withdraw publicly, which he did, albeit reluctantly. Surprisingly, he still managed to gain fifteen thousand votes. Disappointed in Jewish leadership, Samuels recalled: "I felt I received no support from my community … and I thought if I were strong enough to help end segregation, it would be a good thing."[82]

In the following year, 1953, a major anti-Communist incident occurred in Houston involving the Houston School Board. In May, John P. Rogee, a conservative anti-Communist lawyer, announced to the board that its new superintendent, Dr. George Ebey, a Californian by birth, was a threat due to his association with Communist front organizations. Rogee reminded the board of Ebey's opposition to housing discrimination against African Americans and his involvement in the Urban League, which demonstrated his pro–civil rights actions. As an assistant superintendent in Portland, Oregon, Ebey had participated in a joint venture with the Oregon State Department and the Urban League to integrate classes. This involvement led Houstonians to think his plan was to change the face of their city by desegregating the Houston school system. Interestingly, only a year earlier, Ebey had seemed like the perfect candidate to the board because of his upstanding teaching credentials and education at Stanford and Columbia University.[83]

Some Jewish leaders stood behind Ebey, a non-Jew, mostly because of their prior experience with Daily. Instead of focusing on Ebey's involvement with desegregation, the Jews of Houston emphasized his patriotism. Thomas Friedman, executive director of Southwestern Jewish Community Relations, noted his support of Ebey in a letter to Charles Slayman, executive director of the American Veterans Committee (AVC). His work with the AVC led Ebey to become associated with civil rights and anti-segregation— two ideas some Americans had labeled "Communist." The AVC stood as a threat because as an organization it promoted engagement between America and the Soviet Union and improving the rights of African Americans. Friedman and Slayman stressed that, despite close ties with civil rights, the AVC was not a Communist organization. Furthermore, Ebey was a loyal American.[84]

In the *JH-V*, David White also defended Ebey and spoke out against the "injustice done" to him. In addition to writing of how the school board "crucified" Ebey out of fear of Communism, White attacked the Minute Women for attempting to control the board. Like Friedman, White thought Ebey was an American patriot and that a person did not forsake the nation by embracing liberal principles. White believed Ebey acted in line with American ideals and was merely a victim of the same petty attacks against Daily: "We are all being judged. We are all being tried by the same court and with the same evidence." To him, what was happening in Houston was representative of a broader Communist scare. White called on the Jewish community to vote for Ebey and not let Houston "permit this challenge to our freedom."[85] In the end, the school board found insufficient evidence to support Communist claims against Ebey, but he was still dismissed. His dismissal made national news. In fact, *The Nation* reported the Ebey affair was "the zaniest of the poison-pen attacks on public education." Ebey left Houston, never to return.[86]

White wrote numerous features in opposition to the Communist scare occurring in the United States and more specifically in Houston. In his editorial "The Importance of McCarthy," he discussed the difficulty Jews faced from anti-Communists. Not only did they, like Ebey, have to field accusations, they also had to deal with two-pronged attacks against their Jewishness. He acknowledged that McCarthyism was not a "Jewish fight, but it [was] a fight in which Jews have a stake" and that it was destroying "our American way of life."[87]

According to White, all "isms," including anti-Semitism, McCarthyism, and Communism, betrayed American principles.[88] Hostile Americans attacked Jews because they did not fit McCarthy's limited image of an American. White's outspoken voice received mixed reviews from individuals in Houston's Jewish community.[89]

Two years after the Ebey affair, White discussed how anti-Communist fears shaped the level of societal acceptance of Jews. He asked the question, "Can we change this concept of our Jews in the eyes of the rest of the world? In one breath, the hate sheets call us Bolsheviks and Capitalists." The problem, he wrote, was with Jewish names, which were not like "the Smiths, the Joneses, and the Crocketts." When someone had a non-Jewish-sounding last name, his or her actions were "just one of those things," but when a person had a Jewish-sounding last name, that person's actions affected all Jews, as if he or she were representative of the whole. What is more, if a non-Jew saw a prominent street name that sounded Jewish, they associated the "wealth of the country with the Jews," which reinforced long-standing anti-Semitic stereotypes that Jews had money and used it to influence their agendas.[90]

Throughout the 1950s, fear of Communism continued to grow in Houston. In 1956, a member of the Minute Women took it upon herself to compile a list of suspected Communists. Helen Darden Thomas, the niece of Vance Muse, the founder of the *Christian American*, singled out Christians and Jews, educators, religious leaders, labor leaders, lawyers, and activists. Notable people on this list included Rabbi Schachtel, Arthur Mandell, and Lulu White. Using discredited information from the House Committee on Un-American Activities, Thomas's list unwittingly exposed a link between those Houstonians she labeled Communist and those who locally promoted equality for African Americans.[91] Even though Thomas did not include Kahn, later that year the rabbi became the subject of a mysterious anti-Communist attack.

Comrade Circular

Despite Kahn's public stance against Communism, he became a victim of a chain circular that accused him of involvement in the Communist Party. On October 26, 1956, Kahn wrote to D. H. Matherly of Amory, Mississippi, inquiring about an unusual letter that Matherly had sent him about creating better relations between whites and African Americans. Matherly referenced a printing titled the *Comrade Circular*, which ended with the line: "For further information on race relations write Rabbi Robert I. Kahn."[92] Kahn could not comprehend why a man from Mississippi thought he had such information. To prove to Kahn that his name was indeed at the bottom of the printing, Matherly sent Kahn a copy of the circular three days later.

At the top was the phrase "TRUE COPY," obviously an attempt to convince the reader of its legitimacy. In order to sound like a direct report from a Communist Party member, the printing began with "Comrade" instead of "Dear" and used the phrase "WE OF THE PARTY." Another noticeable aspect of the circular was the use of misspelled words and poor grammar, most likely to suggest that the author was uneducated and possibly African American. The author claimed that Mississippians hid behind the "cotton curtain" to excuse their behavior toward African Americans. The circular also suggested that white males were willing to have sexual relations with Black females to demonstrate their "inward love for the colored race."[93]

The author spoke of those "stupid [white] Mississippians" who, believing Blacks were powerless, enabled the NAACP to gain validity and power. In the churches, "Good Comrades" worked to promote "tolerance and brotherly love" toward African Americans. "Stupid ignorant Citizen Council People" thought that southern Blacks were "too ignorant to rule this country." The circular warned that "there [*sic*] deliberate days of rule are numbered" and that current leaders would lose their power because Jews were "spending millions to help us in our political control of this country."[94]

What is more, the Urban League and B'nai B'rith were collecting money to help "the born race that are going to be the American of tomorrow." Praising the superiority of Black culture, especially music, the circular concluded by urging African Americans to break anti-miscegenation laws: "Marry a white person every chance you get. You can satisfy a white person more than another white person." The writer urged those wanting more information to contact Rabbi Kahn at Congregation Emanu El.[95]

In order to halt the spread of the circular, Kahn contacted the ADL and also sent his original copy to Houston FBI agent Mr. W. E. Salisbury. Kahn informed Salisbury that "apparently it was distributed in Amory [Mississippi] during the night, and I do hope that the FBI will do what it can to protect citizens such as myself from being implicated in so vicious and rotten a propaganda message."[96]

A few days later, on November 2, 1956, Kahn again contacted the ADL, which had been in communication with the FBI. Because the circular had first appeared in Mississippi, the ADL connected with the FBI in the New Orleans office. The investigation became a joint effort between the ADL and the FBI. Kahn also asked Matherly to "counteract such a slur on my name."[97]

On November 5, 1956, Kahn received another inquiry about the circular from Ms. Roberta Patterson of Greenwood, Mississippi. In response, Kahn told her to submit the *Comrade Circular* to the FBI because "it would be a favor to me and to America."[98] On November 26, M. M. Taylor, the executive director of the Urban League of Tulsa, received the circular. Kahn received so many requests that by the time L. Williams of San Diego contacted him, he stopped even questioning how the circular made it to California.[99] On January 16, 1957, the *Comrade Circular* made its way to the Elk Temple, a Masonic lodge in Houston. The last and final *Comrade Circular* correspondence arrived in Kahn's mailbox during the first week of March 1957. This time, "the only return address was on the publication itself—there was no return address ... on the envelope."[100] Kahn contacted the Houston FBI office immediately, but with insufficient evidence, the author of the *Comrade Circular* remained a mystery.

To his congregants, Robert Kahn may have spoken about progress for African Americans and preached tolerance as an American value, but he, as well as other Houston Jewish leaders, were not ready to create an activist movement. Instead of fighting to change the status quo, they worked within the broken system, in large part because they did not want to rattle white Gentile society or jeopardize their position within Houston's hierarchy, particularly at the time of increasing white supremacist attitudes in the South. Unaware of the perpetrators of this *Comrade Circular*, the safety of his congregation and his family was foremost on his mind. This letter had the potential to convince others that he was a Communist because of his civil rights activism, especially since it was circulating during the height of Communist fears. Whatever the reason, Kahn believed tremendous risk could potentially come out of this circulation.

The Red Scare in Houston instilled a feeling of insecurity in many of the city's Jews, who did not want to call attention to themselves or appear un-American. Their desire to stand for tolerance was further complicated by the anti-Communist intertwining of Communism and Black rights. Most of Houston's Jews limited their voice to intergroup events or to their synagogues even though some Houston Jewish leaders spoke out publicly for African Americans and encouraged tolerance. In the end, however, the intergroup events Jews attended did not produce substantial inroads or change the African American position in a segregated Houston. They also failed to convince anti-Communists of the importance of tolerance.

In Houston, Jews attempted to prove their American identity in general—and their southern identity in particular—so as not to stand out in segregated Houston. They walked a fine line between embracing their American citizenship and defending those falsely accused of Communism. In this tightrope walk, Jews found themselves occupying several roles: the accuser, the defender, and the accused. After all, when Houston Jews were not careful, they were under the microscope.

The next chapter depicts the reaction, both publicly and privately, of Houston's Jewish leaders during the landmark decision *Brown v. Board of Education* in 1954.

Chapter 3

Brown v. Board of Education: The Houston Jewish Response

For, after all, desegregation is not a Jewish issue but an American issue, and in solving it we must take our place with our fellow-Americans in fighting for equal rights for those who do not at present enjoy them.

Rabbi William Malev
"The Jew of the South in the
Conflict on Desegregation," Fall 1958

A t the outset of the Cold War, Houston's Jews, like other American Jews, wanted to promote the image that the American ideal of tolerance applied to all minorities, even African Americans. The previous two chapters have detailed how they clung to this myth to protect themselves from anti-Semitism and to maintain their position as white Americans of Jewish faith. What such a universal call for tolerance failed to account for were the specific needs of each minority group. African Americans longed for first-class citizenship and fulfillment of their constitutional rights, and Jews wanted the freedom to practice their religion without discrimination. In the end,

Houston's white Gentiles heaped scorn on local Jewish leaders who spoke out against discrimination and accused them of having Communist leanings. For this reason, most of the community shied away from becoming outspoken civil rights activists.

Matters came to a head when desegregation picked up in the 1950s, challenging Houston Jewish ideals of tolerance. While communal leaders promoted integration, the community had acculturated themselves to white Gentile society, which remained strongly opposed to federal desegregation efforts. *Brown v. Board of Education* in 1954 was a watershed moment in the history of race relations in Houston, as it was throughout the South. The Supreme Court ruling prompted Houston's Jewish leaders to consider several serious questions: Were they obligated to be advocates for African Americans in their fight for desegregation? Would they continue to follow the lead of the white Gentile leaders, or would they openly express their own opinions?

Though the initial reaction of Houston's Jewish leaders to the desegregation movement was marked by ambivalence, their commitment to both Judaism and liberalism led them to reevaluate their hands-off approach. Some local Jews involved themselves in political groups, many of which broached the subject of desegregation. However, for the most part Jewish leadership's approach to desegregation was to take a back seat and leave the vocal roles to others. They supported equality at events in the private Jewish sphere yet followed the lead of white desegregationist Christian leaders outside of the synagogue. Congregations and organizations sponsored internal events at which rabbis delivered sermons promoting desegregation. Some of Houston's Jews joined intergroup civil rights organizations like the Houston Community Forum and the Houston Council for Human Relations, both of which had Black members.

The rise of national Jewish defense organizations like AJCongress and the AJC stimulated discussion on desegregation, particularly in the public schools. In Houston, the Jewish leaders' more tepid positions on civil rights caused friction with these organizations, which wanted them to actively seek desegregation. This difference in focus resulted in a backlash from some of Houston's communal leaders, especially from David White of the *JH-V*, Rabbi Robert Kahn, and Rabbi William Malev, all of whom argued that the northern approach to desegregation was wrong for the South and more specifically wrong for Houston. Malev especially believed that the abolition of segregation was an American fight and not a Jewish fight. Leaders like Malev were willing to discuss desegregation within the walls of the synagogue, but in the wider public sphere, they ceded to Christian leaders in order to minimize any chance of anti-Semitic backlash.

Early Desegregation Efforts

The early involvement of the Harris County Council of Organizations changed the path of desegregation efforts. The council's first major endorsement was Judge Roy Hofheinz for mayor in 1952. Hofheinz's mayorship helped African Americans gain appointments to positions on city committees and commissions. His administration also made improvements to the infrastructures of some Black communities, including improving the water supply, paving the streets, and installing proper sewage lines. Mayor Hofheinz also oversaw the desegregation of the Central Library. However, as much as they gained, African Americans still had to rely on whites for political support. It was not until the late 1960s that they were able to run independently for prominent positions in the state and national government.[1]

The rise of a liberal faction within the Democratic Party fueled the success of the Harris County Council. Beginning in 1952, the Harris County Democrats bucked existing discrimination in the local Democratic Party and welcomed whites (including Jews), African Americans, and other minorities. Prior to this integration, the Democratic Party had effectively disenfranchised Blacks in Houston. One of the main founders of the Harris County Democrats was the NAACP administrator, Christia Adair. In her opening address to the integrated faction, she addressed segregation head-on: "You have got to understand the aspirations, needs, hopes, and dreams of the Black people of this community. Until you do that openly, you will never amalgamate with the whole community."[2]

Jewish women in Houston also joined the League of Women Voters, an organization dating back to the time of women's suffrage. By the 1950s, Jewish female involvement was so prominent that the organization worked with Hadassah and often met at the JCC. The league's nonpartisan stance made Jewish women feel safe enough to join. The unbiased information the league provided voters on candidates meant that Jewish women avoided the label of political agitators. Even after *Brown v. Board of Education*, the league did not take a position on integration, nor did it have Black members. It was not until 1956 that the league decided to accept Black women and, even then, they did not "actively solicit such membership."[3]

In addition to Jewish women involving themselves in the voting process, a small contingent of Jews, including prominent anti-Zionist Marjorie Meyer Arsht, were active Republicans. Arsht went so far as to claim that many of the conservative Jewish Democrats in Texas were essentially Republicans who did not want to publicly identify with the Republican Party.[4]

Like Jewish leaders, Christian clergy did not take a strong political stance on Black inequality. Quentin Mease, social activist and executive director of the South Central YMCA, criticized both white and Black, whom he felt "were not really engaged" politically before *Brown*. He questioned, "Why weren't preachers, Black and white, doing their job for the previous two or three hundred years? They should have been out there fighting segregation all those years, but they were quiet."[5] Similarly, Moses Leroy argued, "I think the churches have been slower in the field of race relations than the average."[6] While the overall thrust of Mease and Leroy's criticisms was correct, some of the city's Christian congregations had started to address the desegregation of churches prior to *Brown*. In fact, in many respects, the genesis of Black political rights began in Houston in the church.

Early interest in civil rights started in local Catholic and Episcopal churches in Houston. Since the nineteenth century, the Catholic church in Texas had prioritized Black membership by creating all-Black churches and schools in Galveston and Houston, including Saint Nicholas Catholic Church in the Third Ward. Founded in 1887, Saint Nicholas grew to three thousand members by 1929 and even periodically hosted white pastors.[7] The diversity of the Catholic church in Houston included Blacks, Italians, Mexicans, and Creoles of color. Because they primarily settled in the Fifth Ward, Creoles of color could not easily attend the inclusive Saint Nicholas in the Third Ward. The Immaculate Conception Catholic Church in the Third Ward designated certain pews for Creoles of color and Mexicans. Our Lady of Guadalupe, a Mexican Catholic church, practiced segregation against Creoles of color by making them sit in the back pews. This discrimination led them to create their own church, Our Mother of Mercy, in 1929.[8] Despite Catholic efforts to evangelize Blacks and Creoles of color, the majority of Catholic churches in Houston remained segregated. In the 1940s, the church created a Black hospital, Saint Elizabeth's, but major Catholic inroads to desegregate did not begin until the 1960s.[9] After the Civil War, the freed slaves opted to create their own Episcopal church, but by 1940, only one African American attended Christ Church. Other Episcopal churches initiated integration in diverse neighborhoods like Riverside Terrace in the 1950s.[10]

Synagogues did not go through the same process of integration since there were no known Black Jews who wanted to join them, so many of Houston's Jews believed that integration was not a specific Jewish problem. According to Arsht, the Jews of Congregation Beth Israel "avoided controversial issues of any kind, from integration to their special relationship with the State of Israel."[11]

On December 9, 1951, Rabbi Kahn gave a sermon at his synagogue and later on his radio program, *Emanu El On the Air*, titled "Is Theology Important?" Addressing both Jews and Christians, he recast civil rights as a religious issue rather than a political one. His belief in the "greatest good for the greatest number" led Kahn to argue that the right law was one of majority rule. Most importantly, however, theology trumped law, especially if the law was "discriminatory." Therefore, he believed enforcement of segregation had to end, as it was immoral. Kahn argued that people cloaked the issue of segregation behind "states' rights against the federal usurpation of power," when, in reality, it was not "a question of North or South, nor of big-city Democrats and country-side Democrats. It [was] a theological problem." Kahn's solution was for all to believe that "all men were really the children of God." He encouraged his congregants, and Christian leaders as well, to believe that the support of Blacks did not simply make them pro–civil rights; it made them God-fearing individuals.[12]

Two years later, on January 25, 1953, Kahn rhetorically asked his radio audience how to solve "the negro problem." He stressed the need for more than simply a belief in the principle of equality; one must also support the push for legal change. He went so far as to suggest that solving "the negro problem" would unite Americans and help end the Cold War.[13]

While promising, the initial efforts of Kahn and other clergy, both Jewish and Christian, were not effective in producing any great strides in Houston toward Black equality. As in other parts of the South, there needed to be legislation to begin the process of breaking the well-entrenched system of inequality.

Brown v. Board of Education and Its Aftermath in Houston

The Supreme Court issued its landmark decision on May 17, 1954, making segregation in the public school system unconstitutional. Local Jewish leaders like Kahn believed that *Brown* finally gave progressive Houstonians, Jews included, the legal ability not only to desegregate Houston's schools but to begin to give Black residents full rights. Because Jewish law dictated that Jews follow the law of the land, *Brown* paved the way for their active involvement in eliminating segregation. They were no longer activists standing against the wishes of white Gentile society; they were active followers of the law. As much as many clergy, including rabbis, supported *Brown*, the ambiguity about *when* Houston had to fulfill *Brown* delayed any action. More often than not, Houston's Jewish leaders took their cues from Gentile leaders.[14]

The day after the *Brown* decision, the *Houston Post* featured the article "Churchmen of Houston Favorable." The use of the word "churchmen" excluded Jewish leaders. Along those same lines, the author declared the *Brown* decision a proclamation not only for Americanism and the Declaration of Independence but also for Christianity. When Reverend Virgil E. Lowder, executive director of the Council of Churches of Greater Houston, proclaimed that *Brown* would "guarantee every child has the opportunity to a good education," he emphasized that it was the "Christian spirit to make sure that everyone does what is right."[15]

Many other Houston Christian leaders agreed. When Reverend John Knowles of the First Christian Church, Bishop Wendelin Nold of the Galveston-Houston Diocese, and Bishop A. Frank Smith of the Texas Conference of the Methodist Church heard of the decision, they encouraged Christian Houstonians to unite to create change. The *Brown* decision also brought to the surface prior US failure to consider segregation an outdated practice. "Churchmen of Houston Favorable" offered the example of Reverend Knowles, who argued that desegregation was necessary because scientific evidence had proven there were no "superior races." Reverend Horace F. Westwood of the First Unitarian Church also confirmed that the *Brown* decision would finally put an end to the color line and reveal "America's hypocrisy" of perpetuating segregation.[16]

Despite their support of *Brown*, many clergy in the *Houston Post* article worried that most southerners would not comply with the new ruling, and in expressing their concerns they revealed their own lingering prejudices. The region's history confirmed that too many southerners saw segregation as their right and despised the federal government's interference in a practice that the South had upheld since the 1890s. Local clergy predicted that it would be difficult for a region that had advocated for segregation to become federal law to adopt the opposite without a fight. Even though de facto segregation existed in the North as well, what was custom in the North was law in the South. This distinct ideological difference kept the South at the center of the segregation conflict.[17]

In the article, Dr. E. H. Westmoreland, a pastor of the First Unitarian Church, felt desegregation would "be felt more" in the South. More concerned about the public's reaction to losing their rights than with his faith, Reverend Max R. Gaulke of the First Church of God declared it "socially dangerous in certain parts of the United States" to end segregation, even if the Bible purported "fairness of equality" and even if he was "sympathetic to the idea."[18] Likewise, Lutheran minister Oliver R. Harms illustrated a long-standing attitude dating back to the southern church's justifications of slavery when he argued that he did not expect to see segregation interpreted as "a moral issue" but rather "as a matter of social and political expediency." Despite this, Harms conceded that the church *should* cooperate. In the article, certain members of the clergy may have appeared to be outliers, but their opinions were probably closer to the majority, considering that many churches did not integrate until the 1960s.[19]

Of all the clergy mentioned in the article, only one rabbi and one Black pastor publicly voiced their opinions on desegregation: Rabbi Kahn and Reverend E. J. Davis, president of the African Methodist Episcopal Ministerial Alliance. Rather than emphasizing a Jewish point of view, Kahn spoke of religious leaders as a collective. About desegregation, Kahn was "sure that all Americans who hold to their religious faith and their American ideals will welcome this decision and proceed to implement [it] in good faith."[20] He also stressed that desegregation was the fulfillment of the Declaration of Independence. While Congregation Beth Israel had previously ostracized Kahn in 1942 for being too pro–African American, they stood behind him in 1954 when his views aligned with Christian clergy. Although Reverend Davis was also encouraged by *Brown*, he stressed the time it would take to effectively desegregate the city, since African Americans and whites were not part of the same communities and did not attend the same schools. For that reason, Davis predicted desegregation would take several decades.

Indeed, the progress to equalize education in Houston was slow. The long-standing economic disparities between white and Black schools in the city mirrored that in other parts of the South. One of the reasons was the number of teachers, as well as the higher student-to-teacher ratios in Black schools in Houston. Up until the NAACP demanded equal pay in 1943, Black teachers earned significantly less than white teachers.[21] In addition, Black students received second-rate educational materials that Hattie Mae White, the first Black member of the Houston School Board, rightly described as "dilapidated."[22] Civil rights activist Otis King remembered the books as "hand-me-downs from the white high schools" that were so used that Black students hardly had any space to write their names in the front. King also highlighted how "even playing sports, we noticed that we often got practice equipment that had been used before at the white schools as well."[23] Compounding the inequality was a lack of any access to certain sports activities like swimming, golf, or archery.[24]

Compared to their white counterparts, however, Black teachers tended to have more education. Some were lawyers or doctors who could not find jobs, and many had received training from prestigious historically Black colleges. Black students in Houston benefited from these teachers who augmented their studies, providing them with expertise they would not have received in an integrated school. For instance, teachers implemented dual curriculums in African American history and general history, which instilled a sense of pride in being Black. This dual focus was one casualty of the process of integration.[25]

Shortly after the *Brown* decision in May 1954, David White voiced his opinions about the Houston public school system to the local Jewish community in his article "Our Public Schools— Foundation for Democracy." The *JH-V* editor saw desegregation as an opportunity to create a new public school system. In his vision, the ideal public school would be for everybody, regardless of their religion or the color of their skin, and it would be one in which everyone would "learn to live together, to appreciate one another and understand one another."[26]

David White also used the *Brown* decision to comment on the role of religion in schools as it pertained to Jews. In the article "There Is Religion and There Is Government," he both strongly supported the separation of church and state and urged Jews to be realistic about their minority religious status. Of utmost importance to White was for Jewish parents to educate their children at home, in the synagogue, or in religious schools so they understood their Jewish identity. As a minority religion in Houston, Jewish children needed to be raised to respect Christianity, even as they again fought religious indoctrination in the public schools. In many ways, White used the *Brown* decision as a platform for Jews to advocate for the separation of church and state in Houston's public school system. While desegregation would be the primary focus, religion rose to become a prominent part of the discussion by 1959.[27]

Many cities throughout Texas and the South had to contend with conservative school boards. Each city had its own distinct path toward desegregation. Cities like Houston, however, with large concentrations of African Americans, were especially hesitant to comply with *Brown*, so progress was slow. Still, the school board began the process of discussing a desegregation plan in March 1955. One of the board's members called attention to Saint Louis's successful integration plan as a model or starting point for Houston.

On June 13, 1955, the Biracial Committee formed, as Verna Rogers recalls, to "think and talk things over and work out the best way to handle all our racial problems."[28] Since no local white pastors chose to join, the only white clergyman on the committee was Rabbi Malev. Though the committee developed a plan for school desegregation on July 27, 1955, the plan never came to fruition. The school system had the ability to stall since, at this point, the Supreme Court had only vaguely declared that desegregation should occur "with all deliberate speed." Before the Biracial Committee could implement their plan, conservatives regained control over the school board in 1956.[29]

Even without a direct plan from the school board to implement integration, African Americans tried to attend white schools. However, their efforts were unsuccessful. Confused by why Houston's Black residents did not want to fight for their children to attend white schools, in the summer of 1956 George Nelson of the local NAACP started knocking on the doors of parents to get them to register at a white school. Finally, he met the parents of Delores Ross and Beneva Williams, who had both registered their daughters in white schools. Both the elementary school where Delores registered and the middle school where Beneva registered denied them admittance.

Under the sponsorship of the NAACP, the family filed a class-action lawsuit in December 1956. Despite the Supreme Court–mandated *Brown*, the schools blocked their attendance. Because they had no protection from the city of Houston—and in fear for their lives after they received threatening phone calls—both families decided to abandon the fight. Neither girl ever managed to attend a white school. The process of school desegregation in Houston, it appeared, would be long and drawn out.[30]

The church was not wholly removed from the debate. Some Christian organizations encouraged the city to desegregate its schools more quickly. The Texas Council of Churches, a Protestant organization, came to Houston in 1957 to pressure the Texas Legislature to recognize the Supreme Court decision and end segregation in the public school system. The council adhered to the belief that "guarantee[d] individual rights to citizens of all races in the state."[31] The council also asked the director of the ADL, Theodore Freedman, to promote desegregation in Texas. In the *Chicago Defender*, Freedman stated at a council meeting, "we have a long way to go," referring to bringing equality in the South to all.[32]

The Episcopal General Convention took a different, more severe approach to Houston's school desegregation problems and refused to associate with a segregated Houston. Initial plans for a convention in Houston came about because Diocesan Bishop John Hines had desegregated the diocese in Texas; however, protest from both white and Black Episcopal churches elsewhere led the convention to be moved to Hawaii. If the convention had happened in Houston, it would have been the first Episcopal convention in the South. While the Texas Council of Churches held out hope that the convention could improve white and Black relations in Houston, the irony was that their own clergy were hindering integration by refusing to desegregate their own churches. The one major exception was the Unitarian Universalist Church, which began desegregation immediately after *Brown*. Although full implementation was slow, their actions show that, despite secular pushback, at least a small contingent of churches and synagogues in Houston supported desegregation.[33]

In fact, a group of 173 Houston clergy, including rabbis, issued a proclamation against segregation on October 17, 1957, "urging 'every God-fearing citizen to encourage respect for our courts and obedience to all decisions.'"[34] As a united religious front, the clergy wanted to "bear witness" to the discrimination occurring in the public school system. Rabbis Schachtel, Kahn, Malev, and Max Geller stood alongside Christian clergy, allowing them to appear as part of a larger front rather than as separate Jewish leaders, an approach that unified interreligious leaders. The clergy collectively urged Federal District Judge Ben C. Connally to force the Houston School Board to "end racial segregation in Houston schools" and called for citizens to respect the Supreme Court decision. The proclamation noted that when people "defy decisions," it can lead to "anarchy in which the rights of none are respected."[35]

After joining a larger organized effort for racial integration, Reform and Conservative synagogues in Houston introduced programming to raise local Jewish awareness of desegregation and create a private space in which Jews could voice their concerns. Following the call of the Union of American Hebrew Congregations and the Union of Conservative Judaism for nationwide social justice initiatives, the synagogues became informational centers on civil rights issues. On the surface, it would appear as though the Jewish congregations were far more active toward desegregation in their religious spheres than Christians; however, Christian clergy and congregants faced more difficult decisions over desegregation than the synagogues due to the demographics of their religion.

In Houston, two synagogues—Congregation Emanu El, a Reform synagogue, and Congregation Beth Yeshurun, a Conservative synagogue—initiated this social action programming primarily geared at younger Houstonians. Emanu El hosted

"Integration—Fact and Fancy," an event in 1956 that focused on school integration. Led by Thomas Friedman of the ADL, the synagogue included it in the young adults' social hour.[36] In 1956, Beth Yeshurun held a similar teen-centric event about segregation in the public school system at which school board members Joe Reynolds and Robert Eckhardt gave their opposing perspectives on desegregation. Reynolds spoke in favor, while Eckhardt spoke in opposition.[37]

In addition to these regular talks, Congregation Emanu El created a civic affairs committee focused on many different social justice issues, including "the peace-making role of religion in the areas of racial tension and discrimination."[38] The Sisterhood at Congregation Emanu El took a keen interest in desegregation and formed a World and Peace Committee to discuss "the legal side of integration [as] its first object to study."[39] Like Congregation Beth Yeshurun, the Sisterhood of Congregation Emanu El also invited school board members to discuss integration.

In addition to temple programming, rabbis became one of the central voices of reason in the desegregation struggle. Rabbis—especially southern rabbis—utilized the power of sermons to communicate to their congregants the importance of dismantling segregation. Schachtel's sermon "Religion and Integration," from March 22, 1957, addressed the issue of integration, not just desegregation. Schachtel framed integration as a religious value, though not specifically in Jewish terms, in an attempt to utilize religion as a tool to help individuals accept Black equality as natural if one was a believer in God.[40]

Without differentiating between northern and southern Jews, Schachtel instead expressed his yearning for all Americans to incorporate both their "spiritual and American heritages" into their daily lives. He provided historical examples of the rise of the Ku Klux Klan in the 1920s, the anti-Semitism of Father Charles Coughlin, and the internment of Japanese Americans to demonstrate the historical lack of concern for minorities. While he believed every person "who thinks of himself as a religionist, whether he be a Jew or Christian ... ought to at least sit down and consider this problem carefully in the light of the principles

LEFT FRONT to RIGHT BACK: Rabbi William Malev, Rabbi H. Silver, Rabbi Hyman Schachtel, Rabbi Mose Cahana, Rabbi Raphael Schwartzman, Rabbi Robert Kahn and Rabbi Moshe Cahana at Westwood Country Club for Israel Bonds. Houston, Texas. November 12, 1960. RGD0006N-1960-5472-1, Houston Post Photographs, Houston Metropolitan Research Center, Houston Public Library. Ed Valdez_HP/©Houston Chronicle. Used with permission.

of his faith and country," Schachtel also wanted Americans to not react to world events with violence, in order to present a positive image to the world. If Americans reacted peacefully, he believed the outcome of *Brown* would be "both good religion and good Americanism, and it will work itself out to the satisfaction of all Americans, no matter what their color."[41]

One of the most pivotal speeches that Rabbi Kahn gave on segregation was "Lessons from Little Rock" on October 25, 1957, which considered the challenges that southerners, having grown up in a culture of segregation, faced with the prospect of desegregation. Northerners, who had lived in denial of their own de facto segregation, were unable to understand or fix the problems in the South. Kahn criticized how the Supreme Court had not issued a "uniform pattern of change," which led to noncompliance and disorder throughout the South. The disconnect between what the Supreme Court thought the desegregation process would look like and the reality of the actual situation meant that it was up to everyone, including his Houston congregants, to work toward promoting a smoother desegregation process. In his city, Kahn wanted to avoid a future in which mobs and the National Guard confronted public school children. He encouraged them to embrace the "American Way," and even though southern politicians "did not like the idea," they knew it was the law. The challenge, Kahn articulated, was whether an individual identified first as an American or as a southerner: "As an American, he knew it was right, but as a southerner, he did not like it."[42]

What Kahn's statement overlooked, however, was that while Blacks might have been citizens technically, their treatment was second-class. Nonetheless, Kahn pressed his congregants to treat Black residents as first-class, despite what they may have grown up observing or believing. He also urged them to pressure the school boards to push for a solution. His intent was for Houston to "achieve a quiet transition over the years." Everyone should stand by the police to "prevent civil strife, to keep agitators and troublemakers from destroying our school system."[43]

While some Jewish Houstonians lamented desegregation because of their fear of potential violence, no visible Jewish segregationists fought to preserve segregation. In fact, Kahn noted in a letter to Al Vorspan, the director of the Commission on Social Action of the Religious Action Center in Washington, DC, the preeminent Jewish social justice organization, "the secretary of the Houston White Council [a white supremacist segregationist group] lament[ed] the fact that so few Jews [were] joining their organization."[44] In other parts of the South, Jews were members of the White Citizens' Council, but that was not the case in Houston, most likely because business dominated the city and 80 percent of the city's Jews were in commerce. Cities like Miami, Atlanta, and Houston that did not want to lose the "Negro Market" prioritized economics and progress over white supremacy, causing the White Citizens' Council to have little influence. This was unlike Birmingham in the 1950s, when the White Citizens' Council was able to thwart the Birmingham Interracial Committee in their work to desegregate, causing it to ultimately disband. The council's lack of a stronghold led it to become defunct by the early 1960s.[45]

While Kahn was relieved that Houston's Jews did not actively promote segregation, he was still troubled that they were not fully heeding the "Lessons of Little Rock" and the potential for violence in Houston.[46] He scolded his congregants for romanticizing segregation out of fear or believing it was better for Black-white relations. Instead, he wanted them to become advocates for integration—not necessarily for the sake of Blacks but for the sake of their country.[47]

Jewish organizations hosted wider civil rights events in Houston. On September 12, 1957, the Houston lodge of B'nai B'rith sponsored an event at the JCC focused on the violence in Little Rock. In an attempt to address the question "Can Houston Avert Racial Violence?" Houston police chief Carl Shuptrine discussed how Houston could "maintain law and order in compliance with the law of the land," in order to stop the city from escalating into similar violence. Shuptrine asserted that people who are "sane thinking" understand the inevitability of desegregation, and it was, therefore, important to prevent those who did not accept the change from getting out of hand.[48]

Other outreach events occurred at the local Jewish Chautauqua Society. On January 16, 1956, the society asked Kahn to speak at Prairie View A&M, a historically Black college, about both Judaism and the current situation in Israel. Kahn, a Reform rabbi, was not able to attend, but he suggested Malev, a Conservative rabbi, as his replacement. Kahn's recommendation reveals the extent to which Reform and Conservative rabbis in Houston came together for the common goal of promoting positive interactions with African Americans.[49]

Three years later, on February 13, 1959, Kahn spoke to six hundred students and guests at Prairie View on Black-white interactions and the "Jewish teachings on brotherhood." In May of the same year, Schachtel spoke at an honors event at an all-Black school in Worthing, Texas. He praised the Black students for their academic achievements, regular attendance, and dedication to extracurricular activities.[50] Another interfaith event occurred on the campus of Texas Southern University on November 7, 1959. Rabbi A. Stanley Dreyfus from Temple B'nai Israel in Galveston spoke on "The Contribution of Judaism to American Culture."

Jewish youth groups like the B'nai B'rith Youth Organization (BBYO) Chapter Cyrus Adler AZA also used athletic events to attempt to break down the barriers between Jews, white Gentiles, and African Americans. At one event called "Understanding Your Neighbor," various teams, including an all-Black team, two all-white Christian teams, and an all-Jewish team, joined together for an "Interfaith Basketball Tournament." Though the teams did not play together in integrated teams, the tournament was a significant step forward, considering the historical resistance against Blacks openly playing sports with whites. While this event brought Jews, white Gentiles, and African Americans to the same space for a single sporting event, it was not the most effective long-term way of uniting these groups.[51]

The creation of the Houston Community Forum came the closest to this ideal. Beginning in the early 1950s, YMCA executive director Quentin Mease worked to create the first white and African American dinner group to discuss ways to improve race relations and bring about peaceful desegregation in Houston. There were no fees required to become a member of the forum, but it was only through invitation that one could participate. In total the forum had fifty members, both male and female. Theodore Freedman, the southwest director of the ADL, was responsible for bringing Jews into the organization. Freedman and Mease had worked together to work on police discrimination even in cases where Jews were the culprits. Their collaboration helped prevent certain localized problems from escalating.[52]

The South Central YMCA, which had stood in opposition to segregation, served as an inspiration for the Houston Community Forum. Opened in 1955 on Wheeler Street in Riverside Terrace, the gym hosted Jews who came to play sports and interact socially with Blacks. This center also provided Black residents a place to sleep, exercise, or meet in a city in which most white spaces continued to bar them. Further, all dinners at the South Central YMCA allowed whites and African Americans to sit together. It was also where the Harris County Council of Organizations and the NAACP met to discuss political plans. According to Mease, this YMCA had acted early on "as a crossroad ... it was open to any person of any race or ethnic origin."[53]

Like Mease, Jim Noland, founder of the Houston Council of Churches in 1954, also wanted to improve Black-white interactions. Noland and his friend, Irwin Glatstein, the director of the Jewish Community Relations Council, decided to form the Houston Council on Human Relations in 1958. This integrated group tried to implement social and economic change for minorities in Houston and become involved in day-to-day civil rights activities. Many of the diverse group of founding members—including Adair, Carter Wesley, Gertrude Barnstone, and Eleanor Freed—were from the Houston Community Forum and the Harris County Democrats. Barnstone eventually became a Jewish school board member in the mid-1960s, while Freed, a well-known Jewish art critic, helped found the Harris County Democrats Division for Women in 1956.[54]

The Houston Council on Human Relations was not a Jewish organization, but many Jews supported it, and both Schachtel and Kahn became members. Individuals on the council were not members of Houston's power elite; instead, the council appealed to those who opposed the conservative branch of the Democratic Party and the Houston School Board. For many Jews who supported separation of church and state, the council provided a means of interfaith advocacy outside of a religious setting. Kaplan's Delicatessen and Restaurant, a kosher-style deli located in Riverside Terrace, was one of the places where the council met and at times placed orders for food during meetings.[55] But the council had only a small number of Black members, as many saw the organization as ineffectual. Despite this impression, it was still instrumental in 1958 in helping to elect Hattie Mae White as the first Black school board member and the first African American to win a city election in Houston since Reconstruction.[56]

Houston's Jews took an active interest in the election of Hattie Mae White. The *JH-V* supported her, and some Jews directly involved themselves in her school board campaign. Among them were husband and wife Adie and Jo Marks. Firm supporters of school integration, the Marks believed that one could not separate anti-Semitism and anti-Black sentiment from each other, and thus they fought simultaneously to end both. Their daughter, Dena Marks, associate director of the ADL, recalled her parents' friendships with African Americans, including civil rights activist Reverend William Lawson. Adie Marks ran the first advertising agency to hire a Black photographer and was involved in advertising for Hattie Mae White's campaign. According to Dena Marks, it "was unheard of for a white advertising agency to do the advertising for a Black school board member."[57] Jo Marks also was part of White's election campaign and became involved in the Houston Association for Better Schools.

National Jewish Defense Organizations

Throughout the South, but particularly in Houston, the local chapters of the AJC and the AJCongress hosted meetings to discuss civil rights cases. In Houston, these organizations focused on civil rights violations occurring in the Houston Independent School District. The local chapter of the AJC brought in speakers in 1955, including Margaret Ryan, coauthor of *Schools in Transition*, along with the organization's national president, Irving Engels. Engels spoke to the Houston Jewish community on "how to comply with the Supreme Court decision on desegregation of our public schools."[58] The same year, the national branch of the AJCongress expressed interest in opening a chapter in Houston, especially since there were already B'nai B'rith and AJC chapters in the city. The development, however, of the Houston branch took time and it did not officially open until 1957.[59]

The national office of the AJCongress identified Houston as having the potential to lead change in the segregated South. The temporary head of the Houston branch, Naftalie Abramowitz, sponsored an event with Leo Pfeffer, national director of the AJCongress Commission on Law and Social Action, in which he spoke on the separation of church and state, civil rights, and integration. By October, efforts to enact change via Houston began in earnest. Glatstein, who was a member of the steering committee of the Houston branch, wrote to Richard Cohen, southwest regional director of the AJCongress, requesting "detailed, factual reports on what organized Jewish communities in the South and Southwest were doing as Jewish communities with reference to tensions over the desegregation issues." Glatstein and Cohen wanted to prepare Houston's Jews and their leaders for the desegregation process: "As you know, we are waiting for the Federal Court decision on school desegregation in Houston, and we await the reaction with some trepidation."[60] Prominent constitutional lawyer Will Maslow—whom the organization would refer to as one of the "architects of the AJCongress programs of civil rights and civil liberties"—wrote to Glatstein.[61] Maslow encouraged him to help make Houston into a "model for its sister communities in the South."[62]

Feeling the pressure, the Houston chapter of the AJCongress called a meeting on the topic on February 23, 1958. Due to its kosher kitchen, organizational leaders chose to hold the meeting to discuss Houston's "segregation-integration problem" at the Shamrock Hotel, a sad irony given the fact that the hotel was segregated.[63] Including as two panelists Houston attorney Herbert Finkelstein and Rabbi Malev of Congregation Beth Yeshurun, the meeting addressed establishing a relationship between the Houston chapter and the New York office. Local AJCongress president Abramowitz hoped that this meeting would galvanize Houston's Jews to voice their opinions of educational desegregation publicly. However, the AJCongress and Maslow did not seem to understand the full implications of desegregation or anticipate the arduous process that would later occur in Houston.[64]

A few months later on May 29, 1958, the AJCongress and the AJC held an open meeting at the JCC to discuss school desegregation titled "Current Problems Facing the School Board." The center had become a neutral location for such heated discussions. As *The Informer* noted, the Houston Association for Better Schools regularly hosted their meetings at the JCC as part of the Community Relations Committee. The May 1958 AJCongress and AJC meeting included a panel on desegregation and a showing of *A City Decides*, an Oscar-nominated documentary focusing on integration of the Saint Louis public schools in 1956. The purpose of the post-film discussion was to motivate Houstonians to support school desegregation. A total of 125 people participated, including "about 10 negroes, 25 Jews, and 90 white non-Jews."[65] The AJCongress was disappointed that so few Jews and Blacks attended. Though pro-segregationist members of the White Citizens' Council left before its end, their presence was felt in the public meeting, especially when they asked questions the panel refused to answer. Despite this, the meeting was considered a success, since no violence erupted.[66] However, the wider problem brewing underneath the surface was local disenchantment with the northern Jewish organization's attempts to spearhead southern integration.[67]

Backlash Against the National Jewish Defense Organizations

Not all of Houston's Jews reacted positively to these AJCongress meetings. Rabbi Harry Sky of Congregation Brith Shalom voiced that he felt they caused more problems within the city and antagonized the White Citizens' Council.[68] Even local president Abramowitz was frustrated by the national organization's constant emphasis on integration as the main goal. He had become involved with the AJCongress "because of its militant attitude with respect to Israel" and did not like how desegregation took center stage.[69] Further, Abramowitz sensed a lack of local support for the actions of the northern-based AJCongress among both the city's Jews and Blacks. They could not relate to some of the speakers, such as Maslow, and their emphasis on the Jewish leaders of Houston becoming national representatives of integration. To them, the AJCongress acted as if segregation were an exclusively southern problem. When White of the *JH-V* complained about Maslow to Richard Cohen, Cohen agreed that he and Maslow did not understand "fellow-Jews who have to live with the problem on a day-to-day basis."[70] Cohen believed that when Maslow toured the South, he would gain knowledge of the area and relate better to the particular needs of Houston's Jews.

Between 1956 and 1958, David White regularly opposed the North's involvement in the South's plan to desegregate. Throughout this commentary, he situated school desegregation and the integration crisis as a fight between northern and southern Jews. For instance, White's article "The Season Is Upon Us" in the *JH-V* argued that the North should be patient and stop pressuring the South to integrate. The problem, as Rabbi Kahn also noted, was with the Supreme Court, which "did not arbitrarily set up a date of integration nor did it make integration in the public schools a single national action." From White's perspective, the South was changing, but it was on a different timetable than the North. White opposed the northern Jewish attitude of being "do-gooders" who imposed their values on southerners. Aware of the existence of virulent prejudice and people with "ignorance and mistrust which need to be negated," White nonetheless urged Houston to be cautious and to focus on homegrown efforts: "The strides in better race relations and the acceptance of race equality have outdistanced other parts of the country during the past decade."[71]

White saw northern exceptionalism as one of the factors that encouraged the North to view the South as an "Other." Despite this dichotomy between the two regions, he still trusted northerners would come to realize that they shared the

same fight as southerners and that unity would eventually tran-
spire because "we are one people, one nation." White situated
the plight of southern Jews as precarious. Even though both
northern and southern Jews were minorities, they faced different challenges. Northern Jews had more security than southern
Jews because de jure segregation did not dictate their lives.
Southern Jews, especially Houston's Jewish business members,
had to take into consideration the economic well-being of
their families. What is more, southern Jews did not have the
emotional or financial means to defeat segregation. Regardless
of this reality, White still trusted southerners to "accomplish
much through our own methods than with those suggested by
men living outside of the southern states."[72]

Throughout the 1950s, the *JH-V* published articles from
the Jewish Telegraphic Agency (JTA) focused on the rise of
anti-Semitism, particularly in the South because of desegregation. Many radical southern segregationists blamed the Jews
for instigating integration. In the wake of *Brown*, anti-Jewish
attacks and hate mail escalated. Between 1957 and 1958, temple
bombings occurred in Charlotte, Atlanta, Miami, Gastonia,
Alexandria, and at the Jewish Community Centers in Nashville
and Jacksonville.[73] In May 1958, David White responded by
publishing the ADL's news bulletin, which featured a letter from
the White Citizens' Council leader Robert Pattinson to Senator
Jacob Javits, one of the sponsors of the civil rights bill. Pattinson blatantly blamed national Jewish defense organizations like
the ADL and the AJCongress for the uptick in anti-Semitism
after the *Brown* decision, claiming "many southerners now say,
'If the Jewish organizations, the Jewish propaganda media and
the Jewish individual leadership were removed from the drive
to force integration, there would be no drive.'" Pattinson also
claimed that Blacks felt national Jewish involvement caused
more harm than good. He criticized Jews for making integration
a "Jewish cause." Jews needed to "keep quiet" and not force
integration or there would be consequences.[74]

His ideas and underlying threats encapsulated and reinforced southern Jewish fear of getting involved in the African

American cause. By including this letter in the *JH-V*, White demonstrated that he, too, had reservations about Jewish involvement. The letter validated the local Jewish fears of repercussions and encouraged the need for them to embrace their American and white identity. As a result, Rabbi Kahn and later Rabbi Malev, both integrationists, urged southern Jews to support civil rights privately rather than publicly.

In a letter to his friend Charles Nathan, Kahn complained of certain southern ministers who repetitiously preached on segregation and integration. Kahn described this approach as having the "same effect as the sound of the voice of a nagging wife ... like rain on the roof, and then suddenly it begins to irritate." Because Kahn did not want the Jews of Houston to see him in the same light, he worked proactively behind the scenes through "personal conversations, by letters, by conferences rather than public pronouncement[s]" to promote desegregation. Kahn urged other southern rabbis to embrace his behind-the-scenes resistance. He believed that change came not by being outspoken but rather by opening the channels of communication between whites and African Americans "privately rather than through demonstrations and protest crowds accompanied by banners and shouting."[75] His son, Alfred Kahn, explained that his father did not seek attention like a traditional protester but rather found his activism as a community builder. He put his "personal influence and moral persuasion to bear on community members and leaders to help move them in the right direction, but frequently in private rather than in public."[76]

Rabbi Malev shared Kahn's philosophy of not speaking out publicly. In 1958, Malev wrote an article titled "The Jews of the South in Conflict on Segregation" in *Conservative Judaism*. While some scholars have interpreted Malev as an integrationist speaking in segregationist terms, Malev's point of view was ultimately a liberal in favor of acculturation. He wanted to promote desegregation, but not at the expense of Jewish acculturation. His goal in the article was to present a comprehensive picture of how southern Jews had responded to segregation, in large part to provide northern Jews with a better understanding of what it meant to be a southern Jew, specifically a Houstonian. In particular, Malev did not want civil rights to become a Jewish issue; instead, he wanted it to be an American one. Ultimately, he wanted America to handle the question of race in the United States. It could not be a Jewish problem because Jews had the responsibility of fighting their own battles in a Protestant white world.

As a distinct group, Jews were powerless; however, if southern Jews would define themselves as Americans of Jewish faith, they could align themselves with Christians and be part of a larger faith-based collective. Malev's sentiment echoed Congregation Beth Israel's early attempts to downplay Jewish distinctiveness by advocating for the label of Americans of Jewish faith. And their goals were the same as well: a significant Jewish presence in the public Gentile sphere.[77]

Malev stressed how the southern Jewish experience was not monolithic. In other words, what worked for Jews in Houston might not work in Birmingham. In formulating his ideas, Malev spoke with many southern rabbis, some more experienced in anti-Semitism than others, and some with congregations still divided on the issues of segregation and desegregation. These divisions caused Malev to favor a proactive alignment with white Christians, as they provided southern Jews with the greatest security and societal protection. Aligning directly with African Americans was too risky lest they become an equally vulnerable minority.

Malev also voiced dissent toward national defense organizations like the ADL and AJC. From his perspective, they disrupted Jewish identity. These organizations caused confusion among the non-Jewish population because they were not religiously based. Malev was concerned that this would result in Jews being thought of as an ethnic group rather than a religious group.[78] In other words, if white Gentiles were to define Jews as an ethnic group, they might then associate Jews with African Americans, another ethnic group. Jews as a religious group was safer, since it meant they had more in common with white Gentiles. The problem was that southerners might see national Jewish defense organizations as the same as the NAACP, which was "considered *persona non-grata* by the overwhelming majority of the segregationist leaders." Therefore, the ADL's presence created "conflict" and was "not an advantage but a liability to the Jewish communities in the South."[79]

Moreover, national Jewish defense organizations targeted their programming to the North and not the South. Many southern Jewish leaders, especially Malev, thought the tone of the ADL was condescending—they "[spoke] with arrogance looking down their noses at the backward and timid southern Jews and sometimes committed blunders because of their incomplete knowledge of the situation."[80] Key in Malev's mind was to thwart the national organizations from pushing southern Jews to make immediate change. When a national Jewish defense organization came to Houston to speak to the Jewish community, Malev related how the speaker claimed that desegregation in the South would resolve if "southern Jews [would] have more courage and face the enemies of desegregation without fear or timidity."[81]

The speaker received "considerable notice in the general press," which exacerbated local tensions between Jews and non-Jews. Instead of such public events, Malev believed that these organizations should "continue their splendid work in research, in legal help and in skilled propaganda work on a national level, but let religious leaders of the Jewish communities be the spokesmen for them." He trusted that Houston's Jews would fully support desegregation if they had the support of the rabbis and the greater Christian community. Although Jews were but a small proportion of the Houston population, by identifying as a religious group rather than simply a minority, they could become one of three major faith groups (Protestants, Catholics, and Jews), which would magnify their voice and prevent Jewish marginalization.[82]

When Martin Luther King Jr. criticized southern Jewish complacency in the fight for equality and justice, Malev and other southern Jewish leaders became frustrated with him for "singling out Jews in his accusation against their apparent silence." They asked themselves: Why did King not call out the white Christians? The onus was on northern-based national Jewish defense organizations, which "proclaim[ed] the righteousness of the cause of desegregation" without comprehending that the southern Jew was "caught between the Negro who demanded that they side with them" and the "white population who threatened them with violence if they did."[83] The problem was not Jewish involvement in civil rights; rather, the issue was not defining it as something *all* Americans faced. Although Malev strove to define Jews as similar to white Gentiles, he also feared that if Jews acted independently they might "rouse the sleeping dogs of hate and violence."[84] Southern Jewish leaders needed to decide whether to follow or disregard the orders of national Jewish defense organizations in order to prevent reawakening anti-Semitism.

Glatstein criticized Malev for scapegoating defense organizations and held fast to his position that, if not for them, Houston would not have any "forward movement on race issues." Glatstein was against southern rabbis being the sole communal voices because he did not trust their ability to guide their congregants through the scant efforts already underway on behalf of Black residents. Instead, Glatstein placed his trust in national Jewish organizations to make the changes. In response, Malev reasserted the danger of Houston's Jews becoming the leaders of the civil rights movement. The repercussions of such action "placed emphasis upon the theory that we, as Jews, are closest to the position of the Negro, in our country."[85]

This idea would lead to anti-Semitism in Houston and the South because it was from "the agitator [who] equates the Jew with the Negro, and thereby separates the Jew from the rest of the community, that much of our difficulty has come." While he agreed with Glatstein that Houston did not have adequate leadership, he also felt that progress needed to be slower and focused on rabbinical leadership lest the Jews "upset the applecart and bring tragedy upon themselves and upon the cause of desegregation." He argued that in Houston, "the Jewish Community Council [should work] discreetly and quietly … to prepare the front for desegregation with the help of all, or most, of the religious groups in the community."[86] In other words, Houston's Jews needed to position themselves as white Americans of Jewish faith lest they lose their first-class citizenship in a city and region that strictly defined all of society in white and Black terms.

In the *JH-V*, the regional director of the American Council for Judaism, George Bagrash, supported Malev's argument not only because of the widespread support it had received from southern Jews but also because he felt Malev's philosophy on Jewish involvement in the southern desegregation crisis paralleled the anti-Zionist model that Jews should not separate themselves from the white American majority. Though Malev, a staunch Zionist, agreed that the issue of desegregation was an American problem, not a Jewish one, he did not place Zionism in the same category. This stance was reminiscent of Congregation Beth Israel's institution of the Caucasian clause, which also urged American Jews to conform to the white American majority instead of following the lead of Zionism. They did not intend to be prejudicial toward African Americans, but they wanted the white Gentiles to accept them as white Americans of Jewish faith, not as minority outliers.[87]

In the South, where rabbis had a stronger presence, the ideological conflicts between religious leaders reverberated throughout the community. The ongoing back-and-forth between local rabbis like Malev and the national Jewish defense organizations demonstrated the stark complexities involved in the need for Houston's Jews to define themselves as white while also appearing to be supportive of the civil rights movement.

In Houston during the late 1950s, when the issue of segregation began to reach a climax in the wake of *Brown v. Board of Education*, Houston's Jewish leaders increased their interest in desegregation. However, most of their congregants were unwilling to sacrifice themselves for a cause that did not directly pertain to their plight. As a minority in the South much smaller than the Black minority, they feared public backlash. Instead of creating a unified Jewish front, the entrance of national Jewish defense organizations exacerbated existing schisms.

Houston Jewish leaders may have spoken in favor of desegregation, but none wanted to take the leap the national Jewish defense organizations had recommended to bring about that change. Organizational work was only so effective, especially since the national organizations overlooked key cultural concerns. The different responses during the early desegregation movement around the time of *Brown* helped paint a portrait of what the Houston Jewish leaders thought they needed to do to gain the favor of white Gentile leaders.

In the next chapter, I investigate the historical Jewish enclave of Riverside Terrace during the 1950s and the early 1960s. Even in a time when Blacks were devoid of any power to change the city's structure, the Jews of Houston maintained certain lines that they would not cross to promote integration and full equality for Houston's most vulnerable residents.

Chapter 4

The Houston Jewish Exodus from Riverside to Meyerland

We were more liberal with our ballots than we were with our personal relationships with Blacks. It was a matter of being thoughtful, considerate, and libertarian without becoming too neighborly.

Rabbi Robert Kahn
This Is Our Home, It Is Not for Sale, 1987

Even though the Supreme Court's ruling of *Brown v. Board of Education* propelled Houston's Jewish leaders to support desegregation privately, they avoided a public stance for fear of bringing reprisals to their community. National Jewish defense organizations that pushed for public advocacy failed to understand the degree to which the rise of anti-Semitism in the South and in Houston affected local rabbis and their congregations. While the last chapter addressed broad Jewish involvement in pushing for the desegregation of the city's public schools, this chapter will focus on certain key neighborhoods where separation and eventual integration occurred. Cognizant of the second-class position of Houston's Black residents, the city's

Jewish leaders fought Black encroachment on Jewish neighbor-hoods out of fear that their presence would adversely affect the already tenuous position of Jews in white Gentile society.

Riverside Terrace provided Jewish residents with a sense of security because they were able to form a distinct Jewish presence through the construction of synagogues and the crea-tion of successful businesses. Because of the security their enclave provided, the Jews of Riverside Terrace integrated more successfully with their white Gentile neighbors.

Riverside Terrace welcomed Jews but not African Amer-icans. The restrictive covenant stated that "the property shall never be sold to any person other than the Caucasian race."[1] Although this clause was prejudicial to African Americans—and the Jews could relate—the Jews' main priority was to create a secure environment for their community to flourish in peace. In Riverside Terrace, the Jewish community could establish syna-gogues, Sunday schools, and eventually a Jewish Community Center (JCC). Riverside Terrace became known in Houston as the "Jewish River Oaks," which was surprising considering Jews accounted for less than 30 percent of the Riverside Terrace population. However, by the 1930s, most wealthy Jewish fami-lies, including the Weingartens, Sakowitzes, Battelsteins, and Fingers, had moved into Riverside Terrace.[2]

Houston Jews created religious spaces in Riverside Terrace. They built three Orthodox synagogues: Congregation Beth Jacob developed in 1937, Adath Israel moved from the Fifth Ward in 1939, and Adath Emeth moved from Woodland Heights in 1948. Businessman Joe Weingarten headed the project to create an additional synagogue, Beth Yeshurun, in Riverside Terrace, and its building opened next door to Adath Emeth between 1949 and 1950. It had formed as a merger between two Conservative synagogues, Beth El and Adath Yeshurun, in 1946. The community even developed kosher-style Kaplan's Delicatessen, which became popular for Jewish social events such as bar mitzvahs and secular social gatherings. There were also kosher facilities like M&M Kosher Meat Market and Deli-catessen and Harf's.[3]

While certain neighborhoods excluded Houston Jews, like River Oaks, only the Black population faced extreme segregation in Houston. Jews founded their own country club in 1930, the Westwood Country Club, because the Houston Country Club and River Oaks Country Club barred Jews. However, Jews not affiliated with Reform Judaism were not always welcome in this club either.[4] This reality was in stark contrast to other areas of the city where Jews struggled to interact or integrate. The Jews of Riverside Terrace, however, while supportive of Black civil rights in theory, did not want African Americans to be their neighbors.[5]

The migration of African Americans into Jewish neighborhoods was not unique to Houston. Historically, Blacks felt more at ease moving into Jewish neighborhoods, in large part because they believed that if an area was tolerant enough to allow Jews, they had a chance of acceptance as well. After all, Jews had faced housing discrimination throughout the country, albeit to a lesser degree. Neither in the North nor the South, however, did this similarity of experience inspire Jews to risk living in an integrated neighborhood. Much like their Jewish counterparts elsewhere, Houston's Jews left Riverside Terrace after African Americans began to settle there. They did not retaliate against the Blacks who moved into their neighborhood; they simply left gradually, leaving traces of their Jewish identity behind. Because they had to re-create their community elsewhere, the move came at a heavy cost. Riverside Terrace's Jewish neighborhood thus became a faded memory of a lost Jewish community. As Houston lawyer Harry Brochstein stated, "What was there, is no longer there." Brochstein's comment was a reference to David Meyerowitz's 1926 Yiddish song "*Vos geven iz geven un nito*," which translates to "What Was, Was, and Is No More."[6]

Because of its proximity to the overpopulated Black Third Ward, Riverside Terrace transitioned from a white neighborhood into a Black one beginning in the early 1950s. Middle-class African Americans who wanted nicer homes viewed Riverside Terrace as an ideal choice. As a result, this neighborhood underwent integration, despite the unwillingness of the inhabitants—both Jews and white Gentiles—to share their space. Several important factors influenced Black migration into Riverside Terrace, including the overcrowding of the Third Ward, the expansion of Texas Southern University, and the construction of South Freeway, SH 288. Most importantly, the Caesars, the first Black family who moved to Riverside Terrace in 1953, paved the way for other Black families to follow. These events initiated residential integration, ensuing tensions between the majority Gentile and Houston's Jewish residents, and the eventual flight of white residents.

Jews in the 1950s and 1960s struggled to balance their liberalism and support of tolerance and racial integration with their own desire to acculturate. This struggle affected how Jewish leaders interacted with local Black residents. Houston's Jews did not want to live in integrated neighborhoods even though leaders like Rabbi Kahn promoted integration to the congregants and local Jews participated in social functions with African Americans. Instead, they preferred to support Black causes from a comfortable distance. Voting liberal was different from *acting* liberal. In that sense, the demise of Riverside Terrace as a Jewish center reflects the failure of Jewish liberalism. What purported ideologically to be anti-segregationist was in reality the exact opposite. By leaving Riverside Terrace, Houston's Jews and their leaders chose acculturation over liberal values.[7]

Most of the Jewish population—two-thirds in fact—arrived in Riverside Terrace after 1940. By 1945, it had become a stable community for Jews of different economic means. With so much of the Jewish population in residence there, the neighborhood continued to be the Jewish epicenter for Reform, Conservative, and Orthodox Jews. As the community grew, they developed more social sites, including the JCC, which opened on Herman Drive in 1951.[8] The arts director of the JCC, Marilyn Hassid, recalled that during the 1950s and 1960s, the JCC transformed from a place that was "Jewishly focused" to a center for everyone. As Hassid put it, "The JCC did not see color."[9] By 1958, it became a place where African Americans could play basketball. Also, Houston's JCC became a place where Black blues musicians like John Lomax Jr. and Leadbelly entertained white audiences and performed without any repercussion. Hassid explained that this was often the best break for them during the time of segregation. White blues musicians, like those in the Houston Folklore Group, also played with African American musicians, but because of this collaboration, these white musicians later faced difficulty finding venues for their music.[10]

The Riverside Terrace JCC location also hosted a monthly Folk Music Series, which began on February 14, 1962. One of the first performances featured blues artist Ed Badeaux, who was white, and Mance Lipscomb, who was African American. Later, the African American country blues singer Lightnin' Hopkins first performed at the JCC on March 15, 1962, and went on to play there several times. Hopkins was popular among white middle- to upper-class Jews and even among immigrant Jews. The concert series helped many musicians like Hopkins launch their careers. Before the JCC moved to Meyerland in 1969, Hopkins performed again with John Lomax in 1967.[11]

These interactions between Jews and Blacks, however, were contained to the JCC. Any actual social interactions that took place in the Riverside Terrace neighborhood were between Jews and whites. Jewish and Christian children often played each other in baseball and basketball games. Reverend Tom Bagby of Saint James Church remembered Jewish children coming to the church to play and participate in church activities. Rabbi Kahn also recalled that the neighborhood became a model of Jewish and Christian relations. Residents recalled the existence of two adjacent houses, one with Christmas lights and the other with Hanukkah decorations. Although not representative of the rest of Houston, Riverside Terrace reflected to Jews and Christians alike what was possible. The documentary *This Is Our Home, It Is Not for Sale* depicted Jews and Christians as neighbors who interacted with each other despite their difference in religion.[12]

Because segregation defined the social hierarchy in Houston, Blacks and Jews had very few opportunities to develop personal relationships in Riverside Terrace. The one exception was the Jewish and Gentile employment of Black domestic workers. Aware of this relationship, Kahn even pleaded with his congregants in one of his sermons to treat Black domestic workers with respect.

His son, Alfred Kahn, explained that Jews and African Americans "truly lived in different worlds, and the only contact was commercial, professional, or domestic employment. Mixed neighborhoods were probably 100 percent nonexistent."[13]

One significant problem was that the lack of personal relationships between Jews and Blacks in Houston perpetuated inaccurate perceptions of African Americans. In Jewish enclaves like Riverside Terrace, Jews lacked the personal framework to effectively support civil rights. On the one hand, they followed the call of Jewish leadership to participate in interfaith and Brotherhood events. They listened to, as Alfred Kahn said, "the prophetic vision of equality and social justice [that] was preached and taught and accepted in the Jewish community, by my father among them."[14]

Many Jews clung to their prejudices, but there was a difference between being prejudicial and being discriminatory. Houston's Jews, as Alfred Kahn stated, were "more consistent in [their] opposition to and disdain for legal discrimination and enforced discrimination." Ideologically, they strongly opposed segregation, which according to Alfred Kahn was "antithetical to Jewish values," but realistically, Houston's Jews were not comfortable living with African Americans.[15]

Diverging Living Spaces

In the mid-twentieth century, Houston's Black residents—of both the lower and higher socioeconomic classes—started to migrate closer to the Third Ward from blighted areas like the Fourth Ward. Others of means relocated to Riverside Terrace. Still, many in the lower to middle socioeconomic classes stayed in the Third Ward. As in Boston and other cities, rather than helping African Americans, any urban renewal programs instituted by the city caused greater housing shortages.[16] Houston's public housing struggles caught the attention of Alan Green, a rabbi at Congregation Emanu El. Green supported public housing and slum clearance as a member of the Interfaith Citizen Committee.

In 1946, the committee instituted Housing Sunday to educate Christian and Jewish congregants on Houston's need to clear the city of its blighted slum areas. Green explained that they were "infested with rats and vermin, often without plumbing" and housed "as many as five to eleven in [a] room." He preached to the congregants that it was their duty as Houstonians to make Houston into a "great city."[17] In his sermon notes for Housing Sunday, Green emphasized the pressing need for public housing because, as he reiterated, "1/4 of all Houses in Houston are below living standards." He asked, "Is the Lord building the house when the wealth of the city is poured only into making the beautiful areas more beautiful and nothing to provide better living conditions for those who need them most?"[18]

In Houston, there were two points of view on public housing. Some wanted to take federal funds to clear blighted areas and rebuild; others wanted Houston to remain autonomous. In support of public housing, the Citizens for Slum Clearance, under William Clayton and the oil tycoon R. E. Smith, joined with the Houston Housing Authority (HHA) to promote to the public the dire need for public housing and slum clearance in Houston. Several Jews who were involved in this committee created a documentary film called *Human Harvest* about the "slums," which highlighted the intense disparity between the beautiful parts of Houston and its blighted areas. Despite these efforts, the Houston Home Protection Committee, which opposed public housing, proved to be more powerful. In the end, they won the fight by appealing to irrational fears of Communism. By equating public housing with Socialism, the committee convinced Houstonians that public housing would be a base for recruiting Communists and Socialists.[19]

The Houston Home Protection Committee strongly felt that the city should autonomously raise funds privately to alleviate the slums and not take federal money. In 1950, the city of Houston chose the path of autonomy by voting that money for public housing would come from private funds over public monies. With this vote, Houston became the largest city in America to opt out of funding for public housing.[20]

Because of its defiance toward public housing, Houstonians of the lower socioeconomic classes lacked adequate housing options. Several philanthropists did step up to fundraise and establish housing for African Americans. Adjacent to the Third Ward in Sunnyside, the Eliza Johnson Home for Aged Negroes, founded in 1949, was a joint effort among prominent whites, African Americans, and Jews. Black philanthropists Anna and Clarence Dupree spearheaded the new home, naming it after Anna's mother, Eliza.[21]

The Duprees owned the Eldorado Entertainment Center, which was the social centerpiece of the Third Ward. Opened in 1939, the center housed the Eldorado Ballroom, an upscale social club,[22] which social activist Dr. Ernie Attwell recalled as having "some of the best Jazz and Blues playing at the time in Houston."[23] Among the famous musicians who performed there were Count Basie, Ray Charles, and Big Joe Turner. The Duprees held many functions at the Eldorado Ballroom to raise money for their charities, many of which Jews attended. Philanthropist Hubert S. Finkelstein grew up in the white section of the Third Ward with other Jewish families. In the 1950s, he remembered opening his windows and fondly listening to jazz filtering from the Eldorado Ballroom.[24]

Robert Kahn was one of the incorporators of the Eliza Johnson Home, and Jewish board members included Thomas Friedman, Maurice Hirsch, and Rabbi Schachtel.[25] At the home's dedication in 1952, Schachtel was one of the speakers, calling the place a "Sanctuary for God."[26] After presenting the Duprees with a plaque honoring them for their commitment to the Eliza Johnson Home, he described the prominent Black family as "distinguished citizens, community builders, and humanitarians, respectively."[27] Jewish businessman M.N. Dannenbaum, one of the original organizers of the home, became its president in 1957.[28]

More African Americans settled in the Third Ward in the postwar era, though many remained in the Fourth and Fifth Wards. Those who lived in the Fifth Ward viewed the Third Ward as where more well-to-do professionals, including doctors, lived. In addition to having the nicer restaurants, the Third Ward also housed one of the most well-known Black high schools, Jack Yates Colored High School, which the *Houston Chronicle* described as an "educational anchor" that produced teachers,

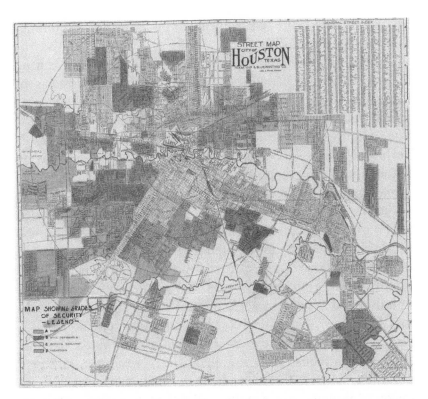

Texas Map & Blueprint Co. (1930): Street Map, City of Houston, Texas, circa 1930.

clergy, lawyers, and many professionals.[29] Despite these assets, the Third Ward also experienced overcrowding in the 1950s.[30] The divide between the Third Ward and the adjacent neighborhood of Riverside Terrace shifted once the Third Ward's Texas Southern University (TSU), formerly known as Texas State University for Negroes, opted to build a new law school in Riverside Terrace in 1947. The state, unconcerned by the potential ramifications of this decision, allotted $2 million for this purpose. The congestion in the Third Ward propelled students and professors in need of housing to consider Riverside Terrace a viable option. The resulting influx of Blacks into the perimeter of Riverside Terrace challenged the invisible border between the two neighborhoods. Riverside resident Sol Weiner called the expansion of TSU the "kiss of death as far as the Jewish community was concerned."[31]

The creation of Houston's new freeway system during the 1940s and 1950s further challenged the homeostasis of Riverside Terrace. The highway plans delineated which areas would face demolition, and in 1959, the city constructed State Highway 288 to cut through the east side of Riverside Terrace. Highway 288 was the last freeway allowed in Houston before a new policy prevented city planners from demolishing minority areas for freeways.[32]

In the 1940s, freeways like Interstate 45, which cut through the Fourth Ward, caused African American cultural and business life to falter. Demolition for the highway not only segmented the neighborhood and destroyed buildings, it separated the Fourth Ward from other wards. In the freeway's wake, the Fourth Ward became a shell of itself. The creation of Highway 59 (1953), Interstate 10 (1956), and Interstate 610 (1952) also greatly affected the Second and Fifth Wards. Neither the neighborhoods' Jews nor their Black residents, however, protested the new freeways. In fact, when the former Jewish mayor of Bellaire, Abe Zindler, had a chance to join an antifreeway protest in 1955, he chose to accept the highway. These new major freeways led to the overcrowding of the Third Ward as displaced Black residents moved there.[33]

The Early Stages of Riverside Terrace Integration

From 1950 to 1960, Houston's Black population grew from 125,400 to 215,037, leading Black residents to find new areas to live in. Riverside Terrace was a logical choice because it was nearby and because redlining practices in other white neighborhoods were more stringent, even after the Supreme Court ruled in 1948 in *Shelly v. Kramer* to outlaw the practice of restricting housing covenants by race. Though Houston's homeowners did not have the legal grounds to stop them from buying homes, Blacks had to find alternative ways to finance their homes, even in Riverside Terrace. In the case of the Tillmans, a Black family, their Jewish doctor provided them the necessary financial assistance to purchase a home in Riverside Terrace. This gesture, however, was an exception to the rule for Black residents. More often than not, whites feared that Black homeownership would decrease their property values.[34]

Riverside Terrace did not change overnight from a Jewish enclave into a majority African American one. However, one particular event did trigger a change: the 1952 arrival of Jack Caesar, a wealthy Black cattle buyer. There was a widespread misconception in both the North and the South that all African Americans were of lower socioeconomic status. When Jack Caesar bought a nice home in Riverside Terrace, he challenged that stereotype. Caesar chose the Jewish neighborhood because traditional Black neighborhoods in Houston did not have a home up to his standards. What is more, he was drawn to the bucolic feeling of the suburb. Caesar had his white male secretary purchase the house under his name and transfer the deed to his employer. Quietly under the guise of night, his family moved into their new home. Clearly, the Caesars knew they were taking a risk. Initially, the neighbors thought he was a chauffeur or that his wife was a domestic worker.[35]

Though there was tension at the Caesars' arrival, no violence occurred. Rumors did circulate about the family, like that they owned nightclubs on Almeda and that their home was possibly a "front" for the NAACP. The *Houston Chronicle* described the relationship between the Caesars and their Riverside Terrace neighbors as a "year-long cold war to force the Negro cattle buyer to move out of the predominantly white neighborhood."[36] The Jews of Riverside Terrace may have pronounced themselves liberals in favor of integration, but they were more concerned about housing values, crime, and their schools. The residents accepted the inevitable change at the perimeter of Riverside Terrace because of its proximity to TSU, but they could not accept African Americans fully integrating into all of Riverside Terrace.

In April 1953, a non-Jewish neighbor, George Howell, altered the tenuous but ultimately peaceful atmosphere of Riverside Terrace when he tried to frighten the Caesar family out of the neighborhood. Howell paid his handyman, Carl Davis, $500 to bomb the Caesars' house. Davis used four sticks of dynamite to bomb their front porch and caused $1,000 in damage. Howell denied his involvement. *The Informer* reported, however, that Davis and Howell were "indicted on three separate counts: possession of a bomb, arson by explosion, and damage to property."[37] Davis then testified that he and Howell had planned the bombing and that they had stored the dynamite in Howell's garage. Though the court found Davis guilty and imprisoned him for two years, it ruled that there was "insufficient evidence" of Howell's involvement and did not prosecute him.[38] For several weeks after the incident, Black "cowboys" affiliated with the Caesars guarded the house with rifles and shotguns until they felt certain the threat had diminished.

The bombing had a ripple effect in the neighborhood, fostering fear of more violence. Those Jewish and white Gentile residents who lived close to Caesar's house wondered whether more unrest might ensue if other Black families moved in.[39]

Black and Jewish Interaction
after the Caesar Bombing

After the April incident in Riverside Terrace, the city's Jewish leadership continued to be involved with Black institutions. Prominent Jews, including Simon Sakowitz and Ray K. Daily, helped in the expansion of TSU. At the October 1954 dedication of three new buildings, Rabbi Schachtel gave the convocation speech, dedicating the buildings to God.[40] Schachtel also showed an interest in Black causes and affection for individual Black residents at other times. In November 1956, Schachtel and his congregation hosted a retirement party for Black employee George Fields, celebrating his fifty years of service. The synagogue's bulletin praised him for his long-term leadership and membership at his Methodist church. The temple encouraged each of its congregants to donate between one and twenty-five dollars on Fields's behalf. On Shabbat, Schachtel honored Fields in a sermon titled "Our Friend George Fields," portraying him not merely as a worker but as a true member of the Temple community.[41]

Though Houston's Jewish leaders were involved in several combined social events near the Third Ward following the Caesar bombing, these interactions did not keep Riverside Terrace's Jews from moving elsewhere when more African Americans settled into their neighborhood. In Houston, as well as in other parts of the country, when Jews sold their homes to Blacks, they found themselves in a precarious position because they were contributing to the changing demographics of the neighborhood and possibly even inciting tension from other white neighbors.[42] However, this risk did not stop many Riverside Terrace Jews who wanted physical distance between themselves and the city's Black residents from selling. Because segregation had become an ingrained mindset, Jews followed the lead of their white Gentile counterparts. Riverside Terrace's Jews did not want to live with the African Americans in an integrated neighborhood because they thought it would erode the image they had culti-vated as being white Americans of Jewish faith. Sustaining their first-class citizenship was paramount.

Some Jewish families faced difficulties in selling their homes. A lawyer named Lionel Schooler remembered how his family struggled when word spread that they might be selling their home to an African American. Schooler recalled "bricks and rocks being thrown against the house, and a cross burned in the front yard."[43] There were also full cans of paint thrown through the window. Riverside resident Jane Silverman "admit-ted bitterness towards Blacks and the way the neighborhood changed."[44] Sid and Mary Smiley recalled that in choosing to leave the neighborhood, Sid "didn't act as a Jew, but as a homeowner." They went on to say that the "bombing created fear—not panic ... [and] concern for families."[45] In his sermon on March 22, 1958, Schachtel recalled that the Ku Klux Klan, located north of the Fifth Ward, harassed Riverside Terrace resi-dents who sold to African Americans. According to Schachtel, "Several weeks ago, after ten o'clock at night, when leaving the home of one of our friends, we were shocked to see two giant crosses and the usual ring of fire burning around them before the homes of two negroes who had purchased these homes from white people in a very nice section of Houston."[46]

On the border of Riverside Terrace, closest to TSU, developers demolished older homes and transformed them into substandard apartments without air-conditioning. They also bought large estates and turned them into two-hundred-family apartment buildings or frat houses for TSU students, as well as strip malls and other types of businesses like bars and nightclubs. Due to Houston's intense humidity, Black residents often sat on their porches or walked down the streets to find comfort. Some homeowners felt that the parts of Riverside Terrace closest to TSU were beginning to resemble the inner city. White homeowners in the wealthier areas of Riverside Terrace worried that low-cost apartments might saturate the market and further change the neighborhood's demographics. One white resident, Dr. Mary Jourdan Atkinson, recalled hearing that it was the Jews and Italians who were behind the creation of these "multiple apartments," which they then gave over to Black real estate agents to rent or sell.[47] One anonymous Black resident of Riverside Terrace commented that "our Black landowners learned from the Jews who lived here that you can optimize money by running the place down and so they did it, we did it and that has caused the neighborhood to go down quite a bit."[48]

By 1959, a significant number of African Americans were living in Riverside Terrace. One Black resident described the process that year as "the whites tipping out and [the] Blacks tipping in." He remembered a Black real estate agent coming to his home. When he answered the door, the agent surprisingly said, "Oh, you're already here."[49] Clearly, the neighborhood was changing even faster than real estate agents expected. In fact, there were homes still vacant because their owners had simply left. In 1950, Riverside Terrace was approximately 97 percent white, but by 1960 it was approximately 23 percent white, and by 1970, it was only 7 percent white. Those whites who stayed did so because of financial constraints, personal attachment to their homes, or because they did not have a problem with living in an integrated neighborhood. In contrast to the rest of Riverside Terrace, the wealthy section remained the last bastion of whiteness, as even in 1960 it was still 99 percent white.[50]

Real estate agents took advantage of the movement of displaced African Americans to Riverside Terrace by using unsavory tactics, such as blockbusting, to incite fear of integration. Blockbusting was a common tactic across the country, used in neighborhoods facing white flight. Jewish, white Gentile, and Black real estate agents would convince white homeowners that they needed to sell in a hurry or risk not selling their homes at all. The goal was to harass white homeowners until they agreed to sell their homes at deflated prices. Realtors would knock on the doors of homes or incessantly call homeowners. Riverside Terrace resident Dr. Atkinson recalled seeing them "standing in the driveway and practically demanding a price."[51] Realtors also used the *Houston Post* and the *Houston Chronicle* "colored sections" to list Riverside homes.[52] Reverend William Lawson, the founder of Wheeler Avenue Baptist Church, remembered "realtors convinc[ing] Blacks that they could get property for them and they could convince Jews that we will give you much more than your house is worth."[53] The agents' goal was to profit off Blacks desperate to buy in Riverside Terrace while at the same time forcing the Jews to move out.

Reverend Lawson observed that this process was a double-edged sword for African Americans because, while they finally lived in better housing, they paid much more for the privilege. He recalled that "For Sale signs popped up on the lawns like dandelions, and people began to move out, and into the vacuum there came Negroes." Lawson's explanation described the cultural effects of segregation. White Riverside Terrace homeowners, including Gentiles and Jews, were so accustomed to seeing Blacks as disadvantaged that, according to Lawson, they were unable to fathom "the kind of Negro who can pay thirty-five or forty thousand dollars for a house and then buy two cars to park outside, hire a gardener and a maid and then take off on impulse on vacation."[54]

By 1964, 165 homes were for sale in the neighborhood. As blockbusting continued to worsen, Jewish and Gentile

PRIDEFUL SIGN IN A PROUD NEIGHBORHOOD
Property Values Have Begun To Stabilize Once More
—Photo by Jerry Click

"Prideful Sign in a Proud Neighborhood," July 6, 1964. Property Values Have Begun to Stabilize Once More. Jerry Click_HP/©Houston Chronicle. Used with permission.

homeowners organized to discuss the problem and attempt to stabilize property values. In the *Houston Post*, Alvin Duvall wrote an article on the backlash titled "Halting an Exodus, Owners Unite, Keep Homes in Mixed Area." While the newspaper did not specify the actual percentages of Jews and Gentiles who faced off against the real estate agents, it did mention that "100 of the 1,100" homes in Riverside Terrace featured the sign "This Is Our Home. It Is Not For Sale." Duvall argued that these signs were "evidence of a working experiment in democracy being conducted by a small but determined group of homeowners who love[d] their homes and want[ed] to keep them."[55]

Not one to mince words, Duvall highlighted the prejudice and corruption of "unscrupulous real estate agents both Negro and white who saw a chance to make a fast buck." The newspaper interpreted the displayed signs as a type of civil rights activism intended "to calm jittery neighbors who wanted to sell out [and] to persuade them to stay and accept desegregation."[56] The article made no mention of the need to preserve the Jewish enclave, nor did it mention how, under similar circumstances, other Jewish communities in Baltimore, Saint Louis, and Detroit used the exact same phrasing on lawn signs. However, the reality was that even some of those homeowners who displayed those signs were also secretly conferring with real estate agents to sell their homes.[57]

Frank Morgan's article a month later in the *Wall Street Journal*, titled "Houston Whites Act to Avoid Selling Panic as an Area Integrates," revealed that the situation was more complicated than the *Houston Post* had suggested. Morgan stressed that the homeowners' plan was exclusively a "campaign by whites" and that the South MacGregor Promotion Committee, which had produced the yard signs, was exclusively composed of white members. The thrust of its mission was to prevent real estate agents from blockbusting. Unlike the *Houston Post*, the *Wall Street Journal* interviewed Black homeowners in Riverside Terrace, one of whom said that while Houston may not be like Birmingham, "it's certainly the Deep South." In other words, Houston still perpetuated Black inequality. A Black biology professor at TSU stated that he supported the South MacGregor Promotion Committee "as long as the promotion committee's effort to maintain the integrity of the neighborhood [had] no racial basis."[58] The reality was, however, that Black residents were not privy to committee discussions and were unable to ask for its assistance.

Morgan also reported that committee members received harassing phone calls from white Houstonians who "complained that Riverside Terrace residents are causing trouble for other all-white sections of town [and] bitterly charged that the residents are 'niggers lovers' because they attempted to have what they considered an 'integrated neighborhood.'"[59] What Morgan did not expose was the violence that African Americans had faced in their transition to Riverside Terrace. As one white real estate agent, Joe Russell, said in 1982, they were being "terrorized." Segregationists broke their windows, fired guns into their homes, and made intimidating phone calls, causing new Black homeowners to string "gold-toned chicken wire across their windows."[60] Instead of highlighting these details, Morgan chose to end on a positive note from Reverend Woodward, a white Episcopal minister, who voiced the following sentiment on Riverside Terrace: "The world is moving toward an era that involves the races' learning how to dwell together, and I wanted my children to experience it."[61]

Despite the strife of integration, certain white families during the 1950s and early 1960s purposely moved into Riverside Terrace because it had the potential of becoming an integrated community, and they saw that as "educational" for their children. Dr. Atkinson recalled that there was some progress in the integration of Riverside Terrace, as one could see mothers sending "their children out to play with the Black children and invited their parents in for tea." Most of all, Atkinson professed that "Blacks don't feel that Blacks are any different than anybody else and that non-Blacks are any different than anybody else."[62]

While some individuals like Atkinson had positive interactions, other Riverside Terrace residents expressed the challenges they faced living in an integrated neighborhood. Edith Eisner, who moved to the area in 1960, remembered that some Jewish families were critical of her decision to move and even warned her "you'll lose your shirt" selling your house.[63] Another resident, Dova Finger, befriended the Graces, a Black family. Before she met them, Finger said that she "would have never call[ed] a Black Mr. or Mrs."[64] Billy Goldberg, another resident, "felt he was in [the] minority because he wanted to stay [because he had] good relations with [the] Black community." He believed that when the Riverside Terrace Jews left, they destroyed the Jewish presence in the area. Goldberg himself felt forced to leave when his synagogue moved in 1962.[65] Dr. Milton Little was angry with the Jewish residents because he saw African Americans as better neighbors than some of the white neighbors because they had more education. He was especially angry at the "Rabbis [who] would preach brotherhood" and then leave the neighborhood with their congregations without trying to change their minds.[66]

Anecdotes drawn from numerous interviews with Black residents of Riverside Terrace reflect the divide that existed between Jews and their new neighbors. When Reverend Lawson first came to TSU in 1955 to become the director of the Baptist Student Union, Riverside Terrace perplexed him. He wondered why "this Black college had been set down in the middle of an old Jewish community."[67] He noticed the synagogues, the Jewish Community Center, and other Jewish cultural institutions surrounding the university but not an active Black church for TSU students and faculty. He contemplated how the two populations, so different in religion, could comfortably coexist, especially since African Americans were pushing their boundaries into the Jewish enclave. He described the Black migration as "simply just kind of a stretching of the Third Ward."[68]

In the same interview, Lawson said he believed the presence of TSU and the Black community was "threatening" to the Jewish community. When Quentin Mease moved into Riverside Terrace, he remembered when the Jewish "holidays came up ... we could look out and look into the window and see them in there with the candles and all."[69] The existence of a community so different from the majority white Gentiles living side by side with them amazed Mease. Lancelin Boliver, a member of one of the first Black families to move into Riverside Terrace, remembered that he did not feel any hostility. However, the "rabbi next door never introduced himself," which disappointed him greatly. Boliver wanted to be "appreciated [as] neighbors—not tolerated."[70]

In the *JH-V* in August 1962, David White wrote of the Jewish perception of the migration away from Riverside Terrace. While he made no mention of Blacks moving into the neighborhood or of any of the resulting complications, he highlighted the momentousness of the move by comparing it to the Biblical exodus of the Jews from Egypt to Israel. White's clear implication was that the Jews were heading for their new homeland and escaping an oppressive situation. White implied the neighborhood's Jews were moving as a cohesive group. By relocating the synagogues as well as the residents, Houston's Jews eventually transported their entire community.[71]

The religious exodus of the Jews from Riverside Terrace did not escape Reverend Lawson's notice, especially the departure of Conservative Jews, who "can't drive to synagogue; they have to walk to synagogues." Lawson understood that even if there were Jews who wanted to stay in Riverside Terrace, once a certain number left, the others left out of a religious duty to follow their communities, especially those who observed the laws of the Sabbath. He did not comment on the Reform or Orthodox Jews; instead, he depicted the Jews as a unified yet mobile cultural group that chose collectively to move. Lawson asserted that "Jews always carry their synagogue and temples with them," as opposed to African Americans, who "do not carry their churches with them."[72]

By the mid-1960s, Riverside Terrace had become a paradox. The area around TSU gradually changed to become a lower socioeconomic African American neighborhood. Nightclubs, frat houses, and cheap new complexes replaced storefronts that once had held thriving Jewish businesses. Crime increased in some parts while, at the same time, middle- and upper-class African Americans replaced the white Gentiles and Jews in the more upscale parts of the neighborhood. Yet because of the increased crime, the wealthier Blacks, according to journalist Lawrence Wright, "lived behind barred windows with expensive security systems."[73] Over time, the entire area of Riverside Terrace merged with the Third Ward. Later, the more opulent part of Riverside Terrace became known as the "Black River Oaks." The Jewish community of Riverside Terrace had indeed become a ghost of the past.[74]

The Development of Black Riverside Terrace and a New Jewish Area

After the Riverside Terrace Jews left the neighborhood, the buildings they left behind that represented Jewish religious life became a part of Black cultural life. Congregation Adath Emeth

sold its building to TSU in 1958, and it became their music building. In the early 1960s, the Houston Independent School District
(HISD) bought Congregation Beth Yeshurun for $500,000 and
turned it into the Lockhart School, which predominantly served
Black students. Lockhart's students confronted traces of Jewish
life every day as they walked floors embedded with Stars of
David and menorah symbols. Congregation Beth Jacob sold its
building, which featured an image of a menorah on the outside
facade, to True Light Baptist Church. The Baptists reappropri-
ated the *mikveh* (Jewish ritual bath) for baptisms. Congregation
Beth Israel later became Houston Community College's Heinen
Theater in 1967. The Star of David with a lit menorah embedded in a stained-glass window is still visible in the theater near
where the ark once stood. In 1969, the JCC became the Judson W.
Robinson, Jr. Community Center, which served Black youth.[75]

The neighborhood of Riverside Terrace had created an
impression of peaceful Jewish-Christian relations, but this
romanticized coexistence did not extend to other neighborhoods.
David McEntire's 1960 report *Residence and Race* addressed
housing disparities, particularly the ways in which Jews continued to face residential restrictions. Houston was one city with
gentlemen's agreements against Jews in certain neighborhoods.[76] Riverside Terrace resident Jackie Proler recalled that
her family sold their house early because they wanted to get the
"best price"; however, when they tried to buy a house on Stella
Link near Meyerland, she said, "[we] were turned down because
we were Jewish—the salesman took my husband aside and told
him the builder didn't sell to Jews."[77] Shayna Turboff, another
resident, complained that when she and her family moved out
of Riverside Terrace, River Oaks still would not accept them:
"River Jews weren't welcome."[78] In the newly created Westbury
subdivision adjacent to Meyerland, at least one builder would
not sell to Jews. Several prominent Jewish business leaders went
to speak with the chairperson of the bank that was providing
financing to the homebuilder and informed him that if the homebuilder's anti-Semitic policy did not stop, they would take their
deposits to a different bank.[79]

Despite these obstacles, Jews continued to leave Riverside Terrace. Over time, a Jewish enclave established itself in Meyerland, an area first established in 1955 by George Meyer. When most of Houston's Jews still lived in Riverside Terrace, Bellaire, adjacent to Meyerland, already had Jewish residents, such as the Zindler family. Bellaire offered new homes with attractive amenities and middle-class pricing. Rumors circulated that businessman Leopold Meyer established this area but, in fact, the founding Meyer family was not Jewish. This rumor continued because so many Jews moved into Meyerland. By 1963, the Meyerland-Bellaire area had evolved into the center of Houston's Jewish life. Though that summer the *Houston Chronicle* advertised Meyerland as an ideal new residential neighborhood, the paper did not mention the growing Jewish presence there. By the early 1970s, the Jewish enclave in Meyerland was larger than the original one in Riverside Terrace.[80]

The Jewish move to Meyerland-Bellaire was not unusual in the scope of American Jewish history. Demographically, American Jews had noticeably different living patterns from African Americans. First-, second-, and third-generation Jews tended to live and grow up in different neighborhoods. Jews, unlike African Americans, had access to property ownership and purchased homes, apartments, and businesses for themselves. Therefore, when Jews left their old neighborhoods, they often retained ownership of their properties. As a result, Jews became landlords in many declining areas. In the case of Houston, Jewish landlords managed property in some of the most blighted wards that the Houston Jews left behind.[81]

In 1965, Saul Friedman, a Jewish reporter at the *Houston Chronicle*, wrote an unpublished series titled "The Black Ghetto in Houston" that explored the landlords in Black neighborhoods. Friedman found that "many of the busiest slum landlords are of Jewish or Italian descent. Names like Silverman, Freedman, Cohen, Pizzitola, Montalbano, Boss, Quarino, Lazzaro, and Sacco are seen most often in the inventories of property in the ghetto slums." In addition to apartments and houses, they owned groceries, pawn shops, clothing stores, and pharmacies.[82]

Friedman found that African Americans did not view Jews and Italians as "pure white" because they were not white and Protestant. While they accepted their presence in their neighborhood as landlords and businesspeople, at the same time, they resented that they were not African American. One story in Saul Friedman's series centered on a Black woman named "Big Mama" who lived in a home owned by Minnie Davis. Big Mama saw Davis as different because she was Jewish: "She owns a bunch of stuff out here. She's an old lady. Comes 'round in that white car and get the rent. She got a son and a sister-in-law, and they got houses out here too. Dey ain't pur white. Dey Jewish." Big Mama's description of Davis as not being "pur white" underscored that the city's Blacks viewed Jews as being different than white Christians.[83]

Friedman described the Black housing situation in the wards in bleak terms. They lived in "shotgun houses" with only a bathtub, a sink, and three rooms (a kitchen and two bedrooms). The rooms were only "12 feet square, and often smaller but rarely larger ... the whole house is 12 by 36, or 432 square feet." Before the early 1950s, Blacks who lived in these homes used outhouses until the Public Health Department went after the landlords. Friedman noted that the landlords did not improve the situation but rather replaced the outhouses with a "closet size toilet tacked on the back, off the kitchen," which did not work well "because the plumbing [was] cheap and the sewerage inadequate." According to Friedman, "as many as 25 were squeezed onto blocks containing 20 lots."[84] Not adequate for human habitation, these squalid shotgun houses often experienced regular roach infestations.

Friedman described the complicated feelings that some Jewish landlords had about the properties they owned. Even though the profits on the businesses and properties they owned were low, Black residents in these areas did not have the means to buy the businesses or properties from them. Furthermore, banks were not willing to give business loans to African Americans. For instance, Minnie Davis and her son "felt trapped by the trap of the slum." By owning property in this area, Davis's son felt like he became as "much a part of the slum as the dweller ...

[though] in the evening he [was] free to leave, to go to his home at 8427 Braes Blvd, in Southwest Houston," also known as Meyerland.[85] The Jews might have created a new enclave in Meyerland-Bellaire away from the old neighborhoods, but for some of them, leaving Riverside Terrace took on a different, more weighted tone.

By the late 1960s, Riverside Terrace had become almost entirely African American. Former resident Frank Goldberg commented, "What happened was a tragedy for the neighborhood, for Jews, for the city because you can't create a neighborhood like that anymore."[86] Jewish social activist Ira Bleiweiss recalled that his wife's family decided to move out of Riverside Terrace once her brother began to adopt Black lingo and assimilate to the new culture.[87] In a *Houston Chronicle* article from 1973, "Mobile Jewish Neighborhood," interviewee Mrs. Nathan Levy speculated that Jews left Riverside Terrace because of the "increasing crime rate in the area." According to Levy, one Sabbath a Jewish woman late to services at Congregation Beth Israel was alone on the front steps when a person knocked her down and stole her purse. Levy did not specify that the perpetrator was African American, but readers of the paper no doubt presumed so given that it happened in Riverside Terrace.[88]

Many of Houston's Jews nostalgically reflected on their previous homes in Riverside Terrace. The Smiley family said, "Our fiddler, this is our home!" in reference to the 1964 Broadway play *Fiddler on the Roof*.[89] For the Smileys, leaving Riverside Terrace evoked the historical memory of when Jews fled their homes in Eastern Europe. In that sense, the loss of Riverside Terrace was a loss of their Jewish past.

Even though this comparison was an exaggeration, some former residents mourned this early center of American Jewish life. Gertrude Barnstone's husband, architect Howard Barnstone, made a similar comment about Riverside Terrace when he described it as a "Jewish ghetto—pale in Europe."[90] Although historically not a positive image, with the help of Hollywood, the pale of Russia and its *shtetls* had become to contemporary American Jews living outside Europe a symbol of cohesive Jewish existence.

Another resident, Allen Becker, stated that Jewish individuals felt "self-pride" and "a sense of continuity; a sense of comfortability in being in a Jewish neighborhood."[91]

Upon later reflection, some of the city's Jews felt they had failed to uphold a sense of moral obligation when they chose to leave Riverside Terrace. One Jewish resident of Riverside Terrace proclaimed that some of the Jews "were really not behaving in the best traditions of our people" in regard to integration.[92] Another thought the history of discrimination against Jews should have deterred them from discriminating against another group and that a person who hated African Americans would also come to hate Jews. However, the misconception that African Americans represented the lowest rung of society, which was perpetuated by segregation, clouded their ability to see beyond skin color.

Because of these prejudices, the Jews thought that new Black residents were changing the climate of their neighborhood and the quality of their schools. As one resident recalled: "There [was] a sense in which we felt that the Blacks had a right to live where they wish, and we had no objections to living next to Blacks, but there was a question as I said before of neighborhoods and schools going."[93]

While these views were prevalent among Jews even outside the South, this prejudice was stronger because of the institution of segregation. Enforcement of segregation in Houston's neighborhoods created the belief that this was necessary to create harmony between whites and African Americans. In reality, the hysteria over integration was more of a destructive force than the integration itself. In the end, however, African Americans—especially those of higher socioeconomic status—had better housing opportunities in Riverside. Ultimately, Houston Jewish concern over how white Gentiles would react to integration came at a heavy price.

The next chapter explores how Houston's Jewish business owners confronted the issue of desegregation in their work environment. Once again, they looked to white Gentiles to lead the way.

Chapter 5

Jewish Commercial Involvement in the Desegregation of Downtown Houston

As a businessman, I know the harm which inequality can do, both in terms of those to whom I sell and those whom I employ. Boycotts, picketing and sit-ins are an economic drain, and a warning sign to prospective new business and industry. I would like to see an organization lend support to all men of good will who are trying to end these problems here forever.

> Houston Council on Human Relations
> *2 Questions*, 1963

By moving to the Meyerland-Bellaire area, Houston's Jews could avoid living alongside the city's Black residents, but Jewish business owners could not avoid interacting with African Americans in the wards and in downtown Houston where they had businesses. In the wards, Jewish owners relied on Black customers, whereas downtown business owners felt dependent on white patronage, which is why they upheld segregation. Houston Jewry, as a whole, never publicly condemned Jewish businesses for practicing segregation. In an interview, social activist Carolyn Litowich noted that they simply accepted the idea that segregation was "the way that it was" in the South.[1] Yet like their fellow white Gentile business owners, Jews found themselves confronted with African Americans who demanded equal economic rights, just as they demanded the right to own homes in Riverside Terrace.

The desegregation of Houston's economic sphere unfolded between 1960 and 1963. Getting to the point of actually calling for equal access to local commerce was not an easy journey. Influential business owners, guided by the dollar, controlled the city. This idea was true for Houston as well as other southern cities. As historian Steven Lawson said, "Southern merchants … calculated that ugly racial incidents did not make good dollars and cents."[2] Because Houston was first and foremost a city of business, what the business leaders said mattered. Of utmost concern was keeping peace in the city so that their businesses thrived.

Houston's Jewish business owners had additional concerns beyond economic solvency because the decision to desegregate had more negative social consequences for them than for their white Gentile peers. Desegregating Jewish-owned department stores in the South varied from city to city. Some were mild transitions like Houston, and others were violent. Jewish-owned department stores in Birmingham such as Parisian and Loveman's faced threats; Parisian received threatening calls and bricks thrown through its windows, and Loveman's experienced smoke bombs thrown through its windows. Even in Memphis, the KKK threatened Shainberg's and other Jewish-owned stores with dire warnings for integrating. However undesirable the experience may have been, though, integration was inevitable.[3]

It took a new generation of African Americans—TSU students exasperated with the status quo—to finally initiate desegregation in Houston. Their sit-in protests shattered the white business world's belief that antiquated, bigoted policies could continue. These protests spurred business and religious leaders—African American, Jewish, and white—to rush behind the scenes to solve the city's looming desegregation crisis. Moreover, since many of their businesses had suffered during the sit-ins, certain Jewish business leaders assisted in the plan to create change. Others adhered to the adage "business is business" and excluded their politics from their work, in large part out of fear that public advocacy for desegregation would link their identity with that of African Americans. The ever-present fear of being labeled a minority drove their actions.[4]

Black clergyman Thomas Griffin publicly criticized the city's Jews for their ethics outside of the synagogue. From his perspective, Judaism was a "beautiful" belief system that did not reflect the Jewish business world. Griffin's statement shed light on the contradiction between the actions of prominent Houston Jewish business owners in their synagogues and in their economic lives, where they shed their core value of social action.[5]

To Griffin, Jews were not adhering to the tenets of *tikkun olam* by conforming to segregation in their downtown stores. This chapter explores this contradiction. I argue that Jewish business owners whose livelihood—and by extension their support of the local Jewish community—depended on conducting business with Gentiles could see no other option but to follow their lead and continue to support segregation. Although sympathetic to the Black cause, they did not feel like they could be at the forefront of the civil rights movement.

Those Jews who had businesses downtown were, for the most part, wealthy but still not fully integrated into Houston's wider business culture. As owners of many of the area's grocery stores and department stores, they faced barriers in their attempts to join white Gentile society. They might have socialized at work with other Gentiles, but after five o'clock, these interactions ended. The primary places where Jews and white Gentiles interacted downtown were meetings of the Retail Merchant Association and at other business functions. Jewish and non-Jewish business owners could commiserate on similar challenges, especially once both started to lose revenue during the height of the sit-ins in the early 1960s.

Yet despite these shared experiences, even Houston's wealthiest Jews never entered the city's top business or professional elite. Most well-to-do Jews found themselves unwelcome in

Gentile country clubs or the enclave of River Oaks, and their children were unable to attend certain private schools. Because the Jew, according to Houstonian Diane Ravitch, "has never been accepted in Houston's Gentile world, he feels insecure in a Gentile setting." According to Ravitch, a Jew "should look and act like a wealthy goy, but within the limits of the Jewish world."[6] When historian Elaine Maas asked select Gentiles in Houston "which Jews they would consider 'society,' most named only one—Maurice Hirsch," a prominent Jewish lawyer and president of the Houston Symphony.[7] Especially downtown, their substantial wealth and business power did not give the city's Jews insider status. Instead, they found their sense of belonging in the confines of the Jewish world. The mimicking of Gentile cultural norms enabled wealthy Jewish business owners to exert their status and social and economic capital in ways they could not outside the community.

Before taking a deeper look at what led Jewish business owners in downtown Houston to integrate their businesses, it is important to explore immigrant-owned stores in the Black wards. Their story of economic and social discrimination illuminates the complexities Jews faced while earning a livelihood in Houston. Starting your own small business became the best choice in a world in which you remained unwelcome.

Immigrant Jewish-Owned Businesses

Immigrant Jews who ran businesses in the wards did not encounter the same pressures of upscale Jewish department store owners downtown. Because English was not their first language and they had not fully Americanized, immigrant Jews felt more comfortable in the wards. And rent was much more affordable.[8] Leon Mucasey, whose Russian family immigrated to Cuba before coming to Houston in 1941, recalled how his small family-owned grocery store in the Third Ward treated African Americans with respect, calling them "Mr." and "Mrs." That white non-Jews did not do the same disturbed Mucasey, especially given his experiences in prerevolution Cuba.[9]

Gloria Ribnick, the director of public relations and marketing for the Jewish Family Service, recalled a similar lack of attention to social hierarchy among her immigrant family. They owned a small grocery store in Houston Heights, a predominantly white neighborhood, and employed Blacks as delivery truck drivers and stock workers. The Ribnick family would eat with all their Black employees, including the family's domestic worker, Lucille. Ribnick claimed, "We were a family."[10]

The Jewish-owned Weingarten's store with three locations in the Third and Fifth Wards and Riverside Terrace was a favorite of Black shoppers because it had a policy of "first come, first served." While Henke & Pillot, a non-Jewish-owned grocery store with two locations, advertised in *The Informer* having a "first come, first served" policy, many Black customers still preferred Weingarten's, in large part because they felt free to

"Big Food Market no. 14." Exterior of Weingarten's grocery store. Bob Bailey Studios Photographic Archive, e_bb_0470, The Dolph Briscoe Center for American History, The University of Texas at Austin.

complain to Jewish managers when the store failed to enforce this policy. Booker Taylor, a Black porter, bought his groceries from Weingarten's because "the store will not allow any discrimination." Taylor explained, "You wait on yourself and everyone lines together (white and negroes) in the same line. If a white woman is behind you, they wait on you first."[11]

Weingarten's, however, came under scrutiny when the Black-sponsored Third Ward Civic Club pressured the city during the 1940s to force businesses in the wards to employ more Blacks. Weingarten's employed them only for menial jobs like carrying out groceries and mopping the floor. The club also fought to have Weingarten's remove an advertisement of a young Black man eating a slice of watermelon because of its promotion of offensive stereotypes. In 1943, the NAACP Legal Redress Committee also protested Weingarten's because one of the store's policemen had struck a Black customer. Until desegregation, Weingarten's also did not permit Black customers to eat at the lunch counter.[12]

Many Holocaust survivors who owned small businesses did not view African Americans as beneath them. They were their clientele, their employees, or, for some Holocaust survivors, a reminder of the painful past they left behind and their own experiences with discriminatory rulings like the Nuremberg Laws. However, Jewish leaders, wanting recent refugees to acculturate to their surroundings, placed pressure on them to act American so they would not stand out and spark anti-Semitism. One part of this was adhering to the hierarchy of segregation. Many survivors tried to adapt, but it proved difficult. For example, their lack of fluency in English led them to drink from water fountains designated only for African Americans or sit in the back of a bus. Whites would yell at them for not understanding their place. Survivors, like Ruth Steinfeld, felt pressured "to be like everyone else"—that is, completely transform into an American.[13] This pressure limited their ability to be vocal in their opposition to segregation.

The children of refugees and Holocaust survivors recounted their particular level of connection with African Americans. The family of Diana Bloom (not her real name), Jewish refugees who had left Poland in the 1930s but lost family members in the Holocaust, owned a furniture manufacturing business with many Black employees. When she went shopping at Foley's department store, Bloom asked her mother why she never saw Black customers in the store. Her mother simply told her, "This is how it is here." Both Diana and her sister, Jaime (also a pseudonym), felt that their parents' experiences had made them aware that they were "different" from their southern Jewish contemporaries in their attitudes toward African Americans.[14]

Bloom's experience was similar to that of David Eisenbaum, whose parents were Holocaust survivors from Poland who went into business almost exclusively with African Americans in the Black wards in the 1960s. Eisenbaum noted that Blacks needed services just like everyone else. His father owned several businesses, including the Zig Zag Grill and Jacob's Fan Mfg. Company, which performed "household repairs for mostly Black customers." Eisenbaum's father also developed the Castle Palace Motel in the 1960s and started a Black nightclub near the motel. In 1969, he sold the nightclub building to a Black community center. At all his businesses, he employed Black salespeople and opposed an industrial supply company for not hiring Blacks to work counter sales. Eisenbaum stated that he did not consider African Americans "different."[15]

Other Jewish immigrants shared this belief in Black equality. Pepi Nichols's father, also a Holocaust survivor, first peddled goods in a Black neighborhood and later ran a grocery store where 90 percent of his customers were Black, one of whom was country blues singer Lightnin' Hopkins, who often used the store's telephone.[16]

These examples suggest that many immigrant Jews found ways to break the color barrier, especially those who had businesses in predominantly Black neighborhoods. Ira Bleiweiss, also a son of Holocaust survivors, recalled that Jews "were well established leaders in many different fields, but primarily in wholesale/retail: groceries, furniture, appliances, [and] plumbing supplies." He recalled that Jews were "the first to hire Blacks for customer facing positions and to not have Jim Crow facilities."[17] Bleiweiss's parents hired African Americans at their wholesale sundries business that "sold to industrial contractors and hardware stores. He later had a business that built commercial spray-painting pumps. His equipment was used to paint the Astrodome and NASA."[18] According to Bleiweiss, his father "would hire Black employees kind of to make a point that he was going to treat them equally, that he is not going to refuse somebody work because of their color." His father believed that if the customer did not like that his employees were Black, then they would just have to "deal with it." Though Bleiweiss recalled that his parents never used the "n-word," he also remembered his father's concerns about exhibiting too much social resistance because of their status as immigrants. When Bleiweiss drank from the "colored" water fountain, he could not understand what he had done wrong, and his mother had to explain to him, "This is just the way they do it here."[19]

Two Jewish food establishments—the Three Brothers Bakery and Alfred's Deli—also hired African Americans. Both were located in Riverside from 1955 to 1960, until the Three Brothers Bakery moved to Meyerland and Alfred's Deli moved to Rice Village. The Jucker family founded the kosher Three Brothers Bakery, which employed Black workers and did not have any form of segregation, even in their attached deli, which never had any separate tables or bathrooms. According to Robert Jucker, son of one of the three brothers, they would never discriminate against African Americans because of their experiences in the Holocaust.[20]

Alfred's Deli, owned by Holocaust survivor Alfred Julius Kahn, also ignored segregationist business practices. When Alfred's celebrated its twenty-fifth anniversary in the 1970s, the *JH-V* featured a two-page spread about the deli. It spoke of Alfred's familial heritage and revealed that the secret behind the deli's cooking was its Black chef, Jack Diggs, who had worked at all three branches of Alfred's. The paper pointed out, "He may be the only Black man in the nation who can make all Jewish dishes better than most Jewish mothers."[21]

Another Jewish business owner who employed Blacks was Bill Morgan, the founder of Global Construction and

Management. Morgan was not a Holocaust survivor, but he did go into hiding during the war and passed as a Christian, even becoming a truck driver in the Polish army when the Russians drafted him. He moved to Houston in 1949 and eventually opened the Kwik Snak Café in 1952, where he employed two Black women, Freddie and Bula. In his café, "Bula worked the counter and washed dishes, and Freddie cooked." Morgan became upset when they came in through the back door and questioned why they did this. Freddie told Bill Morgan: "Yo' let dose Black folk come in da front door, yo' may not have any white folk comin' in. Might hurt yo' business." Morgan "conceded, but not without experiencing great disappointment. He thought he had left discrimination behind in Europe. He could never understand this same attitude in a land where so much opportunity existed."[22] Uncomfortable with the status quo, he still felt he needed to adhere to it because that was the mindset of the city of Houston.

Prior historical accounts have neglected to mention how Houston's Jewish business owners were among the first to integrate.[23] Especially overlooked in the historical narrative is Wheeler's Pharmacy, a Jewish-owned soda fountain in the Third Ward, which integrated in the 1950s. Wheeler's was located in Dowling, a heavily populated Jewish business area in the Third Ward. Evelyn Berkowitz—whose father and uncle owned the store—described the pharmacy as "color blind." In addition to serving Black customers alongside white ones, Wheeler's trained pharmacy students from TSU. One was James Windom, who worked for Wheeler's for thirty-seven years as their manager. The pharmacy delivered to all parts of the city, from River Oaks to the Third Ward. They provided Black residents with credit and never made them pay bills they could not afford.[24] Prominent Black clergymen like Lawson and the NAACP leader D. Leon Everett, as well as Black entertainers from Club Ebony, often visited the pharmacy.[25]

Houston's Jews had the privilege of owning all sorts of businesses, from small stores to well-known department stores, but African Americans could only have stores in Black neighborhoods.

This disparity became a major point of contention for those Blacks who wanted to be able to shop, eat, and work where they wanted without encountering discrimination.

Black-Owned Businesses

Numerous African Americans owned businesses in the wards. Two of the most well-known Black businessmen were the first Black millionaires in Houston: Mack Hannah and Hobart Taylor. Hannah began his career in the funeral home business. Since white funeral homes did not accept African Americans, Hannah had guaranteed Black patronage. Hannah would then go on to own Standard Savings and Loan, the first Black lending business in the city. Hobart Taylor owned H. T. Cab, a thriving taxi business that exclusively transported Black residents from ward to ward, from the wards to downtown businesses, and from the wards to jobs in the suburbs. Both Black executives financially thrived because they had cornered a market created by segregation. Hannah and Taylor would both go on to become philanthropists and activists.[26]

Other Black entrepreneurs became owners of grocery stores, movie theaters, and retail stores. Black women like Anna Dupree became proprietors of beauty salons. One of the more impressive Black-owned retail operations in Houston was the Eldorado Shopping Center, run by the Duprees. In addition to the Eldorado Ballroom discussed in chapter 4, this shopping center held a drugstore, a men's clothing store, a paint store, and an appliance store. Whites rarely patronized Black business owners, but there were exceptions like L. White. Booker Taylor, a porter, recalled how White treated "his white customers just like he does his colored."[27]

Many Black-owned businesses in the wards did not have enough capital or credit to buy better-quality merchandise, which made competition with Jewish immigrant owners in the Black neighborhoods challenging. At times, Black consumers complained about how Black-owned businesses like Hobart Taylor's taxi company had a monopoly because it provided the only available transportation for African Americans. Yet even after integration, Taylor was able to compete with white taxi companies and remained in business until 1970.[28]

Negative Black sentiment toward Black-owned businesses illustrated the economic complexities of segregation. They wanted to support Black businesses; yet at the same time, according to Black civic leader Richard Grovey, "[Black Houstonians] expect[ed] the negro to have better services than the white man before they will even agree to give him a trial."[29] This sentiment did not mean the Black community lacked pride in their businesses, especially in the Third Ward. Indeed, Black restaurants, beauty parlors, funeral parlors, and nightclubs thrived. Despite this success, Black residents perceived the products in white stores to be superior, especially downtown.[30]

Downtown business owners, both Jewish and non-Jewish, united under an organization called the Retail Merchant Association of Houston, which Leopold Meyer reorganized in 1942. Since Black business owners could not belong to this association or the Houston Chamber of Commerce, they formed their own group. With the support of Quentin Mease, they established the Houston Business and Professional Men's Club, which met at the South Central YMCA. This organization provided the economic empowerment that the Negro Chamber of Commerce, which was originally run by whites, never did.[31] By the mid-1950s, Houston had 770 Black-owned businesses, mostly in retail and service-oriented sectors. Very few African Americans thrived in the fields of insurance, wholesale trade, real estate, banking, and finance.[32]

Mistreatment of Black Customers
in Downtown Houston

Downtown Houston catered to white customers. In the department stores, chain groceries, and pharmacies downtown, African Americans continued to face barriers, especially from sales clerks. Oftentimes they had to wait for white shoppers to finish buying their purchases. A small number of stores adhered to such a strict Black and white code that store owners asked

African Americans to leave immediately upon the arrival of any white customer. Some even had Black clerks just for their Black customers, while others only provided services for African Americans in the back of the store, hidden away from white customers. The downtown stores also had separate bathrooms or—still worse—no bathrooms for Black customers. Stores like Sakowitz, Battelstein's, and Neiman Marcus actually hired security guards to prevent Black patrons from allegedly stealing.[33]

Sometimes, African Americans had to pretend to buy products for their white employers in order to purchase merchandise for themselves. When Debra Castleberry was a child, she went to Sakowitz—an upscale department store that primarily catered to upper-class whites—with her uncle to buy a pair of shoes. She recalled that "they were sitting, sitting, and sitting," but still no one came to help them. Her uncle finally went to complain and said to the sales clerk, "I have noticed you have helped several other people, why won't you help us?"[34] Castleberry could not understand why she could not get her shoes, and they left in frustration. This kind of snubbing happened in many stores, both Jewish and non-Jewish, throughout the South.[35]

One of the biggest issues African Americans faced in department stores, like Houston's Sakowitz and Gentile-owned stores like Kress, was the inability to try on clothes, hats, or shoes, forcing them to buy garments they would otherwise not have purchased. Some stores like Burt's allowed them to try on shoes in the back. In fact, Burt's had a clerk at the front door whose sole purpose was to direct Blacks to the back of the store.[36]

NAACP administrator Christia Adair remembered struggling with not being able to have the freedom to try on things in any store in downtown Houston. Adair would choose a hat, and the "sales lady would put it on her own head and then say, 'I think it's pretty; don't you like that?' I'd say, 'Well, I like it on you, but I don't know if I'd like it on me or not. I don't think the same hat that would become you would become me.'"[37] In response, Adair refused to buy anything she could not try on for herself.

She was not the only one to experience these difficulties. When a Black woman complained to Adair that she could not try on hats and had to have a girdle fitted in the alteration room, Adair went herself to Sakowitz to purchase a girdle. The saleswoman led her to the alteration room, and Adair told her, "I don't want anything done to it, I just want to try it on."[38]

The saleswoman replied, "Well, you go in." Adair fought back. "Well I don't want to try it on in the alteration room. I want to try it on in the fitting room." After a second attempt to put Adair into the alteration room, she insisted on seeing the manager. Since the store did not want any problems, the manager allowed her to try on the clothes in the fitting room. When Adair insisted that the saleswoman help her fit it, she remembered the woman touching her like she was "contaminated." Eventually, Adair bought a girdle just to prove that she was indeed a paying customer. Adair's second-class treatment at Sakowitz illustrates the extent to which Black customers in Houston encountered obstacles and social humiliation.[39]

In 1947, after Lazarus purchased the Foley's department store chain, it became known as "the store of tomorrow," despite the fact that it still maintained segregation. Lazarus, a Columbus-based Jewish family, purchased the Houston chain under their company name, Federated Department Stores. Though midwestern Lazarus locations did not have legal segregation, Foley's in Houston did. Under the leadership of Jewish businessman Max Levine, Foley's began to stress Jewish issues. In 1955, the store sponsored a display that portrayed three hundred years of Jewish involvement in the United States. The store's newsletter, *Port-Foley-O*, also acknowledged Jewish events held at their Men's Grill.[40] Early on Foley's hired Blacks, but not for prominent positions. *Port-Foley-O* often praised Black employees for their work or for joining the military. Foley's had Juneteenth picnics for their Black employees on June 19 to commemorate the abolition of slavery in Texas. At times, Foley's and Weingarten's held joint picnics or barbecues for their Black employees where they had games and music.[41]

In the early 1950s, Foley's received several letters from patrons calling for changes in the store's treatment of Blacks. On November 22, 1955, the president of the Retired Teachers

Association of Houston, Pearl W. Sanders, wrote to the Foley's management regarding the store's disrespect for Black consumers: "We believe you intend to be just and liberal. How can you, then, continue to be unjust to the thousands of Negro people who patronize your business? Can you not throw off the shackles of prejudice, and be progressive?"[42] Sanders encouraged Foley's to establish a lunch counter for everyone, regardless of their skin color. Foley's creation of a "colored" restaurant in 1958 in the basement of the store was not enough. On September 11, 1958, individuals staged a protest to urge the chain to integrate the main restaurant.[43] Numerous African Americans complained to Foley's management about their treatment. Mrs. Jacob T. Stewart wrote to the sales manager on February 14, 1957, about how the shoe department had forced her to move to a different section where she had to wait twenty minutes.[44]

In contrast to Foley's attempts to keep peace with their Black customers, Woolworth, a Gentile-owned store, refused services to African Americans at the lunch counter even if a white person ordered for them. Rozelle Kahn, the wife of Rabbi Robert Kahn, commented that, though she grew up with segregation, she never had a personal connection with it until the 1950s when she went to Woolworth and experienced blatant discrimination with Sally, the family's domestic worker. The white world frightened Sally, especially Woolworth's lunch counter. When Rozelle Kahn ordered ice cream for her children and Sally, the server at the counter refused to serve Sally. Infuriated, Kahn did not stop complaining until the server relented. Her first experience with the reality of segregation horrified her.[45]

That Kahn did not understand how degrading segregation was until she saw things through Sally's eyes illustrates the separate spheres in which Jews and Blacks lived. After all, most of the interactions that Jews and white Gentiles had with Black domestic workers were in the privacy of their homes. The mistreatment that Black consumers faced, especially in downtown Houston, defied economic logic, since African Americans were paying customers.

The "Negro Market"

As desegregation loomed, retailers afraid of alienating white customers developed strategies to market to both groups without violating segregation. Through interoffice memorandums, Foley's collected information on the viability of the "Negro market."[46] Foley's also consulted Henry Bullock, the author of *Pathways to the Negro Market*, which examined the city's Black economic system and forecasted the frustration African Americans often had as a neglected economic class. From his perspective, Houston was the southern leader in hiring more Black sales clerks in order to tap into the Black market. However, Bullock did not think this change was enough, arguing instead for an end to segregation to give Blacks the respect they deserved as equal consumers.[47] *The Informer* even produced a special edition for business leaders with the headline "Have You Forgot Houston's $148,800,000 Negro Market?"[48]

Perhaps the most significant aspect of Bullock's study was his discussion of Black buying habits and the effect of "imitative buying."[49] This theory claimed that African Americans wanted to imitate whites in their buying practices because they thought whites had access to and bought better goods. If an African American saw a white person refusing to buy groceries at a certain store, the African American would not shop there either. Since they worked closely with whites, for example as domestics, and lived near Black families of different socioeconomic levels, their neighbors often influenced Black consumers to have a skewed view of quality. Merchandise that African Americans felt was subject to such imitation buying included cars, clothing, appliances, and home furnishings. It was also important to Black consumers to look as though they had means. According to Bullock, "overt consumption rather than wealth, family background, or church affiliation" determined social class within the Black community.[50] The example Bullock gave was a vacuum cleaner salesman who sold one unit on a block one week. By the next week, he had sold ten units because each neighbor told the other neighbor of the purchase.

Bullock discovered that interactions between white employers and Black domestic workers influenced Black buying habits.

Convinced that the key to rising into a higher class was to emulate their white employers, Black domestic workers even went so far as to become experts on high-priced items. Many other African Americans also became interested in buying products that would make them appear high-class, even if they only had low or midlevel incomes.[51] For this reason, Bullock assessed that 86 percent of Blacks chose to shop downtown and face discriminatory practices simply because the stores in Black areas lacked access to the quality items they wanted. Yet Bullock's solution to Black inequality in the consumer market downtown was not to fight the discriminatory policies or call for social activism; rather, he argued for stores in the Black wards to improve their merchandise to attract more consumers.[52]

The privileges Jews had in the marketplace were remarkably better than those African Americans had, but this advantage did not motivate the city's Jewish business leaders to counteract their policies. David White tried to address the inequalities that both Jews and African Americans and other minorities faced in the article "Finding the Pulse of the People," but his priority was with the Jewish predicament.[53] In fact, White never wrote an article disparaging Jewish business compliance with segregation, most likely because most of the city's Jews were business owners and the community, particularly Jewish philanthropic pursuits, relied on their contributions.

While he may not have criticized Houston's Jews directly, White was willing to engage on general issues of inequality. In August 1959, he wrote that Americans feel that they "[had] achieved Democratic living in this country and should leave well enough alone," but from his perspective the United States still had imperfections. Minorities remained under scrutiny because the country conflated class with skin color, religion, and national origin. White was most concerned with the presence of anti-Semitism in Houston, particularly the prejudices Jews still faced in housing, employment, public schools, and social engagements.[54]

White's focus on the economic stability of Houston's Jews was reasonable, especially considering how widespread employment discrimination against Jews remained during the 1950s. He encouraged his coreligionists to recognize the great privilege they had to own a business.[55] Houston Jewish lawyer "Julius Rosenblatt" (an alias) recalled how oil companies and the legal profession excluded Jews. The first Jewish lawyer did not make partner at a major Houston law firm until the 1960s, and it was a slow process even then. Rosenblatt observed that "Jews were not part of the mainstream."[56] Houston Jewish involvement in the business world provided them with some security, but this security relied on compliance with white segregationist standards.

Other minority groups took this same strategy, including Mexican Americans, who practiced segregation in their restaurants. For example, Felix Tijerina, a Mexican American restaurateur with several restaurants, refused to serve African Americans until the day after President Lyndon Johnson signed the Civil Rights Act on July 2, 1964.[57]

Houston's Sit-In Movement

Black discouragement about discrimination in the consumer market grew, especially because they had few allies in Houston. Disenchanted with the status quo, TSU law student Eldrewey Stearns ignited the first sit-in movement. Stearns's story began one evening as he was driving home. The police stopped him and accused him of a burglary he did not commit. A picture of a white woman in his pocket made him appear suspicious to white police. His unjust arrest showed Stearns that it was time for him to initiate real change in Houston. Stearns worked at the South Central YMCA and was a close friend of Quentin Mease, who advised him to arrange a sit-in with TSU students. Mease encouraged him to emulate the sit-in at the Woolworth in Greensboro, North Carolina. By following through on this plan, Stearns designated himself the unofficial leader of the Houston sit-in movement.[58]

The student movement began on March 4, 1960, without the support of TSU. Stearns and a group of TSU students approached William Lawson, the head chaplain of the Baptist Student

Union. While Lawson understood that African Americans felt "mostly fear and frustration" and saw "no hope of finding justice," he opposed the students' plans.[59] Lawson himself avoided any place that maintained segregation, such as department stores, movie theaters, and buses.

However, he was worried that if the students protested, they would put their futures and possibly their lives in jeopardy.[60] Despite Lawson's opposition and the lack of general support from the Black community, the students decided to go forward with their sit-ins. They chose Weingarten's store #26 on Almeda in Riverside Terrace as their first location, a somewhat ironic choice considering Weingarten's policy of "first come, first served." However, choosing Weingarten's #26 in many ways was a symbolic choice, given Riverside Terrace's ongoing transformation from a white Gentile and Jewish neighborhood to a Black one. In fact, in a *Houston Post* article from March 6, 1960, the students mentioned this as their specific reason for choosing Weingarten's.[61]

The students convened in front of the TSU administration building at 4:00 p.m. on March 4 and "held hands around the flagpole. Someone sang the Star-Spangled Banner as the Stars and Stripes waved in the warm March wind."[62] Around thirty-five well-dressed students walked in a group toward Weingarten's #26. Students from Rice and other universities accompanied them. The students protested peacefully, like the sit-ins in Greensboro and Nashville, Tennessee. The Nashville sit-in movement, then considered the model for nonviolent protests, aided the Houston protesters. They used a handout from Fisk University as their guide, which instructed student protesters to remember the teachings of Jesus and Gandhi and not to leave one's seat without the leader's permission.[63]

The protesters moved into the store, sat at the lunch counter at 4:30 p.m., and asked for the manager, Mert Bang. White patrons began to leave. Then three executives from Weingarten's came into the store and had a thirty-minute meeting with six of the protesters.[64] One of the reporters at the meeting reported that a student had said, "Are you going to serve us or are you

Houston in March 1960, before the city's lunch counters were integrated: Student demonstrators, members of the Progressive Youth Association, had a sit-in protest at Weingarten's No. 26, 4110 Almeda. Owen Johnson/©Houston Chronicle. Used with permission.

not ... I don't think you can afford not to—you've got too much money involved." After the meeting, the students stayed. Bang stopped the demonstrators by placing signs saying that the lunch counter would not remain open. However, the students "occupied the 30 stools at the counter until 8:15 p.m." According to the *Houston Post*, this was the "first reported occurrence of its kind in Texas although similar incidents [had] been reported elsewhere in the South."[65]

Weingarten's opened their store the next day, but the lunch counter remained closed. The second day of the sit-in at Weingarten's on March 6 was nine hours long, ending at 6:00 p.m. A separate demonstration took place simultaneously at the lunch counter of Mading's, a non-Jewish drugstore nearby. The Mading's sit-in lasted until 6:45 p.m. After the second sit-in, Weingarten's and Mading's both decided to close their lunch counters to allow for a period of calm. The Weingarten's decision only applied to the Almeda store. Protester John Bland recounted how the Weingarten's sit-in stirred up the students to demand more than the desegregation of the lunch counter.[66] They demanded that Black employees have more opportunities for employment than just to "push the broom." Protesters wanted "to be able to work [the] cash register" and to "be able to wrap [the] meat."[67]

The third sit-in was on March 7 at Henke & Pillot. The same pattern of events followed, including the closing of the lunch counter. These events in Riverside Terrace would inevitably stoke white Gentile and Jewish fear of possible violence and eventually spur them to move. The police participated incognito at these protests along with the help of TSU to prevent violence and protect the protesters. Police Chief Carl Shuptrine, who had been the invited speaker at the B'nai B'rith lodge in 1957 and had a history of wanting to avoid violence in Houston after Little Rock, did not want to arrest the protesters.[68]

The students protested Weingarten's grocery because the family were prominent philanthropists in the Jewish community and among the biggest advertisers in *The Informer*. The protesters perceived Joe Weingarten as hypocritical for having accepted a humanitarian award while acting as a segregationist. To many African Americans, he embodied the contradictions of Houston's Jewish business owners.[69]

Still further complicating Joe Weingarten's image was that he had become a lead promoter of peace after he visited Israel in 1950. While there, he regularly heard the Hebrew *Shalom Aleichem* (peace be unto you), a greeting that inspired him to work toward peace.[70] As a New Year's resolution in a 1958 ad for the *Houston Post*, he stressed, "We Must Start Learning to Live Together," and later in 1959 he proclaimed, "Today the passionate prayer for world peace is in the hearts and on the lips of millions of every nationality—race and religion all over the world of ours."[71] From Joe Weingarten's perspective, the 1960s promised to be drastically different from the 1950s. While he may have appeared to Houstonians as looking forward toward a tolerant tomorrow, his store stayed in the past by maintaining segregation.

The success of the sit-ins at Weingarten's triggered a broader movement. As more students joined, locals started to refer to it as the student protest movement. The students also notified the police every time they demonstrated, and the police then contacted the president of TSU, Samuel Nabrit. Rumors circulated that the TSU administration was behind the sit-ins, particularly since the protests were organized and newsworthy, but Nabrit insisted that TSU was not involved. Black millionaire Mack Hannah and Nabrit spoke privately after the first series of sit-ins to try to prevent future violence in the city. Hannah also spoke with Governor Price Daniel to keep him informed, and with Chief Shuptrine. This movement would accelerate after the Black community faced a horrendous attempted murder and hate crime right in their backyard.[72]

On the night of the third sit-in, March 7, a group of white supremacists kidnapped Felton Turner, an unemployed awning installer, who was walking home at 10:15 p.m. Even though Turner was not involved in the sit-ins, they targeted him as a scapegoat for the movement. The kidnappers first beat him with chains and then held him down and carved "KKK" into his stomach. They hung Turner by his knees from a nearby tree. He survived the attack, freed himself, and reported the assault to the police.[73]

The incident had the opposite effect the white supremacists intended; it galvanized the sit-in movement. Two days later, on March 10, TSU students expanded the protests to a Walgreens in downtown Houston. Turner's abduction and torture also brought unwelcome national attention to Houston and unified more of the city's Black residents behind the student protesters. The movement expanded to lunch counters across Houston. White and Black newspapers throughout the city and state published stories on the Turner incident, stoking fears of more violence.[74]

Just two months prior, white supremacists had also harassed the city's Jews, but not with the severity they had Turner. The *Houston Chronicle* reported in early January 1960, someone hung a towel with a swastika imprinted on it, along with the message "Are you Afraid?" from the front door of Congregation Emanu El. A bomb scare at Congregation Emanu El followed, and a Jewish-owned grocery had a swastika painted on its wall. Throughout Texas, including Houston, white supremacists made threatening phone calls and sent letters that sparked fear in the Jewish community. Also, there was "a threat to blow up the Southwest ADL office" from an anonymous caller. The caller had a "deep voice [and] told the secretary that the office would be blown to smithereens." These harassing calls taunted the city's Jews. The "caller either [says] 'Heil Hitler' or shouts 'Get out Jews'—both men's and women's voices have been reported."[75]

Rabbi Kahn could not believe these acts of hatred toward his synagogue: "'I refuse to believe a Texan or an American would do such a thing,' he said."[76] What Kahn did not know at the time was that white supremacists had the capability of doing something much worse—the abduction and torture of Turner.

While the Turner abduction alerted Black student protesters to the dangers of staying silent and emboldened more TSU activism, some African Americans remained against protesting for fear of subsequent violence. These actions not only reminded Houstonians that segregation was very much alive; they also served to remind the city's Jews that minorities were still subject to hatred. The temple bombings in 1957 and 1958 lingered in their minds and encouraged Jewish business owners to maintain the status quo and continue to follow the lead of white Gentile business leaders. This left African Americans, for the most part, alone in their struggle.

Because the student protest movement did not desist despite all this pressure, Houston's business leaders knew they had to act quickly to defuse the situation. After the initial sit-ins, Foley's senior vice president for advertising, Bob Dundas, held a series of meetings with the Retail Merchants Association. The association's president was Jewish businessman A.D. Grossman. Other prominent Jews in the association were Tobias Sakowitz of Sakowitz, Irving Axelrod of Weingarten's, Abe Battelstein of Battelstein's, and Max Levine of Foley's.[77] Those business leaders, concerned with their city's image, not just in America but internationally, did not want to project to the rest of the world that they did not have peaceful relations with the Black community similar to other business leaders in the South.

Dundas began to meet on a regular basis with Grossman; John T. Jones, editor of the *Houston Chronicle*; and members of Houston's power elite. On March 11, 1960, a day after the Walgreens sit-in, Dundas met with representatives of Sakowitz, Mading's, Walgreens, Weingarten's, Henke & Pillot, Kress, Grants, Schulte-United, Woolworth, and Joske's to discuss the sit-in movement. At the meeting, the retailers agreed on three points: "1) No Negroes would be served at white counters. 2) No changes in policies could be done without contacting the others. 3) Future meetings would be held when plans can be developed."[78] In other words, the business leaders decided to

Students picket outside Foley's in downtown Houston to protest segregation, March 23, 1960. Foley's Department Store Records exhibition poster, courtesy of the Houston History Archives, University of Houston Libraries and Center for Public History.

form a unified front, and one store would not take the lead without the consent of the other stores.

In addition to this effort to reduce the economic impact of the sit-ins, student protesters faced internal resistance. On March 12, C. W. Rice, the owner and editor of the *Negro Labor News*, declared Weingarten's the "proven friends to colored people." Rice argued that it was "unfortunate" that Weingarten's, "a firm that has long been recognized as being fair and interested in the progress ... of the Negro people," was the target of the first sit-in. He defended the establishment as having an "employment ratio of Negro help [that] tops any other firm of its kind in this city" and praised their equal pay practices. Additionally, he praised Weingarten's for employing Blacks in their dining establishment as well as enabling them to buy company stock. To Rice, Joe Weingarten was a business owner working *within* the system of segregation to provide opportunities for African Americans. The *Negro Labor News* went so far as to label Weingarten a "liberal" who aided civil rights and ended the article with this comment: "Let us hope and pray that in our struggle for Civil Rights we will not launch upon a policy of violating Civil Rights of others in order to obtain Civil Rights."[79] Rice's positive portrayal of Weingarten fit in with the newspaper's tendency toward placating local whites. And Rice likely wanted to give credit to Weingarten's "first come, first served" policy. Finally, he may have favored Weingarten's because it was a major advertiser in other Black-sponsored papers.

Regardless of Rice's reasons for supporting the establishment, his article frustrated TSU protesters, who expected immediate action. Even Mayor Lewis Cutrer's speech at TSU on March 14, 1960, in an attempt to thwart student protesters, did not quell student enthusiasm.[80]

Frustrated by a lack of support from the city and TSU administration, the students decided to contact Dr. Martin Luther King Jr. for assistance. King had last visited Houston in 1958, when he delivered a speech at Saint John Missionary Baptist Church. Protester Curtis Graves had his friend Andrew Young initiate contact with King. While the civil rights leader did not offer much help to the student protesters, he did tell them, "I'll tell God about it."[81] King's lack of response underscored to the students that they would have to handle the problem themselves locally.

Toward the middle of March, meetings with several business leaders failed to reach a resolution with student protesters. On March 14, the Houston Restaurant Association and members of the Retail Merchants Association met with Mayor Cutrer. The next day at Foley's, Dundas and Levine discussed privately the sit-in situation, agreeing "to develop a long-range plan directed at integration." But in the short term, efforts still fell short. On March 21, the Retail Merchants Association failed to reach a resolution with student protesters because the association was unwilling to grant the students their demands of equal employment and fair access to dining facilities.[82]

While most individual business owners did not seek out ways to appease the student protesters, Joe Weingarten attempted to do so. His curious solution for integrating the lunch counter at the Almeda store involved removing the barstools. Weingarten's idea was likely drawn from Harry Golden, the publisher of the *Carolina Israelite*. In a satirical article titled "The Vertical Negro Plan," Golden stated that "it is only when the Negro 'sets' that the fur begins to fly."[83] Golden's idea to integrate lunch counters by removing seats was his way of criticizing the nonsensical nature of segregated lunch counters. In the documentary *The Strange Demise of Jim Crow*, Executive Producer Thomas Cole said Golden's article "was a sly dig at segregationists, also noting that race-conscious southerners had trouble only with the idea of sitting down" next to African Americans, not with the idea of standing next to them.[84] In late March, the *New York Times* reported how Golden's irony was lost on southern businessmen, including those in Suffolk, Virginia, and San Antonio, Texas.[85]

Student protesters Otis King and Holly Hogrobrook, offended by the idea of vertical integration, could not conceive why Weingarten's believed that "if they removed the seats and served everybody [standing] then we would no longer have a complaint and people would start shopping there again."[86]

In an interview, Houston historian Cary Wintz noted that "Weingarten was caught between upholding segregation laws still preserved in the city and state and allowing African Americans to have their civil rights."[87] Julius Rosenblatt reflected that Weingarten took these small steps because he knew progress took time.[88] While Weingarten did not favor segregation, he desegregated cautiously so as not to lose customers. Despite his caution, Weingarten's Alameda store suffered financially because of the sit-ins.[89]

Activist Hamah King remembered that it took several demonstrations before student activists met with Joe Weingarten at his home in Riverside Terrace to discuss integration. King felt Weingarten's cooperation had limits and that he had agreed to open the Almeda Street store's lunch counter to African Americans "somewhat reluctantly." To King, this was not real integration, though he granted the opening of the Almeda store lunch counter "had some impact on what later happened in Houston."[90]

In response, students turned their focus to downtown Houston and what King called the "domain of the white business establishment."[91] On March 22, more than 150 Black students protested downtown. While the protesters also targeted Grants and Walgreens, both non-Jewish stores, Foley's took center stage. Protesters went to four out of five of the department store's segregated eating places, congregating in each area, even after Foley's closed the lunch counters.[92] The next day around a dozen protesters came back with placards saying, "We want a Freedom Sandwich." Protests did not end until 5:00 p.m. on March 24.[93]

Students staged another sit-in the next day on March 25 at the city hall lunch counter, a move that retail merchants observed with alarm. Both employees and customers left the coffee shop as the protesters came in. Councilman Louie Welch came into the cafeteria to sit at the table next to the protesters. Welch's action seemed like a positive turn toward desegregation, but the moment did not last. Mayor Cutrer wanted to press charges against the protesters. However, Chief Shuptrine went on air to oppose the mayor, saying the protesters were not breaking the law.[94]

On March 27, student leader Charles Lee tried to recruit students Eldrewey Stearns and Early Allen, as well as Reverend Lawson, to open a dialogue with the mayor. Stearns and Allen were not on board with this plan because it kept the student protesters from being the leaders in the desegregation struggle and allowed the mayor to take the lead. The students who favored Lee's approach sent a letter to Mayor Cutrer saying they would stop sit-ins if he would appoint a biracial committee to discuss an integration strategy. Even though he had wanted them arrested, they commended the mayor for being "as generous as a Caucasian without the experience of segregation can be." They also praised Houston for being the "most discreet and judicious city in the current wave of southern crises." These overtures did not placate the mayor, and the protesters declared, "We are determined. We may lose jobs or friends or life—but we will not lose purpose."[95]

Mayor Cutrer heeded the protesters' call and created a biracial committee on March 29, though it did not meet until April 6. The committee consisted of thirty-seven members, eleven African Americans and twenty-six whites. Prominent lawyer Leon Jaworski was the initial chairman, but eventually J. P. Hamblen became its head.[96] In other words, the mayor assembled a majority white committee with a white chairman to address the issue of Black discrimination. Black members included Reverend L. H. Simpson; entrepreneur Hobart Taylor; Aloysius Wickliff, president of the Harris County Council of Organizations; and A. E. Warner, president of the Negro Chamber of Commerce (now run by Blacks). Jewish members included Rabbi Schachtel and Mrs. Malcom F. Sher, president of the Houston League of Women Voters. The one Mexican American member was Felix Tijerina, a restaurateur who was also the leader of the local branch of the League of United Latin Americans (LULAC). The committee also invited several student protesters from TSU, Rice, Saint Thomas, and the University of Houston.[97]

Committee members were to examine Black-white relations, but they were to avoid the topic of school desegregation. TSU president Samuel Nabrit, who was also on the committee, criticized Mayor Cutrer for not taking control of the situation and accused him of "wash[ing] his hands" of the crisis by creating the committee.[98] One student committee member from the University of Saint Thomas, Tommy J. Domingue, wrote about the Biracial Committee in his unpublished memoir. He described the meetings as "dominated by Jaworski" and "merely a show of fellowship and empathy for the mistreated Blacks." To his knowledge, "no action was taken as a result of the panel's efforts." While he was on the committee, Domingue received "crudely written or typed" letters from the Ku Klux Klan from as far away as Waco, Texas, which contained "crude drawings comparing apes to Blacks ... to demonstrate how Blacks were more similar to simians than humans." He presented all the hate mail at a university assembly and posted it on a bulletin board on the campus for the college community to see.[99]

Domingue's account was correct. The committee was indeed inefficient, in large part because Jaworski's primary concern was Houston's public image. Stopping all protests before violence ensued was top priority. To accomplish this, he wanted committee members to denounce the students for trespassing on private property. Most of the members, however, voted against this proposition. The majority of the Biracial Committee, much to Jaworski's dismay, supported the student protesters. Wickliff and TSU student activist Deanna Lott even called for immediate desegregation in the city. Not wanting to lose control of the committee, Jaworski insisted that all members keep the outcome of their vote secret and away from the prying eyes of reporters until he talked to the mayor.[100]

Ultimately, the mayor decided to never announce the votes for desegregation, which exposed his Biracial Committee as merely a facade to placate Black protesters. The last Biracial Committee meeting on May 9 ended with no resolution. Chairman Hamblen did not even call for a final vote, since he did not believe the mayor could initiate immediate desegregation. Indeed, the mayor preferred to leave the ultimate decision to the lunch-counter owners themselves. The Biracial Committee had been a waste of time and only added to the frustrations of the protesters.[101]

As the members were meeting, protesters took their own initiative. Stearns wrote a letter warning the mayor that the lunch counters must desegregate by April 12 or the student protesters would begin again in earnest. On April 25, fifteen students, under the leadership of Stearns, reignited the protests. The movement showed its strength when the protesters successfully forced the Greyhound Bus Cafeteria to serve them food. Out of this action emerged a formalized group called the Progressive Youth Association (PYA), which included students primarily from TSU but also from Rice University and the University of Houston.[102] Frustrated by a lack of change, PYA demonstrators campaigned to picket large downtown stores like Foley's, Grants, Kress, Weingarten's, and Woolworth beginning on May 7. They urged all African Americans to boycott any stores that did not "give Negroes 'full privileges.'"[103]

The PYA also solicited the help of Black churches to urge their parishioners to cease shopping downtown. The message read: "Remember—do not shop on May 7th. We are together!"[104] They chose the Saturday before Mother's Day, as this day would represent the ultimate "sacrifice," according to Stearns.[105] Reminiscent of the 1930s Harlem "Don't Buy Where You Can't Work" campaign, this initiative was the climax of the lunch counter protest in Houston. The protesters' goal was for business owners to hire African Americans for the same jobs they would give white workers. Stearns noted that during the protest "there [was] a noticeable absence of negroes ... [and] professional people down here ... they're the ones that spend that money."[106]

This protest proved important, as the *Houston Post* reported that 10 percent of Foley's consumer base was African American, and at Woolworth and other downtown stores the figure was as high as 20 percent. Most likely, Foley's became the prime target because it had five white dining facilities.[107]

A week after the Mother's Day protest, Stearns and the student protesters initiated "No Shopping Day." Again, they targeted Foley's, in large part because the department store had a credit card system. Protesters encouraged Black residents to return their Foley's credit cards and pay them off in pennies in protest. The presence of a substantial Black middle class in Houston guaranteed that such a gesture would make an impact on Foley's bottom line. Some Blacks did not support relinquishing their credit cards because they could not buy expensive items without one.[108] Stearns was aware that some of the business leaders affected by "No Shopping Day" were Jewish, such as those for Weingarten's and Foley's.[109]

The desegregation crisis had become a heated issue in Houston, but in the Jewish community, discussions occurred more in private, taking place in the synagogue and Jewish Community Relations Council rather than publicly in the *JH-V*. In fact, both Kahn and Malev had previously suggested that the success of desegregation depended on this privacy. This has obscured the historical record on the desegregation process of downtown Houston. In a private meeting between Jaworski and Levine on May 10, Jaworski revealed his contempt for Schachtel and the non-Jewish lawyer Palmer Hutchinson for being in favor of immediate desegregation. Indeed, Schachtel's support for desegregation exemplified how much he had changed in just a short period. In 1952, he had opposed Joseph Samuels's school board run because of fear of Jewish involvement in desegregation. In 1957, Schachtel supported his good friend, Senator Lyndon Johnson, in the Civil Rights Act of 1957.[110]

Immediate desegregation did not occur in the summer of 1960, despite many pleas, including those by Schachtel and Palmer Hutchinson. Weingarten's took the initiative and made some store policy changes. On June 18, 1960, the *Negro Labor News* announced that all Weingarten's in Black areas would follow "vertical, first come, first serve" for ordering food at lunch counters. Furthermore, Weingarten's began to hire Black cashiers. While the newspaper applauded these actions, it was not the kind of widespread integration the student protesters had envisioned.[111]

Though the city buses, Jeppesen Stadium, and the Houston Public Library had all integrated on May 21, a month before Weingarten's decision, lunch counters in downtown Houston remained segregated.[112] Therefore, student protesters did not stop their efforts and eventually partnered with Black business leaders who became the mediators between the protesters and the white retailers. Welch claimed that Black business leaders became "the unappointed ambassadors to the city's white business establishment." Some of these key figures—Theodore Hogrobrook, Hobart Taylor, attorney George Washington, and Reverend Lawson—had discussions at the segregated Rice Hotel. This was the one time Lawson broke his rule of never entering a segregated space, even though he had to enter through the back door, not through the front lobby with the white business leaders, including those who were Jewish. More meetings would occur at this hotel, and the hotel desegregated two years later in 1962.[113]

On August 4, during a discussion in Levine's office, Dundas proclaimed that "integration was inevitable."[114] The two issues that remained, according to Dundas, were when and how the change would happen. The plan was to have Dundas speak with other downtown business leaders and the mayor. Levine, who claimed that Foley's upheld segregation because it was the "custom of the South; [and] we couldn't go against it," believed the Retail Merchants Association was the key to uniting the downtown businesses and coming up with a solution.[115]

Most involved in these meetings were stores with lunchrooms, including Foley's, Battelstein's, and Woolworth. However, Levine claimed Foley's was the one that actually changed the face of integration in Houston. More specifically, though, it was Dundas who acquired the "cooperation from the stores, from the hotels, and from the Negro community, which agreed not to invade but on a selective basis to try out eating in the various restaurants." Levine asserted that headquarters on the East Coast had pressured many of the stores with lunchrooms to take a position on integration. Levine thus called his "best friends in Houston for advice," and they told him "a man named Max Levine couldn't be the first in the South to make the move." In other words, a Jewish executive could not be the face of desegregation in the South because doing so could lead to anti-Semitism. Levine could not be the face of change, but Dundas, a non-Jewish vice president of publicity,

"Max Levine" (1958). President and general manager of Foley's
Department store Max Levine posing. (Photo by Thomas D. Mcavoy/
The LIFE Picture Collection via Getty Images)

could. Foley's knew they had to be the first to desegregate because it was an "important leading store, the most visible business in Houston, with multiple restaurants." As Levine said, "We had to take a chance and do it."[116]

One rumor of how the stores desegregated centered around an agreement between Jewish business owners. In an interview, Matthew Kahn, the grandson of Robert Kahn, recalled hearing how downtown Jewish business leaders, after deciding to desegregate their stores, told the newspapers they would withdraw their advertisements if they did not keep quiet about their plans.[117] Edward Kahn, son of Robert Kahn, remembered hearing about his father's role doing "behind-the-scenes work to convince Foley's executives to desegregate the downtown store's lunch counter quietly to minimize any disruption."[118] Rozelle Kahn recalled how her husband met with Methodist, Catholic, and Episcopal clergy to discuss strategy. Their plan influenced the business community, but the prevailing Gentile power structure had the ultimate say.[119] Rozelle Kahn believed that Houston was not as violent as the rest of the South because of religious leaders, like her husband, who shaped the city. Rabbi Kahn wanted Houstonians to accept the end of segregation because he did not want Houston to take on the characteristics of Little Rock and Montgomery but instead "build a growing democracy, and present to mankind an inspiring example of interracial cooperation."[120]

Integration of Houston's lunch counters began with a series of private negotiations. Dundas talked with Jones, who then spoke with Jack Harris, the manager of radio station KPRC-AM and television station KPRC-TV. All agreed on an enforced media blackout for a week to allow desegregation to occur. Next Dundas contacted Black community leaders. Nabrit and Hobart Taylor called a meeting to inform all the Black members of the mayor's Biracial Committee, Black newspapers, student leaders, and Black business leaders of the plan.[121]

Levine, who had been given carte blanche by corporate headquarters to solve the issue, recalled how Black leaders had agreed to "infiltrate nice looking people, well-dressed people" into the restaurants. Furthermore, any employee uncomfortable with serving African Americans would face immediate transfer to another department.[122]

In the end, this "experiment" did not lose as many accounts for Foley's as the store had expected. At the end of the week, the news finally reported, "the stores have been integrated in their eating facilities." The retail-store holding company Federated Department Stores wanted to publish a story in a magazine, but Levine would not permit it because the "secret of the success had been the quietness with which this [change]was put across."[123]

The two figures most remembered for the desegregation of Houston's lunch counters were not Jewish leaders, nor the mayor or the Houston police, but Dundas and Jones. Dundas was the one who persuaded business leaders to quietly desegregate seventy lunch counters in department stores, supermarkets, and drugstores. Jones was responsible for keeping the media quiet and compliant. Mayor Cutrer and the Houston police were, first and foremost, focused on Houston as a business city. In an interview with the prominent Jewish Texan businessman and politician Fred Zeidman, he observed, "Houston was driven not by political ideology but by business leadership. What [was] good for business [was] good for the community."[124]

Ultimately, even white Gentile leaders like Dundas and Jones desegregated downtown Houston not because of their passion for civil rights but rather to protect the city's image. As Lawson concluded, "The desegregation of Houston was not white altruism. It was quite frankly, establishment selfishness wanting to protect its image."[125] This preoccupation was reflected in the selection of well-dressed Blacks to integrate the restaurants. Even though the majority of the Houston Jews involved in the effort either owned their own business (e.g., department stores) or were involved in business leadership, they had no real power to override Gentile leaders.[126] Max Levine worked behind the scenes, but in the end it was the Gentile leaders with the power to control the media and all the moving parts.

However, there was a backlash in Houston after this quiet period of desegregation. Citizens bombarded the media with letters questioning why the press had not covered it. The *Negro Labor News* highlighted the ensuing anti-Black and anti-Semitic sentiment. The paper "received an anonymous letter addressed to the three daily papers complaining about news blackout of the sit-ins," which blamed both African Americans and Jews for the desegregation of Houston. The prejudicial author felt the city should have alerted Houstonians about what was happening. By not doing so, Houston complied with only what "suit[ed] the Negroes and the Jews," two groups the author felt had more power than whites. This was the exact reason why Jewish business leaders like Levine had not wanted to be the face of desegregation. The anonymous author further asked the editor, "Was this Country made great by bringing in African Blacks? Is this the way the daily papers see the facts? Really was Booker T. Washington this Country's great Father? To honor him the daily papers may go much farther."[127]

The national press covered Houston's quiet integration. Other cities in the South—such as Columbia, South Carolina, and Dallas and Waco, Texas—also had a mild integration process and used some of the same tactics like silent desegregation and media blackout. However, Houston was the largest city of the Deep South, in 1960, to achieve the first steps toward desegregation without the fanfare of national interest.[128] The *New York Times* reported positively on the events and how Houston had managed to "change in a calm and reasonable manner in the interest of the public."[129] In contrast, *Time* magazine accused Houston of betraying the sanctity of the press: "When does a daily newspaper, even with the best of intentions, have a right to suppress a major news story in its own backyard?" *Time* did not quite understand that the business leaders and the newspapers had collectively decided to do so because they believed it was in the best interest of Houston.[130]

Both Black and white business leaders would argue for the blackout, but shutting down the press would inevitably cause the PYA to become voiceless in the process of desegregating the lunch counters. The PYA, however, did not disappear. The *JH-V*, which had avoided discussion of the sit-ins even though the events affected many Jewish business owners, reported on a joint event between the Jewish community and the PYA. The teen group hosted an open event at the JCC featuring Theodore Freedman of the ADL and Stearns. Both leaders spoke about "discrimination against Negroes and Jews in Houston."[131] The event emphasized the common ground between Jews and Blacks despite the tensions created by the sit-ins. It was as though the Jewish community simply erased Jewish involvement in prior segregation.

After desegregation, Foley's was the department store that most responded to the Retail Merchants Association's call to open more jobs to Blacks. Despite initial complaints from white customers, Foley's did not regress in its treatment of African Americans. Lawson remarked that after Foley's had desegregated, shopping there was a very different experience. The salesperson would ask, "May I help you?" then offer the customer a chance to sit down while he or she went to get the requested merchandise.[132] This major transformation in service happened overnight. Pliny E. Shaw wrote to Levine in August 1961, congratulating him on "upgrading employees regardless of color," which she saw as "certainly a step forward in the right direction."[133] By June 1960, thirty-six Black women had become saleswomen, including Cora Johnson, who later became one of the first Black female store managers at Foley's.[134]

Foley's became the model for change in the Houston business sphere. Congregation Emanu El's Brotherhood committee requested that someone from Foley's speak on a panel about local Black employment opportunities. In 1965, Milton Berman, the next president of Foley's, who was also Jewish, collaborated on a TSU summer workshop to help minority high school students prepare for future employment. Foley's also won an NAACP award in 1969 for having hired seven hundred African Americans. To some Black residents, Foley's was becoming the "store of tomorrow."[135]

Other Jewish stores also had early policies in favor of desegregation. Weiner's department store initiated an integration policy because Isidore Weiner, the president, believed that "all people were created equally in G-d's image."[136] In 1961, Finger Furniture Store hired Black furniture specialist Don Taylor, a decision praised by the Houston Council on Human Relations. In an interview with Cvyia Wolff of Star Furniture, she remembered her husband asking his father sometime in the 1960s to desegregate the store's party and dance.[137] Originally, the store had two parties—one for Blacks and one for whites. Eventually they had one party.[138]

Despite these advances in the retail sector, the fight to end segregation had only begun. A 1961 survey emphasized that, regardless of downtown desegregation, African Americans in Houston remained underrepresented in sales and white-collar managerial positions.[139] In addition, more facilities in Houston needed integration.

Final Stages of Desegregating Downtown Houston

In the early months of 1962, both Jews and African Americans faced their own battles. The PYA increased its protests and focused them on Black inclusion in restaurants, movie theaters, hotels, swimming pools, beaches, and parks. Houston's Jews faced two anti-Semitic incidents that led city and communal leaders to increase their efforts to desegregate quickly and contain simmering prejudice and violence.

The first incident occurred in March 1962 when the leader of the American Nazi Party, George Lincoln Rockwell, came to Houston. In the *JH-V*, White called Rockwell a "self-styled Fuehrer" interested in Houston because he saw the city as a "hot bed of rightism, conservatism, and Nazism." In his pursuit of preserving pure white Christian society, Rockwell targeted the city's Jews for their promotion of Black equality. ADL director Theodore Freedman assured Houston's Jews that Rockwell's visit was not successful because he was not able to "secure large financial support from the so-called 'prominent Houston contributors'" to set up a headquarters for the American Nazi Party. Ultimately, Rockwell was not successful because his plan would have incited violence in a city that prioritized the economy over politics. Rockwell's visit, however, compounded Jewish fear.[140]

The second event occurred a month later in April when agitators painted swastikas at Bellaire High School—another reminder for Jews of prejudice and the need to stay out of the political fray.[141]

Because of the city's prominent role in the US space program, Houston's national and international profile had risen considerably, which put more pressure on officials to complete desegregation and suppress racial violence. As before, Black and white business and city leaders met privately. With the help of major players like Jones, Mease, and Hobart Taylor, the hotels desegregated. Also, Mease struck a deal with Roy Hofheinz and oilman Bob Smith to build the Astrodome, which was to be nonsegregated. This deal also made Houston the first city in the South to have a Major League Baseball team. Other leaders—Dundas, Taylor, and Jones—brokered a deal to desegregate all city restaurants and movie theaters. Once again, it was the city's business leaders, rather than the PYA, who managed to desegregate the city.[142]

Although most downtown businesses had desegregated between May and June of 1963, many held out. Sakowitz's restaurant, the Sky Terrace, was one of the last to desegregate in downtown Houston. According to Mease, "We did not get that cooperation from Sakowitz that we got from Foley's through Bob Dundas's cooperation."[143] In an interview between Cole and Nabrit in February 1993, Nabrit recalled an encounter he had with Bernard Sakowitz.[144] Sakowitz explained that his store did not serve African Americans because the store had prejudicial feelings but rather because, as Sakowitz explained, "we are a Jewish store, and our survival depends upon our providing for our rich Texas clientele, whatever they want." Nabrit recalled Sakowitz saying that "we didn't feel that we could jeopardize that." Even though other owners were willing to desegregate their stores, Sakowitz still feared that he would lose his clients, the upper echelons of white society. While he did relent eventually, he told Nabrit that if the students wanted to come to desegregate Sky Terrace, they needed to wear jackets and ties.[145]

In May 1963, after Houston had mostly desegregated, the Houston Council on Human Relations published a pamphlet focused on how desegregation and improved Black-white relations was good for the economic vitality of the city. Furthermore, the council urged all business owners to exercise fair business practices to all consumers regardless of skin color. The council underscored how working closely with the business community brought more expeditious change than any other method. For this reason, they downplayed the benefits of activist pursuits like "boycotting," "picketing," and "sit-ins," claiming they were an "economic drain" on Houston.[146]

The city of Houston had desegregated numerous public facilities by 1963, but both the schools and neighborhoods remained segregated. In the *Texas Observer*, Saul Friedman declared Houston "the backwater of revolt" and its Black population an ineffective group, saying "the Negroes of Houston are among the most politically docile and backward in the South, if not the nation."[147] In response, *The Informer* scolded Friedman and proclaimed Houston's Black residents effective politically, citing the Democratic white primary election. Moreover, the paper pointed out how Blacks in Houston had gained more rights than they had in other parts of the South because they had worked together with whites to avoid violence. Thus, Houston was not the "backwater of the revolt" but rather a positive "metropolitan and unique city of the South."[148]

Desegregation of white businesses provided more access to goods, transportation, entertainment, and economic opportunities for African Americans, but there was a downside. Black businesses in the wards declined as Black patrons shopped elsewhere, saw movies in integrated theaters, ate in new restaurants, and rode public transportation. They would not have to settle for secondhand merchandise or more expensive groceries. Henry Bullock's analysis on the vitality of the Black economic market became a reality for many department store owners. Although a contingent of white customers stopped patronizing certain businesses after desegregation, the entrance of new Black consumers more than made up for their exit.

Meanwhile, many Black-owned stores suffered. As Jewell McGowen, the wife of Erwin McGowen, one of Houston's first Black city councilmen, said, desegregation produced the "death of Black business."[149] These businesses would continue in the wards into the 1980s, but then they slowly vanished. As the Black middle class moved into suburbs like Riverside, stores in the wards moved or closed due to lack of patrons. In that sense, desegregation fractured the neighborhoods that were the center of African American life. Since white-owned stores, restaurants, and lunch counters could no longer refuse service to Black patrons, Black wards lost their vitality and economic power.[150]

Although Jewish businesses had the privilege of membership in the Retail Merchants Association and having stores downtown, the business world was still discriminatory. In December 1963, the JTA reported how the executive level of the American utility industry barred Jews. Four of the firms discussed in the article were in Houston.[151] Yet despite such discrimination, Houston's Jews disavowed the similarities between their fight and the civil rights movement. Their focus was on the security of the Jewish community, and that focus precluded public activism.

Though business desegregation brought African Americans and whites closer together than ever before, schools remained segregated—and Christian. The next chapter focuses on the collaborative fight of the city's Jews to end religion in the schools and of Black residents to enter white schools. In particular, these two groups came together to dismantle the conservative Houston School Board.

Chapter 6

The Dual Fights against Segregation and Religion in the Schools

Justice is not confined to a minority. If we deprive one of our citizens of these guarantees, if we deny the rights to any single one of our neighbors—we are subject to the same depravation and with these—the demise of our democratic ideals.

David White
"What Problem Is Whose Problem?"
May 30, 1963

While the downtown stores, restaurants, and movie theaters quietly integrated, Houston's Jewish leaders engaged in the coordinated struggle to end religion in the public schools and to usurp the conservative school board. Taking their cue from national Jewish organizations, the city's Jews sought to create a wall between church and state. The contentious fight to remove religion from the public schools was particularly important for American Jews, who were long-standing proponents of public school education. Though the fight to end religion in the schools was a national problem, the public schools in the South reflected the particular Christian values of the Bible Belt.[1]

In 1963, John Slawson, on behalf of the AJC, wrote of the quandary of American Jews who wanted to fit into Christian America but also wanted to retain their Jewish identity: "Have we been so intent on proving our Americanism and integrating into American culture that we have forgotten or minimize our Jewish heritage?" Slawson feared that if Jews did not stand up for their right to public education free of religious indoctrination, they faced the potential of losing their Jewish identity. Accepting that they were both American and Jewish would "instill a sense of surefootedness." In other words, if American Jews did not stand their ground in this particular fight for religious-free public schools, then they ran the danger of becoming "Americans without a past."[2] If they failed to speak up and force the schools to uphold the separation of church and state, Houston's Jewish leaders realized that the cost of acculturation would be very high indeed. Some even began to question their philosophical allegiance to public school education.

By and large, the Jews of Houston felt accepted by their Gentile neighbors in Riverside Terrace, as well as their Gentile business partners. Yet this acceptance did not secure the inclusivity they desired for their children in the city's public schools. They did not want their children to identify as white and American only in school; rather, they wanted their children to feel the strength of their Jewish identity in all of Houston. For Congregation Beth Israel, their prior concern in the 1940s with the Basic Principles about overly identifying as Jews transitioned in the 1960s to a fear that their children might lose touch with their Jewish identity in a white, Christian-dominated public school system. After decades of aligning with their white Gentile peers on most matters, Houston's Jews realized they had to chart their own course.

To accomplish this, Jewish leaders recognized they first had to change the mindset of the conservative school board. And once they realized that their identity as white Americans of Jewish faith did not provide them with complete acceptance in the Gentile world, they started to embrace more publicly the causes of Black residents. They combined their pursuit of ending religion in the public schools with ending segregation. The same people who opposed desegregation in Houston were also against eliminating religion in the schools. This chapter explores how the failure of the Civil Rights Act in 1964 to guarantee a religion-free public school education propelled Houston Jewish leadership to take more direct action in the fight for civil rights, separation of church and state, and the dismantling of the current school board.

Houston's Jews may have been a protected class in the war against segregation, but beginning in the mid-1960s, Jews realized that African Americans were key allies in the battle to end conservativism in the public schools. While one cannot equate the fight for desegregation and integration with trying to end religion in the schools, as there was no Little Rock equivalent in the Jewish fight, the coalescing of these two fights highlights burgeoning change within the Houston Jewish community. For Jews, proselytizing or promoting Christianity was a violation of their First Amendment rights. However, instead of focusing on this particular violation, leaders targeted their efforts toward the fight to end segregation in the public schools and achieve Black equality. In other words, to guarantee their own rights, they came to the assistance of a population fifteen times larger than their own. As in other parts of America where Jews fought for separation of church and state, Houston Jewish leaders wanted Judaism to be seen as equal to Christianity. They may have been a small population and their religion not as widely practiced as Christianity, but as Americans, they believed they should not take a back seat when the First Amendment guaranteed their right to practice their religion.[3]

Early Stages of the Fight to End Religion in the Public School System

Even after *Brown v. Board of Education*, Houston, like other parts of the South, delayed desegregating its schools for as long as possible. The Red Scare may have been over by the late 1950s, but southern segregationists, including those in Houston, still viewed integration as perpetuating Communism. This paranoia fueled the emergence of several radical right-wing groups. The 1960 creation of a headquarters in Houston of the Christian Anti-Communist Crusade alarmed the national AJC, particularly their goal of fighting "communism through education, information, evangelism, and dedication." Since the late 1950s, the John Birch Society, another anti-Communist group, had active members in Houston, although the AJC claimed "no respectable Houstonian" was actually involved in it.[4] Despite the growth of these groups, the US government realized the ramifications of projecting an image of oppression toward African Americans to the rest of the world, especially the Soviet Union. Indeed, Little Rock in 1957 suggested that the South was incapable of desegregating a school system without violence. Still, as much as Houstonians did not want to emulate Little Rock, they also did not want to carry out the Supreme Court's order.[5]

In response to the segregationists, the ACLU opened a branch in Houston under the guidance of Jewish lawyer Ben Levy. Immediately, the school board portrayed the branch as anti-American. The problem the ACLU faced in Houston was the false public perception that it only advocated for the civil liberties of minorities. The Houston School Board in particular doubted the loyalties of the ACLU and, in 1961, required the organization to take an "anti-Communist loyalty oath" to use one of the public school's auditoriums for a meeting. When the ACLU refused, the school board deemed them "un-American." In response, the ACLU sued them and became a more vocal advocate for African Americans in cases of discrimination in the school system, restaurants, and public facilities.[6]

Levy and the ACLU's fight for civil liberties also faced public backlash due to the perception that it was a Communist organization. Four hundred people attended the first meeting of the ACLU in downtown Houston. Upon leaving, participants found flyers plastered on their cars that read "Every Communist in the United States will someday be hanged!" along with a picture of a noose. It further proclaimed, "Being a communist automatically disqualifies your 'civil rights.' And no person will dare defend them … Every person who is a Communist is a traitor and should be summarily disposed of by whatever means necessary."[7]

Ben Levy's daughter, Shanna, remembered from her youth in the 1960s that her father would receive threatening anonymous calls saying, "Well, you tell that nigger-loving Jew …" Such threats underscored the tightrope that Jews and African Americans walked, separately or together, and how easily they could be labeled "un-American."[8]

In Houston, as in other parts of the South, "separate, but equal" public education never actually existed. Moreover, conservative members of the school board gained control in the late 1950s and consistently thwarted desegregation efforts. As the first Black school board member, Hattie Mae White helped speed up the process, but she lacked the authority to upend the system. She remained the lone voice for desegregation in a group of powerful conservatives. Many board members ignored and even disrespected White during meetings. In fact, the televised school board meetings were so contentious that social activist Gertrude Barnstone nicknamed them "Monday at the fights."[9]

In 1958, one of the first initiatives of the HISD to solve the segregation crisis was to create an exercise in which white teachers taught Black students over the summer while Black teachers observed through a one-way mirror so Black students remained unaware of the exercise. Since the HISD believed Black teachers were not as capable as white teachers, they hoped this method would improve their instructional abilities. Black teachers sardonically called the program the "Peeping Tom" or "Peeping Hole" plan.[10] Carter Wesley called it a "humiliation to Negro teachers and an insult to the Negro race" and warned the HISD that if they continued to use the Peeping Tom program, Houston might become another Little Rock.[11] Ultimately the Harris County Council of Organizations worked to defeat the Peeping Tom plan by threatening to boycott all public schools.

By 1959 the Peeping Tom plan had lost favor, but school segregation remained a festering problem. The segregation issue was now in the federal courts. US District Judge Ben Connally oversaw the federal order to administer a desegregation plan for Houston. Connally blocked local NAACP efforts to enforce desegregation through the courts, in large part because he did not want it to become a federal issue that would trigger the involvement of NAACP lawyers from New York. Connally instructed the HISD board to come up with a desegregation plan in July 1959. However, Superintendent John McFarland compiled a 373-page report explaining that the school board was not capable of making this deadline. As a result, Judge Connally extended desegregation until June 1, 1960.[12]

Black efforts to desegregate corresponded with strides Houston Jewish leaders made to bring attention to the question of religion in the public schools. The AJCongress and the AJC both advocated against prayer in the public school system, the handing out of Gideon Bibles, and certain other classroom practices that blurred the boundaries between church and state. Most meetings on religion in the schools took place in private homes. The Jewish Community Relations Council looked to the national AJCongress for a solution to religious violations occurring in Houston's public school system. The council addressed such infractions as teaching the Old and New Testament as part of the school curriculum, visually displaying religious symbols such as crèches and religious materials like posters or statues, staging religious-themed pageants and ceremonies, reciting prayers, and having to register your religion with the school.[13] The chair of the Public Relations Committee of the Jewish Community, Charles Keilin, expressed deep concern to the committee over the "continuing intrusion of sectarian religion in the Houston schools."[14] Rabbi Kahn even intervened at Bellaire High School in the 1950s when the school required students to attend a convocation that had a strong Evangelical presence.[15]

Though communal leaders had always had a problem with religion in public schools, they did not begin to intervene until the late 1950s, when other American Jewish communities called attention to this infringement on their religious rights in courts. In 1959, Rabbi Malev, along with the local branch of

the Zionist Organization of America (ZOA), tried to persuade
the HISD to incorporate Hebrew into the curriculum for high
school seniors.[16]

The plan was that the ZOA would be responsible for paying
for the teacher who would teach the class before or after school.
The *Houston Press* presented this as a community-wide initiative under Malev. However, not all local Jews were completely
on board with introducing Hebrew, especially liberal Jews, who
felt it would cause Jews to appear as if they were advocating for
religion in the public school system. The school board had mixed
feelings over approving Hebrew due to concerns that it promoted
Judaism over Christianity. Yet Superintendent McFarland stated
that the one virtue of Hebrew was its benefit to students interested in Christian ministry. The ZOA received support from
Hattie Mae White, who approved it because she saw it as a right
of the Jewish community. [17] However, David White described
the school board as having "anti-Semitic overtones." The segregationist White Citizens' Council branded Malev a hypocrite
for opposing religion in schools but encouraging the teaching
of Hebrew. They saw "Jewish Zionists"[18] as antagonistic toward
Christians and trying to thwart the right to worship and observe
Christmas in school.[19]

The refusal of the school board to approve the teaching
of Hebrew until 1971 demonstrated their unwillingness to
accommodate minorities. What is more, it foreshadowed the
HISD school board's even greater inflexibility and unwillingness to promote full integration and disrupt the homogenous
community they wanted to preserve. Over time, Houston Jewish
leaders realized their cause was hopeless until existing school
board members were replaced with more liberal members who
supported integration.

To avoid a national scandal, on August 3, 1960, Judge
Connally instituted integration one grade at a time, starting with
first grade. Connally chose a drawn-out desegregation plan not
only because Houston was the largest segregated school system
in the South, but also because he did not want Houston to experience the volatility of other southern cities. In short, Connally

wanted to make the desegregation process as tolerable as possible for white Houstonians. He wanted to provide them with the ability to "adapt" gradually, even though, as noted in the last chapter, business leaders had managed amicably to desegregate the lunch counters in downtown Houston overnight. His plan, called the "stair step system of desegregation," was to end in 1972. Even with this slow approach, he received threatening letters and phone calls from Houston segregationists who wanted to maintain the status quo.[20]

The first group of Black students entered white schools on September 7, 1960. Strict requirements determined which Black children moved. They had to be six years old, live in the area where they were going to school, and could not have a sibling in a Black school. They also had to submit a certificate from a physician that guaranteed they had received diphtheria and small pox vaccinations and were in good health.

HISD also took other precautions, such as having security on call, to prevent any violence. Only twelve students met these requirements, and they became the first African Americans in Houston to attend integrated schools. Thus, even when desegregation occurred, very few Black children benefited.[21] Those who attended white schools did not have an easy time integrating, as even school bathrooms remained segregated until 1962. One of the first African Americans to attend a white school was Anthony Massie, who attended Kashmere Gardens Elementary. His mother, Georgia Massie, received harassing phone calls, and the other schoolchildren bullied her son. Nevertheless, they persevered. Georgia Massie proclaimed, "It (segregation) couldn't go on forever. It wasn't that you walked in easily. I just had decided I just wasn't going to give up."[22]

Only five days after Connally's first steps to implement desegregation in Houston, Senator John F. Kennedy came to the city to address the GHMA on the matter of religion on September 12, 1960. The GHMA wanted to hear why Kennedy thought it permissible for a Catholic like himself to run for president. The Massachusetts senator sought to persuade local Protestant ministers, some of whom had gone to Washington to protest having a Catholic president, not only that the Vatican would not influence him as president; he also wanted to assert religious freedom as an American principle. Kennedy envisioned an America in which no one's father was better than another's.[23] He stated, "I believe in an America that is officially neither Catholic, Protestant nor Jewish ... and where religious liberty is so indivisible that an act against one church is treated as an act against all."[24]

Though Kennedy came to Houston to defend himself and argue that religion had no place in the public sphere, he failed to address the desegregation efforts taking place in Houston, most likely because he knew such a topic would not have endeared him to white Houstonians. To gain political support, he needed to focus exclusively on the separation between church and state. In Houston, Kennedy understood that he had to appeal to the majority Protestants. While Jewish religious leaders were not present at Kennedy's speech, Kahn did urge his congregation, whether they supported him for president or not, to support Kennedy's stance on the separation of church and state.[25]

Although Kennedy's speech did allay Protestant fears and endear him to the local Jewish community, his words failed to eliminate the barriers the public school system had placed on Houston's Jews, nor did it advance integration. It took the efforts of churches and synagogues to begin both the process of desegregation and the removal of religion from the public schools.[26]

Religious Responses

Beginning in September 1961, the Catholic Church was one of the first to initiate a plan for integration. Under Wendelin Nold, the bishop of Galveston-Houston, Catholic schools integrated within three years. According to Nold, location determined the pattern of integration, meaning "any child living in the confines of the parish, if he were Black, could be readily admitted into the Catholic parochial school."[27] This meant if a parish was predominantly African American, it would still be an all-Black Catholic school. Nold declared this scenario inevitable because every parish church was a "definite territory." Archbishop Joseph A. Fiorenza also hailed the Catholic Church's spirit of cooperation not only with the Black community but with synagogues and Protestant churches. Their relationship with the Jewish community would especially coalesce in 1965 during Vatican II's Operation Understanding program in Houston, which increased local Catholic awareness of the intolerance of segregation.[28]

Those Protestant churches that did start to integrate lacked a precise plan or policy. The First Presbyterian Church, currently located in Houston's Museum District, had always welcomed African Americans to worship and attend Sunday School, yet it was not until September 1960 that the church set the policy that ushers needed to welcome and seat Black worshippers just like any other worshippers. This policy was a turning point for Houston's Presbyterian churches on integration. However, some churches, like the First Baptist Church of Houston, did not welcome African Americans until July 1968. This was not surprising, considering that in 1964 the Southern Baptist Convention had decided that individual Baptist churches should formulate their own plans for integration. The churches' mixed responses to integration most likely contributed to a lack of unified Baptist action to push for school integration. Similarly, while some sympathized with local Jews, there was not a cohesive response from Christian clergy of any denomination to end religion in the schools.[29]

The larger issue for Houston Jewish leadership was the persistent indoctrination of Christianity in public schools. Nationally, the religion in school debate would reach its height in the early 1960s; however, Houston, like much of the South, fell behind. Schools continued to present Christmas and Easter ceremonies, hold prayer services, and hand out Bibles. Christian youth movements were also official school functions.[30] When Jaime Bloom was growing up in Houston, she remembered how "uncomfortable [it was] on all the holidays." She recalled that public schools observed Christian holidays and "Jewish holidays were never talked about or acknowledged. Just being Jewish was definitely something the other kids were aware of and made you aware of."[31]

Initially, local Jewish leaders had thought that living with white Gentiles would protect them from discrimination. However, with desegregation underway in the 1960s, Jews became more conscious of how religion divided them from their white Gentile peers. They realized that the predominantly Gentile school board was not going to remove religion from the public schools and that they needed to find a solution on their own. In an attempt to initiate change, Jewish leaders organized numerous meetings on the subject of religion, and Jewish journalists wrote numerous articles.[32] In the *JH-V*, White proclaimed that "education should be left to the schools and to qualified educators—religion to the churches and synagogues and qualified ministers to guide their respective congregations to better understanding."[33]

To persuade white Gentiles that Judaism was neither a lesser religion nor a threat to Christianity, rabbis promoted inter- faith and intergroup programming. In 1961, Kahn led one such community effort to bring Jews together with white and Black Christians called Festival of the Bible Arts. This eighteen-day series featured biblical art as well as biblically themed musical and dramatic performances and dances. TSU's choir also sang "negro spirituals" at one of the events.[34] Kahn thought he could create a space, even if only momentarily, in which everyone shared their common belief in the Hebrew Bible.

The Festival of the Bible Arts was so popular that thousands visited from as far away as sixty miles. All told, forty thousand people came—much more than came to any other interfaith event of the 1950s. In many ways, this festival enabled Houston's Jewish leaders to exert the control they lacked in the city's schools. It also allowed white Gentiles to view Judaism as a religion comparable to Christianity and not fear its inclusion. While Kahn's program did not form a direct alliance with school desegregation activists, it resulted in greater religious connections between groups that reaped later dividends for desegregation efforts.[35]

In February 1963, Congregation Emanu El invited Rabbi William Silverman, a staunch advocate of school integration in Nashville since *Brown*, to speak at an event called Brother- hood and the Rights of Man. The city of Nashville, which had followed the same "stairstep" system of integration as Houston, had experienced violent white supremacist reactions, including the bombing of Nashville's Jewish Community Center. Silverman's wife received threatening phone calls from men who warned her that the rabbi's life was in danger.[36]

Despite these threats, Silverman continued to oppose the white supremacist group the Confederate Underground and stayed firm in his belief in civil rights. Kahn's support of Silverman set an example to his community that when Jews stood on the side of African Americans, they were not in the wrong but were in fact heroes. In addition to Silverman's presentation, the event featured a panel on the economic disadvantages and social prejudices that African Americans faced, which exemplified a change in the Jewish community's participation in civil rights issues. [37] Some of the topics discussed were "fair employment practices, civil rights, restrictive covenants, and other facets of the overall proposition of the Equality of Men."[38]

Houston Jewish Leaders' Attempt to Fight Religion in the Schools

On February 21, 1963, Hattie Mae White spoke at Congregation Beth Yeshurun on behalf of the school board on religion in the public schools and instituting Hebrew as a language in them. White, whose philosophy was to be the voice of all children regardless of their race or ethnicity, was the ideal school board member to speak to the Jewish community. Jewish parents whose children had experienced discrimination in school voiced their concerns. Although White's main work had centered on African Americans, she also recognized the needs of the Jewish community, particularly their concern about religion in schools. They had, after all, voted for her in the school board election. Her decision to come speak to the Jewish community was significant, considering that Jewish business leaders had participated in segregation. Now these same business leaders were seeking the help of a Black woman. This was the first instance of a connection between the Houston Jewish community and a Black political leader. Hattie Mae White was virtually powerless, and yet she came to listen and listened well.[39]

Two months later, on April 18, 1964, Hattie Mae White came to the JCC to discuss school integration. Jewish leaders wanted to highlight to the wider community the problem with the school board. Eventually, many Jews would come to see that any change for themselves would have to include African Americans because the same conservative board discriminated against them both.[40]

Houston Jewish leaders attended several statewide conferences to gain more knowledge about how to end religion in schools. In March, conferences held in Austin and Dallas provided more concrete solutions with the help of the State Commissioner of Education on how to implement the Supreme Court decision of *Engel v. Vitale* to ban school prayer. These meetings may have given local Jews some clear guidelines, but they did not solve the problem.

The Jewish Community Relations Council in Houston issued a call to action to all members of the Jewish community and drafted a statement that opposed religion in public schools, emphasizing "that the relations between man and God are not to be subject to government control, regulation or pressure."[41] B'nai B'rith stood behind this statement, and rabbis read it in their synagogues on April 19, 1963, calling on "all responsible educators and public school officials, as well as religious leaders and laymen, to use every effort to make public school practice conform with fundamental American law and our country's tradition of religious liberty." Believing it to be their First Amendment right, Malev proclaimed: "When we insist upon separation of Church and State, we're not fighting for ourselves alone, but rather for the rights of all Americans."[42]

In May 1963, Melvin Steakley of the *Houston Chronicle* delved into the issue. In his interview with Superintendent McFarland, who favored school prayer, Steakley revealed that "ninety percent of the schools use prayers."[43] On a typical day, it was customary to say a morning prayer, recite the Pledge of Allegiance, sing a patriotic song, and discuss current events.

McFarland claimed that the HISD's intention was not to impose an absolute religious ideal and that prayer was not mandatory. Houston's Jewish community disagreed, arguing that even if their children did not have to participate in religious practice, their teachers made them feel like outsiders. Communal leaders tried to get the GHMA involved in the separation of church and state, but nothing came of this effort.[44] Jewish leaders tabled the issue after Martin Luther King Jr.'s Birmingham campaign took center stage, in large part because the violence in Birmingham had a direct impact on Rabbi Moshe Cahana of Houston's Congregation Brith Shalom.

Rabbi Cahana and the Fight for Civil Rights

Cahana was one of only two southern rabbis who went to Birmingham and eventually joined the Conservative Movement's Rabbinical Assembly to help King. A religious humanist, Cahana saw going to Birmingham as his "obligation to right wrongs" and speak out against human rights violations against African Americans.[45] As a Jew, he also understood the meaning of being the perpetual "other" and could not stand idly by. His wife, Alice, a Holocaust survivor, caused Cahana to feel that what was happening to Blacks in Birmingham, in what became known as the Children's Crusade, was parallel to the Jewish plight in the Holocaust. For Cahana, the ghastly images emerging of dogs attacking Black children and the police beating and using high-pressure hoses on Black teenagers evoked the Holocaust, when police willingly harmed the most innocent without conscience or retribution.[46] At the time, Cahana believed Houston was not facing the same crisis as Birmingham because Houston's religious leaders "had done advance work beforehand"—much like Houston's business owners—to prevent such violence.[47]

When Cahana came home, many local Jews, including his congregants, did not appreciate that he had gone to Birmingham and drawn the wrath of the KKK against both him and his wife. In an interview, Cahana's son remembered his parents received "harassing phone calls in the middle of the night."

He described the calls as "a continuous threat." His father never reacted in fear, however, even when the KKK threatened his life. He believed that the KKK responded more aggressively because of anti-Semitism: "Anti-Semitism [was] as much a part of things as racism was."[48]

In his article "There Are Some Who Remember," David White praised the idealism of Cahana and addressed the Jewish obligation to African Americans. White believed that rabbinic protest was a way to stop a future Holocaust. He further explained that "those who lived through this Holocaust are greatly concerned with the ethics of Little Rock, of Oxford, and now of Birmingham."[49] White's mention of Little Rock emphasized to the Jewish reader that, in order to prevent the eruption of violence in Houston, they needed to be advocates of peaceful integration like Cahana, especially in the schools.

Cahana's actions concerned the Jews of Houston. Insurance consultant Irving Pozmantier recalled speaking with some of the members of Congregation Brith Shalom about Cahana's public stance. Pozmantier said, "We were all uneasy about it." He recalled thinking, "Should we be actively involved, should we be visibly involved, should we be invisibly involved; what is really our role?"[50] Many southern congregants—especially in New Orleans, Jackson, and Memphis who were threatened by white supremacists[51]—felt like Pozmantier and did not want to bring the "wrath of the non-Jewish community" down on them. He felt that second-generation American Jews like himself were simply "trying to find our way in America."[52]

Jewish real estate developer Jenard M. Gross[53] wrote to the *JH-V* about his concerns over Cahana and other rabbis going to Birmingham. Gross strongly felt the Jews should not place themselves in the limelight for the civil rights cause because "we, as Jews, should always keep self-survival uppermost in our minds." Gross was not a segregationist, but he felt that trips to Birmingham to represent Judaism led to "additional anti-Semitism." He rejected Cahana's assertion that helping in Birmingham was a necessary way of preserving Jewish values. Instead, Gross argued that "until we, as Jews, have all of our problems solved, there is no earthly reason to deliberately antagonize people and bring additional plagues upon our houses." He asked White why Jews should help African Americans. After all, "the NAACP and the local Negro Council of Organizations did not feel it necessary to rush to the support of the Jewish Community Council's position on school prayer."[54] For Gross, the Jewish fight to remove religion from HISD was the community's fundamental problem, and he could not understand why rabbis did not make this their foremost fight. The local rise of the Nation of Islam in Houston since 1950 also influenced Gross, who saw them as polluting African Americans against Jews.[55]

In response, David White wrote "What Problem Is Whose Problem?" which attempted to convince Gross and other local Jews that they could both focus on their battle to remove religion from public schools and care about the rights of other minorities, specifically African Americans. White pointed out the common problems facing them. Jewish leaders like Cahana realized that standing quietly against segregation would not gain them the religious rights they so desired for their own children. The Black and Jewish struggles could resolve positively only if both created a united front and vowed to work together rather than separately. As White explained, "If we deny the rights to any single one of our neighbors—we are subject to the same depravation [sic]."[56]

Inspired by his experience in Birmingham, Cahana collaborated with other religious leaders to hold a conference in Houston following the model of the Conference on Religion and Race that had taken place in Chicago earlier in the year. In June 1963, Cahana sent letters inviting the Houston religious community to the conference at Christ Church Episcopal Cathedral. He presented the conference as an urgent matter for all local religious leaders. Two hundred Jews, Protestants, and Catholics attended, including African Americans and Mexican Americans.[57] The conference's theme was "confession of sin and repentance on the part of the White community for the evils imposed on the Negroes."[58] Four speakers—Rabbi Cahana, Reverend Wallace B. Clift Jr., Reverend Thomas J. Griffin, and

Reverend Monsignor John Cassata—spoke of the intersectionality between religion and Black civil rights.

In his speech, Cahana used the term "non-Negro" to describe himself, arguing that he chose to act not based on the color of his skin but because of his Jewish belief system and prioritization of human rights.[59] He felt that solving this problem was urgent because "twenty million people are suffering in America, segregated, humiliated and insulted." Openly placing blame on synagogues and churches for staying quiet in the face of Black discrimination, he claimed, "Segregation is not a Negro problem. It is a white problem. We are the sick. We are the sinners." Because segregation stood in opposition to Judeo-Christian principles, religious leaders should actively declare bigotry a sin.[60]

Reverend Griffin, an African American, also placed blame on the white community for their intolerance and called on all white clergy to ask forgiveness not only of African Americans but of God for their ill-treatment of his people. He called out churches' inaction: "Every large Protestant denomination has passed beautiful, carefully worded resolutions on the race question. Very little has been done to implement the resolutions." From his perspective, all church-sponsored institutions, whether universities, hospitals, or homes for the aged, should have "white only" signs plastered across each building, confirming their failure to integrate. Griffin underscored, "When we see the performance of the white church and its agencies, the Negro is convinced there is little sincerity on the part of the church concerning the struggle for the Negro."[61]

Other conference speakers, including Reverend Clift and Monsignor Cassata, did not focus on the misdeeds of whites. These clergymen took the opposite approach, instead concentrating on the importance of brotherhood and God's call for all humans to love and accept others. This event may not have mentioned religion in public schools, but it did illustrate the way religion could become an effective tool to promote greater tolerance. Such a conference united Judaism and Christianity in action toward civil rights, which was in stark contrast to how the city's public schools exclusively prioritized Christian views.[62]

The *Houston Chronicle* presented Cahana as the face of the Conference on Religion and Race. Yet not everyone thought this conference was a step in the right direction. Cahana received an anti-Semitic and racist letter from Ruby Davis, a visitor to Houston, for his role. Davis rejected Cahana's view that prejudice was a "moral crisis." She believed racial difference was proof of inequality. Davis also accused Cahana and other participating clergy of being Communists, despite the fact that they based their arguments on religious beliefs. She labeled the push for equality as antithetical to her understanding of America and blamed clergy like Cahana for US problems at home and abroad, even going so far as to blame the Cuban Missile Crisis on liberal whites and civil rights activists. Davis highlighted her service as a nurse in World War II, which she claimed made her a real American, unlike Cahana, whom she doubted had served in the military. Most provocatively, she wrote: "By your statements you are proving something I heard years ago (but didn't believe) about a Jew being a nigger (not negroe) turned inside out."[63]

Cahana responded to Davis that "Biblical truth" was the basis for equality, not Communism. He retorted that her "supremacy, prejudice, segregation, and explication muddies our soul and separates us from the Almighty, the Holy One." He ended his letter with a kind of benediction to encourage her to rethink her point of view: "May our Heavenly Father help you to purify your heart and make you free from anti-Negro and anti-Jewish hostility and prejudice."[64]

Taking a cue from David White, Cahana, and other Jewish youth groups, teen editor Norton Shaw of the *JH-V* wrote on behalf of the Jewish Community Center's Youth Council in favor of desegregation. He scolded the Houston Jewish community for politically supporting integration but not practicing it. In a November 1963 article, he declared that if Jews refused to act as Jews—meaning in favor of social justice—then they should "cleanse" their prayer books of all terms like "justice" and "brotherhood."[65]

Shaw may have complained of hypocrisy in the Jewish community, but some Jewish organizations were working to raise awareness of desegregation. From 1959 to 1964, the ADL, in conjunction with the University of Houston, fostered programming to promote better Black-white relations. The Workmen's Circle (Der Arbeter Ring), a mutual aid society originally for Jewish immigrants from Eastern Europe, had a long history of supporting integration and minority rights, including the branch in Houston. They published reports on the March on Washington for Jobs and Freedom and selections from Rabbi Joachim Prinz's famous speech, "The Issue Is Silence," which addressed the parallels between Black civil rights and the Holocaust.[66] The efforts of the ADL and Workmen's Circle, however, did little to stem the tide of Houston's bigotry. Kennedy's assassination in Dallas in November escalated matters even more and unleashed a new wave of intolerance in Houston.

The Kennedy Assassination and the Passing of the Civil Rights Act

Through most of his presidency, Kennedy was not firm on civil rights, except in such cases as his federal protection of the Freedom Riders. When he first proposed a civil rights bill, white southern Democrats perceived it as the beginning of a second Reconstruction. In Dallas, two days before his assassination, anti-Kennedy handbills likely created by southern segregationists circulated with a photo accusing him of creating an anti-Christian government and Communist-inspired civil rights protests. Houstonians shared this antagonism toward their president, despite his visit to Houston a few years earlier to speak at the GHMA.[67]

Many HISD students responded with celebration to news of his assassination. Upon hearing of this reaction, the HISD school board expressed their disbelief. Hattie Mae White, according to Gertrude Barnstone, questioned their surprise during a televised HISD meeting: "How can you pretend [to be] surprise[d]? You sit here week in and week out and you ... [oppose] the Federal Government because of integration/segregation. You do nothing but talk bad about the Federal Government. What do you expect these children to pick up from that?"[68]

Orthodox Rabbi Raphael Schwartzman of Adath Emeth wrote a scathing article addressing the children's celebratory reaction to Kennedy's death and the HISD's ineffectual response to integration. In "The Mosaic of Hate," he addressed the city's lack of respect for the president and thereby the country, especially at two elementary schools where there was a "desecration of American flags." At one high school, "some students cheered" while other "children kneeled to offer thanks that President Kennedy was dead." Schwartzman blamed religious and governmental authorities for defying the legal structure of the United States and promoting anarchy. He wanted Houstonians, especially Jews, to stand up for US policy on civil rights and place their faith in the newly sworn-in President Lyndon Johnson. He saw prejudice toward African Americans as the underlying source of disloyalty. His use of the Hebrew phrase *sinas chinom*, which meant "pointless hatred," communicated to his Jewish audience the degree to which he felt the community had been led astray in their principles.[69]

In the wake of the crisis in Birmingham and the Kennedy assassination, Houston grappled with its embarrassing response. Business leaders and Jewish and Christian clergy tried to change public opinion toward the late president and celebrate his accomplishments. Yet the greater issue at hand was the dangerous precedent being set by the school board's unwillingness to either desegregate or remove Christianity from the schools. Their overall disregard for federal statutes created an environment in which students felt they had permission to disrespect the president.[70]

Ironically, it took a man from Texas—Lyndon Johnson—to pass the Civil Rights Act of 1964. Upon its passing, many Jewish and Christian clergy publicly praised the ruling. According to Tennyson Whorton of the *Houston Post*, their collective goal was "to encourage compliance with its provision and to foster increased interracial brotherhood and understanding" among their congregants. The fourteen ministers and one rabbi from whom Whorton sought reactions to the new act were for the most part in agreement, with some exceptions. Thomas Skaff of Saint

George Orthodox Church questioned whether "the negroes [are] going to become antagonistic." Skaff placed the responsibility on African Americans to fit into churches rather than acknowledging that whites needed to make their churches inclusive.[71]

The two clergy not in favor of the new bill were Milton Richardson of Christ Church Cathedral, even though the cathedral had welcomed Blacks in the nineteenth century, and K. Owen White of First Baptist Church, which upheld segregation until 1967. Though they both saw the Civil Rights Act as a step in the right direction, they nonetheless called it flawed.[72]

Rabbi Malev was the only Jewish clergy Whorton approached. Malev commented that the law was long overdue. He felt it was incumbent on clergy to incorporate this law into their places of worship and "impress upon all people that it is their patriotic and religious duty, not only to obey it, but to accept it with all their hearts." This point was indeed significant, as it not only acknowledged the intersection between civil rights and Jewish rights, but it also indirectly applauded the act for its potential capability of separating church and state. Malev, who had previously disavowed connecting the civil rights movement with American Jewry, had changed his mind.[73]

The passing of the Civil Rights Act of 1964 propelled Houston Jewish leaders and their synagogues to publicly join the fight for Black equality and integration. They also realized that the act might help them win the battle to separate church and state. White's article "The Civil Rights Battle Has Just Begun" had previously discussed the significance a civil rights bill could have for the Jewish community. According to White, no law could end hatred, but it was a piece of legislation for "all minorities," including Jews, who had been waiting patiently for their voice.[74]

Aftermath of the Civil Rights Act of 1964

Shortly after the passing of the act, anti-Jewish sentiment reemerged. Congregation Emanu El received threatening phone calls with recordings of Hitler's voice. Gertrude Barnstone, not even known publicly as a practicing Jew, would also face discrimination when she became a school board member.[75] Barnstone's election reflected a shift in the board toward integration and the promotion of rights and liberties for all individuals. As one of the most active Jewish school board members since Ray K. Daily, Barnstone admired Hattie Mae White's courage to speak out against the board after Kennedy's death and wanted to become her ally. Judge Woodrow Seals, a fellow member of the Houston Council on Human Relations and a friend of Barnstone's, had advised her to organize a tea in Hattie Mae White's honor. Because the event was so successful, the council convinced Barnstone to run for the school board. She campaigned "against what she [believed was] the 'tired and unimaginative' power structure controlling the board" and believed desegregation needed to be "speeded up." To her, segregation was "a tremendous waste of our brainpower and our potential."[76] Barnstone recalled that she had to take up this challenge because she "couldn't live with [herself] if she didn't."[77]

After Barnstone's election to the school board, the Houston Chronicle tried to harm her image by publishing a statement about her opposition to Christmas celebrations and any religious observance in the public school system. Afterward, she received threatening phone calls, and people she assumed were her friends shunned her. Despite the negative press and subsequent backlash, Barnstone continued to voice her opposition in the media, as she felt it was a right of all Americans to attend a public school without religious pressures. The Jewish community responded positively to her views, and the AJC invited her to address the subject of the separation of church and state.[78]

In addition, Barnstone positioned herself on the school board as an integrationist. When the lawyer Asberry Butler became the first Black man on the school board that same year, Barnstone, Hattie Mae White, and Butler formed a small liberal coalition on the nine-member board. Conservative board members resented Butler's arrival, and indeed Butler remembered overhearing that "there must be some kind of way to get this nigger off this board, because he don't deserve to be there." This was in reference to the fact that Houstonians may have elected Butler because they

Gertrude Barnstone with dogs, cats, fish, and birds. RGD0006-0131,
Houston Post Photographs, Houston Metropolitan Research Center,
Houston Public Library. HP staff/©Houston Chronicle. Used with
permission.

confused him with the white conservative Walker Butler, who
was also running for a school board position.[79]

Their three-person coalition collaborated with the Houston
Council on Human Relations to find solutions for African
Americans and lower socioeconomic students. They worked
together to promote free lunches, a program Daily had tried to
implement before. It took time to convince the board to institute
a low-cost breakfast program, but Barnstone presented research
that students perform better in school when they are not hungry.

She also worked with the council to integrate the student orchestra and develop a music scholarship for African Americans. While Barnstone was not very connected to the Jewish community, her initial work with Butler and Hattie Mae White did present to the Jewish community a courageous image. Butler and Barnstone spoke together at the downtown B'nai B'rith lodge about their goals for the HISD. Barnstone also attended other Jewish events to discuss integration.[80]

In addition to Barnstone, Rabbi Cahana continued to be a prominent Jewish communal figure who supported integration. In March 1965, he joined Dr. King in Selma, just as he had two years before in Birmingham—this time with three Episcopal clergy from Houston. The *Houston Post* and *Houston Chronicle* featured stories on the Selma march. According to Saul Friedman of the Chronicle, the clergy wanted to march so they could "do more than talk about justice from the pulpit."[81] David White also praised the religious leaders for their activism in the JH-V. The Houston Rabbinical Association honored Cahana and praised him for his "idealism and courage in participating in the struggle for Negro rights."[82]

Synagogues, Jewish men's clubs, and Jewish youth groups honored Cahana at several events, including the Houston Zionist Organization Association Dinner on April 1, 1965. The organization named him Man of the Year "for his active participation in the field of human relations and his fight for equal rights on behalf of all individuals."[83] Such praise within the Jewish community was a stark departure from earlier attitudes. When Cahana went to Birmingham in 1963, his congregation and members of the Jewish community thought he was placing them in danger of segregationist attacks. Two years later they viewed him as a courageous activist.

In contrast to Cahana's national approach, Kahn believed that the Jews of Houston should work toward solving conflicts between whites and African Americans in their own city first. On April 6, 1965, Kahn introduced a synagogue initiative called "A Call to Conscience." Three years earlier, the Union of American Hebrew Congregations had launched a similar campaign called

"A Call for Racial Justice." The goal was to rally the entire
congregation around support of Black equality. Kahn encouraged
his congregation to think of African Americans as their peers
and not a separate group. He wanted his Jewish congregants
to remember their historical oppression and consider it their
religious duty to stop it from happening again.[84]

The Call to Conscience initiative was in direct contrast to
the Basic Principles, which sought to narrow the definition of
Jews and more closely connect them with the white Christian
majority. Kahn tailored his suggestions to the particulars of the
Houston Jewish experience. For example, he believed local Jews
should not support or be involved in any business or real estate
transaction that allowed discrimination of any kind, including
participating in restrictive covenants or gentlemen's agreements.
This was ironic considering the Jewish community's flight from
Riverside in the early 1960s.[85]

Despite the emerging Jewish call for equality, Houston
remained slow to integrate. By 1965, the HISD had only desegregated up to the fourth grade. Houston's African Americans,
frustrated with the slow process, appealed to Hattie Mae White in
April 1965. The call of civil rights leaders to protest also inspired
the local branch of the NAACP to decide to approach the school
board about their lack of attention to desegregation. Because
the NAACP did not want to be the public face of the protest,
they created People for the Upgrading of Schools in Houston,
or PUSH. However, just as the school board had ignored Hattie
Mae White, Barnstone, and Butler, they ignored the efforts
of PUSH. In response, PUSH organized a march on May 10,
1965. Influential African Americans like Francis William of the
Harris County Council of Organizations, Reverend Griffin of
the Conference of Race and Religion, future Texas state senator
Barbara Jordan, and Reverend William Lawson all took part in
the march.[86]

This march was one of the most public protests since the
student sit-ins of the early 1960s. Because the organizers, including
Lawson, did not anticipate the same violence encountered during
the Children's Crusade of 1963 in Birmingham, they allowed

Houston, 1965: A downtown rally in protest of continuing segregation.
Curtis McGee/©Houston Chronicle. Used with permission.

one thousand children to participate. In fact, 90 percent of Black
school-age children in Houston marched. When the students and
Lawson arrived at Wheeler Street, they were disappointed that no
Black clergy, business leaders, or civic leaders joined them. When
they approached Dowling Street, thousands joined the march-
ers, including people who lived and worked in the area. Lawson
recalled that "there were whites and Jews who joined us because
of all them [*sic*] did not like school segregation."[87]

Along with students from the high schools, TSU, and the
University of Houston, the crowd marched to one of the school
headquarters, which the superintendent closed in response. Two
thousand protesters bore signs with slogans like "Space Age
Houston—Stone Age Schools" and "Jim Crow Must Go."[88]
The protesters made three requests: (1) complete desegregation
of the entire school district must happen and not one grade at a
time, which created a dual system; (2) an end to separate Black

and white schools, which perpetuated segregation; and (3) the use of federal funds to establish certain programs (e.g., school lunches and vocational training). They also asked Houstonians to oppose bond elections that funded white and Black schools separately and perpetuated the dual system. They would only approve of a bond if it funded integrated schools. While the protest did not change HISD's stance, it did speed up deseg-regation. Also, PUSH eventually left the NAACP to become a full-fledged civil rights organization.[89]

In July 1965, Kahn took up the protesters' poignant Space Age/Stone Age distinction in his weekly *Houston Chronicle* series "Lessons for Life." Acknowledging the disparity between the space program and the movement "at oxcart speed" of the desegregation of the city, he saw the swift advancement of space exploration as a reason to be impatient "with the pace of human progress." It took a "hundred years to move from the Emanci-pation Proclamation to the Civil Rights Act." Because this was the way human relations worked, it could take "years, decades, generations, and centuries" for change to occur. By asking Black Houstonians to wait, Kahn revealed his lack of understanding of the challenges and frustrations they faced daily.[90]

As the call for change escalated in the summer of 1965, Houston Jewish leaders attempted to find a solution to the prob-lem of religion in schools. David White, who was also the chair-man of the Community Relations Subcommittee, wrote a letter to Rabbi Marshall Berg, the head of the Houston Rabbinical Association, asking for advice. According to White, the Jews were fighting a losing battle—they either had to devise an effec-tive solution or resign themselves to religion remaining in the schools. In response, Houston Jewish leaders created an education subcommittee to review the same issues that Jewish students had faced before: the distribution of the Gideon Bible, Easter greet-ings in school newspapers, school prayer, observance of Christian holidays, examinations on Jewish holidays, and graduation cere-monies on the Sabbath. Kahn took it upon himself to send letters to various rabbis on behalf of the education subcommittee in order to solicit their opinions on a desired outcome.[91]

Malev found the subcommittee's letter campaign ineffectual because it was focused exclusively on Jewish leaders. He explained that these letters "would be like asking the Negroes whether they believe in Civil Rights." Malev believed rabbinic unity was irrelevant because change would only occur if non-Jewish clergy and the laity assisted in ending religion in the public schools.[92]

In the end, the call of Jewish leaders was indeed ineffectual. Any change regarding religion was difficult, given that board members like Barnstone faced bouts of anti-Semitism not only for her insistence on the separation of church and state but also because of her support of integration. Hattie Mae White recalled that Barnstone began to have problems with the school board when they found out she was Jewish.[93]

On September 15, 1965, Barnstone received an anti-Communist pamphlet about Hubert Humphrey. It was not the article but the letter inside, however, that was the most provocative. The anonymous author evoked European anti-Semitic narratives of Jewish disloyalty, including the post–World War I German view of Jews as traitors: "The dam [sic] jews have stabbed in the back the people of every country where they lived. This is why they finally get kicked out. Hitler had a good idea." The author also tied Jews to Communism by describing them as "natural bolshevicks." Barnstone may not have seen herself as a Jew, but she was still seen as one by others. The author perceived Jews as not capable of being real citizens. Even after the horrors of the Holocaust were exposed twenty years prior, the anonymous author regretted that Jews were not sufficiently wiped out. Jews were seen as the racial other. He blamed Jews for wanting to be "friends" with African Americans and for their "willing[ness] to mix the white Christians with the Niggers." In other words, Jews imposed their integrationist values on Christians. At the end, the author declared to Barnstone that "Houston despise[s] you!"[94] In the author's opinion, if she were a real American, Houstonian, or white, she would not have promoted integration for African Americans.

These attacks did not faze Barnstone; she pressed on. Look magazine featured a spread on Barnstone titled "A Lady Stirs

Her City's Conscience," which described how she broke down barriers in Houston. The magazine described her allies as Black school board members who "battle[d] over Federal aid to schools and the pace of integration." Barnstone soon became recognized as "that school-board lady." She explained to Look her desire for Houston to become a diverse city and for Houstonians to "understand each other's position" and exhibit "mutual tolerance."[95] In response to Look's spread, William Worrilow Jr., of the Protestant-centric Organized Minorities Association based in Lebanon, Pennsylvania, asked the editor how Houston, the Space City, could have allowed one person to deprive the city of its Christian spirit—that is, Protestantism. Barnstone, he felt, should not represent the city of Houston in a popular international magazine like Look.[96]

In November 1965, Barnstone received another anti-Semitic letter in which the author addressed her not by name but as "Jew." Accusing Barnstone of being a "Christ Killer," the author saw her as a threat to Christianity, particularly because of her rejection of religion in the schools. The author wanted to create a billboard exposing her anti-Christian values, which would read: "Don't vote for 'Jew'= They are not Christians they wont [sic] let your kid have a Xmas play—." Like Worrilow, the author did not want Barnstone, a non-Christian, to become the face of Houston and therefore threatened to rally other Christians to fight against her to restore the city's true Christian values.[97]

Black school board members Hattie Mae White and Butler also faced harassment. During White's first year, white supremacists fired a gun at her car's windshield, splintering the glass, and burned a cross in her front yard. The police never apprehended the perpetrators. Butler faced so many threats that his wife tried to persuade him to leave the school board after his first year. Some of the more extreme incidents his family experienced were rocks thrown at his house and a bomb set off outside.[98] There were also political investigations aimed at sabotaging him, and Louis Moore, a reporter from the *Houston Post*, accused Butler of such crimes as bigamy and rape. According to Butler, because he was a lawyer, he was "very vulnerable," unlike Hattie Mae White, who was less threatening as a wife and mother.[99] Even their coalition of three (with Barnstone) could not protect them, and they continued to be regular recipients of threats. However, they were not alone in their battle. Other organizations would eventually help them with the transition to desegregation. One of these organizations was the AJC.

The Broussard Case

After years of encouraging Houston's Jews to take an active role in desegregation, the AJC discussed the possibility of opening an office in Houston at a national meeting on July 27, 1964. The AJC already had a presence in the city, but this move made it official. The AJC felt that a local branch was important because "Houston, a city of considerable intergroup tension and conflict, [was] also a stronghold of discrimination against Jews in civic and industrial enterprises and the center of considerable extremist and Fundamentalist activity."[100] A full-fledged office in Houston enabled the AJC to assist in the fight for school desegregation. In fact, it was the AJC that eventually stepped in to push the HISD to desegregate unconditionally.

The Houston chapter of the AJC acquired its first full-time director, Milton Feiner, in the spring of 1966. Under his leadership, the Houston AJC changed its focus from being an educational discussion group to an active communal organization. Between 1966 and 1967, several items on their agenda, including "social discrimination," "Jewish-Negro relations," "Jewish identity," "extremism," and "education and public relations," revealed their shift in approach.[101] To halt discrimination, they planned to create surveys to better understand the hiring process of Houston corporations. The committee also devoted its efforts to Jewish and Black interactions, including dialogue groups, working with Black organizations to combat Black anti-Semitism. Their ultimate mission, however, was still the school system and its desegregation.[102]

With 225,000 students—30 percent of whom were African American—the HISD was the sixth largest school system in the

United States, but by 1966 it still had not fulfilled the *Brown v. Board of Education* decision of 1954. The "freedom of choice" plan, enacted in 1966, offered students the ability to choose their school as long as it was not overcrowded. The plan, however, did not "provide for the transportation of students, made no change in teacher assignments, and did not provide for notifying parents and students of their rights under this plan."[103] Lack of access to buses made it difficult for Black children to go to schools in other neighborhoods. For this reason, white students in the same neighborhoods continued together throughout their schooling and never experienced integration. Also, stairstep desegregation only allowed the lower grades to integrate, which meant older Black and white students did not interact with each other.[104]

In March 1966, a new school desegregation problem emerged. Houston voters had approved a $60 million bond for a school construction project in a predominantly Black neighborhood. A Black couple, Onesephor Peter and Yvonne Broussard, sued HISD on behalf of their six children and other Black families to stop the construction of the new school, maintaining that such a move would lead to even more segregation. They feared most Black families would opt to attend the neighborhood school rather than an integrated school. Considering that in June 1966, 95 percent of Black students attended segregated schools, this was a valid concern. Judge Allen B. Hannay denied the Broussard amily's claim on July 13, 1966, and the US District Court would not agree to stop the construction of the school.[105]

Not long after, AJC director Milton Feiner came across this case and wondered if the Houston branch should help the Broussard family in their quest. Though sympathetic, Feiner worried that Jewish involvement might garner unwanted publicity. He asked the national office to review the case. In May 1966, Harry Fleischman, the Director of Labor and Race Relations, learned about the case and convinced Feiner that the Houston AJC should support the Broussard family. Since not all members were on board, they decided that the decision would be up to individual members. AJC members who wanted to be involved took the lead with the backing of the Houston Jewish

Community Relations Council, which voted unanimously to support the Broussard family's suit. Houston AJC lawyers Ronald Cohen, Al Schulman, and Arthur Mandell worked with the lawyers who represented the Broussard family—Joe Tita, a white, and Bill Wood, an African American in the same firm as Mandell.[106]

The national offices of both the AJC and the NAACP lent their full support and contacted other civil rights organizations, including the ACLU, to support the case. AJC lawyers qualified their argument for the Broussard family by stating that "they were not opposed to the concept of neighborhood schools but would support the suit on the general legal and moral grounds that segregation, de facto or de jure, was illegal and harmful."[107] In other words, the HISD could build a new neighborhood school if that school did not perpetuate segregation. Ultimately, Judge Connally sided with the defendant and the Broussard family lost the case.[108]

The case, however, was the first time that Houston Jewish leaders set aside their fears of exposing themselves to antagonism from Houston's white Gentile community and openly involved themselves in creating a legal partnership with groups like the NAACP to fight segregation. It would also be the first time the local chapter of the AJC would willingly combine efforts with national Jewish and civil rights organizations. Feiner believed if the local and national AJC worked together, their united front would lessen repercussions. Indeed, members of local Jewish organizations started to see the importance of fighting not just on behalf of Jews but also for Black equality. Feiner would later comment in a private letter to the general counsel of the New York AJC, Ed Lukas, that there was a noticeable change in the Houston Jewish community, as they had "previously been fearful of 'sticking their necks out.'"[109]

National leadership of the AJC applauded Houston's branch for their work with the Broussard case, especially because it was a southern city. Irving Engel, former national president of the AJC, remarked to Lukas about the communal shift toward action: "How things have changed since 1955 when, with very few exceptions,

Jewish leaders throughout the South, including members of the AJC, were insisting that national Jewish organizations stay out of the Civil Rights field!"[110] Lukas wrote back on April 5, 1967, saying that the Houston AJC's involvement in the Broussard case was a "landmark event."[111] The Houston Jewish community had become an open and firm supporter of Black rights.

Another example of Jewish leaders spearheading change was in the predominantly Black area of Settegast—near the Third Ward—where two-thirds of residents lacked a high school diploma. Houston Jewish leadership worked to create Head Start and adult education programs to help bridge this education gap. Beginning in 1965, the National Council of Jewish Women (NCJW) joined with the Council of Negro Women, the Council of Catholic Women, United Church Women, and Women, Infants, and Children (WIC) to implement a Women's Job Corps to help women and their families rise out of poverty. This program provided women with training and additional education. In addition, the group instituted Literacy Instruction for Texas (LIFT) to help combat illiteracy in Houston among minorities and immigrants by using televised literacy programs on KTRK Channel 13.[112]

The school of Congregation Emanu El, under the leadership of Kahn, also created a local branch of Head Start for underprivileged preschoolers. Alongside certified teachers, volunteers from the congregation helped tutor Black and white children.[113] The AJC and area synagogues also held food drives for the hungry. Congregation Brith Shalom, under Cahana, instituted a tutoring program in the Third Ward and worked to clean up areas of the inner city. Similar programs developed under Bishop L. Morkovsky of the Catholic-Galveston-Houston Diocese and the First Presbyterian Church.[114]

Houston Jewish leaders began to realize that hiding behind the white majority would not help gain the rights they desired as Houstonians and as American Jews. Those Jews who publicly spoke on behalf of civil rights enabled the community to begin to change its unified response to the civil rights movement and also its Jewish identity within the white Gentile public sphere.

The fight over religion in the public schools awakened the city's Jews to the reality that to make a change, they could not stay quiet. The dual fights over religion in the schools and desegregation would continue, but change would be slow to come for both groups.

In the next chapter, I explore the rise of self-interest politics for both the city's Jews and African Americans. Houston's Jews began to embrace their identity as Jews and to reach out to African Americans in an ongoing way, even when the Black Power movement gave rise to concerns.

Chapter 7

Self-Interest Politics

Times change, moods change, needs change. We must
respond accordingly, but ... we are standing on the shoulders
of those who came before us.

Rabbi Samuel Karff
A Tribute to Spirit:
The Beth Israel Experience, 1975

hroughout the 1940s and 1950s, a fear of discrimination
from the white majority led Houston Jewish leaders to
differentiate themselves from African Americans. One important effort was Congregation Beth Israel's creation of the Basic
Principles in 1943, which defined Jews as white Americans of
Jewish faith. Moreover, the prospect of Israel's statehood raised
concerns that white Gentiles might see them as a non-American
minority. As one synagogue member put it, they thought whites
would say, "You now have a country of your own ... go there."[1]
Houston Jewish leadership also feared that expressing their
opinions on civil rights in public would hurt their social standing. Their approach only began to shift in the mid- to late 1950s

as local Jewish leaders considered what their role should be in the burgeoning civil rights movement. Still, they remained in the background, looking toward white Gentile leaders to make the first move.

The mid-1960s marked the beginning of change. Houston's Jews began to publicly express their interest in the Holocaust and Israel. In 1965, around 150 Jews protested at the German consulate in Houston regarding the potential end of the prosecution of Nazi war criminals.[2] Jewish Community Relations Council (JCRC) president Harold Falik signed a protest letter to German consul Ludwig Fabel: "The people of Jewish faith deserve all sympathy and support for what they suffered during World War II during Hitler's mass extermination of Jews."[3] Houston's Jews not only wanted justice for their past but also for their future. In 1966, a year before the Six-Day War, the formerly anti-Zionist Schachtel articulated his support of Israel and Jewish nationalism: "We must support Israel. It has nothing to do with whether you are a Jewish nationalist, a Zionist; it has to do with the fact that this is your people."[4] Schachtel's words corresponded with increased vocal support among Houston's Jews for Black rights, particularly for the desegregation of city schools. After the passing of the Civil Rights Act in 1964, they realized that equality for one meant equality for all.

But by the late 1960s, the mood in Houston had shifted again. The needs of local Jews and Black residents diverged. Two separate movements developed simultaneously: the Black Power movement and a new wave of American Zionism. In Houston, Jewish leaders tried to balance their concern for the rise of Black Power with their ongoing attention to the need of African Americans to voice their injustices and seek equality, especially after the TSU riot of 1967. At the same time, Jews began to embrace Zionism with more zeal, despite anti-Zionist sentiment looming in Houston. This period laid the foundation for how these two groups, with the assistance of their leaders, began to pursue group identity politics.

In the United States, Jews had gone through various political stages. During the period known as the Politics of Accommodation,

Jews took an interest in civil rights. After the Six-Day War, they shifted into the "politics of self-interest," focusing on international Jewish issues like Israel. Around the same time, many African Americans shifted away from civil rights activism to a focus on the emerging Black Power movement.[5] The following charts how this new era of self-interest politics changed the way Jewish and African American leaders interacted with each other.

Black Power Responses in Houston

African Americans continued to be disillusioned and frustrated with their second-class citizen status and the fact that they still faced poverty, blighted neighborhoods, lower wages, and higher unemployment rates. The Civil Rights Act of 1964 had not guaranteed a better life, and to many African Americans, Martin Luther King Jr.'s nonviolent approach appeared ineffectual. The Watts riots in Los Angeles in August 1965 were not the first racial riots the country had ever seen, yet their intensity paved the way for the Black Power movement.[6]

Even though the movement never became a powerful force in Houston, news reports of its development elsewhere frightened many residents. Many feared a local riot on Labor Day in 1965. In response to these fears, Mayor Louie Welch hired Houston sociologist Blair Justice to observe the city during the summer of 1965. Justice conducted interviews with Black residents living in blighted areas, including those who believed the solution to their problems was to riot. Justice was one among many sociologists after the Watts riots who visited Black communities throughout the country. When he published Violence in the City in 1969, he mentioned the disbelief one sociologist from California had when he came to Houston and saw the intense squalor of some Black residents, squalor the West Coast sociologist considered far worse than the conditions in Watts. He even went so far as to state that he seemed surprised that no rioting had ever occurred in Houston before, especially since the "abject conditions in some areas compared only with the squalor of slaves in the Old South."[7]

Such poverty spurred the growth of the Nation of Islam in Houston, which focused on empowering Black youth through education, particularly through learning Black history. Because the Nation of Islam saw public schools as perpetuating white supremacy, local members wanted to self-segregate and open a private school in Houston. Like other religious schools, they wanted to avoid government interference.[8]

Rabbi Schachtel addressed local plans to build a school and the rise of the Nation of Islam in Texas in his New Year sermon, "Some Predictions for 1966." He opposed the opening of a Nation of Islam school because he believed it would ignite trouble. Since the movement advocated separatism as a response to white oppression, Schachtel worried that disenfranchised Blacks would gravitate to the Nation of Islam in their quest for equality. He compared the youth in the Nation of Islam school to Ku Klux Klan youth, saying that both "are being trained night and day in this extreme philosophy [and] you are bound to have violence and we had better expect it." What concerned Schachtel most was Houston's stability and security. In response, he encouraged synagogues and churches to halt this movement through congregants becoming more inclusive of African Americans in religious life. This approach would diminish the Nation of Islam as a religious movement. Schachtel cautioned that if white Americans did not change their treatment of African Americans and accept them as equals, then the violence would continue and grow, as would the Nation of Islam.[9]

Between 1967 and 1971, the Nation of Islam took center stage in Houston when Muhammad Ali, the legendary boxer who famously fought in the Astrodome, moved to the city. Ali, a conscientious objector and a Nation of Islam minister, declared his residency in Houston because he thought he could evade the draft more easily in a city that had been more welcoming to him than any other city in the United States. In fact, Houston honored Ali by naming a street after him. After declaring residency, Ali announced he was going to fight there, preach there, live there, and help uplift the city's Black communities. In addition, he sought to prevent any wide-scale protest in his name because he did not want to incite violence in Houston. In order to avoid the draft, Ali hired a civil liberties lawyer to help him fight for recognition as a Nation of Islam minister, but Local Board No. 47 in Kentucky denied Ali's conscientious objector claim in June 1967.[10] Ali eventually received a five-year jail sentence and a $10,000 penalty for draft evasion. Judge Roy Hofheinz offered to throw out the conviction if Ali signed a five-year boxing contract with Houston, but Ali refused. The US Supreme Court eventually overturned the decision.[11]

In addition to Ali and the Nation of Islam, the Houston press focused on the racial tensions radiating from the city's college campuses. Tensions rose as African Americans faced hostility from police and persistent inequality.

On February 21, 1967, J. B. Stoner, the vice chairman of the white supremacist National States' Rights Party, spoke against Jews and African Americans at Rice University. At this small event—with only thirty-five people in attendance—Stoner advocated that Houston was about to undergo demographic change, and this new population wanted change and equal opportunity. The country would now become a nation of "faceless brown skinned, kinky-headed mongrels."[12] Not only did he want to keep African Americans jobless and politically disempowered; he also wanted to rid Jews of their wealth, which he claimed they used to control the United States and the NAACP.

Upon hearing of this event, seventeen Black students from the Student Nonviolent Coordinating Committee (SNCC), under the leadership of Reverend F. D. Kirkpatrick, came to Rice to condemn Stoner. These students successfully chased Stoner off the Rice campus, as reported in the school's newspaper.[13]

On March 21, 1967, Bernard Friedberg, the South Texas regional director of the ADL, spoke at the University of Texas at Austin Hillel about the failures of integration in Texas. He stressed that because African Americans consistently faced inequality, it would not surprise him if "young Negroes in Houston [were] willing to set the torch to communities until something is done."[14]

Black discontent and the Black Power movement came to a head on Houston campuses two months later, in May 1967.

It was then that TSU students rose to action. The media blamed Black Power leader Stokely Carmichael—who had spoken at the University of Houston and TSU the previous month—for influencing events, as he had in Nashville at Fisk University.[15]

TSU had already kicked the Friends of SNCC off campus for protesting police brutality in Houston and inciting students. Administrators tried to thwart any discontent on campus, but TSU students—like the student protesters before them—seethed with anger over the inequality that African Americans still faced from the police and the city of Houston. They saw Chief Herman Short as the embodiment of all the violent injustices that the Houston police had committed against African Americans. Moreover, the students protested the presence of landfills and dumps in Black neighborhoods and the city's lack of attention to health and safety concerns. Mayor Welch did nothing to stop the influx of garbage into their neighborhood, nor did he install any security measures. As a result, an eleven-year-old Black child drowned in a pond filled with garbage. Despite their fears having become a reality, the police instead arrested the protesters, including Reverend Lawson.[16]

Anger intensified when a false rumor circulated that a white police officer had shot a six-year-old Black child. The child was white, but the enraged students protested, leading police to surround the campus. Some students threw rocks, bottles, and watermelon rinds in the streets. Lawson and Mayor Welch tried to stop the riot, but chaos ensued after the police heard a shot.[17]

In reaction, Chief Short led a police raid, with officers shooting some three thousand rounds on campus. In response, many students hid in the dorms. Five hundred police officers entered the men's dormitory. The police arrested 488 students, an excessive number considering not all the students who'd been arrested had been participating in the protests.[18] According to Lawson, "There was never any evidence that there had been guns inside the dormitory. The only thing that was going on was all the loud epithets by these students, mostly outside the dormitories."[19] He recalled that "the cops were enraged, they cut up their beds, tore down doors."[20] In the aftermath of the riot, two police officers were wounded, one officer died from a bullet wound to the forehead, and one student was injured.[21]

Despite the police destroying radios, televisions, and students' textbooks and papers just one week prior to exams, the media portrayed the students as villains. In response, Lawson wrote in the Forward Times, "It has been called a riot, but most of the ingredients of a riot were absent. There was no evidence of looting ... there was no evidence of widespread resistance to arrest, even though brutality by police was painfully obvious."[22] From his perspective, what occurred was "police terrorism."[23] In the end, the Houston police charged five students with instigating a riot and causing the death of the police officer. The Houston Legal Defense Fund Committee Public Rally program supported all the legal fees for the arrested students. In the officer shooting, the evidence proved that a ricocheted bullet had killed him, and the trial ended in a mistrial due to lack of evidence.[24]

In response, former Houston Chronicle journalist Saul Friedman spoke to the Houston Council on Human Relations to draw a parallel between the TSU protesters and the Jews of Nazi Germany because both had faced extreme prejudice and second-class treatment. From his perspective, the hatred toward African Americans was not any different from Nazi Germany's treatment of Jews. Friedman also wanted to press upon his audience that TSU students did not riot solely because of economics—since most protesters came from middle-class Black families—but rather out of frustration with the burden of institutionalized prejudice. Friedman emphasized to the white liberals in the audience that one can have lectures and create programs targeting poverty and talk about Black discrimination, but the real solution had to come from listening to Black voices and changing one's attitude.[25]

The crux of protester frustration was the Houston Police Department's disrespect and treatment of them as criminals. The TSU riot also brought to the surface the Black community's overwhelming contempt for Chief Short, whom they saw as the instigator of police brutality. Short ran his department, according to Mimi Swartz, like a "stereotypical Alabama State Trooper."[26]

Many, including African Americans, were positive he was a member of the Klan. The Jewish civil rights lawyer David Berg even accused Short of being a "Klansman"[27] and took on "the Klan ridden Houston Police Department" in several high-profile cases, many with the ACLU.[28] Chief Short refuted Berg's portrayal: "I am not a Klansman, and I know of no police officer who is a Klansman. You can't fault a man, however, for praising God, country, and obedience to law and order."[29] The *New York Times* challenged Short's statement that the police did not have Klan involvement. Social activist Laurence Payne argued, "Short did more harm to race relations than anyone else." He simply "put fuel on the fire."[30]

As much as discontent with the police brewed after the TSU riots, certain efforts to change Houston's social climate gained traction. One Jewish activist by the name of Jo Marks took it upon herself to seek the input of Martin Luther King Jr. himself.

Martin Luther King Jr.'s Impact in Houston

Jo and Adie Marks had a long history of working with local Black activists. They were involved in the public relations campaign to elect Hattie Mae White to the school board. In addition to wanting to deliver aid to Houston's Black community, they sought to increase social awareness of Black causes and the ongoing fight for equality. To this end, Jo Marks contacted King through his public relations manager, Carol Hoover.

King agreed to hold a benefit concert in Houston to support local Black programs with the assistance of the Southern Christian Leadership Conference. King felt that the Black Power movement had deterred some white liberals from funding civil rights programs and believed that a concert would help bring them back to the fold.[31] Most of all, Jo and Adie Marks and other organizers wanted this concert to be a positive step toward making Houston a model for civil rights activism. Houston could no longer hide behind its international Space City image; it needed to innovate in other ways. The Markses wanted "Houston to become an example to the Nation" by establishing "a new, sensible and positive approach to the civil rights problem."[32]

The concert, starring Harry Belafonte and Aretha Franklin, took place on October 17, 1967, at the Sam Houston Coliseum, with four thousand in attendance. While it set out to be a uniting event, divisive protesters broke their way into the event. The Houston Chronicle reported that "with no warning, the acrid fumes from two stink bombs wafted through the hall. Hundreds stumbled toward the exits." Though prejudice could have led to another Selma, King was able to calm the situation and turn it into a teachable moment: "We have problems here tonight ... The forces of evil are always around."[33] In his last visit to Houston before he died, he pleaded for national unity. He may not have come to help the PYA during the sit-ins, but his final appearance made a lasting impact on the city.

After King's assassination on April 4, 1968, many African Americans held a memorial service at Emancipation Park on April 14. One speaker was former SNCC member Lee Otis Johnson, a known activist on TSU's campus. Johnson spoke disparagingly about Mayor Welch and Chief Short, holding them responsible for Black mistreatment. Three days later, on April 17, the police arrested and charged Johnson with possession and distribution of marijuana.

Abbie Lipschutz, a Jewish diamond wholesaler and left-wing activist, created the Lee Otis Johnson Defense Fund. Lipschutz and others believed the police unfairly framed Johnson because of the defamatory statements he made about city officials. Lipschutz thought the justice system was unable to fairly try any African Americans. He felt that "it was time for Blacks to take their struggle into their own hands."[34] Lipschutz's committee brought in over one hundred supporters. In fact, his committee was so effective that when the governor of Texas, Preston Smith, came to speak at the University of Houston, the crowd began chanting "free Lee Otis now!" The AJC's legal committee, after hearing about the Johnson case, prepared an appeal and eventually prevailed. After a federal judge had determined the sentence to be unfair, he reduced his thirty-year sentence to four years.[35]

Overall, King's death did not usher in a period of violence in Houston, as occurred in other parts of the country; however, Jewish Houstonians remained concerned. Theodore Freedman, the Southwest director of the ADL, saw King's death as the beginning of possible new problems. He blamed white Americans for not working toward equal rights for African Americans. As much as he disapproved of rioting, he saw it as a likely product of prejudice. Melvin Waxler, then editor of the Jewish teen column for the *JH-V*, feared that the civil rights movement would become a movement "for revenge" because of the death of Dr. King and the rise of Black Power.[36]

As much as many Jews feared the possibility of riots, they also took the time to reflect on King's impact. A peaceful march of Black and white religious leaders—Jewish and Christian alike—occurred, during which several Houston Jewish leaders paid tribute to the late Dr. King. In a sermon at Congregation Beth Yeshurun, Malev described him as a prophet. In The Informer, Cahana noted King's impact on American history as a parallel to that of Moses and the Israelites. He wanted people to continue the fight, even if King, like Moses, could not lead African Americans to the promised land of freedom.[37]

In the summer of 1968, the Houston JCC made an unprecedented move when it opened its doors to disadvantaged Black youth on Saturdays. Since the program was on the Sabbath, the Houston Rabbinical Council and the Jewish Community Council had to approve it. The opening of the center made international Jewish news. The Houston Jewish leaders agreed to proceed, according to the JTA, "as a measure to fight racial divisiveness" and to "establish a close understanding of the concern of the Jewish community for the welfare of the underprivileged." The compromise made was that none of the JCC staff would receive payment for their work—because of the Sabbath—but some of the staff members would volunteer at the center on Saturdays to train African Americans to be program directors. The president of the JCC, Harold Falik, reported to the JH-V that the decision to welcome African Americans on the Sabbath was "following the wishes of a vast majority of our community."[38]

In 1969, Black Houstonians created a community center similar to the JCC called SHAPE. Based on Black Power ideology, its purpose was to help families, children, and parents by promoting programs that fortified Black empowerment, promoted health and wellness, honored African celebrations like Kwanzaa, and provided an open forum for community discussion. Its mission statement was "to improve the quality of life for people of African descent (all people) through programs and activities, with emphasis on Unity, Self-Determination, Collective Work & Responsibility, Cooperative Economics, Purpose, Creativity, and Faith."[39]

The JCC initiative brought international attention to Houston's Jews because it demonstrated that Jews and African Americans could interact peacefully with each other in the midst of this social unrest. This perception was in stark contrast to cities throughout the United States that faced riots out of reaction to King's death. For example, Black protesters in Cincinnati damaged and burned the Rockdale Temple, a Reformed synagogue.[40] However, Houston was different. Although prejudice did exist between these two communities, it did not result in open antagonism. In fact, in the late 1960s the city's Black and Jewish leaders collaborated to join the organization Citizens for Good Schools. Both groups wanted to replace the members of the school board who prevented Jews and Blacks from having a voice in the public school system. Carter Wesley joined the fight to oust the school board, placing the majority of the blame for the "infectious running sores" in the city on their negative influence. In his opinion, they "had not taken a single positive step in the direction of racial understanding but had antagonized the Negro community constantly."[41]

Citizens for Good Schools and Crossover Programs

In the spring of 1967, Houston Jewish businessman Vic Samuels emerged as a significant leader in the school desegregation movement. This was when Samuels saw firsthand the problems on the school board. He was concerned over teacher salaries, lack of air-conditioning in the schools, and slow integration. These concerns led Samuels to form a small group focused on replacing outgoing board members. The group backed George Oser, a white Catholic physicist. However, before the election even took place, Oser's name mysteriously disappeared from the ballot, most likely because of his devotion to integration.[42]

Frustrated with school board politics, Samuels and a few other residents started Citizens for Good Schools (CGS) in December 1967. The group eventually grew to have 3,500 members, some of whom were Jews and African Americans. A number of Jews from Cahana's Congregation Brith Shalom joined.[43] The mission of CGS was to "engage in comprehensive research into educational issues and to wage another political campaign."[44] Most concerned with the lack of diversity and integration in Houston's public schools, the group produced newsletters, implemented research committees, and organized public meetings where they voiced the need for change in Houston's educational system. The CGS not only promoted the "orderly and legal process of desegregation of the schools," it sought to create a "total environment" in which students learned effectively. In addition, it also advocated for particular teacher training that focused on "crossing over from a segregated teaching situation to an integrated one."[45] They asked Regina Goff, the assistant commissioner of the Office of Disadvantaged, to provide funding for teacher training workshops and conferences.[46]

CGS members held debates all over Houston, from people's houses to the Miller Amphitheater, which could seat one thousand. Not surprisingly, Samuels faced discrimination during these debates. One person even asked him whether he had gone to Brandeis—which Samuels had learned was code for being Jewish—and he said yes. An attendee later told him that he lost the debate because he revealed his identity as a Jew. He learned, even in school politics, that whenever he debated, he had to be careful about revealing any personal information.[47]

Coinciding with CGS was the Faculty Crossover Program, a 1967 program started by the HISD board of trustees to initiate integration of the public schools. The program's goal was to recruit new teachers, both white and African American, to teach in a school where they would be the minority. The HISD referred to the teachers who volunteered for this program as "voluntary Crossover teachers." Former "voluntary" Jewish Crossover teacher Susan Septimus remembered that these "teachers were arbitrarily assigned schools to meet racial parity goals." According to Septimus, one of the major flaws of the program was that often "newly graduated, inexperienced Caucasian teachers were going into Black schools, while *experienced* Black teachers were transferring to predominantly Caucasian schools." Septimus first became a Crossover teacher after she finished college in 1969. The HISD assigned her to teach fifth grade at Frederick Douglass Elementary. All her life she had attended segregated schools in Houston. Being a Crossover teacher was a "total culture shock." Everyone in her class was African American, and all the teachers were African American except for two Jewish Crossover teachers. Despite Principal Lawrence Marshall's support, Septimus still felt like a "misfit."[48]

The disparity in education was striking to Septimus, as was the disturbing degree of poverty. She remembered children often coming to school hungry. Out of his own salary, Principal Marshall paid for student breakfasts. Many students did not have the funds for school supplies, so Septimus paid for those materials out of her own salary of $5,600. Her fifth-grade students read at a third-grade level. Also, as she remarked, "many of the students had never been outside the confines of their school neighborhood." Septimus redeveloped the curriculum and used "maps and other materials, instead of social studies textbooks, using reading materials appropriate to students' abilities and interests, and teaching geography and history relevant to the children's neighborhood." She even brought in speakers like Judge Andrew Jefferson to introduce the students to the leaders of their community. The experience enlightened her to the educational differences between white schools and predominantly Black schools.[49]

One of the most publicized stories from the Crossover Program was of Ernestine Stewart Mitchell, an African American elementary school teacher who worked for the HISD starting in 1957 at the all-Black Gregory School in the Fourth Ward. Mitchell had worked there for ten years, until 1967, when she decided to participate in the Crossover Program. The HISD sent Mitchell to Kolter Elementary School in southwest Houston, which at the time had a significant population of "mostly prominent Jews."[50]

She was apprehensive about transferring to Kolter because she felt that she had a moral obligation to teach disadvantaged Black children. However, her college professors persuaded her to take the leap. At Kolter, she taught some of the children from the families who ran the Jewish department stores in Houston, including the Levits, the Battelsteins, and the Weiners. She was the first Black teacher ever employed at the school. She said, "I really worried that one of them might call me a nigger. They can become very angry with you and say almost anything. But do you know, I have never heard that word in all the time I've been here?"[51]

Through her experience in the Crossover Program, Mitchell discovered a way to mitigate differences without causing tensions between whites and African Americans. Her plan was to discuss the topic of "differences." When the subject came up during a lesson on colors, she remembered, "We were talking about colors one day, you know, 'Red—an apple is red.' We came to brown and they all said, 'We know what's brown, Mrs. Mitchell. You're brown!'" The children shocked Mitchell when they simply stated she was brown. As she said, however, "It couldn't have been simpler." She had expected them to say more—to define her based on the Black stereotypes that resulted from segregation. She realized that to teach the children effectively, she should not concentrate on how they might negatively perceive her. She needed to have pride in herself so the children would respect her. She believed her experience was exceptional because "not everyone is going to move into a situation as ideal as this one."[52]

While Septimus and Mitchell did have fulfilling learning experiences in the Crossover Program, the initiative overall was a failure. Black teacher Howard Jefferson was a voluntary

Crossover teacher at Bellaire High School. In 1969, the predominantly white and Jewish school had only ten Black students.
Jefferson saw firsthand the disparity between Houston's white
and Black schools. What was missing in Black schools was
parental support, better facilities, and better academics.[53]

The CGS was aware of these realities and knew that for
change to happen they had to change the mentality of the school
board. In 1969, CGS created a ticket for the upcoming school
board election. Hattie Mae White had already lost her reelection
in 1967. Butler's term was up, and he had chosen not to run
again. Barnstone had won awards for her outstanding service
from Jewish, Catholic, and Black organizations, but she could
not bring herself to serve a second term. As Vic Samuels recalled,
CGS's tagline was "quality integrated education" with a focus
on financial stability.[54]

The JH-V endorsed CGS's proposed board for the year
1970. It included the Jewish medical doctor Leonard Robbins,
Reverend Leon Everett, Eleanor Tinsley, and—in his second
attempt at candidacy—Dr. Oser.[55] According to Samuels, it
"was the first time in Houston a multiracial ticket had been put
together."[56] Everett was not a politician, but he had a strong
influence in the Baptist Ministers Association and was the
leader of the NAACP. The Black community, including Reverend
Lawson and Judge Andrew Jefferson, strongly supported CGS
and helped mobilize voters.[57]

The JH-V reported on the anti-Semitism that Robbins faced
during the election. At the National Cash Register building on
November 24, 1969, 125 individuals attended a Houston School
Board election debate. Afterward, someone remarked, "all that was
lacking at the close of the meeting was 'Heil Hitler.'" Bob Eckles,
a former president of the Houston School Board, and H.W. Lois
Cullen, a school board member, expelled the "venom." The *JH-V*
perceived the event as "a call to open hatred, a call for prejudice
and antagonism. It was directed against the Jewish candidate—
Dr. Leonard Robbins." The newspaper exclaimed to its readers,
"*They must be defeated*—this old bunch of mud-rakers. If you
want sound education, if you want decency in our schools," voters

needed to vote for Tinsley, Everett, Robbins, and Oser. At the debate, Cullen had said, "Ask Robinovitz or whatever he calls himself—How does he feel about those skits at Christmas?"[58] Religion in the schools was still a problem, but the members of CGS had tabled this fight until they changed the makeup of the board.

In the end, Houstonians voted to elect CGS candidates. These changes to the school board, however, did not alter the lack of quality community educational spaces for the city's African Americans. For this reason, Black Power advocates continued to advocate for change. While Houston's Jews remained supportive of Black educational causes—even those based on Black Power ideology—they continued to have an uneasy relationship with the local Black Power movement.

HISD school board members taking oath of office; includes Eleanor Tinsley. January 5, 1970. RGD0006N-1970-0027-28, Houston Post Photographs, Houston Metropolitan Research Center, Houston Public Library. Bill Thompson_HP/©Houston Chronicle. Used with permission.

From the Black Power Movement to Zionism

Despite comparing Black Power to the Jewish fight for recognition of the State of Israel, Rabbi William Malev criticized what he saw as the reckless decision of the Black Power movement to reject alliances with other groups. He did not believe that the movement would be able to bring about equality for African Americans on its own. Malev argued that "no minority has ever achieved liberation without the help and cooperation of the right-thinking groups in the general community."[59] Just as the Jews could not solve their problems on their own, African Americans also required outside support. He gave the example of Israel, which had required the support of non-Jews like Harry Truman to acknowledge Israel as an independent state.

Malev's perspective on Israel did not consider the political climate in Houston after the Six-Day War. The war empowered American Jews but also isolated them from those Americans who viewed Israel more as an aggressor than a victor. Many Black and white Houstonians did not support Israel. The 1943 predictions of Congregation Beth Israel that Zionism would isolate local Jews from their white Gentile peers had come true. Yet over the course of twenty years, the calculus had changed for the city's Jews who had prioritized the issues of Israel and their community above their desire to fit in. They committed themselves to the cause of Israel through raising money and promoting awareness in synagogues and the Jewish press.[60]

In 1967, one of the greatest challenges affecting the American Jewish community was anti-Zionism, a broad term that encompassed both religious intolerance and political opposition to the State of Israel. Anti-Zionism also took on economic significance as Israel became entangled in the oil crisis. As the home to the largest petrochemical complex in the world, Houston was the epicenter of the oil industry. Because of this, Houston's thriving economy often mirrored the global economy's relationship with OPEC and thus the ongoing Arab-Israeli crisis.[61]

Tensions between the Arab nations and Israel would bring about US oil shortages and shifting oil prices, and Houston had to use reserves to make up for shortages when Arab oil compa-nies instituted embargoes against the United States for its rela-tionship with Israel. The Arab oil embargo after the Six-Day War forced Houston's oil industry to make up the shortages again, which caused profits to fall and gas prices to increase in the city. The average Houston consumer did not care about Israel and was instead focused on how oil prices affected their daily lives. Boiling frustration led members of the Houston Jewish commu-nity to receive hate mail.

On November 30, 1967, the JH-V sent out a warning to the Jewish community about a hate letter called "The Patriot" circu-lating throughout Houston. The letter, issuing a security threat to the Jewish community, was mailed anonymously to all the Jews in Houston as well as Jews in other Texan cities. It warned them—"Jews Beware"—and threatened death through cyanide gas fumes, arsenic, shooting, strangling, or stabbing. By calling themselves "patriots," the writers placed themselves in oppo-sition to Jews. Although the letter did not say so explicitly, some believed that American support for the State of Israel had prompted the hostile letter. The oil crisis was directly harming the Houston economy, as well as that of other Texan cities.[62]

The JH-V investigated and discovered the authors: the anti-Communist Minutemen, which had close ties with the National States' Rights Party, a white supremacist group founded in 1958 in Tennessee. A month earlier, the national director of the ADL, Benjamin R. Epstein, had spoken in Houston about how the Palestine Liberation Organization (PLO) and the Palestine Arab Delegation used the National States' Rights Party to disseminate anti-Semitic and anti-Zionist propaganda. The PLO had a history of utilizing white supremacists in this way. Thus, the Minute-men's hate letter to the Jews of Houston was part of a larger trend of using scare tactics to defuse American Jewish support for Israel and redirect Jewish loyalties. It was certainly no coincidence that the letter appeared only six months after the Six-Day War.[63]

In the summer of 1967, the SNCC addressed Jewish support of Israel in one of their newsletters. Curtis Graves, the first Black Texas representative since 1899, responded to the newsletter with a "strongly worded" editorial in the Houston Informer.[64] The JH-V discussed how Graves labeled the SNCC visibly anti-Zionist and anti-Semitic. Graves did not understand why the SNCC had sided with the Arabs against Israel, and he compared the SNCC's position on Jews to that of the John Birch Society or the Ku Klux Klan. He questioned what the SNCC had to gain from their hostility. Yet the SNCC's reason for aligning with the Arab position was that many Black Power leaders with whom the SNCC identified saw their marginalized status in the United States as comparable to the Palestinian cause. For Black Power leaders, Israel's victory transformed that state from being a victim to being colonialist.[65]

Graves was less concerned about the Israeli-Palestinian conflict than he was about engaging the city's Jews about national media coverage of the tension between Jews and African Americans. On November 16, 1968, Graves spoke at the JCC about "The Image of the Jew in the Negro Community."[66] He addressed "Negro Anti-Semitism, Jewish store owners and landlords, Jewish influence in the ghetto, and Negro identification with the Jews."[67] To reach individuals in both the Black and Jewish communities, both *The Informer* and the *JH-V* advertised the event.

By the late 1960s, the *JH-V* had become a consistent voice against the rise of Black anti-Semitism in the United States. Though it did not report on this phenomenon in Houston specifically, the city's Jews were aware of its effects and wanted to promote peace and reconciliation between the two communities. They had a lot in common. Both faced antagonism in their pursuit of carving out their identity in a predominantly white and Christian city. Both saw self-interest politics as integral to being heard. While African Americans fought for full representation, the city's Jews confronted anti-Zionism.

Anti-Zionism in Houston

The rise of anti-Zionism in Houston was not directly correlated with the rise of Black Power, perhaps because interest in Black Power waxed and waned among Black residents so much that it did not become a widespread movement. Additionally, African Americans continued to be focused on the struggle for their civil rights, which left little time for anti-Zionism. Most of all, Black political leadership gradually began to see the value of securing connections within the Houston Jewish community. Reverend Lawson had already made huge inroads in developing a connection with the local Jewish community through attendance at numerous events and regular interactions with Jewish leaders.[68]

Despite this progress, Jewish leaders knew Israel remained a source of contention since they continued to receive hate mail. In "A New Approach Needed," David White commented that by the end of 1968, the public mindset toward Israel had rapidly changed because of the Six-Day War.[69] In a subsequent article in the JH-V on January 30, 1969, White reported that several Jews who had written editorials for local newspapers in defense of Israel found themselves "deluged" with hate mail. Additionally, other Jewish residents received "crude handwritten" hate letters, post-marked with a Bellaire zip code. According to Theodore Freedman of the ADL, these letters "denounce[d] Jews and state[d] 'we should complete Hitler's job and rid the world of Jews.'"[70]

Freedman sent the letters to the FBI for analysis, but the culprits remained a mystery. Furthermore, additional hate letters arrived, likely from the small and relatively new Arab population in Houston. These letters were written under the guise of prominent Houston oil business leaders accusing Jews of being "exploiters and saying Americans have been brainwashed in favor of this communistic country."[71] In February 1969, Freedman blamed the Houston Arab Chamber of Commerce in the JH-V for these letters, claiming it had instigated a conspiracy that linked Israel with Communism. Their letters implied that support of Israel endangered the safety of the United States. In response to the influx of hate mail, the Houston Jewish community hosted several events to educate the city and garner solid support for the State of Israel.[72]

The Six-Day War evoked a sense of pride among American Jews. Jews had emerged as the victors—for better or for worse—in contrast to their prior image as victims of the Holocaust.

This made Houston's Jews more confident about declaring themselves publicly as Jewish. Congregation Beth Israel's Basic
Principles, which had decreed that its members were "Caucasian"
and had rejected the State of Israel, were now obsolete, and on
December 9, 1968, the congregation eliminated them.[73]

On February 23, 1969, the community sponsored a city-
wide public event at Congregation Beth Israel. The goal was to
promote awareness of the crisis in the Middle East and how it
affected local Jews. JCRC president Leo Horvitz stressed how
many Jews in Arab countries lived in constant fear, bound by
severe daily restrictions. JCRC director Albert Goldstein told the
community at large that one did not need to be Jewish to support
Israel. Rather, he stated, "humane considerations of the plight
of a country whose civilian population is constantly subject to
attack from armed terrorists are compelling."[74] Additionally,
Goldstein explained that the Soviet Union was sending weapons
and advisers and training Arab countries to fight Israel. The intent
of this statement was to garner support of Israel from non-Jewish Americans and to demonstrate that Israel was on the side of
American democracy, while Arabs were pro-Communism.

Israel remained the JCRC's primary concern. As its president stated, "Israel's victory in the '67 war, instead of being
followed by lasting peace, was leading instead to the reawakening of anti-Semitism."[75] This reemergence led the JCRC to initiate educational programs to provide accurate information about
Israel to Houstonians.

In 1970, the Jewish Community Council began to hear
complaints from Jewish parents in Houston about the disturbing
rise of anti-Semitism in the public schools. At Bellaire High School
in 1969, Jewish parents had protested unsuccessfully about the
school scheduling graduation on the Jewish Sabbath. In response
to this and other incidents, Congregation Beth Yeshurun initiated
a series of interfaith panel discussions called Ladder of Learning.
One discussion titled "Religion in the School" brought together
a panel of Jews, Catholics, and Protestants to discuss issues like
Christmas, the closing of schools in Jewish neighborhoods on
Jewish holidays, the removal of "non-denominational" prayers,

religious speakers in the schools, and religious education. When Houston Jewish leaders began to consider the role of religion in schools, once again they realized that for change to occur they needed to not only work within the Jewish community; they also had to gain the support of non-Jews.[76]

Rabbi Robert Kahn once described the process of desegregation as "swallowing a bitter pill" to convince Houstonians to move forward and not let their prejudices dictate what was best for all of Houston. However, after watching along with the rest of the world as Neil Armstrong walked on the moon, he had a different perspective. Kahn could not believe that in his lifetime an astronaut would walk on the moon. It prompted him to realize: if NASA could put an astronaut on the moon, the country should be able to come together to solve the problem of Black inequality.[77]

In his 1969 Rosh Hashanah sermon, Kahn described NASA's achievement as a symbol of the potential of humans to create tremendous change over a short period of time to benefit humankind. Throughout his sermon, he repeated the mantra "we can do anything" to help his audience internalize that they could be the change makers. He encouraged the Jewish community to be the "we" for social change, just as scientists were the "we" for technological advancement. Putting an astronaut on the moon took a decade. Integration might take even longer. Kahn criticized African Americans for losing their patience and turning to "revolutionary" movements like Black Power that could only lead to white backlash. What Kahn failed to account for, however, was the ongoing economic degradation of Houston's Black residents and how that fueled an interest in Black Power.[78]

Black Economic Disparity in Houston

In Houston, desegregation and the passing of the Civil Rights Act had not granted the largest Black population in the South full access to the economic sphere. Higher unemployment rates and ongoing discrimination led to further efforts to demand that companies employ Black workers with equal pay and that unions fairly represent African Americans in all sectors of industry.[79] To address the issue, the US Equal Employment Opportunity Commission held public hearings on employment in Houston, Los Angeles, and New York in 1970. While some corporations refused to participate, several did, including Foley's.

The commission assessed the top private companies in Houston that did not employ minorities, specifically those in the chemical, liquid hydrocarbon, and petroleum industries. While they employed forty thousand people collectively, only 4.4 percent of the employees were African American. The commission also revealed the disparities in the oil industry's hiring structure. Approximately 9 percent of hires were minorities, but the oil industry had yet to elevate a minority to an executive position. Only 2 percent of African Americans had white-collar jobs. Further, the commission revealed that out of the forty-six major urban areas in the United States, Houston ranked at the bottom in hiring minorities.[80]

In the local commission meeting, Reverend Lawson stated, "Houston is a City that is built around the Anglo Man." By defining the "Anglo man" as white, Christian, and male, he excluded Jews from this category, in large part because Jews experienced bigotry as well. Despite the role that Houston's Jewish business owners played in segregation, Lawson still perceived them—even a decade later—as a group that the "Anglo man discriminated against" economically.[81] While Houston Jews had seen larger gains—for example, in the 1960s, they were slowly gaining employment into major law firms—the AJC and the ADL struggled to obtain employment for Jews at oil companies like Humble Oil. In the 1970s, Jews still had problems gaining access to the oil, banking, and gas industries. One reason they failed to gain traction in the oil industry was because of the industry's ties to the Arab world.[82] Companies feared hiring Jews in managerial positions because, as one Jewish Houstonian explained, "the big insurance firms, banks, oil, and gas [were] still very much WASP controlled. They are afraid that if a Jew buys, he'll put in three Jewish vice presidents and, then, there go[es] the three slots for *their* boys."[83]

While Houston's Jews experienced job discrimination, it was not to the degree of African Americans. Foley's had Jewish executives, a status an African American would not achieve until much later. Moreover, the focus of Jews' anger was that they could not always attain higher positions, like at Humble Oil, whereas African Americans struggled to even ascend above the lowest ranked positions.

The commission hosted a session on the local Jewish community, but for unknown reasons, the proceedings were not included in the final report. The most provocative point made at the commission came from Yolanda Birdwell, a representative of the Mexican American Youth Organization. Birdwell argued: "We want change, and we want this discrimination to stop." She knew that it would be difficult because "the ones that have the power, they're out there and they have all got the lawyers on their side. They have everything, but I'd like to tell them this: we got the people, you know."[84]

Birdwell spoke on behalf of all minorities, especially Mexican Americans, who were part of the city's emerging Chicano movement that wanted Houston to recognize them as a minority that was neither Black nor white. This and other movements revealed the extent to which Houston's Black-white divide was beginning to be dismantled.[85]

When Laurence Payne first came to Houston in 1968, he was involved in activism at Saint Thomas University and TSU. He connected early on with Houston Jewish leaders, joined the JCC, and met the staff of the *JH-V*, the ADL, and the National Council for Christians and Jews. He understood the relationship between Black and Jewish leaders to be individual and based on "mutual trust and respect." Payne recalled that the first dialogue between Jewish and Black leaders in the 1970s came through the Houston Metropolitan Ministries, an organization he felt enabled people to come together across "ethnic" and "religious" boundaries. He noted that when it came to Black-Jewish interactions, "if you cared to get involved there were opportunities."[86]

One unexpected place for dialogue was Alfred's Delicatessen. Payne commented that Alfred's had become the "unofficial" place

for Black-Jewish dialogue. He remembered the table in the back
where these discussions occurred. They had "heavy integration
and racial" discussions "over food and fellowship," including
Jewish lox and bagels. At Alfred's, they could have the kinds of
discussions that they could not have "over the phone."[87]

These open discussions, however, were few and far between.
In 1970, *Black Enterprise* published a profile of Houston
in which it said the city appeared to the world as "a model
of success in contemporary America." However, the author
claimed that Houston was "among the most backward of U.S.
cities." Economics always took center stage in Houston, and
"in Houston, prosperity [was] labeled 'white only.'" The city
spent millions of dollars to build the Astrodome and the Space
Center but neglected the blighted and poverty-stricken areas
where minorities resided. The city of progress was a facade.[88]

In addition to grappling with employment disparity, African
Americans who owned businesses in Houston struggled to entice
consumers who still favored white-owned stores. Even African
Americans did not always patronize Black businesses. According to *Black Enterprise*, Black business owners faced two major
hurdles: a lack of a central Black community and the fact that
African Americans only bought goods from Black business to
meet specific African American needs, like beauty items. One
frustrated Black business owner said, "They'd rather trade with
the same racist and Klansman who is oppressing us now and who
use the money that they give him to pay his dues in the Klan."[89]

Moreover, Blacks also had trouble getting loans to expand or
start new businesses. In response, several Black leaders created
organizations to assist the failing Black businesses. Reverend
Earl Allen, the founder of Human, Organizational, Political,
Economic Development, Inc. (HOPE), worked to help African
Americans of lower socioeconomic status start businesses. They
also created an antipoverty organization, launched a newspaper called *Voice of Hope*, and contributed to the development
of housing projects. Reverend Lawson and Pluria Marshall
developed Operation Breadbasket, under the Southern Christian Leadership of Houston, to promote economic growth in the

Black community. One of their achievements was convincing several businesses to give a percentage of their earnings back to the Black community. They also forced Burger King to give franchises to African Americans. Bill Lawton, a business adviser interviewed by *Black Enterprise*, detailed how crime pushed out Italian and Jewish grocers and stores and that Black entrepreneurs filled the gap. African Americans in high-crime areas encouraged whites, including Jewish and Italian landlords, to leave the neighborhood, in large part so that they could claim ownership of their space.[90]

But there were definite hurdles to Black economic and social advancement. In 1970, the Ku Klux Klan bombed the Pacifica Foundation Radio Station in the first and only bombing of a radio transmitter in an act of terrorism. Founded by Jo Marks, Pacifica Radio promoted free speech and activism. A Black listener explained, "There's a lot of people who want to be heard and they can't be heard. All they have to do is let Pacifica know about it and they'll be heard."[91]

Pacifica gave anyone a voice. This integrated station welcomed everyone. In the same year as the bombing, the People's Party II, which was part of the Black Panther Party, witnessed the fatal police shooting of the party's leader, Carl Hampton. A champion of anyone who wanted to fight the white power structure, Hampton implemented Black Panther Party ideals of self-protection, helped to feed and clothe the poor, and fought against police brutality. In reaction to Hampton's death, the Black Coalition boycotted downtown stores to convince white business leaders to pressure the Houston Police Department to end its brutality.[92]

Despite the efforts of the Black Coalition, Black Power activism was not widespread in the city. Houston, which prided itself on avoiding large-scale conflict, never had an incident on par with the Watts riots in Los Angeles, as it quickly used mediation to prevent escalation. Spread across neighborhoods, the city's Black residents were unable to form a cohesive community. And many of Houston's African Americans did not support activism. In 1974, Lawson reflected on the way Houston never "really produced a major crisis, never really produced a riot, never really produced the kind of charismatic leaders that came out of some of the other southern states," such as Dr. King in Georgia and the brothers Medgar and Charles Evers in Mississippi. Lawson believed this was because Houston—like Texas as a whole—wanted "to solve its own problems" without allowing the government to intervene. Houston churches had a "'let me do it myself' mentality," which did not foster interchurch alliances. The community had "shared very, very little in an organized Civil Rights organization" because the leadership handled the crisis before national civil rights leaders arrived to mediate the situation.[93] The city, thus, had gained the reputation of being asleep during the civil rights movement.

Black and Jewish self-interest politics defined the mid-1960s to 1970s as both groups wanted attention placed on their struggles. The city's Jews became preoccupied with their intrinsic international concerns, especially Israel. While they still wanted to change the public school system, they mostly oriented their efforts toward the Arab-Israeli conflict. The focus for the Houston Black community, on the other hand, centered on domestic issues and gaining first-class citizenship. At times leaders came together on certain issues, including the school board and civil rights, which helped to usher in the beginning of an alliance.

Still, Houston was about to undergo demographic change and the influx of new minorities who wanted change and equal opportunity. The period from 1970 to 1989 marked the onset of more substantive interactions between Jews and African Americans. The next chapter will show the ingenious way that politicians Barbara Jordan and especially Mickey Leland furthered this cross-cultural initiative as the climate of Houston changed into an international city.

Chapter 8

Black-Jewish Encounters in Houston

We are now a microcosm of America and the world.
Rabbi Samuel Karff
Interview with David Goldstein
December 4, 2007

he previous chapter detailed how Israel and the rise of Black Power failed to create a wedge between Houston's Jews and African Americans. Rather, the two communities managed to interact and even unite in the attempt to change the makeup of the school board. Beginning in the late 1960s, Houston started to undergo a transformation as a city. The migration of individuals from all over the world to work in the oil, petrochemical, and aerospace industries, coupled with the rise of Black political power, transformed Houston into a diverse and more welcoming city. Houston would remain conservative, but as the city's population changed and new minorities like Arabs, Vietnamese, Indians, and South Africans arrived, the city could no longer divide all its inhabitants into just Black and white.

Houston would become, as Rabbi Samuel Karff said, "a microcosm of America and the world."[1] This demographic shift demolished many of the color barriers that stood between Jews and African Americans and enabled them to realize they both had causes for which they needed to advocate. Although discrimination still existed, Jews no longer felt the same pressure from white Gentiles to conform. Moreover, in the 1970s, American Jews began to think about their identity in relation to Israel. Houston's Jews realized that, as a minority with specific political interests, they needed an active political presence.

At the same time, African Americans intensified their fight against discrimination and ongoing social and economic barriers. They realized the limitations of activism and began to transition to political leadership. Blacks may have been a minority in Houston, but redistricting in 1965 increased their political bargaining power. In the process, Black politicians reached out to the city's Jews to help facilitate interactions—a concept foreign under segregation. Houston's transformation from segregationist to culturally diverse spurred Black politicians to craft a political platform that benefited both Jews and African Americans. In this new environment of cultural diversity, Black politicians saw that self-interest politics could turn into mutual politics.

The rise of congressional leaders like Barbara Jordan and Mickey Leland solidified the emergence of an alliance as these leaders openly supported Israel. This dynamic between Houston's African Americans and Jews exemplified how much had changed in the city since Congregation Beth Israel's creation of the Basic Principles in 1943. The desire of Houston's Jews to increase Israel's security outweighed their need to conform to the status quo. The interactions between the Black and Jewish communities would reach its apex with Mickey Leland and his creation of the Mickey Leland Kibbutzim Internship. Many of the city's Jews publicly supported these representatives, despite the fact that the majority of Houston's Jews did not live in Congressional District 18 and could not vote for them.

Between the 1960s and 1980s, immigrants from all over the world, including Muslims, Buddhists, Hindus, and Zoroastrians,

Congresswoman Barbara Jordan and Mickey Leland at Wheatley High
School Alumni Day at "Deluxe Show," Delux Theater, 1971. Photo
Hickey-Robertson. Courtesy of Menil Archives, The Menil Collection,
Houston.

started moving to Houston to work for NASA and the petrochemical industry. Since Houston had become an international
business center in the 1970s, it was an ideal place for immigrants to find work. Another wave of immigrants, beginning in
the 1970s through the 1980s, came from Asia, the Middle East,

Europe, Central America, and Africa. By the 1980s, Houston became an international epicenter where Houstonians could experience world cultures without ever leaving the city proper. All in one city were specialty stores from around the world, diverse cuisines, and music and art from various cultures.[2] In the 1960s, whites accounted for 70 percent of the Houston population, African Americans 22.9 percent, Latinos 6.7 percent, and Asians 0.4 percent. However, by the 1970s whites comprised only 62.1 percent of Houston's population. The Black population grew to 25.7 percent; Latinos were 11.3 percent, and 0.9 percent were Asian. By the 1980s, whites decreased to 52.2 percent, whereas African Americans were 27.6 percent, Latinos 17.6 percent, and Asians 2.1 percent.[3]

From 1970 to 1980, Houston's Jewish population only grew from 1.67 percent to 1.69 percent.[4] Roslyn Barr of *Hadassah Magazine* wrote in the 1980s that the Houston Jewish population had become "a microcosm of American Jewry in its diversity of origins."[5] They came from the Soviet Union, South Africa, Iran, and Israel. Minority populations continued to increase as more immigrants from India and Pakistan arrived.[6] One highly visible symbol of Houston's increasing diversity was the construction of the nondenominational Rothko Chapel.

The Influence of Houston as an International City: From the Rothko Chapel to Its Effects on African Americans and Jews

On February 27, 1971, the dedication of the Rothko Chapel— a sanctuary for all religions—ushered in a new era for Houston as a multicultural city. John and Dominique de Menil, a prominent Catholic couple, became the chapel's patrons. They also happened to be supporters of the civil rights movement and one of the main financial supporters of the Black Panthers.

The Rothko Chapel was the physical representation of the aspirations of the civil rights movement. When Rabbi Cahana retired from Congregation Brith Shalom for health reasons, the de Menils asked him to become the chapel's director.

Even though it embodied everything he had dreamed of for the city, Cahana declined the offer.[7] According to his son Michael Cahana, his father saw the Rothko Chapel as a "platform to now build and expand on" the civil rights movement. Michael Cahana stated that Houston was "exactly the right place" for the chapel because it "did not have the race problems that other southern towns" had.[8]

The chapel became the first such ecumenical religious setting in the world. Without religious icons or symbols, its only connection with religion was the shape of the building, which looked like a Greek cross, but in design it was representative of many backgrounds. One of the architects was the Jewish Houstonian Howard Barnstone, and Mark Rothko, a Russian-born Jewish abstract painter, designed the panels inside the chapel. Chosen by the de Menils to represent the late Dr. King, *Broken Obelisk* by Jewish sculptor Barnett Newman stood on a wooden platform adjacent to the reflecting pool.[9] The Rothko Chapel became known as "an 'oasis of stillness' in busy, noisy Houston" where people could silently meditate or unite to pray.[10] As a symbol of religious and cultural plurality, the chapel broke down remaining barriers in the city. Events such as a bar mitzvah ceremony, a lecture on the "World Fellowship of Religions" by a Jain monk, a Buddhist wedding, a Quaker meeting, a Christian memorial service, a Muslim celebration (Eid al-Adha), and an annual observance of Dr. King's birthday all took place at the Rothko Chapel. It became a symbol of the civil rights movement with its annual observance of Dr. Martin Luther King Jr.'s birthday, which began January 15, 1979, seven years before this date became a national holiday.[11]

The philosophy of the Rothko Chapel likely influenced Houston's Jewish leaders. While some collaborative civil rights events between African Americans and Jews occurred prior to Rothko, they increased after the chapel's dedication. On April 4, 1971, Congregation Beth Yeshurun hosted the first Black-Jewish Seder in Houston. Reminiscent of the Freedom Seder in 1969 spearheaded by Rabbi Arthur Waskow to memorialize Dr. King in Washington, DC, Congregation Beth Yeshurun joined with the Julia C. Hester House, a Black community center in the Fifth Ward, to create this model Seder. In a city in which only a decade earlier whites and African Americans could not eat together at a lunch counter, they sat down to break matzo and engage in a Jewish ritual. The director of the Julia C. Hester House, Besselle Atwell, believed that Jews and African Americans had certain preconceptions of each other that could be broken down through interaction. To Atwell, this Seder created the "real contact" that hitherto had been lacking. These Seders would continue under Rabbi Jack Segal's leadership even into the 2000s.[12]

On October 13, 1971, Congregation Beth Yeshurun's Akiba Institute invited Robert T. Coleman, director of the Social Justice Department for the Synagogue Council of America, to speak. Coleman was both African American and Hassidic and had previously been a Baptist minister. He was the first Black Jew to attain an executive position in a national Jewish agency. His primary purpose was to be a liaison for Black Jews and help ease the tension between Jews and African Americans in urban areas. It was significant that in 1979, a Congregation Beth Yeshurun advertisement for the Early Shabbat program featured one white and one Black family to represent Jewish diversity.[13]

In November 1971, the Urban Affairs Department of the national ADL invited the presidents of five Black colleges, including TSU president Granville Sawyer, on a sixteen-day trip to Israel, which eventually initiated a student exchange program. Black educators observed Israel's "methods of education" toward "the disadvantaged" and the "country's youth" as well as learned about Israel's approach to "health and immigration projects" and "its handling of ethnic problems."[14] They met with Israeli educators at Hebrew University's Weizmann Institute and Israel's Afro-Asian Institute.

While Houston's diversity accelerated relations between Jews and African Americans in the 1970s, the city's Jewish community still faced barriers. It was not until the late 1970s and early 1980s that Jews started to break through the glass ceiling. Prior to that, wealthy Jews might have been able to live in River Oaks, but they remained outside the upper echelon of Gentile society. Most Jews still lived in the southwestern enclave of Meyerland-Bellaire, and in 1970, only 10 percent of Jews lived in the predominantly Gentile areas of Highland Village, Memorial, and River Oaks.[15] They established Jewish day schools, which minimized their exposure to Christian indoctrination in the public schools, including the founding of the Robert M. Beren Academy in 1969, Torah Day School of Houston in 1977, and Emery/Weiner School in 1978. Even though many perceived all the city's Jews to be middle and upper class, 7.5 percent of the Jewish population in 1971 made less than $7,000 a year. Rather than arrange for public housing for poor Jewish families, however, beginning in the 1960s the JCRC worked through the Houston Housing Authority to set up apartments for disadvantaged Jews. As much as Houston's Jews wanted to be supportive of non-Jewish causes, they also realized they needed to support their community first, as they felt no one else would help them. Most of all, the issue still on the minds of the majority of the community was Israel and its survival.[16]

To gain a better understanding of the dynamics of the community over the past five years, the Jewish Community Council of Metropolitan Houston commissioned a sociological study through the University of Houston in 1976. The study asked myriad questions on the topics of religion, employment, Israel, and anti-Semitism. It revealed that out of 543 Houston Jewish respondents, 97.3 percent believed that Israel's existence and prowess in war had provided American Jews with a sense of pride in their Jewish identity. Out of 480 respondents, 86.6 percent of Houston Jews felt that the State of Israel connected them to their culture, history, and religion. Furthermore, approximately 93 percent of Houston Jews believed "that American Jews have a responsibility toward Israel and should shoulder this responsibility by helping Israel in some significant way."[17] Clearly, Houston Jews felt an affinity to Israel.

The sociologists determined that 33 percent of Houston Jews had experienced anti-Semitism or had family members who had experienced anti-Semitism. The study proved that Houston Jewish business leaders still faced discrimination in business and professional dealings. Yet despite the anti-Semitism they faced, whether it was because of the Arab-Israeli conflict or just being Jewish, Houston's Jews still felt secure enough to openly identify as Jews. This study revealed that, for the city's Jews, Israel was top priority. This was a significant break from their prior focus on self-protection through identifying themselves as white.[18]

Around the same time as this survey, the Jewish portrait photographer Gay Block, who was born and raised in Houston, produced a black-and-white film in 1975 called *A Tribute to Spirit: The Beth Israel Experience* for America's upcoming bicentennial. The film sought to present the Houston Jewish story and its place in the American Jewish experience. Block traced how Congregation Beth Israel's mindset changed from anti-Zionist to pro-Zionist. Ultimately the film was a story of how the Six-Day War empowered young Jewish Houstonians to connect with their Jewish identity. They began to wear Stars of David in public. One young adult in the film said he wore a Star of David because "I decided I was Jewish and I might as well show it."[19]

The makeup of the HISD began to change when Houstonians voted to elect CGS's candidates. By 1970, Houston had a new school board, a new superintendent, and, most importantly, a new court order to integrate. Federal Judge John Singleton replaced Judge Connally and mandated that every school follow the Singleton Ratio, a percentage-based system to help ensure diversity for faculty and students. The new school board had a commitment to public school education for everybody, not just whites. In the 1970s, CGS was also involved in implementing a magnet school program, which would help to initiate more integration. When the CGS-chosen school board took over, the district was 49.9 percent white, 35.7 percent African American, and 14.4 percent Latino. However, complete integration would still falter until 1984.[20]

The 1970s was also when Houston became known for its affordable living and increased job opportunities. Black residents had better employment rates than they did in other US cities, but their unemployment rate was still double that of whites. Even though more African Americans owned homes than before, rising from 21.7 percent to 44.7 percent, many lived in blighted areas that did not have paved roads, functioning water sources, or garbage collection services. The HHA still did not provide enough public housing—a problem that persisted even into the 1990s. Some African Americans who could afford to move out of the old neighborhoods faced barriers buying homes in new neighborhoods. As a result, 93 percent of all African Americans in Houston lived in majority Black neighborhoods in the 1970s. Riverside Terrace, known as "Black River Oaks," was one of the higher socioeconomic minority neighborhoods found in the United States. Thus, while housing and employment were improving, the major issue African Americans still faced was how to gain equal representation at all levels and in all venues. This made political representation all the more important for the city's Black residents.[21]

The Rise of Black Political Power

After Congress passed the Voting Rights Act of 1965 and ended the poll tax in 1966, voter turnout in Houston increased as citizens from lower socioeconomic backgrounds, which included a significant portion of African Americans, could finally vote. In addition, the Supreme Court's approval of redistricting the southern states, specifically Houston in 1965, enabled the division of Harris County into new congressional districts. This not only allowed Black residents to vote and run for political office; it also increased their political power by creating a new Black voter bloc. Both Texas House of Representatives member Curtis Graves and Judson Robinson, the first Black city councilman, benefited from redistricting. Despite experiencing bigotry by other representatives, Graves initiated altering Black representation in history textbooks. Robinson increased Black representation in the city's police and fire departments and became the voice of poor Blacks whose neighborhoods were fragmented by the new Houston freeways.[22]

Redistricting also led to the rise of Barbara Jordan, who initiated relations with the Jewish community in the political sphere. In 1966, Jordan broke the color barrier when Congressional District 18 elected her to the Texas Senate. In 1972, she became the first Black woman from the South ever elected to the US House of Representatives. Though she did not consider herself a feminist, Jordan espoused feminist ideas, such as supporting the Equal Rights Amendment. As she put it, "I am neither a Black politician nor a female politician ... Just a politician. A professional politician."[23] An opponent of all kinds of discrimination, Jordan fought for a fair minimum wage, helped unions fight for better teacher salaries and fair labor practices, and promoted workers' compensation acts, voting rights, and equal rights for all.[24]

D. Z. Cofield, the senior pastor of Good Hope Missionary Baptist Church, saw Jordan as the successor to Martin Luther King Jr.: "If Dr. King opened the doors of segregation, she taught us how to walk in and hold our heads high."[25] In 1976, Jordan became the first African American and the first woman keynote speaker at a major party national convention, declaring, in the spirit of King, that "we believe in equality for all, and privileges for none. This is a belief that each American, regardless of background, has equal standing in the public forum, all of us."[26] Jordan exemplified these words spoken in support of the Democratic Party in the way she approached Houston's Jewish minority.

While African Americans were making political advancements, Houston's Jews continued to lack a political foothold due to the strong influence of Christianity and an ongoing fear that public exposure would exacerbate anti-Semitism. The entire state of Texas had only a small percentage of Jews in positions at the state and national level. Texas had never had a Jewish governor, and Martin Frost, the only Jewish congressman from Texas, was not elected until 1978. Plus, Frost represented Arlington, Dallas, and Forth Worth—not Houston. In 1970, City Councilman Dick Gottlieb became the city's first Jewish politician. In 1973, Gottlieb attempted to run for mayor but failed because he became, as *Texas Monthly* said, "a good old boy's candidate" instead of reaching out for the African American and Mexican American vote.[27] He aligned himself with Chief Short, a man

despised by both minorities because of his alleged ties to the Ku
Klux Klan and history of not curbing police brutality. This was
a foolish move on the part of Gottlieb, considering the minority
vote secured his first election to the city council.[28]

Unlike Gottlieb, Jordan saw the validity of making connections with other minorities, especially the city's Jews. Through
her early work with the Houston Council on Human Relations
and Congregation Beth Israel, Jordan secured Houston's Jews as
her supporters. In 1993, after she received the Joseph Prize for
Human Rights through the ADL of Detroit, Jordan said, "When
I first ran for public office 30 years ago in Houston, Texas,
I could count on support from two groups. My neighbors in the
fifth ward and the congregation of Temple Beth Israel, led by
Rabbi Hyman Schachtel."[29] During her time in the Texas Senate,
Jordan lent her voice to the cause of Soviet Jewry.[30]

A few years later, during her term in Congress, Jordan spoke
at the Women's Plea for Human Rights for Soviet Jewry at
Congregation Emanu El. Sponsored by several Houston Jewish
women's organizations, the event sought to highlight the ongoing discrimination Soviet Jews faced.[31] The *JH-V* stated that
"Representative Jordan [was] well recognized for her humanitarian interests and is known to be keenly aware of the problems of all minorities and active on behalf of their needs."[32]
Eight hundred people listened to Jordan's speech, in which she
"compared the struggle for freedom of her own people with the
plight of Soviet Jews."[33] At this event, Jordan received a menorah in appreciation of her support of human rights.

Perhaps Jordan's greatest accomplishment was fostering a
rapport with the Jewish community in Houston. Yet for all her
active involvement in building bridges between the two communities, the city's Jews still experienced insecurity when the topic
of Israel emerged at the National Black Political Convention
of 1972. Held in Gary, Indiana, in March, the event sought to
unify Black political leadership. At the convention, the attend-
ees voted to "dismantle" Israel and condemn the country for its
"expansionist policy" and "forceful occupation" of the Palestinian territory.[34] This event concerned not only American Jews

but also Black politicians and Black organizations that did not support this anti-Zionist agenda. The media also played a role in heavily publicizing the vote. Even though it had nothing to do with Houston, the *JH-V* reported on the event, stoking local Jewish fears that anti-Zionist sentiment was rampant among Blacks in Houston: "It would seem that insofar as the State of Israel has been and remains a haven for Jewish victims of oppression ... Black people in America who likewise have been victims of centuries of oppression should demonstrate a great understanding and support for the State of Israel."[35]

Following the resolution in Gary, the JCRC contacted both Jordan and Graves, and, according to the *JH-V*, both then "immediately sent telegrams disassociating themselves with the statement which was extremely critical of Israel, and associated themselves with a very positive statement issued by 13 Black congressmen."[36] Their stance in favor of Israel affirmed to Houston's Jewish leaders that they could count on the support of local Black leadership.

Like Dr. King, Jordan believed that Israel had the right to exist. King had said in 1967, after the Six-Day War, "Israel must exist. [It] has a right to exist and is one of the great outposts of democracy in the world."[37] Jordan also maintained this stance. This did not mean that she considered herself anti-Palestinian but rather that she felt it was her obligation to support Israel's security as a state. Nevertheless, she did not receive unanimous praise in Houston for her support of Israel and, in fact, experienced backlash for it, just as many of Houston's Jews did.

One reason Jordan supported Israel was her firm belief in uniting these two communities. She saw the relationship as a means for both groups to gain a voice. In a speech to Congregation Beth Israel in 1992, she said that, in unity, both groups have the power to make a change. She cited Dr. King: "Where do we go from here, chaos or community?" Jordan thought Jews and African Americans needed each other not just because they shared a history of subjugation and being the objects of prejudice, but because together they formed a larger voting constituency. She thought that Jews had "been instrumental in electing many Black political leaders in America," primarily because "Blacks represented an electoral strength that Jews did not have."[38] This was both because Jews were a smaller minority and because redistricting favored the Black vote. Additionally, Mexican Americans were less likely to vote for African Americans, according to a 1972 study by the Houston Council on Human Relations, which made Jews more reliable allies.[39]

The Yom Kippur War of 1973 increased anti-Zionism and led Arab oil producers to establish an oil embargo in 1973. As a result, Houstonians experienced rising gas and electricity prices. In retaliation for supplying Israel with military equipment, the Arab embargo extended to any US businesses that had a relationship with Israel or had Jewish owners. In Houston, Arab students organized debates over the Arab-Israeli conflict at Rice University and the University of Houston. Still, Jordan remained steadfast in her support of Israel's right to exist. From her perspective, it was in the best interest of the United States to have and support economically a Middle Eastern ally.[40] Many of the city's Jews wrote to Jordan praising her commitment, though many other non-Jewish residents responded with inflammatory letters. On October 25, 1973—in the middle of the Yom Kippur War—Jordan received a letter from Richard Monell urging her not to support Israel because the United States had not benefited from the relationship and Israel was unconcerned with Christian Americans. Perceiving Israel as a "permanent aggressor in the Middle East," Monell worried that the United States would send their "sons to die for the Rothschilds and other Jewish international bankers."[41]

Monell wrote Jordan a year later to complain how "the high oil prices can be blamed on Israel because Israel refused to return the occupied lands that rightfully belonged to Syria and Egypt. Please don't be influenced by the international Jew."[42] Until dwindling supply during the embargo quadrupled the price, Houstonians had access to cheap oil. This change, coupled with the prominence of the oil industry, increased resentment toward Israel more in Houston than in other cities.

Aware of the concerns of Houston Jewish leadership over possible anti-Semitic or anti-Zionist backlash due to the

Arab-Israeli conflict, Jordan met with the Houston JCRC to reiterate her support for Israel. The council praised her for being a loyal ally and for supporting the "funding for Israel."[43] Jordan's support of Israel influenced the views of many Black residents who respected her beliefs. In 1974, the Israeli invitational basketball tournament invited the basketball team at Wheatley, a predominantly Black high school in Houston, to play in Tel Aviv. Principal A. C. Herald, concerned for the team's safety, contacted White at the *JH-V* for advice. White informed Herald "that there was less hazard to their trip than the day-to-day traversing of our own city streets," given Houston's high murder rate, understaffed police force, and history of police brutality.[44]

Wheatley was able to raise only $14,000 of the $15,000 they needed for their trip. When the JCRC heard of their financial woes, they raised extra money, in large part because the council was proud to see Wheatley go to Israel as a representative of Houston and hoped that the experience would reshape their perspective on Israel. The *JH-V* featured an article on this donation and a photograph of Joseph Hiller, a representative of the JCRC, giving a check to Coach Jackie Carr.[45]

Jordan's membership in BASIC, the Black Americans to Support Israel Committee, positioned her as both a local and a national supporter of Israel. BASIC opposed the Arab Economic Boycott of 1973, arguing that Arab countries should not be able to use their "newly acquired oil wealth to boycott business firms that deal with Israel or have Jewish owners, executives, or directors." BASIC noted that African Americans had fought endlessly to "root out discrimination," and so to "sit idly while foreign interests import bigotry into America" was wrong. They also observed that the high prices caused by Arab oil embargoes disproportionately hurt lower socioeconomic Blacks and further weakened poverty-stricken African countries already suffering from drought.[46]

Rabbi Cahana corresponded with Jordan, praising her for her commitment to Israel: "During the long years of my involvement in the Civil Rights Movement in Houston I came to know you and admire your courage to stand up forcefully for your moral convictions." Cahana saw his work in the local civil rights movement as comparable to Jordan's public stance on Israel. He saw Jordan as he saw himself, as a believer in human rights for all. A little more than a decade earlier, he had characterized Jews as white and as part of the group that permitted the oppression of African Americans. However, now he saw how Jordan stood up for Jews as he had stood up for African Americans in Houston, Birmingham, and Selma. It was no longer only about Jews coming to the aid of Blacks but also about Blacks like Jordan coming to the aid of Jews—both groups on equal footing, neither one dominating the other. Cahana ended his letter to Jordan with a simple note: "Eternal God should grant you health and long years that you may continue to tender His goodness promoting justice for all."[47]

When the United Nations passed Resolution 3379 on November 10, 1975, pronouncing Zionism "a form of racism and racial discrimination," it fueled anger within both the Jewish and Black communities of Houston. An open dialogue on Resolution 3379 emerged in both the *JH-V* and *The Informer*. Kahn saw the resolution as an "obscene joke." How was it possible, Kahn asked, that a group of people who were "the victims of the most vicious racism in the history of mankind, should be labeled racists?" He felt that the use of the term "racism" in Resolution 3379 made a mockery of the slavery and segregation Blacks had endured. Kahn further stated "Zionism was a liberation movement" similar to King's civil rights movement or Cesar Chavez's United Farm Workers. In fact, Kahn said, "Zionism ... was the direct opposite of Racism."[48]

The Informer published editorials also voicing frustration with the United Nations asserting ownership of the term "racism." Using racism to describe Zionism diminished the prejudice imposed on African Americans and the people of Africa. After all, the United Nations had never declared segregation an example of racism. *The Informer* described how the United Nations had not condemned Arab discrimination against Black Christians in the Middle East as racism. The resolution was "an insult to the generation of Blacks who have struggled against real racism. From our 400 year experience with slavery, segregation, and discrimination we know that

Zionism is not racism."[49] The articles in *The Informer* and the *JH-V* stressed that the fight against anti-Zionism was not only about Jews but was rather a larger fight to end all bigotry. *The Informer* did not want the United Nations to have the authority to define what bigotry was because in doing so it could affect African Americans, who had, since the time of enslavement, experienced prejudice in its purest form.

In 1975, Jordan spoke at a meeting of the Houston Council on Human Relations, where she received an award for her work. She wanted the board, whose members were African American, white, Latino, and Jewish, to understand why the resolution stating "Zionism is racism" was against the cause of civil rights. Jordan praised how the members' work on behalf of civil rights in Houston had brought about an era of "mutual respect and understanding" between "African Americans, Latinos, and Whites."[50]

But now it was time for the members of the board to once again stand up and fight for civil rights—this time for Israel. Jordan saw Resolution 3379 as incongruent with the civil rights movement. It was not a call to end prejudice but to reinforce it. She urged Houstonians to recognize that Jews needed their support, not only for the sake of Israel but because the UN resolution condemned all Jews who supported Zionism. Also, Jordan feared that the effect of the boycotts on Houston's economy would increase anti-Semitism.[51]

A year later, during an event to honor prominent Jewish Houstonians Peggy and Leon Samet for their commitment to Israel, Jordan once again spoke about Resolution 3379, but this time she focused on Black identity and the meaning of bigotry. As an African American, Jordan was aware of what bigotry was and firmly stated, "It makes no sense to equate it with Zionism."[52] Instead, she equated it with Jewish identity. To Jordan, the Jewish people were allies in the civil rights movement.

Although Houston's Jews may not have had a powerful presence during the movement's height, Jordan did not define Jewish involvement in terms of one community; rather, she viewed it in terms of the collective Jewish response. In other words, Jordan did not look to specific Jewish communities to determine their contribution to the civil rights movement, as King did when he criticized Birmingham's Jews for not participating. Instead, she related to them as one unified group. In this respect, Jordan saw Houston's Jews not as a group trying to fit into the white majority as in the past but instead as a distinct minority. Because Jews had responded to the Black fight for equal rights, Jordan proclaimed that it was the turn of Blacks to support Jews. She promised, "We Black Americans can be counted on to support you. I make that statement, not only because we are in your debt, and we are ... but I make that statement because our pursuit is common."[53]

Jordan presented the relationship between Blacks and Jews as an alliance of peers, a partnership that existed because both faced persecution and discrimination. She explained that "there is a sameness, there is a commonality about it, and we will continue our pursuit of freedom despite any discomfort we cause some countries."[54]

While Jordan's pro-Israel stance created more inroads between the Black and Jewish communities in Houston, relations would not fully coalesce until Mickey Leland's appearance in the city's political landscape.

The Rise of Mickey Leland

Mickey Leland emerged on the Houston political scene in 1972 when he became a Texas state representative. Like Jordan, Dr. King influenced Leland, but it was the Black Power movement, especially the Black Panthers, that led him to activism. Eventually he realized that to create real change in Houston, he needed to work within the political system.

With the support of the de Menils, Leland began his quest to become a Black political leader. At the young age of twenty-seven, he shocked many white politicians when he walked into the Texas legislature sporting an Afro and wearing a dashiki and platform shoes.[55] During his time in the state legislature, Leland advocated for health care for disadvantaged African Americans as well as for the city's homeless. Later, in Congress, he established the National Commission on AIDS and introduced bills that would provide medical care and food stamps for African American and Mexican American homeless and low-income families. This assistance even included providing low-income families access to fresh vegetables.[56]

While he never wavered in his attention to these two groups, as a congressman he expanded his alliances to include other minorities as well. Initially, however, Houston's Jews and Israel were not among his priorities. In fact, like most Black Power leaders, Leland opposed supporting the State of Israel. On October 8, 1975, he wrote a letter to Philip Randolph, chairman of BASIC, opposing Black involvement with Israel. He perceived Jews to be white and therefore saw Israel as a "white cause."[57] In his view, African Americans needed to prioritize African American and African causes. When the United Nations recognized the PLO in 1974, some Black Houstonians voiced opinions in favor of the Palestinian cause, seeing it as a civil rights issue. For instance, Black resident Dan Moriarty viewed Israelis as occupiers, claiming, "The Palestinians [were] the terror-evicted 'Blacks' of the Middle East!"[58]

Editorials in the *Houston Chronicle* had similar anti-Zionist discussions, arguing that Jordan's promotion of the fight for Israel as a joint Black and Jewish cause against bigotry was not an effective means of uniting the two groups since some African Americans compared the plight of Palestinians to that of themselves. As a result, some—including Leland—viewed Israel exclusively as a white Jewish cause.

After a visit to Israel, however, Leland changed his views and publicly framed Israel's fight for survival as a symbol for both Jews and African Americans. In 1977, ADL executive director Tom Neuman had suggested that Leland travel to Israel to form his own opinion rather than base it on media speculation or the idea that Israel was an exclusively Jewish issue.[59]

The Israeli government invited Leland and several journalists to attend a ten-day tour of the country. Upon arrival, Israeli airport security arrested him because they thought he was a Black Hebrew. At the time, Black Hebrews had a tense relationship with the State of Israel, as the former were known to be anti-Semitic and had threatened the Israeli government.[60]

After being released, Leland decided to continue with the tour. He learned about the country's politics, economy, and history and saw firsthand what it was like to live in Israel. Leland had candid discussions with Israelis on the Arab-Israeli conflict and their philosophy on what the country needed to maintain its survival. The trip gave him new insight into the struggle of worldwide Jewry and the significance of having a Jewish homeland. After visiting the Kibbutz Kfar Hahoresh, he stated, "I think the theory of communal living and shared responsibility set forth in the kibbutzim could hold the answer for world survival. I would like to introduce the idea in Africa or for that matter in the United States."[61] Leland came back from Israel believing that America should continue to aid the country and that the political situation there was far more complicated than he had previously supposed.

After his experience in Israel, Leland described himself as "Israel's newest ambassador to the Jewish community," and he began to inspire others to travel there as well.[62] A year after his trip, his advocacy for Israel spurred Reverend Lawson to visit the country. As a preacher, Lawson viewed Israel as the center of spirituality. In a life-changing moment, Lawson said, in an article for the *JH-V* titled "Israel: History by the Inch," "I fell on my knees in my hotel room and thanked God for the privilege of praying in the Land of Abraham." Lawson stressed Israel's diminutive size and how its widest point was the distance between Houston and Dallas. He challenged the anti-Zionist image of Israel as a colonizer. Instead, Israel was the underdog. The country represented religion, courage, and a new beginning for a group of people who had historically suffered persecution.[63]

Leland's transformation greatly affected his future leadership. He realized that to have unity among all minorities, "we [first] must destroy the line that separates humanity and learn to appreciate the differences among people."[64] Change would not occur for his community, the nation, or the world if he saw the matters only in terms of Black and white. He needed to help create a society in which everyone mattered. Leland's revelation caused him to see the validity in facilitating relations between the two communities in the emerging multicultural Houston. In doing so, he could help to lay the foundation for a new and better Houston, despite a conservative effort to maintain unofficial segregation.

Leland wanted to spend a year living on a kibbutz, but when he discovered that Barbara Jordan was not going to run for Congress again in 1978, he decided to seize the opportunity to replace her and returned to Houston. Leland was eager to have the platform that Jordan's seat would give him. He wanted to be the one to empower the city to embrace its diversity—a goal he hoped to expand eventually to the nation and the world.

Yet while Leland and Lawson extolled the virtues of Israel, they were also confronted with the local rise of the American Nazi Party. With the increase in new immigrant groups coming to Houston, the American Nazi Party feared losing its white majority status. As a result, it emerged onto the public scene to exert its power through hatred. In 1977, the Houston branch of the American Nazi Party sent out phone messages to scare local Black and Jewish communities. According to Rabbi Segal, these messages called for "an 'all-white war against Jews and other non-whites.' ... it even offered a $5,000 bounty to persons who killed non-whites attacking whites."[65]

The threatening messages continued, alarming both the Black and Jewish communities.[66] As Segal proclaimed, the party continued "their vituperative, abusive, and poisonous statements about Jews and Blacks and preaching the principles of Nazism."[67] The AJC asked Southwestern Bell for help, but they refused, citing the First Amendment. Eventually, several local Jews tried to take legal action, including Segal and well-known journalist Marvin Zindler. In February 1978, Houston's chapters of the ADL, the AJC, the Jewish Federation, and Zindler fought for an injunction from the Texas Supreme Court, but the court denied their efforts. Both the *JH-V* and *The Informer* followed the case, especially after it made national headlines.[68]

The American Nazi Party caused unease not only because of the party's presence during World War II and the 1960s but also because its reemergence showed that extremist groups still saw Jews as the same as African Americans.[69] Segal warned Congregation Beth Yeshurun's congregants that the communities faced a *"clear danger* and *present danger* to Jewish and Black lives and property in the city of Houston because of this recording and other similar Nazi recordings."[70] Most of all, Segal was disappointed that Houston was "a city in which Nazis [were] legally permitted to broadcast over the telephone a $5,000 reward for dead Jews and Blacks."[71] This proved that Houston was still very much a conservative city and that Jews and African Americans needed, now more than ever, to unify and speak out for their rights.

In Houston, Leland rose to become the political broker who would advocate for relations between the two communities. He further solidified his affiliation with the city's Jews when they supported his run for Congress. A campaign ad in the April 6, 1978, *JH-V* displayed a photograph of Leland shaking hands with the mayor of Jerusalem, Teddy Kollek. Below the photograph, the caption read, "Mickey Leland is a friend. We believe he belongs in Congress."

The *JH-V* also ran an editorial titled "Mickey Leland, the Making of a Congressman" that asked, "Who is worthy of succeeding Representative Barbara Jordan in the 18th Congressional District?" The newspaper strongly endorsed Leland, stressing that he was the one congressional candidate who had been to Israel and had a desire to help facilitate peace in the Middle East. The *JH-V* urged its Jewish readers to be a voice for Leland, stating, "Many *Herald-Voice* readers cannot vote in the 18th Congressional District. But you *can* give support. Houston needs strong leadership in Congress, and Israel needs continued strong support from its friends. *Help Mickey Leland.*"[72]

One of Leland's first projects in Congress was to develop the Mickey Leland Kibbutzim Internship for inner-city teens, which changed the face of Black and Jewish interactions in Houston. He established it with J. Kent Friedman, a longtime friend, and Vic Samuels, who had led CGS. Since Friedman was involved with the Jewish Federation, the Mickey Leland project was first under its auspices, and funding came from private sources in both the Black and Jewish communities. Today it is under the leadership of the AJC. Leland's experience growing up in poverty inspired him to create an Israel trip distinctly for non-Jewish minority teens from inner-city Houston.[73]

Friedman, who became the president of the Mickey Leland Kibbutzim Internship Foundation, recalled Leland's connection rested in "the land, the people, the immigrants' stories, and the success which had been accomplished by that small state."[74] Leland found his inspiration in the ideals behind the kibbutzim "concept of socialized living. He thought it would be life-changing for young people to have the opportunity to see what he had seen."[75] In other words, he thought it would benefit inner-city teens to see an economic system in which individuals in a community shared their economic resources, living space, clothing, and child care. Before Leland's development of the internship, there had been individual trips to Israel organized for local teens, but his program became a permanent institution.[76]

The Mickey Leland Kibbutzim Internship selected ten minority students from Congressional District 18 to go to Israel for six weeks starting on June 25, 1980. To be eligible, students needed to be eleventh graders who had displayed leadership in extracurricular activities, achieved academic success, and were exceptionally creative.[77]

The ADL and the AJC developed a six-hour class to prepare the students for their trips. A press release for the Mickey Leland Kibbutzim Internship from June 25, 1981, stated that the aim of these trips was for the students to have an educational, social, and cultural experience in Israel and to consider the differences and similarities between Israel and the United States.[78] One of the more significant goals was for students to "develop positive ways of dealing with people of other races, cultures, religious and ethnic backgrounds."[79] The teens stayed with Israeli host families in Haifa and studied Hebrew at the Leo Baeck School. Afterward, the students spent three weeks working on a kibbutz and then traveled around Israel learning about its diverse cultures. The teens also visited the religious sites of Christians, Jews, and

Muslims. Additionally, because Leland wanted them to meet Jews who were not white, they visited an absorption center for Ethiopian immigrants coming to Israel.[80]

The students who participated in the internship spoke about their experiences on television, in newspapers, and on the radio. Leland described the students as becoming "ambassadors of good will and advocates for peace for Israel."[81] In the *JH-V*, Karin Burling, who accompanied one of the groups, wrote about the impact of the trip, explaining that the kibbutz closed the "gap between Jews and these energetic minority students." It helped to abolish the prejudices minority students might have had of Jews and sparked an interest in Jewish culture. Burling observed that some of the interns even became interested in learning Hebrew and participating in Jewish events.[82]

By the time Leland died in 1989, around one hundred students had participated in the program. Many of them went on to become National Merit finalists or receive other academic honors. On a social level, the program broke the barrier that had existed between Jews and African Americans because of segregation.[83]

In 1983, Al Vorspan asked Leland to write to David Saperstein, director of the Union of American Hebrew Congregation's Religious Action Center, "to work out ways and means of spreading the super Mickey Leland kibbutz intern program to other parts of the country." Vorspan envisioned Leland's Kibbutzim Internship as the widespread solution to cultivate a relationship between the two groups. After the North had cast the South as being passive at the height of the classic civil rights movement, Leland provided a new image of a proactive southern city.[84]

In addition to improving relations, Mickey Leland's internship program highlighted the need for alliances between Jews and other minorities, such as Latinos. The Houston AJC paired with the Latino community to hold the conference "Jews and Hispanics in America: The Meeting of Two Historic Cultures." This was a complete turnaround from the 1920s, when Jews and Blacks, let alone Latinos, had no formal alliance to fight against bigotry or white supremacy.[85]

In April 1983, the US Department of Justice had the Houston Council on Human Relations convene a meeting of the main human rights organizations for African Americans, Latinos, and Jews, as well as business and religious leaders, to discuss the Ku Klux Klan. The group's goal was to protect the changing culture of Houston from white supremacy. As a show of unity, they held Human Fellowship Day on April 2, 1983. Its slogan was "Say 'No to Racism, No to the KKK—Yes to Human Dignity.'"[86]

The following month, they hosted a workshop on the Ku Klux Klan. Before, Jews would have handled this issue in their own community and African Americans in theirs, but now the groups worked together alongside the Latino community. In large part, Leland's devotion to breaking down boundaries and creating alliances solidified these intergroup relations.[87]

In Houston, the Kibbutzim Internship received much praise. In 1989, the *Houston Chronicle* touted the program as a "personal success story in Black/Jewish relations." As one of the participating students said, "If you're born in the Black community, all you know is the Black community ... Israel is my chance to experience something different. I'll become more responsible because I won't have my parents telling me everything." Leland, however, felt that Black and Jewish interaction could not alone mitigate the division between the communities; rather, these interactions could help "young people develop a better understanding of each other."[88]

Alison Leland, the wife of Mickey Leland, recalled that the students who went to Israel saw it as a "way to bridge understanding between major religious groups." These students had never been on an airplane, let alone left the country.[89]

When people asked Leland, "'Israel? Why don't you start a program that takes students to Africa?' he would say, 'That would be a great trip, but that's not this trip. I want to do something a little bit different but also something that is personally important to me.'" When he thought about Israel, he remembered his experience of growing up in the Fifth Ward in a single-parent home and how an opportunity like the one he was providing would have made a difference for him. He believed that in helping

Houston's teens, he was also changing the world. Israel became a symbol for local Black teens to see they could transcend the ward in which they lived. As he explained, "If I time these Israel trips so that it's between 11th and 12th grade they will come back and they will imagine they could go to any college because they have been on an airplane now, they've been to Israel and now leaving home is not going to be so daunting."[90]

On April 11, 1989, the Religious Action Center awarded Leland the prestigious Peter and Marjorie Kovler Award for Black-Jewish Relations. He was its first recipient, and C-SPAN broadcast the ceremony. Vorspan described Leland as "a living symbol of the deep and abiding bond between the Black and Jewish communities in America."[91] His hope was to nationalize this program. In the 1980s and 1990s, Leland's internship greatly influenced both Black and Jewish communities throughout the country.

While other cities had kibbutzim programs, the program in Houston was exceptional because of Leland himself. He had become the embodiment of hope that these communities could unite under a cause through his leadership. Former interns who participated in the Mickey Leland program thirty years prior still acknowledge the impact it had on them. For instance, Judge Ursula Hall, when she ran for judge for Harris County 189th Civil District Court in 2010, wrote in her campaign advertisement in the *JH-V*, "Ursula regards the summer during which she lived and worked in Israel, among the greatest of her life. As a former Mickey Leland Kibbutz Intern, Ursula spoke at synagogues and other gatherings about the significance of her time in the Holy Land."[92]

Leland's legacy continues to live on. As of 2020, the program was forty years old. Other kibbutz programs influenced by his internship program include Operation Understanding in Philadelphia and Washington, DC, Youthworks in New York, Operation Unity in Los Angeles, and Children of the Dream in San Francisco and New York.[93]

By the mid-1980s, Houston had transformed into a city that was less white and less Christian-centric. Redistricting had created an African American voting bloc that laid the foundation for interethnic alliances—in this case, Blacks and Jews. Jordan and Leland built on this foundation and gave minorities a stronger political voice. The change was best seen in Albert Goldstein, who captured the new collaborative climate in the city: "Jews are a minority, Black people are a minority, and Chicanos are minorities. We don't protect—We work together."[94]

Leland especially embodied the new Houston. His relationship with Israel showed how much had changed since 1943, when Congregation Beth Israel espoused anti-Zionism and distanced itself from African Americans to assert Jewish whiteness. In Leland's Houston, Jews could look to Zionism as a way of connecting with African Americans. And while Jews and African Americans would sometimes be divided over the question of Israel in the post-Leland era, nevertheless during the period from the 1960s through the mid-1980s, African Americans and Jews connected and identified with one another as two oppressed minorities. Through a series of small yet powerful moments, leaders like Leland initiated relations in a city that had once prevented such interactions. Through his work with Israel and collaboration with local Jewish leadership, they put to rest the controversy of the Basic Principles. Indeed, Leland's political rise buried Principle 2—"Our religion is Judaism. Our nation is the United States of America. Our nationality is American. Our flag is the 'Stars and Stripes.' Our race is Caucasian …"—into history.

Conclusion

"Together or Apart?"

The transformation of Congressman Mickey Leland from an anti-Zionist to an advocate of Israel encapsulated the wider shift in the relationship between African Americans and Jews in Houston between the 1930s and 1980s. During the summer of 1987, Leland posed for a photograph at a refugee camp located on the Ethiopian-Sudanese border. At the time, he was on a mission to assist the persecuted Beta Israel Jews who wanted to immigrate to Israel because of widespread starvation, persecution, and discrimination.[1] A viewer seeing this photograph might assume that the picture was a political photo op, but his simple navy-blue T-shirt emblazoned with white Hebrew words spread across its front that read "האג וטסוי," adjacent to its English translation, "Houston Proud," exemplified Leland's devotion to the Jewish community. His longtime friend J. Kent Friedman said: "Mickey could have a bunch of T-shirts printed up with the 'Houston Proud' in Hebrew, and pass them on to a group of Americans having dinner in an Arab restaurant in Jerusalem—a dinner that he was hosting, no less."[2]

Throughout the 1980s, Leland continued to serve as a voice for Israel and the promotion of relations between both

Mickey Leland wearing "Houston Proud" T-shirt in English and Hebrew.
The Mickey Leland Papers & Collection Addendum. (Texas Southern
University, 2018), "Mickey Leland on African Ethiopian trips" (1987).
Series 14 : The Mickey Leland Audio Video Collection – Box 17 Images.
104. https://digitalscholarship.tsu.edu/mla_mlavc_photos17/104.
Courtesy of the George Thomas "Mickey" Leland Collection, Mickey
Leland Center on Hunger, Poverty, and World Peace, Texas Southern
University, Houston, Texas.

communities. He often cited the line from the Talmud, "And whoever saves a life, it is considered as if he saved an entire world."[3] Active in the fight for Soviet Jewry, Leland sat on a panel with Congressman Steny Hoyer addressing the Soviet Union's human rights violations toward its Jews. According to Hoyer, "Mickey demonstrated on that trip and on countless other occasions that his concern for the human condition knew no geographic, racial, or religious bounds."[4] J. Kent Friedman explained that Leland "always seemed to connect on a 'gut' level with the centuries of suffering and persecution that Jews had endured."[5]

For this reason and for the work Leland did for Ethiopian Jews and Israel in general, he received the Righteous Gentile Award on April 26, 1987. Traditionally, Houston's Jewish community gave this award to those who had saved Jews during the Holocaust; however, the city's Jews honored Leland because, before his death in 1989, he had arranged to have eight thousand Ethiopian Jews airlifted to Israel.[6]

Leland continued to advocate for Black and Jewish relations beyond his Kibbutzim Internship. His reputation, however, as an unofficial ambassador of the Jewish community within and beyond Houston never caused Leland to shy away from criticizing the Jewish community. Regarding Louis Farrakhan, the head of the Nation of Islam, he told a Houston Jewish audience, "We [Black leaders] can't be responsible for Minister Farrakhan any more than you can be responsible for Rabbi Kahane [the head of the Jewish Defense League]."[7] Leland explained that Jews needed to recognize their community's role in fueling prejudice and insensitivity toward Blacks just as much as his community needed to recognize their anti-Semitism. He described the "Black-Jewish Coalition … as a two-way street." At the American Israel Public Affairs Committee in Washington, DC, in 1986, Leland professed, "I don't help Israel because I want you to help us. I would help Israel whether you help me or not." But he also called upon his Jewish constituents to become more involved in the "remaining battles that concern American Blacks."[8]

In August 1989, Leland's plane crashed on its way to the refugee camp Fugindo on the Ethiopian-Sudanese border. The Houston AJC executive director said upon his death that Leland "was not only a link between the Jewish communities, but between all people."[9] At his funeral, Houston's Jews mourned him and praised his advocacy for their community and the Jewish world at large. At a memorial service at Congregation Emanu El, Rabbi Roy Walter, Kahn's replacement, described the importance of Leland: "In a sense, Mickey and the Jewish community were bound together by vocabulary; we spoke the same language ... In no less real and powerful a fashion [was] his memory etched not only into our hearts but into Jewish history."[10]

Walter's admiration for Leland demonstrated how far the city's Jews had come in their relations with African Americans. Friedman commented on Leland's bond with Israel in his eulogy: "Having traveled there many times ... Mickey felt it to be a place of solace and comfort ... There was a rapport between Mickey and the Israelis that was impossible to analyze but beautiful to behold."[11] To memorialize Leland, the city's Jews established the Mickey Leland Memorial Fund, the funds for which were "channeled to the Mickey Leland Kibbutzim Internship Foundation, which was for building a better understanding between Blacks and Jews in Houston."[12]

Leland's memory also had an impact on many other Jewish organizations. The Jewish National Fund created the Mickey Leland Parkland outside of Jerusalem. Max Goldfield, past president of B'nai B'rith District 7, compared Leland's life to the B'nai B'rith mission of helping those in need, supporting Israel, and fighting bigotry. The Southwest Regional Office of the ADL sent their sympathy to Leland's family, expressing appreciation for his efforts in pushing forward relations between both communities. AJC president David Mincberg sent the family condolences and praised Leland for his devotion to civil rights and his role in helping Soviet Jewry and supporting Israel. According to the *JH-V*, both the Israeli government and Washington sent condolences, and "tributes from around the world were heard."[13] The Israeli embassy's Fifth Annual Commemoration of Martin Luther King Jr.'s birthday, which the Jewish National Fund cosponsored, announced an award in memory of Leland. Moshe Arad, the Israeli ambassador, proclaimed "Leland a 'mensch' and likened his tragic death to that of Dr. King."[14]

After Leland's death, the Houston City Council suggested naming the airport in honor of him. City Councilman Jim Westmoreland joked that Houston should call the airport "Nigger International."[15] As a result of this racist comment, Houston's Jews and African Americans joined to get Westmoreland removed from office. According to Congressman Al Green, then president of the Houston NAACP, "That [comment] cost him the seat on the city council because Blacks and Jews coalesced and demanded his resignation." Green saw this coordinated effort by both minorities as an example of when the "African-American-Jewish political alliance forged" as a result of Leland's efforts. The fact that both groups converged to get Westmoreland removed further illustrated Leland's lasting influence. As Green explained, "Having these common experiences of being rebuffed and discriminated against caused us to realize there were greater opportunities for us together than apart."[16]

If one were to ask a Jewish Houstonian today about the relationship between Jews and African Americans, one might hear, "Have you heard of Mickey Leland? He was a congressman from Houston from 1980 to 1989. He supported the State of Israel, the local Jewish community, and Jewish interests abroad." But if one asked a Jewish Houstonian what the interactions were between Jews and African Americans *before* Leland took leadership, the same consensus would remain: "Nothing happened in Houston." One might also hear a generalized answer about Jewish participation in the civil rights movement. However, Leland's T-shirt with "Houston Proud" emblazoned across it, as simple as it may seem, symbolized the pinnacle of the larger story of Houston's African American and Jewish narrative, as something important did happen between the two populations.

Glimpses into Houston's history through a Jewish lens over the long civil rights movement does not paint a romantic or disappointing image but rather illustrates how these two distinct communities could not find unity until they found commonality. Houston's Jewish leaders struggled between their liberalism and passion for civil rights and their desire for themselves and their community to acculturate. As the city became more international, the divide between Black and white broke down and propelled Black politicians like Barbara Jordan and Mickey Leland to initiate relations between these two groups. Two communities that had developed separately now developed in tandem. These relations would eventually lead to a political alliance between Jewish and Black leaders and Leland's eventual establishment of the Mickey Leland Kibbutzim Internship.

An alliance between Jews and Blacks in Houston did not emerge at one single moment in time but rather developed over the long civil rights period. Most narratives on Jewish and African American interactions have concentrated on the classic timeline of the civil rights movement, especially in the North, but Houston has shown the importance of expanding that story to include those cities that developed over a longer trajectory. Although segregation existed in other parts of the South, one cannot monolithically define the Houston African American and Jewish narrative as the same as narratives in other parts of the South. After all, as Alan Tigay of *Hadassah Magazine* once claimed, each city throughout the world has shaped Jewish identity in its own way: "Each city has its own ethos, and in each city Jews [were] affected by, and [had] an impact on the surrounding community."[17]

Historians need to broaden their view of the history between these two dynamic groups, which is often from a northern perspective. The history of relations in southern cities like Houston complicate this narrative and illustrate a more nuanced picture of this bond. Houston emerged from a segregationist city divided between those deemed white and Black to become a diverse city with a plurality of cultures. Changes within Houston led to a new bond between African Americans and Jews. Unlike the traditional trajectory of African American and Jewish relations in the North, which peaked at the height of the civil rights movement and then fell apart in the 1960s at the height of Black Power, in Houston, a political alliance blossomed in the mid- to late twentieth century. By examining specific and important moments in Houston's history, one realizes the value of Jewish history at a local level, not only to fully understand the civil rights period but also to better examine the way individual cities have shaped the African American and Jewish experience.

In order to be accepted by white Gentiles, Houston Jewish leaders felt pressure to acculturate, even as they demonstrated an interest in promoting Black civil rights. The rigidity of segregation propelled Congregation Beth Israel's Policy Formulation Committee to create a Caucasian clause to secure their status within the white Gentile majority. Completely denied access to that kind of security due to the color of their skin, African Americans continued to languish politically, economically, and socially.

In Houston, the interconnection between white and first-class citizenship solidified during the Red Scare. While the city's Jewish leaders promoted tolerance for all minorities as an American value, fear of Communism overshadowed this spirit of liberalism, particularly when Houston segregationists saw civil rights as an act of Communism. Local leaders might have tried to promote the city's Jews as white Americans of Jewish faith to protect their communal interests, but external perceptions complicated the situation more than anticipated. Though Houston Jewish leaders supported the *Brown v. Board of Education* outcome, they did not want desegregation to be labeled a Jewish issue.

Areas in the Third Ward, Riverside Terrace, and downtown Houston became the central areas of contention between Jews and African Americans. Initially, Jewish leaders sacrificed their liberalism and acculturated to the white Gentile majority when they elected to live in neighborhoods that restricted African Americans and opened segregated businesses. When African

Americans from the Third Ward attempted to integrate peacefully with whites in Riverside, white and Jewish neighbors did not give them a chance to be equal neighbors. Eventually, a lack of access to the economic sphere propelled Black student protesters to fight for equality. Once again, Houston Jewish leaders followed the lead of white Gentile leaders, choosing self-protection for their community over equality.

For communal leaders, beginning to align themselves with a segregated minority was not an easy shift to make. Houston's Jews, like other southern Jews, had the illusion that if white Gentiles perceived them as white, they could live seamlessly among them, free from discrimination. After all, as Eli Evans stated, southern Jews believed African Americans were the "lightning rod" of southern society, which protected Jews from widespread discrimination.[18]

The Black plight, however, remained a constant reminder of what their lives could become. Therefore, when the Houston School Board refused to remove Christianity from the schools, while also being painfully slow to integrate the school system, Houston Jewish leaders began to understand that white Gentiles were not their allies. As a result, in an attempt to change the makeup of Houston's school board, Jews forged an overt alliance with the city's African Americans.

Interactions between both communities solidified throughout the mid- to late 1960s through the 1980s as both groups explored identity politics. Jews were a welcomed—but small—minority in need of a larger presence; African Americans were a large—but discriminated against—minority that needed support. Through the redistricting of Harris County, Black politicians gained political power, which enhanced their relations with the Jewish community in Houston. For the Jewish community, the Six-Day War motivated the city's Jews to become more interested in identifying as Jewish Americans over white Americans of Jewish faith. This victory evoked a sense of pride as Israel was no longer just the home of lost Jewish refugees but a symbol of Jewish power. It caused local Jewish leaders and residents—even Congregation Beth Israel, the anti-Zionist synagogue of the 1940s—to realize that they were part of something greater: the Jewish world.

The changing environment of the city shaped encounters between both groups for the better. As segregation lessened and Houston became a more diverse city, Jews and Blacks deepened their connection. Black political leaders, first Barbara Jordan and then Mickey Leland, stood by the city's Jews in their support of Israel, and Houston's Jews supported them politically in return. Ultimately, unity emerged out of commonality. Houston Jewish leaders may have faced similar experiences to those in other parts of the South and the North, but it was their involvement and later collaboration with Black politicians that cumulatively shaped their relations over the long civil rights period from the 1930s to 1980s. It was this partnership that sets Houston apart in the greater American Jewish and African American story.

After Leland's death, Houston became a model of a new multicultural United States no longer divided between Black and white. A 1990 edition of *Time*, "America's Changing Colors," highlighted Houston's diversity. In "Beyond the Melting Pot," William A. Henry narrowed in on evidence of the city's multi-culturalism: "At the Sesame Hut restaurant in Houston, a Korean immigrant owner trains Hispanic immigrant workers to prepare Chinese-style food for a largely Black clientele." This was a striking illustration of how in Houston different groups merged without losing their own cultural identities.[19]

It was in this environment that Houston's African Americans and Jews continued to strengthen their relations with each other as well as with other groups. Notably, Jordan, who had retired from politics in 1979, spoke at Congregation Beth Israel in Houston in 1992 about future interactions between both communities. Her speech would become emblematic of their relations moving forward. Jordan situated local relations in a national context by tracing past encounters of Jews and African Americans during the civil rights movement and contrasting them with emerging tensions, including Jesse Jackson's derogatory remarks about "Hymietown" and Israel's economic relationship with South Africa under apartheid.[20]

She reminded Houston's Jews that their struggles were one and the same and that the two communities should stop blaming each other for prejudicial views. To reinforce how the communities' fates were intertwined, she cited the Director of the Commission on Social Action of Reform Judaism Leonard Fein, who claimed that "an America that is not safe for Jews cannot be safe for Blacks; an America that is not safe for Blacks will not stay fair to Jews."[21]

Jordan urged Houston's Jews to build on and expand existing ties. In her perspective, African Americans and Jews should "seek and achieve a comity, a loose alliance that is built upon mutual respect and that is not exclusive to Blacks and Jews but that is inclusive of all our brothers and sisters." She saw this bond as a foundation for changing America. Together they were the solution to bringing America closer to its original ideal as a diverse nation. Future leaders in both communities would heed Jordan's ideal.[22]

In the 1990s and early 2000s, local Jewish and Black leadership worked to preserve their relationship and Houston's status as a defining city for creating an alliance between both communities. In 1995, Pam Geyer, along with her Black colleague Wendy Rawlins, instituted dialogue groups for "building relationships with each other and 'unlearning' racism and anti-Semitism."[23] Through Bridge Houston, Ira Bleiweiss not only fought against anti-Zionism but also worked to create bridges with different local communities. Bleiweiss also worked jointly with Quanell X, the leader of the New Black Panther Nation of Houston, to protest Holocaust denier David Irving when he spoke at the LaQuinta Inn in Houston.[24] Black politicians like Congresswoman Sheila Jackson Lee and Congressman Al Green have consistently supported Israel in Houston and in Congress through their votes and by attending numerous local Jewish events for Israel. Lee has been acting director of the Mickey Leland Kibbutzim Internship since 1987. Green also became involved on the national and local level when he fought the Texas Association of Private and Parochial Schools to change the day of the state championship so the Jewish basketball team did not have to play on the Sabbath.[25]

The new Brigitte and Bashar Kalai Plaza of Respect at the Interfaith Ministries for Greater Houston campus featuring three monuments of dichroic glass to honor Rabbi Samuel Karff, Rev. William Lawson, and Archbishop A. Joseph Fiorenza. April 2, 2019. Melissa Phillip/©Houston Chronicle. Used with permission.

The so-called "Three Amigos"[26]—Reverend William Lawson, Rabbi Samuel Karff, and Archbishop Joseph Fiorenza—have become the embodiment of Jordan's call to make relations between Blacks and Jews more inclusive by including other cultural and minority groups in the twenty-first century. The three leaders have advocated to stop homelessness, improve the court and prison systems, and stop truancy.[27] They also instituted the Coalition of Mutual Respect, which, according to Jayme Fraser of the *Houston Chronicle*, "combat[ed] anti-Semitism, rallied diverse faith leaders to condemn the bombing of a local Islamic mosque, called for high schools with large minority populations to offer college prep courses … and fought for fair housing standards."[28] They have redefined interfaith activism through their work with TRUTH Houston, a peace and justice organization wanting to create a future generation of leaders who promote alliances between Blacks and Jews.[29]

More recent collaborations suggest that the alliance between minorities in Houston continues. In 2009, Jews, African Americans, Latinos, and white non-Jews stood together to oppose an anti-Israel protest at the Holocaust Museum Houston, in which protesters dressed in concentration camp garb to equate Israel's treatment of Palestinians with Nazi Germany.[30]

Will the next generation of Black and Jewish youth, further away from the struggles of the civil rights movement and the memories of Jordan and Leland, still be able to preserve these relations in light of more recent movements like Black Lives Matter? When Aaron Howard of the *JH-V* asked Congressman Al Green whether young African Americans were cognizant of Jewish activism during the civil rights movement, he responded that "my belief is the average young Black under 18 does not ... It's not been widely passed on. But we're getting there." Green likewise felt the Houston Jewish community needed to do more to educate young Jews on this history and that the solution for both communities was "to work harder passing down this history, particularly the history that binds us together. And not focus on the things that set us apart."[31]

Rabbi Walter of Congregation Emanu El said in an interview concerning Houston Jews' commitment to social justice that "the Jewish Community has stepped up and always been an important part of the social change that was taking place in the world around us as well as in our world." Walter noted that the virtue of Houston's Jewish community was that it was "very close." As he poignantly expressed, "We're Jews. We're a community. We're a people."[32]

No matter what happens, the preservation of the Mickey Leland Kibbutzim Internship keeps Leland's dreams of a "two-way" street between Jews and African Americans alive.[33] The true test of relations, however, will be whether leaders continue to believe, as Green claimed, that they are stronger "together than apart."[34] Leland's commitment to building lasting relations between the two communities hinged on this same rejection of the notion that collaboration cannot last because of what sets the two groups apart. The days when Houston Jewish leaders felt the need to value acculturation over liberalism will hopefully remain a memory, because Jews will recall how anti-Semitism still bloomed even in the soils of segregation. Yet only time will tell if the city's Jews and African Americans will remain together for the foreseeable future or simply drift apart.

Endnotes

Introduction

1. Allan Turner, "Exhibit Opening Tonight Examines Jim Crow," *Houston Chronicle*, August 4, 2011, http://www.chron.com/news/houston-texas/article/Exhibit-opening-tonight-examines-Jim-Crow-2079427.php.
2. Peter Novick, *The Holocaust in American Life* (Boston: Houghton Mifflin, 1999), conclusion; Eric Goldstein, *The Price of Whiteness: Jews, Race, and American Identity* (Princeton, NJ: Princeton University Press, 2008), 221–223.
3. Marc Schneier and Martin Luther King III, *Shared Dreams: Martin Luther King, Jr. and the Jewish Community* (Woodstock, VT: Jewish Lights, 2009), 34, 97; Clive Webb, *Fight Against Fear: Southern Jews and Black Civil Rights* (Athens: University of Georgia Press, 2001), 23–24.
4. Deborah Dash Moore, "Separate Paths: Blacks and Jews in the Twentieth-Century South," in *Struggles in the Promised Land: Toward a History of Black-Jewish Relations in the United States*, eds. Jack Salzman and Cornel West (New York: Oxford University Press, 1997), 284; "Atlanta Jewish and Black Coalitions," *AJC*, September 25, 2017, accessed September 25, 2017, https://www.ajc.org/news/atlanta-Black-jewish-coalition.
5. Elaine Maas, "The Jews of Houston: An Ethnographic Study" (PhD diss., Rice University, 1973), 179–180.
6. Maas, "The Jews of Houston," 116.
7. Alfred O. Hero, Jr. "Southern Jews, Race Relations, and Foreign Policy," in *Anti-Semitism in America*, ed. Jeffrey S. Gurock. Vol. 2 of *American Jewish History* (New York: Routledge, 1998), 816; Hasia Diner, "If I Am Not for Myself/ If I Am Only for Myself: Jews, the American South, and the Quandary of Self Interest," in *Jews and the State: Dangerous Alliances and the Perils of Privilege*, ed. Ezra Mendelsohn, vol. 19 of *Studies in Contemporary Jewry* (New York: Oxford University Press, 2003), 62; Charles Reagan Wilson, ed., *Religion in the South: Essays* (Jackson: University Press of Mississippi, 1985), 3; Leonard Dinnerstein, "Southern Jewry and the Desegregation Crisis, 1954–1970," in *Anti-Semitism in America*, ed. Jeffery Gurock, vol. 6, pt. 2 of *American Jewish History* (New York: Routledge, 1998), 233.
8. Gary A. Tobin, *Jewish Perceptions of Antisemitism* (New York: Plenum Press, 1988), 179–182.
9. See: Clive Webb, *Fight Against Fear*, 88–113.

10. Maas, "Jews of Houston," 99; "About," BYDS.org, accessed October 7, 2017, http://byds.org/; Congregation Beth Yeshurun Dedication Book Houston, Texas, September, 1962, Congregation Beth Yeshurun Archives.

11. Esther Hecht, "Houston," *Hadassah Magazine*, October & November 2014, http://www.hadassahmagazine.org/2014/10/22/houston/; "Jews Separate Selves at High School Lunch," *Jewish Post* (Indianapolis), February 1969, 31.

12. Sam Schulman, David Gottlieb, and Sheila Sheinberg, *Jewish Community Council of Metropolitan Houston: A Social and Demographic Survey of the Jewish Community of Houston, Texas* (Houston, TX: The Demographic Study Committee, 1976), 2.

13. Diner, "If I Am Not for Myself," 63.

14. Dana Evan Kaplan, *American Reform Judaism: An Introduction* (Piscataway, NJ: Rutgers University Press, 2003), 31–32.

15. Diner, "If I Am Not for Myself," 63.

16. Eric Foner, *Forever Free: The Story of Emancipation and Reconstruction* (New York: Knopf Doubleday Publishing Group, 2013), 238.

17. Willi Goetschel, "Mendelssohn and the State," MLN 122, no. 3 (April 2007): 488.

18. Kenneth D. Roseman, "Six-Tenths of a Percent of Texas," in *Lone Stars of David: The Jews of Texas*, eds. Hollace Ava Weiner and Kenneth Roseman (Waltham, MA: Brandeis University Press, 2007), 207; Cary Wintz, "Blacks," in *The Ethnic Groups of Houston*, ed. Fred R. Von Der Mehden (Houston: Rice University Studies, 1984), 20.

19. Quoted in Schneier and King III, *Shared Dreams*, 23.

20. Maas, "Jews of Houston," 179.

21. Mallory Robinson, interview by author, Houston, May 19, 2014.

22. Marc Dollinger, *Quest for Inclusion: Jews and Liberalism in Modern American* (Princeton, NJ: Princeton University Press, 2000), 3–18.

23. See: Goldstein, *The Price of Whiteness*.

24. "Hebrew Words Every Jews Should Know/ IX Hebrew, Israelite, Jew," April 15, 1955. Box 1, Folder 1945 Sow, MS-853, Robert I. Kahn Papers, American Jewish Archives, Cincinnati, Ohio [hereafter AJA].

25. Dollinger, *Quest for Inclusion*, 4.

26. Eli Evans, *The Provincials: A Personal History of Jews in the South* (New York: Free Press Paperbacks, 1997), 188.

27. Eric J. Sundquist, *Stranger in the Land: Blacks, Jews, Post-Holocaust America* (Cambridge, MA: Belknap Press of Harvard University Press, 2005), 3.

28. Norton Shaw, ed. "Teen Community Jewish Community Center Youth Council," *Jewish Herald Voice* [hereafter JH-V] (Houston, Texas), August 29, 1963, 9.

29. Jonathan Sarna, "What's the Use of Local Jewish History?" *Rhode Island Jewish Historical Notes* 12, part B, no. 1 (November 1995): 77–83; Carol Kammen, *On Doing Local History* (Walnut Creek, CA: AltaMira Press, 2003), 4.

30. Marc Lee Raphael, ed. *Columbia Anthology of Jews and Judaism in America* (New York: Columbia University Press, 2008), 2.

31. Cheryl Greenberg, "Black-Jewish Relations in the United States," in *Encyclopaedia Judaica, eds.* Michael Berenbaum and Fred Skolnik, 2nd ed., vol. 3 (Detroit: Macmillan Reference USA, 2007), 734–737.

32. Hasia Diner, *The Jews of the United States, 1654 to 2000* (Berkeley: University of California Press, 2004), 268; Cheryl Lynn Greenberg, *Troubling the Waters: Black-Jewish Relations in the American Century* (Princeton, NJ: Princeton University Press, 2006), 1.

33. Jack Salzman, "Introduction," in *Struggles in the Promised Land: Toward a History of Black-Jewish Relations in the United States*, eds. Jack Salzman and Cornel West (New York: Oxford University Press, 1997), 1.

34. Greenberg, *Troubling the Waters*, 1.

35. Greenberg, *Troubling the Waters*, 1.

36. Clayborne Carson, "The Politics of Relations between African-Americans and Jews," in *Blacks and Jews: Alliances and Arguments*, ed. Paul Berman (New York: Delacorte Press, 1994), 135.

37. Greenberg, *Troubling the Waters*, 1.

38. Marc Dollinger, *Black Power, Jewish Politics: Reinventing the Alliance in Jewish Politics in the 1960s* (Waltham, MA: Brandeis University Press, 2018), xiv. See: Dollinger, *Quest for Inclusion.*

39. See: Leonard Dinnerstein, "A Neglected Aspect of Southern Jewish History," *American Jewish Historical Quarterly* 61, no. 1 (September 1971); Dinnerstein, "Southern Jewry and the Desegregation Crisis"; Allen Krause, "Rabbi and Negro Rights in the South, 1954–1967," in *Jews in the South*, eds. Leonard Dinnerstein and Mary Dale Palsson (Baton Rouge: Louisiana State University Press, 1973); Evans, *The Provincials*; Cheryl Lynn Greenberg, "The Southern Jewish Community and Struggle for Civil Rights," in *African Americans and Jews in Twentieth Century: Studies in Convergence and Conflict*, eds. V.P. Franklin, Nancy J. Grant, Harold M. Kletnick, and Genna Rae Meneil (Columbia: University of Missouri Press, 1998); Webb, *Fight Against Fear*, 24; Clive Webb, "Closing Ranks: Montgomery Jews and Civil Rights, 1954–1960," in *Dixie Diaspora: An Anthology of Southern Jewish History*, ed. Mark K. Bauman (Tuscaloosa: University of Alabama Press, 2006); Mary Stanton, *The Hand of Essau* (Montgomery, AL: River City Publication, 2006).

40. See: Webb, *Fight Against Fear*, xvi; Mark Bauman, "Part V: Identity," in *Dixie Diaspora: An Anthology of Southern Jewish History*, ed. Mark K. Bauman (Tuscaloosa: University of Alabama Press, 2006), 355. See: Dollinger, *Quest for Inclusion*; Greenberg, "Southern Jewish Community."

41. Dollinger, *Black Power, Jewish Politics*, Introduction; Micah D. Greenstein and Howard Greenstein, "'Then and Now': Southern Rabbis and Civil Rights," in *The Quiet Voices: Southern Rabbis and Black Civil Rights, 1880s to 1990s* (Tuscaloosa: University of Alabama Press, 1997), 325–339. Seth Forman, Introduction, *Blacks in the Jewish Mind: A Crisis of Liberalism* (New York: NYU Press, 1998).

42. See: David G. McComb, *Houston: A History* (Austin: University of Texas Press, 1981); Howard Beeth and Cary D. Wintz, eds., *Black Dixie: Afro-Texan History and Culture in Houston* (College Station: Texas A&M University Press, 1992); Thomas Cole, *No Color Is My Kind: The Life of Eldrewey Stearns and the Integration of Houston* (Austin: University of Texas Press, 2012); William Henry Kellar, *Make Haste Slowly: Moderates, Conservatives, and School Desegregation in Houston* (College Station: Texas A&M University Press, 1999); Dwight Watson, *Race, and the Houston Police Department, 1930–1990* (College Station: Texas A&M University Press, 2005); Tynia Steptoe, *Houston Bound: Culture and Color in a Jim Crow City* (Oakland: University of California Press, 2015).

43. See: Maas, "Jews of Houston."

44. See: Bryan Stone, *Chosen Folks: Jews on the Frontiers of Texas* (Austin: University of Texas Press, 2011); See: Maas, "Jews of Houston."

45. Brian Behnken, *Fighting Their Own Battles: Mexican Americans, African Americans, and the Struggle for Civil Rights in Texas* (Chapel Hill: University of North Carolina Press, 2011); Max Krochmal, *Blue Texas: The Making of a Multiracial Democratic Coalition in the Civil Rights Era* (Chapel Hill: The University of North Carolina Press, 2016).

Prologue

1. James Martin SoRelle, "The Darker Side of 'Heaven': The Black Community in Houston, Texas, 1917–1945" (PhD diss., Kent State University, 1980), 4; Cary Wintz, "Blacks," 20; Betty Trapp Chapman, "A System of Government Where Business Ruled," *Houston History Magazine* 8, no. 1 (July 12, 2011): 30–31; Tamara Miner Haygood, "Use and Distribution of Slave Labor in Harris County, Texas, 1836–60," in *Black Dixie: Afro-Texan History and Culture in Houston*, eds. Howard Beeth and Cary D. Wintz (College Station: Texas A&M University Press, 1992), 49; "ISJL-Texas Houston Encyclopedia," *Institute of*

Southern Jewish Life, 2014, accessed August 10, 2016, http://www.isjl. org/texas-houston-encyclopedia.html.

2. Maas, "The Jews of Houston," 29; "ISJL-Texas Houston Encyclopedia"; Stone, *Chosen Folks*, 44; Aaron Howard, "Texas Jews: A History on Two Frontiers," JH-V (Houston, Texas), March 25, 2010, 8.

3. Anne Nathan Cohen, *The Centenary History: Congregation Beth Israel of Houston, Texas, 1854–1954* (Houston, TX: s.n., 1954), 1; Maas, "The Jews of Houston" 37, 30; Stone, 44; "ISJL-Texas Houston Encyclopedia."

4. Maas, "The Jews of Houston," 27–34.

5. Quoted in "ISJL-Texas Houston Encyclopedia."

6. Maas, "The Jews of Houston," 29.

7. Howard Jones, *The Red Diary: A Chronological History of Black Americans in Houston and Some Neighboring Harris County Communities—122 Years Later* (Austin, TX: Nortex Press, 1991), 36; Elaine Maas, "Jews," in *The Ethnics Groups of Houston*, ed. Fred R. von der Mehden (Houston: Rice University Studies, 1984), 20; Howard Jones, *The Red Diary*, 36; SoRelle, "The Darker Side of 'Heaven,'" 34; Michael R. Botson, Jr., *Labor, Civil Rights, and the Hughes Tool Company* (College Station: Texas A&M University Press, 2005), 122.

8. Benjamin Ross, *Dead End: Suburban Sprawl and the Rebirth of American Urbanism* (Oxford: Oxford University Press, 2014), 22; SoRelle, "The Darker Side 'Heaven,'" 35–36; "Mrs. Gladys House and Mrs. Holly Hogrobrook," interview by Gary Houston, The Institute of Texas Cultures Oral History Collection, January 21, 1994, accessed October 25, 2016, transcript, digital.utsa.edu/cdm/ref/collection/ p15125coll4/id/1628; Bernadette Pruitt, *The Other Great Migration: The Movement of Rural African Americans to Houston, 1900–1941* (College Station: Texas A&M University Press, 2013), 75.

9. SoRelle, "The Darker Side 'Heaven,'" 58, 97–99; John Ingram Gilderbloom, *Invisible City: Poverty, Housing, and New Urbanism* (Austin: University of Texas Press, 2008), 149; Donna M. DeBlasio, "Architecture," in *Encyclopedia of African American History, 1619–1895: From the Colonial Period to the Age of Frederick Douglass*, ed. Paul Finkleman (New York: Oxford University Press, 2009), 92–94; "Historic Marker: The Emancipation Park Project Marks a Special Place in the Celebration of Juneteenth," *Houston Chronicle*, June 19, 2015, accessed October 20, 2016, http://www.chron.com/opinion/editorials/ article/Historic-marker-6336420.php; The City of Houston, "Emancipation Park," *The City of Houston Official Site for Houston, Texas*, accessed October 20, 2016, http://www.houstontx.gov/parks/parksites/ emancipationpark.html.

10. "Race, Income, and Ethnicity Residential Change in a Houston Community, 1920–1970, by Barry J. Kaplan," Box 1 Folder 16: Source 2, 1981–2010, This is Our Home, It Is Not for Sale Film Collection. Courtesy of Special Collection. University of Houston Libraries; Anne Nathan Cohen, 36, 45.

11. Pruitt, *The Other Great Migration*,75; Wendy H. Bergoffen, "Taking Care of Our Own: Narratives of Jewish Giving and the Galveston Movement," *Shofar* 34, no. 2 (2016): 26, 33, 50; Maas, "The Jews of Houston," 39, 59; Gerald Salzman, "A History of Zionism in Houston 1897–1975" (Master's thesis, University of Houston, 1976), 46; Maas, "The Jews of Houston," 45–46.

12. Pruitt, *The Other Great Migration*, 75;Thomas McWhorter, "From Das Zweiter to El Segundo, A Brief History of Houston's Second Ward," *Houston History Magazine* 8, no. 1 (December 2010): 42; Maria Cristinia Garcia, "Agents of Americanization: Rusk Settlement and the Houston Mexicano Community, 1907–1950," in *Mexican Americans in Texas History*, eds. Emilo Zamoro, Cynthia Orozco, and Rodolfo Rocha (Austin: Texas State Historical Association, 2000), 125; "Ernest Equia," interview by Thomas Kreneck, HMRC Oral History Collection, February 25, 1988, accessed October 25, 2016, audio, http://digital.houstonlibrary.net/oral-history/ernest-equia_OH369.php.

13. "Jewish Population in the United States—Census 1917," in *American Jewish Yearbook*, 20 (1917–1918) (Philadelphia, PA: Jewish Publication Society, 1917): 412, accessed October 20, 2016, http://www.ajcarchives.org/AJC_DATA/Files/1917_1918_7_Statistics.pdf; "Barry Kaplan," HMRC Oral History Collection, April 29, 1979, audio, http://digital.houstonlibrary.net/oral-history/barry-kaplan_OHB27.php; Maas, "The Jews of Houston," 52.

14. Kaplan, interview; McComb, *Houston: A History*, 110; Ezell Wilson, "Third Ward, Steeped in Tradition of Self-Reliance and Achievement," *Houston History Magazine*, April 18, 2011, vol. 8, no. 2, 31–35; Equia, interview.

15. McComb, *Houston: A History*, 110; SoRelle,"The Darker Side of 'Heaven,'" 30–31; Naomi W. Lede and Constance Houston Thompson, *Precious Memories of a Black Socialite: A Narrative of the Life and Times of Constance Houston Thompson* (Houston: N.W. Lede, 1991), 122, 168; SoRelle, "The Darker Side of 'Heaven,'" 30–31; Mass, "The Jews of Houston," 54; Lede and Thompson, 156; U.S. Congress, Senate Committee on Banking, Housing, and Urban Affairs, *Club Membership Practices of Financial Institutions, Congressional Hearings, 1979–07–13*, 1979.

16. Steptoe, *Houston Bound*, 65; Henry Allen Bullock, *Pathways to the Houston Negro Market* (Ann Arbor, MI: JW Edwards, 1957), 28; Pruitt, 53.

17. Ruthe Winegarten, Cathy Schechter, and Jimmy Kessler, *Deep in the Heart: The Lives and Legends of Texas Jews: A Photographic History* (Austin, TX: Eakin Press), 76, 77; "ISJL-Texas Houston Encyclopedia."

18. Quoted in Anne Nathan Cohen, *The Centenary History*, 44.

19. Kellar, *Make Haste Slowly*, 18; Howard Beeth and Cary Wintz, eds.,"Part III: Economic and Social Development in Black Houston During the Era of Segregation Introduction," in *Black Dixie: Afro-Texan History and Culture in Houston* (College Station: Texas A&M University Press, 1992), 94; Lede and Thompson, *Precious Memories of a Black Socialite*, 122, 168.

20. SoRelle, "The Darker Side of 'Heaven,'" 285–287, 294.

21. James SoRelle, "The Emergence of Black Business in Houston, Texas: A Study of Race and Ideology, 1919–45," in *Black Dixie: Afro-Texan History and Culture in Houston*, eds., Howard Beeth and Cary D.Wintz (College Station: Texas A&M University Press, 1992), 93, 94, 98, 109; Howard Beeth and Cary Wintz, eds., "Part IV: Segregation, Violence, and Civil Rights: Race Relations in Twentieth-Century Houston Introduction," in *Black Dixie: Afro-Texan History and Culture in Houston*, eds., Howard Beeth and Cary D.Wintz (College Station: Texas A&M University Press, 1992), 94; *Handbook of Texas Online*, Douglas Hales, "Nickerson, William N., Jr.," accessed July 04, 2017, http://www.tshaonline.org/handbook/online/articles/fnifp; Pruitt, 240; "O'neta 'Pink' Cavitt," interview by Nicolas Castellanos, Gregory School Oral Histories, May 22, 2010, accessed October 25, 2016, film, http://digital.houstonlibrary.net/oral-history/oneta-cavitt_OH_GS_0013.php.

22. Mitchel P. Roth, Tom Kennedy, and Ray Hunt, *Houston Blue: The Story of the Houston Police Department* (Denton: University of North Texas Press, 2012), 233; Watson, *Race and the Houston Police*, 3; Alwyn Barr, *Black Texans: A History of African Americans in Texas, 1528–1995*, 2nd ed. (Norman: University of Oklahoma Press, 1996), 152; Pruitt, 36.

23. James SoRelle, "Race Relations in "Heavenly Houston, 1919–45," in *Black Dixie: Afro-Texan History and Culture in Houston*, eds., Howard Beeth and Cary D. Wintz (College Station: Texas A&M University Press, 1992), 175; Beeth and Wintz, eds., "Part IV: Segregation, Violence, and Civil Rights: Race Relations in Twentieth-Century Houston Introduction," 161; Karen Kossie-Chernyshev, "Houston Riot of 1917," in *The Jim Crow Encyclopedia*, eds. Nikki L.M. Brown and Barry M. Stentiford, vol. 1 (Westport, CT: Greenwood Press, 2008), 386–387.

24. Stone, *Chosen Folks*, 98, 118; Winegarten, Schechter, and Kessler, *Deep in the Heart*, 77.

25. Quoted in Merline Pitre, *In Struggle Against Jim Crow: Lulu B. White and the NAACP, 1900–1957* (College Station: Texas A&M University Press, 1999), 18.
26. "The Colonel Gives Up-To-Date Study of World-Wide Sentiment Against Jew and Shows Why," *Colonel Mayfield Weekly*, April 21, 1923, Colonel Mayfield's Weekly, The Dolph Briscoe Center for American History [herafter DBCAH), The University of Texas at Austin [CAH], Box Newspaper Column Folder 4/21/1923.
27. "The Colonel Scents a Note of Danger in the Jewish and Catholic Combine," *Colonel Mayfield Weekly*, March 25, 1922, Colonel Mayfield's Weekly, DBCAH, The University of Texas at Austin [CAH], Box Newspaper Column Folder 3/25/1923; Casey Greene, "Guardians Against Change: The Ku Klux Klan in Houston and Harris County, 1920–1925," *Houston History Magazine* 8, no. 1 (Fall 2010), 2; Stone, 123, 127; Greene, 4; Steptoe, 105–107.
28. *Colonel Mayfield Weekly*, April 1, 1922, Colonel Mayfield's Weekly, DBCAH, The University of Texas at Austin [CAH], Box Newspaper Column Folder 4/1/1922.
29. "ISJL-Texas Houston Encyclopedia"; Steptoe, *Houston Bound*, 105–107; Clifton Richardson, Jr. Interview by Louis Marchiafava, HMRC Oral History Collection, June 9, 1975, accessed October 25, 2016, audio. http://digital.houstonlibrary.net/oral-history/clif-richardson.php.
30. *Handbook of Texas Online*, Diana J. Kleiner, "Houston Informer and Texas Freeman," accessed May 27, 2017, http://www.tsaonline.org/handbook/online/articles/eeh11.
31. Clifton Richardson, "A Lesson from the Jewish Race," *The Houston Informer* (Houston, Texas), June 7, 1919.
32. Clifton Richardson, editorial, *The Houston Informer* (Houston, Texas), May 28, 1921.
33. "Cora Johnson," interview by Adrienne Cain, HMRC Oral History Collection, April 16, 2013, accessed October 25, 2016, film, http://digital.houstonlibrary.net/oral-history/cora-johnson_OHGS0061.php.
34. Saul Friedman. Box 3 Folder 27: Saul Friedman Research, 1993–1997, Thomas R. Cole Desegregation Papers. Courtesy of Houston History Archives, Special Collections, University of Houston Libraries.
35. Bullock, 209; Wintz and Beeth, eds., "Part III: Economic and Social Development in Black Houston During the Era of Segregation," 93.
36. Charles S. Johnson, "Source Material for Patterns of Negro Segregation 12-Houston, Tex.," Reel 7 Box 1, SC Micro R-6534. Carnegie-Myrdal Study of the Negro in America Research Memoranda Collection, Schomburg Center for Research in Black Culture [hereafter SCRBC], The New York Public Library [hereafter NYPL].

37. Charles S. Johnson, "Source Material for Patterns of Negro Segregation 12-Houston, Tex."; Gloria Darrow, interview by Vince Lee, Gregory School Oral Histories, December 8, 2010, accessed October 25, 2016, film, http://digital.houstonlibrary.net/oral-history/Gloria-Darrow_ OHGS0023.php; Clive Webb, "A Tangled Web: Black-Jewish Relations in the Twentieth-Century South," in *Jewish Roots in Southern Soil: A New History*, eds., Marcie Cohen Ferris and Mark I. Greenberg (Waltham, MA: Brandeis University Press, 2006), 193.
38. SoRelle, "The Emergence of Black Business in Houston, Texas," 108.
39. Charles S. Johnson, "Source Material for Patterns of Negro Segregation 12-Houston, Tex.," Reel 7 Box 1, SC Micro R-6534. Carnegie-Myrdal Study of the Negro in America Research Memoranda Collection, SCRBC, NYPL.
40. Sarah S. Malino, "Southern Jewish Retailers (1840–2000)," in *Encyclopedia of American Jewish History*, eds. Stephen H. Norwood and Eunice G. Pollack, vol. 2 (Santa Barbara: CA: ABC-CLIO, 2008), 400; "Serra Gordon," interview by Josh Parshall, Goldring/Woldenberg Institute of Southern Jewish Life, July 14, 2011; "Harold Wiesenthal," interview by David Goldstein, Houston Oral History Project, July 8, 2008, accessed October 25, 2016, film, http://digital.houstonlibrary. net/oral-history/harold-wiesenthal.php; Gordon, interview.
41. Kaplan, interview; Maas, "The Jews of Houston," 58; Archeological and Historical Commission, "Landmark Designation Report," City of Houston Planning and Development Department, January 12, 2012, accessed October 12, 2016, http:///www.houstontx.gov/planning/ Commissions.docs_pdfs/hahc/reprots_ACTION/JunAction?B2_2622_ Riverside Terrace _PLM_Action.pdf; "Race, Income, and Ethnicity Residential Change in a Houston Community, 1920–1970, by Barry J. Kaplan," Box 1 Folder 16: Source 2, 1981–2010, This Is Our Home, It Is Not for Sale Film Collection. Courtesy of Special Collection, University of Houston Libraries; "Much history flows through Riverside Terrace" by Katherine Feser, *Houston Chronicle*, April 3, 1994, Box 1 Folder 18: Newspaper Article about Riverside Terrace part 1 of 2, 1953–1995, This Is Our Home, It Is Not for Sale Film Collection. Courtesy of Special Collections, University of Houston Libraries.
42. Kaplan, interview; Malevna Weingarten, Box 1 Folder 22: Preliminary Interview Notes on Index Cards (2), undated, This Is Our Home, It Is Not for Sale Film Collection. Courtesy of Special Collections, University of Houston Libraries; Example of use of Restrictive Covenants: Celia Morris, *Finding Celia's Place* (College Station:: Texas A&M University Press, 2000), 50.
43. Susan Rogers, "Hazardous: "The Redlining of Houston Neighborhoods," *Cite: The Architecture + Design Review of Houston*, October 4,

2016, accessed October 20, 2016, http://offcite.org/hazardous-the-redlining-of-houston-neighborhoods.

44. Robert Fairbanks, *The War on Slums in the Southwest: Public Housing and Slum Clearance in Texas, Arizona, and New Mexico, 1935–1965* (Philadelphia: Temple University Press, 2016), 59–60; Rogers, "Hazardous: The Redlining of Houston Neighborhoods."

45. Fairbanks, *War on Slums in the Southwest*, 17, 47; "History of HHA," *Housing Communities*, 2009, accessed August 8, 2016, http://www.housingforhouston.com/about-hha/history-of-hha.aspx; Fairbanks, *War on Slums in the Southwest*, 56.

46. Fairbanks, *War on Slums in the Southwest*, 58; NAACP 1940–55, General Office File. 1980.Frederick, MD: University Publications of America; Fairbanks, 57, 58, 59; SoRelle, "The Darker Side of 'Heaven,'" 248; Fairbanks, *War on Slums in the Southwest*, 55, 57; "Geraldine Pittman-Wooten," interview by Adrienne Cain, Gregory School Oral Histories, February 5, 2013, accessed October 25, 2016, film, http://digital.houstonlibrary.net/oral-history/geraldine-wooten_OHGS0055.php; Fairbanks, *War on Slums in the Southwest*, 59.

47. SoRelle, "The Darker Side of 'Heaven,'" 246; Fairbanks, *War on Slums in the Southwest*, 59–60.

48. Fairbanks, *War on Slums in the Southwest*, 59, 60.

49. *The Informer* (Houston, Texas), December 14, 1940.

50. SoRelle, "The Darker Side of 'Heaven,'" 248; Fairbanks, *War on Slums in the Southwest*, 59; SoRelle, "The Darker Side of 'Heaven,'" 248.

51. Roger Wood, *Down in Houston: Bayou City Blues* (Austin: University of Texas Press, 2003), 71; University of Houston, *Attwell, Ernie— Attwell transcript 1 of 1, November 12, 2004, Oral Histories from the Houston History Project, Special Collections, University of Houston Libraries*, accessed March 25, 2017, http://digital.lib.uh.edu/collection/houshistory/item/570/show/567; Steptoe, *Houston Bound*, 171–173; Roger Wood, *Down in Houston*, 30.

52. "Benny Joseph," interview by Cheri Wolfe, The Institute of Texan Cultures, December 16, 1993, accessed October 25, 2016, transcript, http://digital.utsa.edu/cdm/ref/collection/p15125coll4/id/1651.

53. "Race, Income, and Ethnicity Residential Change in a Houston Community, 1920–1970, by Barry J. Kaplan," Box 1 Folder 16: Source 2, 1981–2010. This Is Our Home, It Is Not For Sale Film Collection. Courtesy of Special Collection, University of Houston Libraries; Kaplan, interview; Thurman W. Robins, *Aspire, Act, Achieve* (Bloomington, IN: AuthorHouse, 2014), 1.

54. *This Is Our Home, It Is Not for Sale*, directed by Jon Schwartz (1987); Houston, Texas: Riverside Terrace Productions, 2007), DVD.

Chapter One

1. *The History of the Official Adoption of "The Basic Principles,"* by Congregation Beth Israel and Israel Friedlander, Policy Formulation Committee Papers, 1943–1968, Box 1, MS-132, Congregation Beth Israel [hereafter CBI] (Houston) Records, AJA.
2. Conference of Reform Rabbis, "The Pittsburgh Platform (1885)," in *The Jews in the Modern World: A Documentary History*, eds. Paul Mendes-Flohr and Jehuda Reinharz, 3rd ed. (Durham, NC: Duke University Press, 2011), 521–522.
3. Howard R. Greenstein, *Turning Point: Zionism and Reform Judaism*, vol. 12 of *Brown Judaic Studies* (Chico, CA: Scholars Press, 1981), 51–73; Bobby Brownstein, "The Battle of the 'Basic Principles:' Congregation Beth Israel and Anti-Zionist Revolt in American Reform Judaism" (master's thesis, University of Houston, 1991), 83; Gerald Salzman, "History of Zionism in Houston 1897–1975" (master's thesis, University of Houston, 1976), 83; Hollace Ava Weiner, *Jewish Stars in Texas: Rabbis and Their Works* (College Station: Texas A&M University Press, 1999), 193.
4. Jonathan D. Sarna and Jonathan Golden, "The American Jewish Experience through the Nineteenth Century: Immigration and Acculturation," *National Humanities Center*, 1999, accessed October 20, 2016, http://nationalhumanitiescenter.org/tserve/twenty/tkeyinfo/jewishexp.htm; Jewish Federation of Greater Houston, *Golden Jubilee: A Half Century of the Houston Jewish Federation 1936–1986* (Houston: Jewish Federation of Greater Houston, 1986), 1; Jewish Community Council of Metropolitan Houston, *A Six Year History of the Jewish Community Council of Metropolitan Houston: A Chronicle of Community Organization and Accomplishment* (Houston, TX: Jewish Community Council of Metropolitan Houston, 1943), 35–36.
5. Alison Cook, "Robert Sakowitz and His Fraying Empire: Why the Sakowitz Stores Went Bust," *Texas Monthly*, December 1985, 136.
6. *Handbook of Texas Online*, Sanford N. Greenberg, "White Primary," accessed October 20, 2016, http://www.tshaonline.org/handbook/online/articles/wdw01.
7. *The History of the Official Adoption of 'The Basic Principles,'* by Congregation Beth Israel and Israel Friedlander, Policy Formulation Committee Papers, 1943–1968, Box 1, MS-132, CBI (Houston) Records, AJA.
8. Jonathan Kaufman, "Blacks and Jews: The Struggle in the Cities," in *Struggles in the Promised Land: Toward a History of Black-Jewish Relations in the United States*, eds. Jack Salzman and Cornel West (New York: Oxford University Press, 1997), 109; Don E. Carleton,

Red Scare! Right Wing Hysteria Fifties Fanaticism and Their Legacy in Texas (Austin, TX: Texas Monthly Press, 1985), 63.

9. Paul Buhle and Robin D.G. Kelley, "Allies of Different Sorts," in *Struggles in the Promised Land: Toward a History of Black-Jewish Relations in the United States*, eds. Jack Saltzman and Cornel West (New York: Oxford University Press, 1997), 206–207; Margaret Nunnelley Olsen, "Teaching Americanism: Ray K. Daily and the Persistence of Conservatism in Houston School Politics 1943–1952," *Southwestern Historical Quarterly* 110, no. 2 (2006): 248; J.A. Zumoff, "The American Communist Party and the 'Negro Question' from the Founding of the Party to the Fourth Congress of the Communist International," *Journal for the Study of Radicalism* 6, no. 2 (Fall 2012): 53–89.

10. Howard Jones, 140; Robert V. Haynes, "Black Houstonians and the White Democratic Primary 1920–45," in *Black Dixie: Afro-Texan History and Culture in Houston*, eds. Howard Beeth and Cary D. Wintz (College Station, TX: Texas A&M University Press, 1992), 196–199; Pitre, 21–27.

11. Pitre, *In Struggle Against Jim Crow*, 2–27.

12. Quoted in Darlene Clark Hine, "The Elusive Ballot: The Black Struggle Against the Texas Democratic White Primary, 1932–1945," in *The African American Experience in Texas: An Anthology*, eds. Bruce A. Glasrud and James M. Smallwood (Lubbock: Texas Tech University Press, 2007), 283.

13. Quoted in Charles S. Johnson, "Source Material for Patterns of Negro Segregation 12-Houston, Tex.," Reel 7, Box 1, SC Micro R-6534, Carnegie-Myrdal Study of the Negro in America Research Memoranda Collection, SCRBC, NYPL.

14. Carter Wesley, "The Primary and Hitlerism," *The Informer* (Houston), November 5, 1938.

15. Lunabelle Wedlock, "Comparison by Negro Publications of the Plight of the Jews in Germany with that of the Negro in America (1942)," in *Relations Between Blacks and Jews in the United States*, eds. Maurianne Adams and John Bracey (Amherst: University of Massachusetts Press, 1999), 427–443.

16. Quoted in Thomas A. Guglielmo, "Fighting for Caucasian Rights: Mexicans, Mexican Americans, and the Transnational Struggle for Civil Rights in World War II Texas," *Journal of American History* 92, no. 4 (March 2006): 1212.

17. Tudor Parfitt, *Black Jews in Africa and the Americas* (Cambridge, MA: Harvard University Press, 2013), 93.

18. Communist Party of the United States of America, Texas State Committee, *Free Texas From Monopoly Control! Bring the New Deal to Texas!*

For Democracy, Security, Jobs, Peace (Houston, TX, 1938), https:// archive.org/details/FreeTexasFromMonopolyControlBringTheNewD- ealToTexasForDemocracy.

19. Communist Party of the United States of America, Texas State Commit-tee, *Communist Party of Texas 1940 State Platform*, https://archive.org/ details/1940StatePlatform_621.

20. Cecil B. Robinett, "An Open Letter," *The Houston Vanguard*, December 1, 1940, Q-JK2391C5H687m, Folder Houston Vanguard, no. 4 (Dec. 1, 1940), Texas Collection, DBCAH, The University of Texas at Austin [CAH].

21. E. A. Piller, *Time Bomb: America's Sinister New Fascism: Will It Explode on Schedule* (New York: Arco Publishing Company, 1945), 46.

22. Christian American, November 1936, BR 526 C464 Folder, Chris-tian American, vol 1, nos. 4–5 (1936), Texas Collection, DBCAH, The University of Texas at Austin [CAH]. See also: George Green, *The Establishment in Texas Politics: The Primitive Years, 1938–1957* (Norman: University of Oklahoma, 1979), 63; Michael Pierce, "The Origins of Right-to-Work: Vance Muse, Anti-Semitism, and the Maintenance of Jim Crow Labor Relations" *LAWCHA*, January 12, 2017, https://www.lawcha.org/2017/01/12/origins-right-work-vance-muse-anti-semitism-maintenance-jim-crow-labor-relations/; Bryan Burrough, *The Big Rich: The Rise and Fall of the Greatest Texas Oil Fortunes* (London: Penguin Group, 2009), 135–136.

23. Piller, *Time Bomb*, 54.

24. Quoted in Green, *The Establishment in Texas Politics*, 59.

25. Quoted in Piller, *Time Bomb*, 62.

26. Carleton, *Red Scare!*, 155.

27. "Mrs. Davis Charges Dr. Daily Defended Rugg Source Books," *Houston Post*, March 21, 1943.

28. Lynwood Abram, "Minority Report: Dr. Ray K. Daily Battles the Houston School Board," in *Lone Star of David: The Jews of Texas*, eds. Hollace Ava Weiner and Kenneth D. Roseman (Lebanon, NH: University Press of New England, 2007), 227–230; Olsen, "Teaching Americanism," 255; *Handbook of Texas Online*, Virginia Bernhard, "Hogg, Ima," accessed February 04, 2016, http://www.tshaonline.org/ handbook/online/articles/fho16.

29. Advertisement "Attention!! Colored Voters," Ray K. Daily Collec-tion, MS 9, Box 3, ScrapBook (Xerox copy), Houston Metropolitan Research Center, Houston Public Library [hereafter HMRC HPL]; *Handbook of Texas Online*, Diana J. Kleiner, "Fifth Ward, Houston," assessed October 16, 2016, https://tshaonline.org/handbook/online/ articles/hpfhk.

30. Quoted in Kellar, *Make Haste Slowly*, 37. See also: Pitre, *The Other Great Migration*, 27.

31. Pitre, *The Other Great Migration*, 71; Carleton, *Red Scare!*, *38*.

32. Letter from Arthur Mandell and Herman Wright to Miss Ima Hogg, April 13, 1943, Box 4w237, Folder 3, Ima Hogg Papers, 1924–1977, DBCAH, University of Texas at Austin [CAH].

33. Election Notice, Box 4w237, Folder 3, Ima Hogg Papers. See also Letter from Ima Hogg to Arthur J. Mandell, April 20, 1943, Box 4w237, Folder 3, Ima Hogg Papers.

34. Letter from Ray K. Daily to Miss Ima Hogg, February 16, 1943, Box 4W237, Folder 3, Ima Hog Papers. See also: Jewish Community Council of Metropolitan Houston, *A Six Year History*, inside front cover.

35. Larry Ceplair, *Anti-Communism in Twentieth Century America: A Critical History* (Santa Barbara, CA: Praeger, 2011), 56.

36. Letter from Ray K. Daily to Miss Ima Hogg, February 16, 1943, Box 4W237, Folder 3, Ima Hog Papers.

37. Letter from Mrs. Milby Porter to Miss Hogg, March 8, 1943, Box 4w237, Folder 3, Ima Hogg Papers.

38. Letter from Mrs. Milby Porter to Miss Hogg; Olsen, 243.

39. Letter from Ima Hogg to Mrs. Milby Porter, March 11, 1943, Box 4w237, Folder 11, Ima Hogg Papers.

40. Ray K. Daily, interview by Don Carleton, HMRC Oral History Collection, December 10, 1974, audio, http://digital.houstonlibrary.org/cdm/singleitem/collection/Interviews/id/343/rec/1.

41. Circular, Ray K. Daily, MS 9, Box 2, Folder 1: School Affairs Houston School Board, Pamphlets, Circulars, 1951 Election Returns, HMRC, HPL; Daily, interview.

42. Sarna and Golden, "American Jewish Experience;" H. Raphael Gold, ed., *The Book of Redemption*, comp. Jewish National Fund Council of Texas (Houston, TX: D.H. White Co.,1939); Maas, "Jews of Houston," 44; Stuart Rockoff, "Deep in the Heart of Palestine: Zionism in Early Texas," in *Lone Star of David: The Jews of Texas*, eds. Hollace Ava Weiner and Kenneth D. Roseman (Lebanon, NH: University Press of New England, 2007), 103; Salzman, "A History of Zionism in Houston 1897–1975," 73; Stone, 161.

43. Central Conference of American Rabbis, "The Guiding Principles of Reform Judaism: 'The Columbus Platform'—1937," https://www.ccarnet.org/rabbinic-voice/platforms/article-guiding-principles-reform-judaism/.

44. Gold, *Book of Redemption*, 19.

45. W. Gunther Plaut, *The Growth of Reform Judaism: American and European Sources until 1948* (Philadelphia: Jewish Publication Society, 2015), 144; Thomas A. Kolsky, *Jews Against Zionism:*

The American Council for Judaism, 1942–1948 (Philadelphia: Temple University Press, 1990), 75, 68, 4; Rockoff, "Deep in the Heart of Palestine," 103; Rafael Medoff, *Jewish Americans and Political Participation: A Reference Handbook* (Santa Barbara, CA: ABC-CLIO, 2002), 35, 34; Melvin Urofsky, *A Voice That Spoke for Justice: The Life and Times of Stephen S. Wise* (Albany: State University of New York Press, 1982), 335.

46. Goldstein, *Price of Whiteness*, 27–29, 93, 102–106; Steven J. Belluscio, *To Be Suddenly White: Literary Realism and Racial Passing* (Columbia: University of Missouri Press, 2006), 31; *The Eugenics Crusade: What's Wrong with Perfect?*, directed by Michelle Ferrari (2018. Arlington, VA: PBS), DVD.

47. Kolsky, *Jews Against Zionism*, 70, 72,83.

48. Lessing J. Rosenwald, "Reply to Zionism: Why Many Americans of Jewish Faith Are Opposed to the Establishment of a Jewish State in Palestine," *Life Magazine*, July 28, 1943, 11.

49. Kolsky, *Jews Against Zionism*, 72.

50. "Hyman Judah Schachtel," interview by Gay Block and Linda May, Congregation Beth Israel, October 27, 1975, audio, http://www.beth-israel.org/learning-programs/library.

51. *The History of the Official Adoption of 'The Basic Principles'* by Congregation Beth Israel and Israel Friedlander, Policy Formulation Committee Papers, 1943–1968, Box 1, MS-132, CBI (Houston) Records, AJA.

52. Leopold Meyer, *Days of My Years: Autobiographical Reflection* (Houston TX: privately published, 1975), 195.

53. Letter from Israel Friedlander to Leopold Meyer, May 30, 1944, in *The History of the Official Adoption of 'The Basic Principles,'* Policy Formulation Committee Papers.

54. Letter from Israel Friedlander to Leopold Meyer, May 30, 1944.

55. Letter from Israel Friedlander to Leopold Meyer, May 30, 1944.

56. Letter from Israel Friedlander to Leopold Meyer, May 30, 1944.

57. Jewish Community Council of Metropolitan Houston, *A Six Year History*, 15–16; Winegarten, Schechter, and Kessler, *Deep in the Heart*, 123.

58. "Negro Wants Normal Life, Meeting Told: Rabbi Compares Plight of Colored Race in U.S. to That of Persecuted Jews in Ancient Egypt," *Houston Chronicle*, February 9, 1942, in *The History of the Official Adoption of 'The Basic Principles,'* Policy Formulation Committee Papers; Thomas A. Guglielmo, "'Red Cross, Double Cross': Race and America's World War II-Era Blood Donor Service," *Journal of American History* 97, no 1 (June 2010): 63–90.

59. "Lack of Negro Training Called Defense Handicap: 1000 Hear Rabbi Kahn At Meeting Here," *Houston Post*, February 9, 1942, in *The History*

of the Official Adoption of 'The Basic Principles,' Policy Formulation Committee Papers.

60. Carter Wesley, "Interracial Meet Is Minus All Prejudice," *The Informer* (Houston), February 14, 1942, 1, 10. See also: "Prejudice Cuts Both Ways, Rabbi Declares," *The Informer* (Houston), February 14, 1942, 1.

61. "Report of the Policy Formulation Committee," *The History of the Official Adoption of 'The Basic Principles,'* by Congregation Beth Israel and Israel Friedlander, Policy Formulation Committee, 1943–1968, Box 1, MS-132, CBI (Houston) Records, AJA.

62. "Report of the Policy Formulation Committee."

63. "Report of the Policy Formulation Committee."

64. "Report of the Policy Formulation Committee."

65. Richard Lloyd Jones, "The American Flag for All of Us," *Tulsa Tribune,* February 27, 1943; copy of editorial in *The History of the Official Adoption of 'The Basic Principles,'* by Congregation Beth Israel and Israel Friedlander, Policy Formulation Committee, 1943–1968, Box 1, MS-132, CBI (Houston) Records, AJA.

66. Board and Recommendation of Board of Trustees of Congregation Beth Israel, Box 7, Folder 254, MS 67, Leopold Meyer Papers, HMRC, HPL.

67. "1980, Kahn notes for TV Interview," Congregation Emanu El archives; Lucas Wall, "Rabbi Kahn, Integration Leader, Dies," *Houston Chronicle,* November 22, 2002, http://www.chron.com/news/houston-texas/article/Rabbi-Kahn-integration-leader-dies-2085638.php; Weiner, *Jewish Stars in Texas,* 184; Rockoff, *Deep in the Heart of* Palestine, 104.

68. David Aronson, "An Open Letter to Rabbi Schachtel," *The American Jewish World,* November 19, 1943, *The History of the Official Adoption of 'The Basic Principles'* by Congregation Beth Israel and Israel Friedlander, Policy Formulation Committee, 1943–1968, Box 1, MS-132, CBI (Houston) Records, AJA.

69. Stone, *Chosen Folks,* 167.

70. "In Memoriam D.H. White 1903–1972," *JH-V* (Houston), January 20, 1972; "Beth Israel Adopts Basic Principles; Membership Votes for 612 to 168," *JH-V* (Houston), November 25, 1943; "The Basic Principles of Cong. Beth Israel," *JH-V* (Houston), December 2, 1943; "Comments from Many Sources," *JH-V* (Houston), December 2, 1943.

71. Israel Goldstein, "Pathological Jews," *New Palestine,* in *The History of the Official Adoption of 'The Basic Principles'* by Congregation Beth Israel and Israel Friedlander, Policy Formulation Committee, 1943–1968, Box 1, MS-132, CBI (Houston) Records, AJA.

72. Rabbi Louis I. Neuman, "Houston 'Reform Judaism': Folly in Masquerade," *Independent Jewish Press Services,* January 23, 1944,

in *The History of the Official Adoption of 'The Basic Principles'* by Congregation Beth Israel and Israel Friedlander, Policy Formulation Committee, 1943–1968, Box 1, MS-132, CBI (Houston) Records, AJA.

73. Neuman, "Houston 'Reform Judaism': Folly in Masquerade."

74. Rabbi Fred Isserman, "Jim Crowism—A Temple Creed?" *Temple Israel Bulletin*, in *The History of the Official Adoption of 'The Basic Principles'* by Congregation Beth Israel and Israel Friedlander, Policy Formulation Committee, 1943–1968, Box 1, MS-132, CBI (Houston) Records, AJA.

75. "Religion: Storm over Zion," *Time Magazine*, January 17, 1944. See also: *The History of the Official Adoption of 'The Basic Principles,'* by Congregation Beth Israel and Israel Friedlander, Policy Formulation Committee, 1943–1968, Box 1, MS-132. CBI (Houston) Records. AJA.

76. Letter of Resignation from Congregation Beth Israel, Box A, Folder: A-13/17, Kahn, Robert I. 1931; 1933; 1944–1946, MS-5, Hebrew Union College [hereafter HUC] Records, 1873–1955, AJA. See also: Congregation Emanu El, Houston, Texas, "The First Fifty Years an Adventure of the Spirit 1944–1994," Nearprint: Congregation Emanu El, Nearprint Geography, AJA.

77. CBI (Houston), Policy Formulation Committee, *A Handbook of True Facts concerning the Basic Principles of Congregation Beth Israel, Houston, Texas (organized 1856) an American Reform Congregation* (Houston, TX: Congregation Beth Israel, 1944), 1.

78. CBI (Houston), *A Handbook of True Facts*, 1.

79. CBI (Houston), *A Handbook of True Facts* 6–7.

80. CBI (Houston), *A Handbook of True Facts*, 16.

81. CBI (Houston), *A Handbook of True Facts*, 16.

82. Herbert S. Lewis, "The Passion of Franz Boas," *American Anthropologist* 103, no. 2 (June 2001): 447; Douglas R. Parks and Ruthe E. Pathe, "Gene Weltfish 1902–1980," *Plains Anthropologist* 30, no. 107 (February 1985): 62.

83. CBI (Houston), *A Handbook of True Facts*, 16–17.

84. Laurence C. Thompson, "Melville Jacob, 1902–1971," *American Anthropologist* 80, no. 3, (1978): 642; Robert E. Park, "Jews in the Gentile World: The Problem of Anti-Semitism," review of *Jews in the Gentile World: The Problem of Anti-Semitism*, by Isacque Graeber and Stuart Henderson Britt, *American Sociological Review* 9, no. 6 (Dec., 1944): 711; CBI (Houston), *A Handbook of True Facts*, 17.

85. Quoted in CBI (Houston), *A Handbook of True Facts*, 17.

86. Charles Gordon, "The Racial Barrier to American Citizenship," *University of Pennsylvania Law Review* 93, no. 3 (March 1945): 242–245.

87. The Jewish Community Relations Council found homes in Houston for 120 German refugees. Nathan Klein, an influential Jew in Houston, also used his own funds to sponsor the immigration of 100 European Jews. See: Jewish Community Council of Metropolitan Houston, *A Six Year History*, 15–16; Winegarten, Schechter, and Kessler, *Deep in the Heart*, 123; Stone, *Chosen Folk*, 176; Roseman, "Six-Tenths of a Percent of Texas," 207.

88. Goldstein, *Price of Whiteness*, 102; Sarna, *American Judaism*, 216; David Brody, "American Jewry, the Refugees, and Immigration Restriction (1932–1942)," in *America, American Jews, and The Holocaust*, ed. Jeffery S. Gurock (New York: Routledge, 1998), 197, 200.

89. CBI (Houston), *A Handbook of True Facts*, 17; John Tehranian, "Compulsory Whiteness: Towards a Middle Eastern Legal Scholarship," *Indiana Law Journal* 82, no. 1 (Winter 2007): 15.

90. Easurk Emsen Charr, *The Golden Mountain: The Autobiography of a Korean Immigrant 1895–1960*, ed. Wayne Patterson, 2nd ed. (Urbana: University of Illinois Press, 1961); Jacqueline Jones, *A Dreadful Deceit: The Myth of Race from the Colonial Era to Obama's America* (New York: Basic Books, 2015), chapter 4; CBI (Houston), *A Handbook of True Facts*, 18.

91. "The Jews—Nation, Race or Religion," by H. J. Schachtel, March 1944, MS 0172, Box B, Rabbi Hyman Judah Schachtel Papers, HMRC, HPL.

92. "Rabbi Schachtel Opposes National State for Jews," *JH-V* (Houston), June 7, 1945, 1; "Rabbinical Ass'n Rebukes Rabbi Hyman J. Schachtel," *JH-V* (Houston), June 7, 1945, 1; Weiner, 203.

93. "Hyman Judah Schachtel," interview by Gay Block and Linda May, Congregation Beth Israel, October 27, 1975, audio, http://www.beth-israel.org/learning-programs/library. See also: "Rabbi Hyman Judah Schachtel of Beth Israel Vigorously Opposes Jewish National State," Box 1, Folder, Houston, Tex-Cong Beth Israel Clippings re Basic Principles 1943–1945; 1949 n.d. MS-132. CBI (Houston) Records, AJA; Weiner, 200.

94. Box 45, Folder 8, MS-724. Alan S. Green Papers, American Jewish Archives, Cincinnati, Ohio.

95. "Rabbi Tofield Takes Exception," *JH-V* (Houston), June 7, 1945, 1.

96. "Houston Papers," Box 45, Folder 8, MS-724, Alan S. Green Papers, AJA.

97. Stephen S. Wise, "The Shame of Houston," *Opinion: A Journal of Jewish Life and Letter* 19 no. 4 (February 1944): 5.

98. Weingarten's Letter of Resignation to Congregation Beth Israel, July 20, 1945, in *The History of the Official Adoption of 'The Basic Principles,'* Policy Formulation Committee Papers.

99. Stone, *Chosen Folk*, 167.

100. "Rabbi H. Schachtel Quits Council," *National Jewish Post* (Indianapolis), April 15, 1949.

Chapter Two

1. Stuart Svonkin, *Jews Against Prejudice: American Jews and the Fight for Civil Liberties* (New York: Columbia University Press, 1997), 1–11.
2. *The House I Live In*, YouTube video, 10:15, posted by "KRT1934," November 10, 2008, https://www.youtube.com/watch?v=vhPwtnGviyg.
3. Quoted in Svonkin, *Jews Against Prejudice*, 11.
4. David White, "Let Us Be Careful of Labels," *JH-V* (Houston), December 26, 1946, 4.
5. McComb, 131–135; Carleton, *Red Scare!*, 8,16.
6. David Berg, *Run, Brother, Run: A Memoir* (New York: Scribner, 2013), 18.
7. Wintz, "Blacks," 20; "Statistics of the Jews," in *American Jewish Yearbook*, vol. 43, 1941–1942 (Philadelphia: Jewish Publication Society, 1941–1942), 660, http://www.ajcarchives.org/AJC_DATA/Files/1941_1942_9_ Statistics.pdf; Roseman, "Six-Tenths of a Percent of Texas," 207.
8. Carleton, *Red Scare!*, 72; Jeff Woods, *Black Struggle, Red Scare: Segregation and Anti-Communism in the South, 1948–1968* (Baton Rouge: Louisiana University Press, 2004), 1–11.
9. Chandler Davidson, "Negro Politics and the Rise of the Civil Rights Movement in Houston, Texas" (PhD diss., Princeton University, 1968), 86; Carleton, *Red Scare!*, 63–100, 125, 134.
10. Jewish Federation of Greater Houston, *Golden Jubilee*, 11–13, 15; Maas, "Jews of Houston," 59; Alice Bruce Currlin, *Community Welfare Houston, Texas* (Houston: Community Chest and Council of Houston and Harris County, 1946), 28; "Executive Directors Guide JFS for Over 100 Years," *JH-V* (Houston), May 30, 2013, 14.
11. Quoted in Jewish Federation of Greater Houston, *Golden Jubilee*, 13.
12. David White, "Are We So Blind," *JH-V* (Houston), February 21, 1946.
13. Jewish Federation of Greater Houston, *Golden Jubilee*, 17.
14. Leon J. Taubenhaus, "Says We Can't Use the Silent Treatment," *JH-V* (Houston), November 2, 1946, 2.
15. David White, "Are We Selling 'Fear Judaism'?," *JH-V* (Houston), November 21, 1946, 2.
16. "Thos. Friedman to Discuss A.D. Program at Symposium Series," *JH-V* (Houston), December 5, 1946, 13. See also: Sarna, *American Judaism*, 276; Jewish Federation of Greater Houston, *Golden Jubilee*, 12.
17. "Center Social Group Reviews Vocational Anti-Semitism," *JH-V* (Houston), December 18, 1947, 8.
18. Jewish Federation of Greater Houston, *Golden Jubilee*, 15.
19. "'Which Way Anti-Semitism in This Country' Panel Discussion at Houston Lodge Meeting April 21st," *JH-V* 43rd Anniversary—Passover

Edition (Houston), vol. 44 (1949–50); "'Is Prejudice Increasing or Decreasing in Country?' Topic for Houston Lodge Meeting," *JH-V* (Houston), May 18, 1950, 6.

20. Arnold Forster, *A Measure of Freedom: An Anti-Defamation League Report* (Garden City, NY: Doubleday, 1950).

21. Charles S. Johnson, "Source Material for Patterns of Negro Segregation 12-Houston, Tex.," Reel 7, Box 1, SC Micro R-6534, Carnegie-Myrdal Study of the Negro in America Research Memoranda Collection, SCRBC, NYPL.

22. Charles S. Johnson, "Source Material for Patterns of Negro Segregation 12-Houston, Tex."

23. Watson, *Race and the Houston Police*, 35, 49; Wintz and Beeth, eds., *Black Dixie*, 98–99.

24. F. Kenneth Jensen, "The Houston Sit-In Movement of 1960–61," in *Black Dixie: Afro-Texan History and Culture in Houston*, eds. Howard Beeth and Cary D. Wintz (College Station: Texas A&M University Press, 1992), 211.

25. Carter Wesley, *The Informer* (Houston), March 20, 1943. See also: Amicar Shabazz, "Carter Wesley and the Making of Houston's Civic Culture before the Reconstruction," *Houston Review of History and Culture* 1, no. 2 (Summer 2004): 13.

26. Attwell, interview.

27. See the following oral histories for first-hand accounts of segregation in Houston: University of Houston, *Williams, Beneva—Williams audio, 1 of 3*, July 13, 2006, Oral Histories from the Houston History Project, SC, UHL, http://digital.lib.uh.edu/collection/houhistory/item/786/show/782; "Patricia Smith Prather," interview by Gary Houston, Institute of Texas Cultures Oral History Collection, January 21, 1994, transcript, http://digital.utsa.edu/cdm/ref/collection/p15125coll4/id/1747; "Isaac Bryant," interview by Jacqueline Bartha, Gregory School Oral Histories, July 27, 2011, film, http://digital.houstonlibrary.net/oral-history/isaac-bryant_OHGS0034.php.

28. Pitre, *The Other Great Migration*, chapter 4; Richard West, "Only the Strong Survive," *Texas Monthly*, February 1979, accessed October 20, 2016, http://www.texasmonthly.com/articles/only-the-strong-survive/; Wintz and Beeth, *Black Dixie*, 159; Jensen, "The Houston Sit-In Movement of 1960–61," 212.

29. "Dr. Merline Pitre," HMRC Oral History Collection, 1980, audio, http://digital.houstonlibrary.net/oral-history/merline-pitre_OHB45.php.

30. Jack Feinsilver, "Education for Minorities Discussed at Sunday Night Social," *JH-V* (Houston), November 6, 1947, 4.

31. "Sixteen Student Organizations Represented," *Informer* (Houston), November 23, 1946; "Jewish Groups File Brief with Supreme Court

on Denial of Admission of Negro to School," *JTA* (New York), May 25, 1949; "Daniel Claims Strong Groups Behind Sweatt," *Dallas Morning News* (Dallas), December 3, 1949.

32. Matt Nichter, "The Old Left and the Rise of the Civil Rights Movement, 1930–1964" (Master's thesis, University of Wisconsin-Madison, 2005), 48.

33. Moses Leroy, interview by Florence Coleman, HMRC Oral History Collection, October 30, 1974, audio, http://digital.houstonlibrary.net/ oral-history/moses-leroy_OH102.php.

34. Eleanor Tinsley, interview by Jane Ely, HMRC Oral History Collection, October 16, 2007, film, http://digital.houstonlibrary.net/oral-history/ eleanor-tinsley.php.

35. Rev. Lee Haywood Simpson Papers, MS 0239, Box 5, Folder 5: "Profile of the Houston Negro Community with Special Tribute to Barbara Jordan," Harris County Council of Organizations, 1967, HMRC, HPL; Abner Anderson, interview by Adrienne Cain, Gregory School Oral Histories, August 22, 2013, film, http://digital.houstonlibrary.org/cdm/ singleitem/collection/gsinterview/id/59/rec/16.

36. "Race Relations Sunday," in *Holidays, Festivals, and Celebrations of the World Dictionary*, 3rd ed., ed. Helene Henderson (Detroit: Omni-graphics, 2005), 437; "Brotherhood/Sisterhood Week," in Henderson, *Holidays, Festivals, and Celebrations*, 68; Benny Kraut, "Towards the Establishment of the National Conference of Christians and Jews: The Tenuous Road to Religious Goodwill in the 1920s," *American Jewish History* 77, no. 3 (March 1988): 388–412.

37. Melton J. Gordon, ed., "National Conference for Community and Justice," *Encyclopedia of American Religions*, 7th ed. (Detroit: Gale Division of Cengage Learning Inc, 2003), 214.

38. Greenberg, *Troubling the Waters*, 149, 152.

39. Though the exact date of Batiste's memory is unknown, she did remember that Schachtel of Congregation Beth Israel conducted the Brother-hood Week service. Gertrude Beatrice Scott Batiste, interview by Maria Nora Olivares, Institute of Texan Cultures, February 8, 1995, transcript, http://digital.utsa.edu/cdm/ref/collection/p15125coll4/id/587.

40. "'Race Relations' to Be Observed Here Feb. 9, 4 p.m.," *The JH-V* (Houston), February 6, 1947, 8.

41. Congregation Beth Yeshurun, "Rabbi Malev to Speak at Inter-Racial Service," *The Message* 2 (November 21, 1947): 1; U.S. Congress, *In Recognition of an Interfaith Celebration of Thanksgiving* (Washington, DC: Congressional Record Daily Edition, 2003).

42. "Council on Education in Race Relations to Hold Community Service Feb. 8," *JH-V* (Houston), January 29, 1952, 2.

43. See, for example: "Two Inter-Racial Services to Be Held: Rabbi Marcus and Frank to Speak," *JH-V* (Houston), November 19, 1953, 12; "Council

on Education in Race Relations to Have Thanksgiving Service," *JH-V* (Houston), November 18, 1954, 2; "Race Relations to Be Observed Sunday, Feb. 8th, 3:30 p.m. at the First Christian Church with Many Groups Participating," *JH-V* (Houston), February 5, 1959.

44. "Interfaith Thanksgiving Service Set for Thursday in City-Wide Observance," *JH-V* (Houston), November 17, 1955, 10.

45. "Preliminary Report on My Ed.D Thesis by Hyman Judah Schachtel," Box E, Folder: Thesis-Ed.D Degree University of Houston Light of Liberty—A Guide to Better Human Relations, MS 172, Hyman Judah Schachtel Papers, HMRC, HPL.

46. Susan J. Douglas, *Listening In: Radio and the American Imagination* (Minneapolis: University of Minnesota Press, 2004), 5.

47. Congregation Beth Yeshurun, "Rabbi Malev, Chairman of 'American Way' Program," *The Message* 3 (January 14, 1949): 3. See also: Congregation Beth Yeshurun, "Race Relations Program Starts December 3," *The Message* 4 (December 2, 1949): 3; Congregation Beth Yeshurun, "Radio Program Worth Listening To," *The Message* 4 (February 10, 1950): 5.

48. Congregation Beth Yeshurun, "Race Relations Program Starts December 3," *The Message* 4 (December 2, 1949): 3.

49. Congregation Beth Yeshurun, "Radio Program Worth Listening To," *The Message* 4 (February 10, 1950): 5.

50. "The Humanitarian Hour 'The Change We Really Need,'" by Dr. Hyman Judah Schachtel, November 2, 1952, Box 61 2/B/3, Folder 2: Photocopied articles Rabbi Schachtel, 1950 and 1960s, CBI Archives, Houston, Texas.

51. "The Humanitarian Hour 'The Change We Really Need."

52. "The Humanitarian Hour: The Family of Mankind, February 26, 1955," by Hyman Judah Schachtel, Box Nearprint, Folder: Schachtel. Hyman Judah, Nearprint File, AJA.

53. Hyman Schachtel, *The Life You Want to Live* (New York: E.P. Dutton & CO., Inc., 1956), 60, 65, 217, 218.

54. Schachtel, *The Life You Want to Live*, 224.

55. "The Promise of America Rabbi Robert I. Kahn Rosh Hashonah a.m," sermon, October 1, 1951, Box 1, Folder SMS-SMU, MS-853, Robert I. Kahn Papers, AJA.

56. "Rabbi Kahn to Give Series of Sermons on 'Communism' Beginning March 28," *JH-V* (Houston), March 20, 1952, 8.

57. Robert I. Kahn, *An Affirmative Answer to Communism: A Series of Four Sermons* (Houston, TX: Congregation Emanu El, 1952), 6.

58. Mary L. Dudziak, *Cold War Civil Rights: Race and the Image of American Democracy* (Princeton, NJ: Princeton University Press, 2000), 8, 13.

59. "Am Yisorel Chai": Emanu El Service of the Air Dr. Robert I. Kahn," March 1, 1953, Box 3, Folder Emanu El Services of the Air 1952–1953, Rabbi Kahn's Copies, MS-853, Robert I. Kahn Papers, AJA.

60. Pepi Nichols, interview by author, Houston, May 21, 2014.
61. Leopold Meyer to Albert Parker, December 12, 1953, Box 9, Folder 124, MS-67, Leopold Meyer Papers, HMRC, HPL; Leopold Meyer to George Alpert, December 15, 1953, Box 9, Folder 124, MS-67, Leopold Meyer Papers, HMRC, HPL.
62. Pitre, *In Struggle against Jim Crow*, 72–73.
63. Carter Wesley, *The Informer* (Houston), July 19, 1947.
64. Pitre, *In Struggle against Jim Crow*, 72, 89, 118; Jeff Woods, *Black Struggle, Red Scare*, 50, 61, 62; "Negro U. Branded Red Target," *Houston Post*, March 9, 1948; "Negro U. Case Up to Regents," *Houston Post*, March 10, 1948.
65. Ralph O'Leary, "Teacher Ran into Volley of Epithets," *Houston Post*, October 18, 1953, 1.
66. Carleton, *Red Scare!*, 142–143; June Melby Benowitz, "Minute Women of the U.S.A.," *Handbook of Texas Online*, accessed September 12, 2016, http://www.tshaonline.org/handbook/online/articles/pwm01.
67. Ralph O'Leary, "Teacher Ran into Volley of Epithets," *Houston Post*, October 18, 1953, 1.
68. Letter from R.A. Childers to Mr. Holger Jeppeson, President Houston School Board, March 22, 1952, Box 6, Folder 3: Misc. Speeches Houston's Reactions March, 1952–August, 1953, MS 40, Ralph S. O'Leary Papers, HMRC, HPL.
69. Congregation Beth Yeshurun, "Hats off to Drs. Louis and Ray K. Daily," *The Message* 3 (April 22, 1949): 5.
70. "Dr. Daily, Mrs. Rogers Address Beth Yeshurun Forum," *JH-V* (Houston), October 23, 1952, 1.
71. Ray K. Daily, interview by Don Carleton; "'Socialism' Charges Fire School Race by John Spano Houston Press October 29, 1952," Box 2, Folder 9: Minute Women—Newspaper Clippings, April 19, 1951–December, 1952, MS 40, Ralph S. O'Leary Papers, HMRC, HPL; Carleton, *Red Scare!*, 171.
72. Olsen, "Teaching Americanism," 264; Abram, "Minority Report: Ray K. Daily Battles the Houston School Board," 230; Kate S. Kirkland, "For All Houston's Children: Ima Hogg and the Board of Education, 1943–1949," *The Southwestern Historical Quarterly* 101, no. 4 (Apr.,1998), 467; Daily, interview.
73. David White, "Our Schools—The Backbone of American Democracy," *JH-V* (Houston) October 16, 1952, 3.
74. White, "Our Schools—The Backbone of American Democracy."
75. White, "Our Schools—The Backbone of American Democracy."
76. Olsen, "Teaching Americanism," 241; "Ray K. Daily" (*Houston Post*, Jan 20, 1976), Box 1, Folder 2: Biographical Newspaper Clippings Concerning Dr. Louis Daily Sr. and Dr. Ray K. Daily, MS 9, Ray K. Daily Collection, HMRC, HPL.

77. Ruthe Winegarten, "Congregation Emanu El, Houston Nov 21, 1991," Box: 3J146 Folder November 21, 1991 ORT and Temple Emanuel Houston, Texas Jewish Historical Society, DBCAH, University of Texas at Austin [CAH].

78. Olsen, "Teaching Americanism," 265–266.

79. Quoted in "Dr. Ray K. Daily: A Woman of Valor," *JH-V* (Houston), December 3, 1975, 4.

80. The two individuals who ask Samuels were W.W. Kemmerer, president of the University of Houston, and John Schwarzwalder, the head of the university's radio station.

81. Jeanne Samuels, interview by author, Houston, June 19, 2014.

82. Alice Adams, "Joseph W. Samuels: Visionary—Communicator: JH-V Publisher's Dream for the Houston Jewish Community," *Jewish Herald Voice 100th Anniversary Passover Edition*, April 20, 2008, 69–70.

83. Don Carleton, "McCarthyism in Houston: The George Ebey Affair," *Southwestern Quarterly* 80, no. 2 (October 1976): 163, 166; Carleton, *Red Scare!*, 181; Kellar, *Make Haste Slowly*, 58.

84. Carleton, *Red Scare!*, 184; Letter from Charles H. Slayman, Jr. to Tom Friedman, February 23, 1953, Box 1, Folder 6: Letters of Recommendation—May 1953 Attack Houston, MS 70, Dr. George Ebey Collection, HMRC, HPL.

85. David White, "Is Time an Ally of Bigotry?," *JH-V* (Houston) July 30, 1953, 2.

86. Quoted in Carleton, *Red Scare!*, 219.

87. David White, "The Importance of McCarthyism," *JH-V* (Houston), April 8, 1954, 2. "Individuals from Texas Reported as having been affiliated with Communist or Communist-front organizations—as compiled from official government records" compiled by Helen Thomas, Houston, Texas 1956," State of Texas vs. NAACP, Box 3N160, Folder 4, DBCAH, University of Texas at Austin [CAH]; Carleton, *Red Scare!*, 129.

88. White, "The Importance of McCarthyism."

89. "'Letters to the Editor': Meyer Kaplan to David White," *JH-V* (Houston), April 22, 1954, 2; "Letters to the Editor: Sonia Gorelik," *JH-V* (Houston), April 22, 1954, 2.

90. David White, "Jews Are a Normal People," *JH-V* (Houston) July 14, 1955, 2.

91. "Individuals from Texas Reported as having been affiliated with Communist or Communist-front organizations—as compiled from official government records" compiled by Helen Thomas, Houston, Texas 1956," State of Texas vs. NAACP, Box 3N160, Folder 4, DBCAH, University of Texas at Austin [CAH]; Carleton, *Red Scare!*, 129.

92. Letter from Mr. D.H Matherly to Rabbi Robert I. Kahn, October 26, 1956, Box 2, Folder 32 FBI, MS 186, Robert I. Kahn Papers, HMRC, HPL; Letter from Dr. Kahn to D. H. Matherly, October 29, 1956, Box 2, Folder 32 FBI, MS 186, Robert I. Kahn Papers, HMRC, HPL.

93. "'Comrade' By Committee of Centralized Government," Box 2, Folder 32 FBI, MS 186, Robert I. Kahn Papers HMRC, HPL. See also: Bernard K. Johnpoll, ed. *A Documentary History of the Communist Party of the United States-Vol 2*, (Westport, CT: Greenwood Press, 1994), xv–1; Kerri Allen, "A Digital Cotton Curtain? What Selma Means to Silicon Valley," *Public Relations Tactics* 22, no. 5 (May 2015): 8.

94. "'Comrade' By Committee of Centralized Government," Box 2, Folder 32 FBI, MS 186, Robert I. Kahn Papers, HMRC, HPL.

95. "'Comrade' By Committee of Centralized Government."

96. Letter from Robert Kahn to W. E. Salisbury, October 31, 1956, Box 2, Folder 32 FBI, MS 186, Robert I. Kahn Papers, HMRC, HPL.

97. Letter from Mr. Matherly to Robert Kahn, October 31, 1956, Box 2, Folder 32 FBI, MS 186, Robert I. Kahn Papers, HMRC HPL. See also: Letter from Theodore Freedman to Robert Kahn, November 2, 1956, Box 2, Folder 32 FBI, MS 186, Robert I. Kahn Papers, HMRC, HPL; Letter from Mr. Matherly to Robert Kahn, November 2, 1956, Box 2, Folder 32 FBI, MS 186, Robert I. Kahn Papers, HMRC, HPL.

98. Letter from Miss Robert Patterson to Robert Kahn, November 5, 1956, Box 2, Folder 32 FBI, MS 186, Robert I. Kahn Papers, HMRC, HPL.

99. Letter from Robert Kahn to Mr. Williams, November 20, 1956, Box 2, Folder 32 FBI, MS 186, Robert I. Kahn Papers, HMRC, HPL.

100. Letter from Robert Kahn to Mr. Burton, March 8, 1957, Box 2, Folder 32 FBI, MS 186, Robert I. Kahn Papers, HMRC, HPL.

Chapter Three

1. Rev. Lee Haywood Simpson Papers, MS 0239, Box 5, Folder 5: "Profile of the Houston Negro Community with Special Tribute to Barbara Jordan," by the Harris County Council of Organizations, 1967. Houston Metropolitan Research Center, Houston Public Library.

2. Jack Bass, *The Transformation of Southern Politics: Social Change and Political Consequence since 1945* (Athens: University of Georgia Press, 1995), 326, 332; "Interview with Eleanor Freed by Ruthe Winegarten 6–18 and 6-19-88," Texas Jewish Historical Society, The Dolph Briscoe Center for American History, The University of Texas at Austin (CAH), Box 3A171 Folder 6; Christia Adair, HMRC Oral History Collection, October 22, 1977, audio, http://digital.houstonlibrary.net/oral-history/christie-adair_OHC14.php. See also: "Interview Black

Women Oral History Project Interview Christia Adair, April 25, 1977,"
Box 4 Folder 2, MS 109, Christia V. Adair Collection, HMRC, HPL;
"Thelma Scott Bryant," interview by Patricia Smith Prather, Houston
Oral History Project, August 3, 2007, transcript, http://digital.houston-
library.net/oral-history/thelma-scott-bryant.php.

3. Letter from Malcom F. Sher to Horton W. Smith, May 17, 1956,
    League of Women Voters, RG.E.0013, Box 1, Folder 13: Mrs. Malcom
    F. Sher, correspondence, 1956–1957, HMRC, HPL. See also: League
    of Women Voters, RG.E.0013, Box 1, Folder 12: Mrs. Malcom F. Sher,
    correspondence, 1955, Folder 13: Mrs. Malcom F. Sher, correspond-
    ence, 1956–1957, HMRC, HPL.

4. Marjorie Meyer Arsht, *All the Way from Yoakum: The Personal
    Journey of a Political Insider* (College Station: Texas A&M Univer-
    sity Press, 2006), 132–133.

5. Quentin Mease, *On Equal Footing: A Memoir* (Austin, TX: Eakin
    Press, 2010), 58.

6. "Interview Mr. Moses Leroy, Nationally Recognized Civil Rights
    Leader, Former Present Houston Black Community Leader," Margue-
    rite Johnston Barnes Research Material for "Houston, The Unknown
    City, 1836–1946," MS 455, Box 2, Folder 28: Leroy, Moses, Woodson
    Research Center [hereafter WRC], Fondren Library, Rice University
    [hereafter RU].

7. Robert C. Giles, *Changing Times: The Story of the Diocese of Galves-
    ton Houston in Commemoration of Its Founding* (Houston, TX: J.L.
    Morkovsky, 1972), 104; Pruitt, *Other Great Migration*, 115; Texas
    Historical Commission, *Historic Marker Application: St. Nicholas
    Catholic Church*, January 13, 1988, text, from the Portal to Texas
    History, Recorded Texas Historic Landmark Files, texashistory.unt.
    edu/ark:/67531/metapth477610/m1/7/?q=DaytonSalisbury.

8. Steptoe, *Houston Bound*, 112–116; Pruitt, *Other Great Migration*,
    114–115; "Our Mother of Mercy Catholic Church," accessed October 20,
    2016, http://www.ourmotherofmercy.net/history.html.

9. Pruitt, *Other Great Migration*, 116; "To Bear Fruit For Our Race—
    Department of History at the University of Houston," http://classweb.
    uh.edu/cph/tobearfruit/story.html; *Handbook of Texas Online*, William E.
    Montgomery, "African-American Churches," accessed December 16,
    2016, http://www.tshaonline.org/handbook/online/articles/pkatz.

10. Marguerite Johnston, *A Happy Worldly Abode: Christ Church Cathedral
    1839–1964* (Houston: Cathedral Press, 1989), 187; Howard Thurman,
    *Footprints of Dream: The Story of the Church for the Fellowship of All
    Peoples* (Eugene, OR.: Wipft & Stock, 2009), 148–150; "Texas Church
    Council Asks Integration Help," *Chicago Defender*, January 7, 1957, 7.

11. Arsht, *All the Way from Yoakum*, 129
12. "Is Theology Important?" by Rabbi Robert I. Kahn, December 9, 1951, Box 1, Folder: SOR-SOT, MS-853, Robert I. Kahn Papers, AJA.
13. Untitled Sermon for Emanu El Services of the Air by Rabbi Robert I. Kahn, January 25, 1953, Box 3, Folder: Emanu El Services of the Air, 1952–1953, Rabbi Kahn's Copies, MS-853, Robert I. Kahn Papers, AJA.
14. "Tell It Again," Rosh Hashanah, Box 1, Folder SMZ, MS-853, Robert I. Kahn Papers, AJA.
15. "Churchmen of Houston Favorable," *Houston Post*, May 18, 1954.
16. "Churchmen of Houston Favorable." Not all local Christian leaders were that supportive. In the *Houston Post* article, Bishop Clinton S. Quin of the Episcopal diocese refused to comment because he wanted further clarification of Supreme Court parameters.
17. Abraham L. Davis and Barbara Luck Graham, *The Supreme Court, Race, and Civil Rights: From Marshall to Rehnquist* (Thousand Oaks, CA: Sage, 1995), 221.
18. "Churchmen of Houston Favorable."
19. "Churchmen of Houston Favorable."
20. "Churchmen of Houston Favorable."
21. John A. Kirk, "The NAACP Campaign for Teachers' Salary Equalization: African American Women Educators and the Early Civil Rights Struggle," *Journal of African American History* 94, no. 4 (2009): 529–552.
22. Hattie Mae White, interview by Louis Marchiafava, Houston Oral History Project, August 9, 1974, audio, http://digital.houstonlibrary.net/oral-history/hattie-mae-white_OH192a.php.
23. Otis King, interview by David Goldstein, Houston Oral History Project, August 6, 2008, film, http://digital.houstonlibrary.org/cdm/singleitem/collection/oralhistory/id/78/rec/1.
24. "Charles S. Johnson, "'Source Material for Patterns of Negro Segregation 12-Houston, Tex.," Reel 7, Box 1, SC Micro R-6534, Carnegie-Myrdal Study of the Negro in America Research Memoranda Collection, SCRBC, NYPL.
25. Debbi Z. Harwell, "William S. Holland: A Mighty Loan at Yates High School," *Houston History Magazine*, 8 no. 1 (December 20, 2010): 12; Hattie Mae White, interview; Isaac Bryant, interview by Jacqueline Bartha, Gregory School Oral Histories, July 27, 2011, film, http://digital.houstonlibrary.net/oral-history/isaac-bryant_OHGS0034.php.
26. David White, "Our Public Schools—Foundation for Democracy," JH-V (Houston) May 27, 1954, 2.
27. David White, "There Is Religion and There Is Government," *JH-V* (Houston), June 24, 1954, 2.
28. Quoted in Kellar, *Make Haste Slowly*, 70–71.

29. Kellar, 134.
30. McComb, *Houston: A History*, 166; Salatheia Bryant, "30 Years After Desegregation, Some Things Same," *Houston Chronicle*, May 17, 2004, http://www.chron.com/news/nation-world/article/30-years-after-desegregation-some-things-same-1978582.php.
31. "Texas Church Council Asks Integration Help," *Chicago Defender*, January 7, 1957, 7.
32. "Texas Church Council Asks Integration Help."
33. "Convention Not Houston," *The Living Church*, June 20, 1954, 6–7; Gardiner H. Shattuck, *Episcopalians and Race Civil War to Civil Rights* (Lexington: University Press of Kentucky, 2015), 41–42, 65; "The Church Awakens: African Americans and the Search for Justice," accessed October 20, 2016, http://www.episcopalarchives.org/Afro-Anglican_history/exhibit/transitions/; "Looking Back," *UU World: Landmark Desegregation Ruling at Fifty*, accessed October 20, 2016, http://archive.uuworld.org/2004/03/lookingback.html.
34. "173 Houston Area Ministers Back Desegregation Decision," Box 2, Folder 9, Civic Affairs Committee, MS 186, Robert I. Kahn Papers, HMRC, HPL.
35. "173 Houston Area Ministers Back Desegregation Decision."
36. "Integration Discussion Topic of Emanu El Young Adults Friday," *JH-V* (Houston), March 22, 1956, 4; Congregation Emanu El, "Young Adults," *Emanu El Bulletin* 11 (March 1956): 5.
37. Congregation Beth Israel, "Dr. Hyman Judah Schachtel will preach on 'Religion and Integration," *Temple Bulletin* 102 (March 11, 1957): 1; "Segregation Topic of Beth Yeshurun Young People League," *JH-V* (Houston), March 22, 1956, 7.
38. "Tentative plan for Civic Affairs Committee—Rabbi Robert I. Kahn," (March 28, 1955), Box 2, Folder 9: Civic Affairs Committee, MS 186, Robert I. Kahn Papers, HMRC, HPL.
39. Letter to Al Vorspan from Rabbi Robert I. Kahn, November 8, 1957, Box 2, Folder 9 Civic Affairs Committee, MS 186, Robert I. Kahn Papers, HMRC, HPL.
40. "'Religion and Integration,' March 22, 1957," Box A2, Folder: Sermons and Outlines 1956–1957, MS 172, Hyman Judah Schachtel Papers, HMRC, HPL.
41. "'Religion and Integration.'"
42. "The Lessons of Little Rock Preached in Congregation Emanu El, Houston," by Rabbi Robert I. Kahn, October 25, 1957, Box 2, Folder: SPB-SPF, MS-853, Robert I. Kahn Papers, AJA.
43. "The Lessons of Little Rock Preached in Congregation Emanu El, Houston."

44. Letter to Al Vorspan from Rabbi Robert I. Kahn, November 8, 1957, Box 2, Folder 9: Civic Affairs Committee, MS 186, Robert I. Kahn Papers, HMRC, HPL.
45. The FBI utilized the ADL of Houston to attain information on the White Citizens' Council, even sending someone undercover to investigate their meetings and report their findings. See: FBI: "Citizen Council Houston," Citizen Council, accessed August 30, 2016, http://archive. org/details/CitizensCouncilMovement. See also: Chanelle Nyree Rose, *The Struggle for Black Freedom in Miami: Civil Rights and America's Tourist Paradise, 1896–1968* (Baton Rouge: Louisiana State University Press, 2015), 193; ISJL-Alabama Birmingham Encyclopedia," *Institute of Southern Jewish Life*, 2014, accessed August 10, 2016, https://www.isjl.org/alabama-birmingham-encyclopedia.html.
46. "The Lessons of Little Rock Preached in Congregation Emanu El, Houston," by Rabbi Robert I. Kahn, October 25, 1957, Box 2, Folder: SPB-SPF, MS-853, Robert I. Kahn Papers, AJA.
47. "The Forward Look," Rosh Hashanah 1958, Box 1, Folder: SMZ, MS 853, Robert I. Kahn Papers, AJA.
48. "Houston Police Chief to Address Houston Lodge September 17," *JH-V* (Houston), September 12, 1957, 1, 9.
49. Letter from Sylvan Lebow to Rabbi Kahn, January 16, 1956, Box 3, Folder 28: Jewish Chautauqua Society, MS-186, Robert I. Kahn Papers, HMRC, HPL; Letter from Rabbi Kahn to Mr. Sylvan Lebow, January 19, 1956, Box 3, Folder 28: Jewish Chautauqua Society, MS-186, Robert I. Kahn Papers, HMRC, HPL.
50. "Dr. Schachtel Speaker at Worthing's Honor Day," *The Informer* (Houston), May 16, 1959, 10.
51. "Cyrus Adler AZA," *JH-V* (Houston), February 6, 1958, 10.
52. Mease, *On Equal Footing*, 74–75; Mallory Robinson, interview, Houston, May 19, 2014.
53. Mease, *On Equal Footing*, 49–52.
54. Eleanor Freed to Ann, March 1964, Community Services H.C.O.H.R. Correspondence 1959–1975, letterhead, unprocessed, Series 7, MS 28, Frank and Eleanor Freed Papers, 1814–1996, Museum of Fine Arts Archives, Houston, Texas. See also: "The Heart of Houston: The Early History of the Houston Council on Human Relations 1958–1972," by Barbara Thompson Day, Marguerite Johnston Barnes Research Materials for "Houston, The Unknown City, 1836–1946," MS 455, Box 16, Folder 2: *The Houston Review History and Culture of the Gulf Coast*, Woodson Center, Fondren Library, RU; Mease, *On Equal Footing*, 75–77; "Interview with Eleanor Freed by Ruthe Winegarten 6–18 and 6-19-88," Box 3A171, Folder 6, Texas Jewish Historical Society, DBCAH, University of Texas at Austin [CAH].

55. Letter from Miss Frankie M. Austin to Mrs. Kaplan, December 30, 1965, Houston Council on Human Relations. RG E 64, Box 1, Folder 23, HMRC, HPL; "Kaplan Famous Sandwiches," Judge Woodrow Seals, MS 414, Box 62 Folder 24: Houston Council Human Relations Correspondence (October-December 1965), HMRC, HPL.

56. Davidson, "Negro Politics," 122; Hattie Mae White, interview; Mildred Hubert Meltzer, "Chapters in the Struggle for Negro Rights in Houston, 1944–1962" (Master's thesis, University of Houston, August 1963), 57–59; Kellar, *Make Haste Slowly*, 110.

57. Dena Marks, interview by author, Houston, March 12, 2014.

58. "Houston Chapter AJC Announces January 20 Program On 'Desegregation in Our School,'" *JH-V* (Houston), January 13, 1955, 9.

59. Letter to Mr. Isaac Toubin, June 5, 1956; American Jewish Congress, records; I–77; Box 104, Folder 2: Houston, Texas, 1955–1956, American Jewish Historical Society, New York, New York [hereafter AJHS]; Letter from Morton Gottschall to Mr. Abramowitz, May 23, 1957; American Jewish Congress, records; I–77; Box 104, Folder 3: Houston, Texas, 1956–1957, AJHS.

60. Letter from Dick to Irwin L. Glatstein, October 4, 1957, American Jewish Congress, records; I–77; Box 104, Folder 3: Houston, Texas, 1956–1957, AJHS. See also: "Richard Cohen, 71, an Adviser to Major Jewish Organizations," *New York Times*, November 1, 1994, B8.

61. "Announcement from American Jewish Congress, February 17, 1958," American Jewish Congress, records; I–77; Box 104, Folder 4: Houston, Texas Chapter, 1958–1959, AJHS.

62. Letter from Will Maslow to Irwin Glatstein, December 24, 1957, American Jewish Congress, records; I–77; Box 104, Folder 3: Houston, Texas, 1956–1957, AJHS.

63. "Dear Friends," February 17, 1958, American Jewish Congress, records; I–77; Box 104, Folder 4: Houston, Texas Chapter, 1958–1959, AJHS.

64. For Immediate Release, February 23, 1958, American Jewish Congress, records; I–77, Box 104, Folder 4: Houston, Texas Chapter, 1958–1959, AJHS; Letter from Irwin Glatstein to Public Relations Committee, Jewish Community Relations Council, February 13, 1958, American Jewish Congress, records; I–77, Box 104, Folder 4: Houston, Texas Chapter, 1958–1959, AJHS; "Segregation Topic of Amer. Jewish Congress Meeting Sunday, Feb. 23," *JH-V* (Houston), February 20, 1958, 1; "Non-Sectarian Panel to Discuss Question of Integration May 29th," *JH-V* (Houston), May 22, 1958, 3.

65. Letter from Herbert Finkelstein to Richard Cohen, June 3, 1958, American Jewish Congress, records; I–77, Box 104, Folder 4: Houston, Texas Chapter, 1958–1959, AJHS.

66. "W. Kilgarlin and Rev James Noland on Civil Rights Panel Discussion Thursday, May 29," *JH-V* (Houston), May 29, 1958, 4; "Community Relations Committee memorandum February 11, 1959," Subject Files Collection, n.d., various dates; I–424, Box 38, Folder: Jewish Community Council of Metropolitan Houston, AJHS.

67. For more information on Southern Jewish reaction to the National Jewish Defense Organizations, see: Michael Staub, *Torn at the Roots: The Crisis of Jewish Liberalism in Postwar America* (New York: Columbia University Press, 2002), 53.

68. Richard Cohen to Rabbi Sky, June 7, 1957, American Jewish Congress, records; I–77, Box 104, Folder 2: Houston, Texas, 1955–1956, AJHS.

69. Letter from Natafali Abramowitz to Boris Bell, June 17, 1958, American Jewish Congress, records; I–77, Box 104, Folder 4: Houston, Texas Chapter, 1958–1959, AJHS.

70. Letter from Richard Cohen to David White, February 14, 1958, American Jewish Congress, records; I–77, Box 104, Folder 4: Houston, Texas Chapter, 1958–1959, AJHS.

71. David White, "The Season is Upon Us," *JH-V* (Houston), June 28, 1956, 2.

72. White, "The Season is Upon Us."

73. "Anti-Semitism in U.S. Discussed at Anti-Defamation League Parley," *JTA* (New York), December 4, 1958; "Jewish Congress Attacks 'Panic Proposals' on Synagogue Bombings Synagogue Bombings," *JTA* (New York), November 24, 1958; Diner, *Jews of the United States*, 272.

74. "Exchange of Correspondence': A Senator and a Citizens' Council Leader Differs Sharply on a Crucial Issue," *JH-V* (Houston), June 19, 1958, 6.

75. Letter from Rabbi Robert I. Kahn to Charles Nathan, May 13, 1957, Box 4, Folder 21: Miscellaneous N, MS-186. Robert I. Kahn Papers, HMRC, HPL.

76. Alfred Kahn and Matt Kahn, interview by author, Houston, February 1, 2014.

77. William S. Malev, "The Jew of the South in the Conflict of Segregation," *Conservative Judaism* 13, no. 1 (1958): 35–36.

78. To understand Jewish ethnic and race identity: Goldstein, *Price of Whiteness*, 210–211.

79. Malev, "The Jews of the South," 37.

80. Malev, 36–37.

81. Malev, 39–40.

82. Malev, 39–40; See also: Will Herberg, *Protestant, Catholic, Jew: An Essay in American Religious Sociology* (Chicago: University of Chicago Press, 1960).

83. Malev, "The Jew of the South," 39–40.

84. Malev, 39–40.

85. Irwin Glatstein, "Letters to the Editor," *Conservative Judaism* 13, no. 1 (Fall 1958): 47.
86. William S. Malev, "Letters to the Editor," *Conservative Judaism* 13, no. 1 (Fall 1958): 49–51.
87. "Letter to the Editor," *JH-V* (Houston), December 18, 1958, 2; "Letter to the Editor," *JH-V* (Houston), January 1, 1959.

Chapter Four

1. Quoted in "Race, Income, and Ethnicity Residential Change in a Houston Community, 1920–1970, by Barry J. Kaplan," Box 1, Folder 16: Source 2, 1981–2010, This Is Our Home, It Is Not for Sale Film Collection, SC, UHL.
2. "XII Script Treatment," Box 1, Folder 7: Texas Committee for the Humanities (3rd Proposal). This Is Our Home, It Is Not for Sale Film Collection, SC, UHL; "Much History Flows through River-side Terrace" by Katherine Feser, *Houston Chronicle*, April 3, 1994, Box 1, Folder 18: Newspaper Article about Riverside Terrace part 1 of 2, 1953–1995, This Is Our Home, It Is Not for Sale Film Collection, SC, UHL; Winegarten, Schechter, and Kessler, *Deep in the Heart*, 173.
3. "ISJL-Texas Houston Encyclopedia"; This Is Our Home, It Is Not for Sale; Hecht, "Houston"; "M&M Kosher Meat Market and Delicatessen," "Harf's," *The Message* 1 (March 22, 1947): 5,6.
4. Alison Cook, "Robert Sakowitz and the Fraying Empire," *Texas Monthly*, December 1985, 136; Mass, "Jews of Houston," 54.
5. "Questionnaire Response for MEDIA," Box 1, Folder 3: Grant Proposal #2, 1984–1986, This Is Our Home, It Is Not for Sale Film Collection, SC, UHL; Samuel Gruber, "The Continuing Exodus: The Synagogue and Jewish Urban Migration," *Religion* 35 (2012): 14–17, http://surface.syr.edu/rel/35; Archeological and Historical Commission, "Landmark Designation Report," City of Houston Planning and Development Department, January 12, 2012, http:///www.houstontx.gov/planning/Commissions.docs_pdfs/hahc/reprots_ACTION/JunAction?B2_2622_Riverside Terrace_PLM_Action.pdf; Nathan Glazer, "The American Jewish Urban Experience," in *The Cambridge Companion to American Judaism*, ed. Dana Evan Kaplan (New York: Cambridge University Press, 2005), 273.
6. Harry Brochstein, Box 1, Folder 22: Preliminary Interview Notes on Index Cards, undated, This Is Our Home, It Is Not for Sale Film Collection, SC, UHL; David Meyerowitz, "Vos geven iz geven un nito," Milken Archive of Jewish Music, 1926, http://www.milkenarchive.org/music/volumes/view/great-songs-of-the-american-yiddish-stage/work/

vos-geven-iz-geven-un-nito/. See also: Glazer, "American Jewish Urban Experience," 273–74.

7. Alfred and Matt Kahn, interview by author, Houston, February 1, 2014; *This Is Our Home, It Is Not for Sale.*

8. "Race, Income, and Ethnicity Residential Change in a Houston Community, 1920–1970, by Barry J. Kaplan," Box 1, Folder 16: Source 2, 1981–2010, This Is Our Home, It Is Not for Sale Film Collection, SC, UHL; "Questionnaire Response for MEDIA," Box 1, Folder 3: Grant Proposal #2, 1984–1986. This Is Our Home, It Is Not for Sale Film Collection, SC, UHL; *This Is Our Home, It Is Not for Sale*; Hecht, "Houston."

9. Marilyn Hassid, interview by author, Houston, January 28, 2014.

10. Robert D. Jacobus, *Houston Cougars in the 1960s: Death Threats, the Veer Offense, and the Game of the Century* (College Station: Texas A&M University Press, 2015), 47; Marilyn Hassid, "Jewish Community Center: An Arts and Culture for the Houston Community" (unpublished essay, January 28, 2014), Microsoft file; Alan Govenar, *Lightnin' Hopkins: His Life and Blues* (Chicago: Chicago Review Press, 2010), 79; John A. Lomax, "History of the Society (June, 1966)," *Houston Folk Music*, http://www.houstonfolkmusic.org/audio_files/; John Lomax, III, "John A. Lomax, Jr. (1907–1974): A Success in All He Did," *Cultural Equity*, http://www.culturalequity.org/alanlomax/ce_alanlomax_profile_johnlomaxjr.php.

11. "Second Annual Houston Blues Concert Scheduled at Center," *JH-V* (Houston), June 27, 1968, 8. See also: "First J.C.C. Folksong Concert February 15," *JH-V* (Houston), February 8, 1962, 12; Govenar, *Lightnin' Hopkins*, 121.

12. Lisa Gray, "A Revisit to Riverside Terrace," *Houston Chronicle*, April 18, 2008, http://www.chron.com/entertainment/article/A-revisit-to-Riverside-Terrace-1781683.php; This Is Our Home, It Is Not for Sale.

13. Alfred Kahn, email message to author, August 24, 2017. See also: "Sermon" Passover April 4, 1941, Box 1, Folder Sermons: 1936–1941, MS 853, Robert I. Kahn Papers, AJA; See also: Albert Vorspan, "Blacks and Jews," in *Black Anti-Semitism and Jewish Racism*, by Nat Hentoff, James Baldwin, et al. (New York: Schocken Books, 1969), 209.

14. Alfred Kahn, email message to author, August 24, 2017.

15. Alfred Kahn, email message to author, August 24, 2017.

16. See: Lawrence Harmon and Hillel Levine, *Death of American Jewish Community: A Tragedy of Good Intentions* (New York: Macmillan International, 1992), 5.

17. Build a Better Houston, 1946, Box 45, Folder Houston Papers, MS 724, Alan S. Green Papers, AJA.

18. (Suggested Sermonic Material for Housing Sunday, May 5, 1946), Box 45, Folder Houston Papers, MS 724, Alan S. Green Papers, AJA.

19. Fairbanks, *The War on the Slums in the Southwest*, 103–105; "The Citizens Committee for Slum Clearance," Advertisement, *Southwest Citizen* (Houston), July 13, 1950, 8; "Why Was Captured Communist Leader in San Felipe Courts?" *Bellaire Citizen* (Bellaire, Texas) July 6, 1950, 8.

20. Fairbanks, *War on Slums in the Southwest*, 104.

21. Fairbanks, 104; Anna Dupree, a beautician, owned a beauty salon and Clarence Dupree was a successful businessman. A few years earlier in 1940, they contributed $20,000—the equivalent of $345,000 today—to create the Anna Dupree Cottage of the Negro Child Center in the Fifth Ward for parentless children. See: *Handbook of Texas Online*, Nancy Baker Jones, "Dupree, Anna Johnson," accessed May 17, 2017, http://www.tshaonline.org/handbook/online/articles/fdu39; "Dream of Home for Negro Aged to Come True for Anna Dupree," November 20, 1949, Box 1, Folder 5 Clippings, MS 110, Anna Dupree Collection, HMRC, HPL.

22. Yvette Jones, "Seeds of Compassion," *Texas Historian* 37, no. 2 (November 1976): 18, https://texashistory.unt.edu/ark:/67531/metapth391307/m1/18/?q=%22anna%20dupree%22; Chris Gray, "Eldorado Ballroom: A Concise History By Dr. Roger Wood," *Houston Press*, March 7, 2011, http://www.houstonpress.com/music/eldorado-ballroom-a-concise-history-by-dr-roger-wood-6755634.

23. Attwell, interview.

24. "It's Official: The Eldorado Ballroom Is Historic," *Houstonia*, April 29, 2014, http://www.houstoniamag.com/articles/2014/4/29/its-official-the-eldorado-ballroom-is-historic-april-2014.

25. Incorporation Papers and Land Deed, 1949–50, 1956, July 30, 1949, Box 1, File 1, Charter, RG E-47, Eliza Johnson Home for Aged Negroes Collection, HMRC, HPL; Folder: Negroes, Eliza Johnson Home for the Aged, Box H1, MS 172, Hyman Judah Schachtel Papers, HMRC, HPL; Letter from Hyman Judah Schachtel to Mrs. Dupree, June 12, 1950, Box H1, MS 172, Hyman Judah Schachtel Papers, HMRC, HPL; "Home for Negroes Dedicated by Ted Williams," June 23, 1952, Chronicles Correspondents, Box 1, Folder 5, MS 110, Anna Dupree Collection, HMRC, HPL.

26. "Home for Negroes Dedicated by Ted Williams," June 23, 1952, Chronicles Correspondents, Box 1, Folder 5, MS 110, Anna Dupree Collection, HMRC, HPL.

27. "Testimonial Banquet at Texas Southern University," Box 3, Scrapbook, RG E-47, Eliza Johnson Home for Aged Negroes Collection, HMRC, HPL.

28. "Houstonite to Address Brotherhood Assembly," February 10, 1957, American Statesmen, Box 1, Folder: News Clippings, MS 1120, Maurice Nathan Dannenbaum Papers, HMRC, HPL.

29. Allan Turner, "UH Exhibit Focuses on Third Ward History, People," *Houston Chronicle*, March 23, 2011, http://www.chron.com/news/houston-texas/article/UH-exhibit-focuses-on-Third-Ward-history-people-1617407.php.

30. Doris Peavey, interview by Nicholas Castellanos, Gregory School Oral Histories, February 26, 2010, film, http://digital.houstonlibrary.net/oral-history/doris-peavey_OHGS_11.php; "History," *Texas Southern University*, http://www.tsu.edu/about/history.php; James SoRelle, "The Darker Side of 'Heaven': The Black Community in Houston, Texas, 1917–1945" (PhD diss., Kent State University, 1980), 233; Wintz, "Blacks," 34.

31. Sol Weiner, Box 1, Folder 22: Preliminary Interview Notes on Index Cards (1), undated, This Is Our Home, It Is Not for Sale Film Collection, SC, UHL; Kaplan, Interview; Cary D. Wintz, "Texas Southern University," *Handbook of Texas Online*, accessed May 17, 2017, http://www.tsaonline.org/handbook/online/articles/kct27.

32. Erik Slotboom, *Houston Freeways: A Historical and Visual Journey* (Cincinnati, OH: Oscar F. Slotboom; printed by C.J Krehbiel, 2003), 3, 11–19, 187–188.

33. "Race, Income, and Ethnicity Residential Change in a Houston Community, 1920–1970, by Barry J. Kaplan," Box 1, Folder 16: Source 2, 1981–2010, This Is Our Home, It Is Not for Sale Film Collection, SC, UHL; Robert D. Bullard, *Invisible Houston: The Black Experience in Boom and Bust* (College Station: Texas A&M University Press, 1987), 15; *Who Killed the 4th Ward*, prod. James Blue, 1978, https://www.uhd.edu/academics/humanities/news-community/filmfest/Pages/Who-Killed-the-4th-Ward.aspx; "Vivid History Highlights Three Decades of Progress for Rapidly Expanding City," *Southwestern Times* (Houston), June 24, 1948, 5; "Bellairites Outspoken on P.O. Freeway," *Bellaire Texan* (Bellaire, Texas), November 16, 1955, 8; Steptoe, *Houston Bound*, 204; Slotboom, *Houston Freeways*, 187–88, 205, 226.

34. Wintz, "Blacks," 20; "Race, Income, and Ethnicity Residential Change in a Houston Community, 1920–1970, by Barry J. Kaplan," Box 1, Folder 16: Source 2, 1981–2010, This Is Our Home, It Is Not for Sale Film Collection, SC, UHL; Antero Pietila, *Not in My Neighborhood: How Bigotry Shaped a Great American City* (Chicago: Ivan R Dee, Inc., 2012), 105–110; Shannon Buggs, "March 15, 2004: Buggs: Third Ward Residents Fighting Gentrification Efforts," *Houston Chronicle*, March 15, 2004, http://www.chron.com/business/article/March-15-2004-Buggs-Third ward-residents-1976061.php; Lawrence Wright, "Easy Street," *Texas Monthly Magazine*, November 1982, http://www.texasmonthly.com/articles/easy-street/.

35. Albert Vorspan, *Negroes and Jews, Journal of Jewish Communal Service* (Spring 1966): 239–242, http://www.bjpa.org/Publications/details.cfm? PublicationID=5031; *This Is Our Home, It Is Not for Sale*; Chris Lane, "The Changing Face of Houston-Riverside Terrace," *Houston Press*, October 13, 2014, Lisa Gray, "A Revisit to Riverside Terrace;" Friends of MacGregor, "Riverside Terrace," https://friendsofmacgregorpark.org/Riverside Terrace-terrace/."

36. "Explosion Rocks Home in Riverside Terrace: Cattle Buyer Sees Violence as Warning, By Jim Whisenant," *Houston Chronicle*, April 17, 1953. See also: Lisa Gray, "A Revisit to Riverside Terrace."

37. "Indict Two in Caesar Blast," *The Informer* (Houston), June 20, 1953, 1.

38. *This Is Our Home, It Is Not for Sale*. See also: "Beacon Company: Press Release," Box 2, Folder 26: Critiques and Press Release, 1987–1989, This Is Our Home, It Is Not for Sale Film Collection, SC, UHL; "Davis Gets 2 Years in Bombing," *The Informer* (Houston), July 25, 1953, 1.

39. Friends of MacGregor, "Riverside Terrace"; Aaron Howard, "How Meyerland Became the Center of Jewish Houston," *JH-V* (Houston), September 29, 2016, http://jhvonline.com/how-meyerland-became-the-center-of-jewish-houston-p21650-89.htm.

40. "Catalogue Regular Session 1946–1948," Box T.S.U History 1947–1973, TSU Archives, SC, TSU; "Catalogue Houston College for Negroes Regular Session 1942–1944," Box T.S.U History 1947–1973, TSU Archives, SC, TSU; "Dedicate New Buildings October 17 Dr. Schachtel Convocation Speaker (The TSU Clarion)," Box News Clippings, Dr. R. O'Hara Lanier 1951–1959, Folder: Texas southern University-News Clippings 1951–1955, TSU Archives, SC, TSU.

41. Congregation Beth Israel, "Fifty Years of George Fields by Dr. Hyman Judah Schachtel," *Temple Bulletin* 102 (October 22, 1956): 1; Congregation Beth Israel, "George Field Fund Committee," *Temple Bulletin* 102 (October 22, 1956): 2; Congregation Beth Israel, "Sabbath Services November 23 through December 1," *Temple Bulletin* 102 (November 19, 1956): 1.

42. "Race, Income, and Ethnicity Residential Change in a Houston Community, 1920–1970, by Barry J. Kaplan," Box 1, Folder 16: Source 2, 1981–2010, This Is Our Home, It Is Not for Sale Film Collection, SC, UHL.

43. Lionel Schooler, email message to author, April 21, 2014.

44. Jane Silverman, Box 1, Folder 22: Preliminary Interview Notes on Index Cards (1), undated, This Is Our Home, It Is Not for Sale Film Collection, SC, UHL.

45. Sid and Mary Smiley, Box 1, Folder 22: Preliminary Interview Notes on Index Cards (2), undated, This Is Our Home, It Is Not for Sale Film

Collection, SC, UHL. See also: "Race, Income, and Ethnicity Residential Change in a Houston Community, 1920–1970, by Barry J. Kaplan," Box 1, Folder 16: Source 2, 1981–2010, This Is Our Home, It Is Not for Sale Film Collection, SC, UHL.

46. "Religion and Integration, March 22, 1957," Box A2, Folder: Sermons and Outlines 1956–1957, MS 172, Hyman Judah Schachtel Papers, HMRC, HPL.

47. Mary Jourdan Atkinson, interview by Margaret Henson, HMRC Oral History Collection, October 1, 1974, audio, http://digital.houstonlibrary.net/oral-history/mary-jourdan-atkinson_OH003.php.

48. *This Is Our Home, It Is Not for Sale.* See also: Lisa Gray, "A Revisit to Riverside Terrace"; Slotboom, *Houston Freeways*, 185.

49. *This Is Our Home, It Is Not for Sale.*

50. "Race, Income, and Ethnicity Residential Change in a Houston Community, 1920–1970, by Barry J. Kaplan," Box 1, Folder 16: Source 2, 1981–2010, This Is Our Home, It Is Not for Sale Film Collection, SC, UHL.

51. Atkinson, interview.

52. Frank Morgan, "Houston Whites Act to Avoid Selling Panic as an Area Integrates," *Wall Street Journal*, August 19, 1964.

53. 'Bill' Lawson (Reverend), interview by Jane Ely, Houston Oral History Project, March 14, 2008, film, http://digital.houstonlibrary.net/oral-history/bill-lawson.php.

54. "Mission Conference, April 17, 1960," Box 2, Folder 8: "Sermon & Lecture Materials," MS 532, William Lawson Papers, WRC, Fondren Library, RU.

55. Alvin I. Duvall, "Halting an Exodus: Owners Unite, Keep Homes in Mixed Areas," *Houston Post*, July 6, 1964, 7.

56. Duvall, "Halting an Exodus: Owners Unite, Keep Homes in Mixed Areas."

57. See: Albert Vorspan and Eugene Lipman, *Justice and Judaism: The Work of Social Action* (New York.: Union of American Hebrew Congregations, 1956), 36; Lila Corwin Berman "Jewish Urban Politics in the City and Beyond," *Journal of American History* 99, no. 2 (2012): 505–506; Pietila, *Not in My Neighborhood*, 102.

58. Morgan, "Houston Whites Act to Avoid Selling Panic as an Area Integrates."

59. Morgan, "Houston Whites Act to Avoid Selling Panic as an Area Integrates."

60. Wright, "Easy Street."

61. Morgan, "Houston Whites Act to Avoid Selling Panic as an Area Integrates."

62. Atkinson, interview.

63. Edith Eisner, Box 1, Folder 21: Preliminary Interview Notes on Index Cards (1) undated, This Is Our Home, It Is Not for Sale Film Collection, SC, UHL.

64. Dova Finger, Box 1, Folder 21: Preliminary Interview Notes on Index Cards (1) undated, This Is Our Home, It Is Not for Sale Film Collection, SC, UHL.

65. Billy Goldberg, Box 1, Folder 21: Preliminary Interview Notes on Index Cards (1) undated, This Is Our Home, It Is Not for Sale Film Collection, SC, UHL.

66. Dr. Milton Little, Box 1, Folder 21: Preliminary Interview Notes on Index Cards (1) undated, This Is Our Home, It Is Not for Sale Film Collection, SC, UHL.

67. University of Houston, *Lawson, William Rev.-Lawson transcript*, 1 of 1, October 20, 2004. Oral Histories from the Houston History Project, SC, UHL, http://digital.lib.uh.ed/collection/houhistory/item/500/show/499.

68. "Bill" Lawson (Reverend), interview by Jane Ely.

69. Interview with Quentin Mease, Houston, Texas At HELP Office on Wheeler, January 17, 1997, Box 17, Folder 5: Transcript: Quentin Mease, 10-17-97 and 1-24-97, Thomas R. Cole Desegregation Papers, SC, UHL.

70. Lancelin Boliver, Box 1, Folder 21: Preliminary Interview Notes on Index Cards (1) undated, This Is Our Home, It Is Not for Sale Film Collection, SC, UHL.

71. David White, "Religious Services for Families East of Main Street," *JH-V* (Houston), August 9, 1962, 2.

72. Lawson, interview by University of Houston. See also: "Beth Yeshurun to Hold Services in New Building," *JH-V* (Houston, Texas), August 23, 1963, 12.

73. Wright, "Easy Street."

74. This Is Our Home, It Is Not for Sale; "Beacon Company: Press Release," Box 2, Folder 26: Critiques and Press Release, 1987–1989, This Is Our Home, It Is Not for Sale Film Collection, SC, UHL; Lane, "Changing Face of Houston-Riverside Terrace."

75. "TSU Buying Building of Adath Emeth," *Houston Chronicle* (Houston, Texas), February 11, 1958; *This is Our Home, It is Not For Sale*; Houston Independent School Board, "School Board Meeting August 8, 1960 meeting"(meeting, Houston Independent School Board, Houston, Texas, August 8, 1960); Hescht, "Houston."

76. "Report Discloses American Jews Still Suffer Discrimination in Housing," *JTA* (New York), October 31, 1960.

77. Mrs. Jackie Proler, Box 1, Folder 22: Preliminary Interview Notes on Index Cards (2), undated, This Is Our Home, It Is Not for Sale Film Collection, SC, UHL.

78. Mrs. Shayna Turboff, Box 1, Folder 22: Preliminary Interview Notes on Index Cards (2), undated, This Is Our Home, It Is Not for Sale Film Collection, SC, UHL.
79. Julius Rosenblatt, interview by author, Houston, April 21, 2014.
80. Meyerland Community Association, "History of Meyerland," *Meyerland,* http://meyerland.net/en/tx/index.php/general-information/about-meyerland; Aaron Howard, "How Meyerland Became the Center of Jewish Houston," *JH-V,* September 29, 2016, http://jhvonline.com/how-meyerland-became-the-center-of-jewish-houston-p21650-89.htm; Maas, "Jews of Houston," 68; "Meyerland Springs Upon Prairie," *Houston Chronicle,* August 28, 1963, 12.
81. Lila Corwin Berman, "The Death and Life of Jewish Neighborhoods," *Sh'ma: A Journal of Jewish Ideas,* June 1, 2014, http://shma.com/2014/06/the-death-and-life-of-jewish-neighborhoods/; Janice Goldstein, "Jewish Neighborhoods in Transition," *Our Stake in the Urban Conditions: Pertinent Papers,* American Jewish Committee (AJC), October 1980: 1, http://ww.bjpa.org/Publications/details.cfm?PublicationID=13937.
82. Saul Friedman, Box 3, Folder 27: Saul Friedman Research, 1993-1997, Thomas R. Cole Desegregation Papers, SC, UHL.
83. Interview by telephone with Dr. Sam Nabrit, by Tom Cole, February 10, 1993, Box 17, Folder 41: Cole, Tom, Voices from Houston (1 of 2), 1998–2001, Thomas R. Cole Desegregation Papers, SC, UHL; Saul Friedman, Box 3, Folder 27: Saul Friedman Research, 1993–1997, Thomas R. Cole Desegregation Papers, SC, UHL.
84. Saul Friedman, Box 3, Folder 27: Saul Friedman Research, 1993–1997, Thomas R. Cole Desegregation Papers, SC, UHL.
85. Saul Friedman.
86. Frank Goldberg, Box 1, Folder 21: Preliminary Interview Notes on Index Cards (1), undated, This Is Our Home, It Is Not for Sale Film Collection, SC, UHL.
87. Ira Bleiweiss, interview by author, Houston, February 17, 2014.
88. Louis Moore, "The Mobile Jewish Neighborhoods," *Houston Chronicle,* August 3, 1973, 17.
89. In *Fiddler on the Roof,* the Russian government forced Jews to leave their town, Anatevka. See: Sid and Mary Smiley, Box 1, Folder 22: Preliminary Interview Notes on Index Cards (2), undated, This Is Our Home, It Is Not for Sale Film Collection, SC, UHL.
90. Howard Barnstone, Box 1, Folder 22: Preliminary Interview Notes on Index Cards (2), This Is Our Home, It Is Not for Sale Film Collection, SC, UHL.
91. Allen Becker, Box 1 Folder 22: Preliminary Interview Notes on Index Cards (2), This Is Our Home, It Is Not for Sale Film Collection. SC, UHL.

92. *This Is Our Home, It Is Not for Sale.*
93. *This Is Our Home, It Is Not for Sale.*

Chapter Five

1. Carolyn Litowich, interview by author, Houston, June 24, 2016.
2. Quoted by Elizabeth Jacoway, *Southern Businessmen and Desegregation* (Baton Rouge: Louisiana State University Press, 1982), 10. Originally in Steven F. Lawson, *Civil Rights Crossroads: Nation, Community, and the Black Freedom Struggle* (Lexington: University Press of Kentucky, 2014), 233.
3. "ISJL-Alabama Birmingham Encyclopedia"; "ISJL-Tennessee Memphis," *Institute of Southern Jewish Life*, 2014, accessed August 10, 2016, https://www.isjl.org/tennessee-memphis-encyclopedia.html.
4. For more on business desegregation in Houston, see: Cole, *No Color Is My Kind*; Fran Dressman, *Gus Wortham: A Portrait of a Leader* (College Station: Texas A&M University Press, 1994), 40; Hank V. Savitch and John Clayton Thomas, *Big City Politics in Transition* (Newbury Park, CA: Sage Publications, 1992), 182.
5. "Conference on Religion and Race," Folder: Metropolitan Houston Conference on Religion and Race 1963, SC-2850, AJA.
6. Diane Ravitch, "My Ghetto and Yours," *Texas Observer* (Houston), August 20, 1965, 4–5.
7. Quoted in Maas, "Jews of Houston," 188.
8. Jenna T. Berger, "From the Ashes of Europe to the Opportunity City: Immigration and Resettlement of Holocaust Survivors in Houston (Master's thesis, University of Houston, 2005), 52–65.
9. Leon Mucasey, interview by author, Houston, March 28, 2014. For more on Cuba, see: Timothy B. Tyson, *Radio Free Dixie: Robert F. Williams & The Roots of Black Power* (Chapel Hill: University of North Carolina Press, 1999), 293–294.
10. Gloria Ribnick, interview by author, Houston, March 20, 2014; Gloria Ribnick, email message to author, March 10, 2014.
11. Charles S. Johnson, "Source Material for Patterns of Negro Segregation 12-Houston, Tex.," Reel 7, Box 1, SC Micro R-6534, Carnegie-Myrdal Study of the Negro in America Research Memoranda Collection, SCRBC, NYPL.
12. SoRelle, "Darker Side of 'Heaven,'" 383, 390; University of Houston, *Williams, Beneva - Williams audio, 1 of 3*, July 13, 2006, Oral Histories from the Houston History Project, SC, UHL, http://digital.lib.uh.edu/collection/houhistory/item/786/show/782.
13. Quoted in Berger, "From the Ashes of Europe," 59, 52–60, 82. See also: William B. Helmreich, "Research Report: Postwar Adaptation

of Holocaust Survivors in the United States," *Holocaust and Genocide Studies* 2, no. 2 (1987): 307–315.

14. Diana Bloom, interview by author, Chicago, March 26, 2014; aka Jaime Bloom, interview by author, Austin, February 28, 2014.
15. David Eisenbaum, interview by author, Houston, April 28, 2013; David Eisenbaum, email message to author, May 9, 2013. The community center was run by S.H.A.P.E. (Self-Help African People through Education).
16. Nichols, interview.
17. Ira Bleiweiss, email message to author, January 31, 2017.
18. Ira Bleiweiss, email message to author, August 6, 2016. The involvement of Bleiweiss's father with NASA was not unusual, as many Jewish business owners worked with the government agency. See: Michael Kevin Brady, "NASA Launches Houston into Orbit: The Political, Economic, and Social Impact of the Space Agency on Southeast Texas, 1961–1969" (PhD diss., Baylor University, 2009), 52.
19. Ira Bleiweiss, interview by author, Houston, February 16, 17, 2014.
20. The three brothers were Sigmund, Sol, and Max Jucker. "Our History: Three Brothers Bakery Houston, TX." *Three Brothers Bakery*, April 25, 2016, accessed October 20, 2016, http://3brothersbakery.com/history/; Robert Jucker and Sigmund Jucker, interview by author, Houston, June 11, 2014.
21. "Alfred's, A Tradition in Houston, Celebrates 25th Anniversary," *JH-V* (Houston), April 5, 1976, 12.
22. Quoted in C. S. Ragsdale, *Living Longer than Hate: A Story of Survival and Success* (Houston: D. Armstrong Printing Co., Inc., 1997), 95. See also: "The Morgan Story," *Morgan Group*, accessed August 6, 2016, http://www.morgangroup.com/history.php.
23. Alfred and Matt Kahn, interview.
24. Evelyn Berkowitz, interview by David Goldstein, Neighborhood Voices Oral Histories, April 12, 2008, film, http://digital.houstonlibrary.net/oral-history/evelyn-berkowitz.php.
25. Behnken, *Fighting Their Own Battles*, 1–2; Berkowitz, interview.
26. Larry J. Jackson, "The Development of Black Business in Texas, 1919–1969: From Houston Perspective" (Master's thesis, Texas Tech University, 1979), 58.
27. Charles S. Johnson, "Source Material for Patterns of Negro Segregation 12-Houston, Tex.," Reel 7, Box 1, SC Micro R-6534, Carnegie-Myrdal Study of the Negro in America Research Memoranda Collection, SCRBC, NYPL.
28. "Taylor, Hobart T. Sr.," in *Encyclopedia of African American Business History*, ed. Juliet E. K. Walker (Westport, CT: Greenwood Publishing Group, 1999), 555–556; Howard Beeth and Cary D.

Wintz, "Introduction: Historical Overview," in *Black Dixie: Afro-Texan History and Culture in Houston*, eds., Howard Beeth and Cary D.Wintz (College Station: Texas A&M University Press, 1992), 92; SoRelle, "The Emergence of Black Business in Houston, Texas," 112; SoRelle, "Darker Side of Heaven," 252–282.

29. Charles S. Johnson, "Source Material for Patterns of Negro Segregation 12-Houston, Tex.," Reel 7, Box 1, SC Micro R-6534, Carnegie-Myrdal Study of the Negro in America Research Memoranda Collection, SCRBC, NYPL.

30. Bettie M. Patterson, "My Neighborhood in the 1950s and 1960s," University of Houston, http://www.uh.edu/honors/Programs-Minors/honors-and-the-schools/houston-teachers-institute/curriculum-units/pdfs/1999/the-history-economic-base-and-politics-of-houston/patterson-99-houston.pdf; Beeth and Wintz, "Introduction," 93.

31. Leopold Meyer Retail Merchant Association, 1941-1942, Box 1, Folder 3, MS 67, Leopold Meyer Papers, HMRC, HPL; SoRelle, "The Emergence of Black Business in Houston, Texas," 111; Mease, *On Equal Footing*, 73.

32. Most African Americans in Houston had employment as follows: 8% professionals, 9.8% in personal services, 10.5% in construction, 11.3% in transportation, 23.0% in manufacturing, 23.9% in wholesale and retail. Pitre, interview; Henry Bullock, *Pathways to the Negro Market* (Ann Arbor, MI: JW Edwards, 1957), 48.

33. Steptoe, *Houston Bound*, 135–136; Attwell, interview; Charles S. Johnson, "Source Material for Patterns of Negro Segregation 12-Houston, Tex.," Reel 7, Box 1, SC Micro R-6534, Carnegie-Myrdal Study of the Negro in America Research Memoranda Collection, SCRBC, NYPL; Bettie M. Patterson, "My Neighborhood."

34. Debra Castleberry, interview by Patricia Prather, Gregory School Oral Histories, March 22, 2011, film, http://digital.houstonlibrary.net/oral-history/debra-castleberry_OHGS0030.php.

35. See: Leon F. Litwak, "Jim Crow Blues," *OAH Magazine of History*, 18, no. 2 (2004). 7–58.

36. Charles S. Johnson, "Source Material for Patterns of Negro Segregation 12-Houston, Tex.," Reel 7, Box 1, SC Micro R-6534, Carnegie-Myrdal Study of the Negro in America Research Memoranda Collection, SCRBC, NYPL.

37. Interview Christia Adair, April 25, 1977, Box 4, Folder 2, Black Women Oral History Project, MS 109, Christia V. Adair Collection, HMRC, HPL.

38. Adair, interview.

39. Adair, interview.

40. "Foley's 'The Store of Tomorrow,'" *Houston History Magazine*, 10–47, Box 3A172, Folder 3, Texas Jewish Historical Society, DBCAH,

University of Texas at Austin [CAH]; Max Levine, Retired Chairman
of the Board, Foley's of Houston, interviewed by Oral Business History
Project, Floyd S. Brandt, Direct of Interview Series Conducted by John F.
Burnham, "A Venturing in Retailing Federated 'Foley's of Houston,'"
University Business Oral History Records, Box 3J246, Folder 7, DBCAH,
University of Texas at Austin [CAH]; Jewish Federation of Greater
Houston, *Golden Jubilee*, 19; "Rabbi Benjamin Marcus to Address Book
Club," Box 30, Folder 1: Newsletters: Misc. Port-Foley-O's-Magazine
(Bound), 1953–1957, Foley's Department Store Records, SC, UHL.
41. "Foley's Colored Associates Celebrate June 19th with Annual Family
Picnic," Box 29, Folder 4: Newsletters: Misc. Port-Foley-O's-Magazine
(Bound), 1948, Foley's Department Store Records, SC, UHL; "F.C.A.A.
Cardinal Win Two Games Juneteenth," Box 29, Folder 4: Newsletters:
Misc. Port-Foley-O's-Magazine (Bound), 1948, Foley's Department
Store Records, SC, UHL.
42. Letter from Mrs. Pearl W. Sanders to Foley's Management, November 22,
1955, Box 11, Folder 12, Integration—Segregation Issues, Foley's
Department Store Records, SC, UHL.
43. Box 12, Folder 11, and Box 13 Folder 15, Foley's Department Store
Records, SC, UHL; Note 11-12-58, Box 14, Folder 17, Foley's Department Store Records, SC, UHL; Transcription of Telephone Conver-
sation After Your Call, Box 14, Folder 16: Integration—Colored
Facilities, 1958, Foley's Department Store Records, SC, UHL.
44. Letter from Mrs. Jacob T. Stewart to Foley's Management, February 14,
1957, Box 13, Folder 15: Integration—Negro Marketing, 1957, Foley's
Department Store Records, SC, UHL.
45. Rozelle Kahn, interview, Congregation Emanu El Houston, Texas,
January 20, 1983, AJA. See also: Jacoway, *Southern Businessmen and
Desegregation*, 5, 6.
46. Box 13, Folder 15: Integration—Negro Marketing, 1957, Foley's
Department Store Records, SC, UHL.
47. For more information, see: Bullock, *Pathways to the Negro Market*.
48. "The Houston Negro Market," Box 16, Folder 21: Integration—
The Negro Market (Analysis from 1954), Foley's Department Store
Records, SC, UHL.
49. Bullock, *Pathways to the Negro Market*, 190.
50. Bullock, 193.
51. Bullock, 192–95.
52. Bullock, 210.
53. David White, "Finding the Pulse of the People," *JH-V* (Houston),
August 27, 1959, 2.
54. White, "Finding the Pulse of the People." See also: Jewish Federation
of Greater Houston, *Golden Jubilee*, 57–58.

55. David White, "Employment Discrimination," *JH-V* (Houston), November 15, 1956, 5.
56. Rosenblatt, interview by author, Houston, April 21, 2014.
57. Dr. Tatcho Mindiola, interview by David Goldstein, Houston Oral History Project, June 4, 2008, film, http://digital.houstonlibrary.org/cdm/singleitem/collection/oralhistory/id/88/rec/1. See also: Box 1, Folder 4: Felix Mexican Restaurant, Personnel and Policy Directives, 1950s–1960s, MS 108, Felix Tijerina Sr. Family Paper, HMRC, HPL.
58. Cole, *No Color Is My Kind*, 110, 197; "The Strange Demise of Jim Crow: How Houston Desegregated Its Public Accommodations, 1960–63," Box 2, Folder 4: Draft 2.0, 1993–1997, Thomas R. Cole Desegregation Papers, SC, UHL; "I'll Tell God About It: How Houston Integrated Its Public Accommodations, 1960–63," Box 2, Folder 1 Draft 1.0, 1993–1997, Thomas R. Cole Desegregation Papers, SC, UHL.
59. Cole, *No Color Is My Kind*, 26; Quoted in Zeke Minaya, "Houston Man, 1960 KKK Victim, Dies," *Houston Chronicle*, April 28, 2006, http://www.chron.com/news/houston-texas/article/Houston-man-1960-KKK-victim-dies-1876503.php.
60. Lisa Gray, "Gray: The Quiet Revolution to Open Segregation's Doors," *Houston Chronicle*, January 12, 2012, http://www.chron.com/life/gray/article/Gray-The-quiet-revolution-to-open-segregations-2494635.php.
61. "The Strange Demise of Jim Crow: How Houston Desegregated Its Public Accommodations, 1959–63," Box 2 Folder 7 Draft: 3.0, 1993–1997, Thomas R. Cole Desegregation Papers. Courtesy of Houston History Archives, Special Collections, University of Houston Libraries; "TSU Student Group Widens Its Sitdown: Drug Store Counter Is Visited; Supermarket Is Closed Early," *Houston Post*, March 6, 1960, 1.
62. "The Strange Demise of Jim Crow: How Houston Desegregated Its Public Accommodations, 1959–63," Box 2, Folders 4 and 7, Draft: 3.0, 1993–1997, Thomas R. Cole Desegregation Papers, SC, UHL.
63. "I'll Tell God About It: How Houston Integrated Its Public Accommodations, 1960–3," Box 2, Folder 1: Draft 1.0, 1993–1997, Thomas R. Cole Desegregation Papers, SC, UHL; Guy Carwan, writer, *Nashville Sit-in Story: Songs & Scenes of Nashville Lunch Counter Desegregation*, Folkways, 1960, CD; Clayborne Carson, *In Struggle: SNCC and the Black Awakening of the 1960s* (Cambridge, MA: Harvard University Press, 1995), 16, 28, 36; Stone, *Chosen Folks*, 193.
64. Cole, *No Color is My Kind*, 29.
65. "TSU Student Group Widens Its Sitdown: Drug Store Counter Is Visited; Supermarket Is Closed Early," *Houston Post*, March 6, 1960, 1.
66. Cole, *No Color Is My Kind*, 30–32; "I'll Tell God About It: How Houston Integrated Its Public Accommodations, 1960–63," Box 2,

Folders 1 and 2, Drafts 1.0 and 1.1, 1993–1997, Thomas R. Cole Desegregation Papers, SC, UHL. See also: Cole, *No Color Is My Kind*, 30–32; "TSU Student Group Widens Its Sitdown: Drug Store Counter Is Visited; Supermarket Is Closed Early," *Houston Post*, March 6, 1960, 1; "'Negro Knifed Near 'Sit-Down' T.S.U Students Force Early Closing of Weingarten's Store," *Houston Chronicle*, March 6, 1960, 1.

67. "I'll Tell God About It: How Houston Integrated Its Public Accommodations, 1960–63," Box 2 Folder 1: Draft 1.0 1993–1997, Thomas R. Cole Desegregation Papers. Courtesy of Houston History Archives, Special Collections, University of Houston Libraries.

68. "Third Lunch Counter Closed After Sitdown by Thomas Mahr," Houston Press (Houston, Texas), March 7, 1960, 1; "Sit-Down Spreads to Fourth Store," Houston Chronicle (Houston, Texas), March 8, 1960, 1; "Houston Police Chief to Address Houston Lodge September 17," JH-V (Houston, Texas), September 12, 1957; Cole, *No Color is My Kind*, 31.

69. *This is Our Home, It Is Not for Sale.* In the film, it says it was B'nai Brith Award, but most likely it was the Brotherhood Award he received through the National Conference of Christians and Jews. See: WBAP-TV (Television station: Fort Worth, Tex.), News Script: Sitdown strike, item, March 5, 1960, from The Portal to Texas History, KXAS-NBC 5 News Collection. texashistory.unt.edu/ark:/67531/metadc936149, accessed October 20, 2016.

70. "Joseph Weingarten, February 1959," Texas Jewish Historical Society, Box 3A, Folder 3, February 1959, DBCAH, The University of Texas at Austin [CAH]; "Man With a Dream Don't Bet Against It Becoming a Reality, July 25, 1959," Scrapbook Highlights of 1958, 1959, 1960, 1961, 1962, 1963, 1964, 1965, MS 136, Sig Frucht Collection, HMRC, HPL; Today is the Dawn, (Houston Post), New Years 1959, Nearprint: Joe Weingarten, Nearprint Biographies, AJA.

71. "In the New Year of 1958 … "(Houston Post), New Years 1959, Nearprint: Joe Weingarten, Nearprint Biographies, AJA.

72. Cole, *No Color Is My Kind*, 32, 36; "I Tell God about It: How Houston Integrated Its Public Accommodations, 1960–63," Box 2, Folder 1: Draft 1.0 1993–1997, Thomas R. Cole Desegregation Papers, SC, UHL.

73. "T.S.U. Students' 'Sit-Ins,'" *Texas Observer* (Houston), March 11, 1960, 1; Zeke Minaya, "Houston Man, 1960 KKK Victim, dies," *Houston Chronicle*, April 28, 2006, http://www.chron.com/news/houston-texas/article/Houston-man-1960-KKK-victim-dies-1876503.php.

74. "Sit-in Spreads to Fourth Store," *Houston Chronicle*, March 8, 1960; Minaya, "Houston Man, 1960 KKK victim, dies"; "Negro Teenagers Sought in Carving of White Man"[sic], *Indianapolis Recorder*, March 9, 1960, 1–2.

75. "Smear Swastika on Emanu El," *JH-V* (Houston), January 14, 1960, 1.

76. "Houston Jewish Heads Plan Fight on Anti-Semitism: Alarmed by Outbreak of Smears," *Houston Chronicle*, January 15, 1960, 1.
77. Some of the important white Gentile business leaders were J. T. Baker Jr., manager of Grants; Groce Lallier of Madding's Drug Store; J. M. Burns, of Montgomery Ward and Company; H. H. Hocher, manager of Woolworths; and S. W. Shipnes, area manager for the Sears, Roebuck, and Company. Sam Weiner, "Grossman Is Reelected Retail Merchants' Head," *Houston Post*, March 17, 1960, 1, 10; "The Strange Demise of Jim Crow: How Houston Desegregated Its Public Accommodations, 1960–63," Box 2 Folder 4: Draft 2.0, 1993–1997, Thomas R. Cole Desegregation Papers, SC, UHL.
78. "Bob Dundas Diary 4/3/97," Box 3 Folder 3: Research and Consultants, 1993–1997, Thomas R. Cole Desegregation Papers, SC, UHL.
79. "The Weingarten's: Proven Friends to Colored People," *Negro Labor News* (Houston), March 12, 1960, 1.
80. Cole, *No Color Is My Kind*, 37–39.
81. I'll Tell God About It, Box 2 Folder 1: Draft 1.0, 1993–1997, Thomas R. Cole Desegregation Papers, SC, UHL.
82. "Bob Dundas Diary 4/3/97," Box 3, Folder: Research and Consultants, 1993–1997, Thomas R. Cole Desegregation Papers, SC, UHL.
83. Harry Golden, "The Vertical Negro Plan," *Race & Education in Charlotte*, https://speccollexhibit.omeka.net/items/show/74. See also: Kimberly Marlowe Hartnett, *Carolina Israelite: How Harry Golden Made Us Care about Jews, the South, and Civil Rights* (Chapel Hill: University of North Carolina Press, 2015).
84. "The Strange Demise of Jim Crow: How Houston Desegregated Its Public Accommodations, 1960-63," Box 2, Folder 4: Draft 2.0, 1993–1997, Thomas R. Cole Desegregation Papers, SC, UHL.
85. "Vertical Integration," *New York Times*, March 24, 1960, 32.
86. *This Is Our Home, It Is Not for Sale.*
87. Cary Wintz, interview by author, Houston, May 27, 2014.
88. Rosenblatt, interview.
89. "I Tell God About It: How Houston Integrated Its Public Accommodations, 1960–63," Box 2, Folder 1: Draft 1.0, 1993–1997, Thomas R. Cole Desegregation Papers, SC, UHL.
90. "The Strange Demise of Jim Crow: How Houston Desegregated Its Public Accommodations, 1960–63," Box 2, Folder 21: Sit-ins, 1993–1997, Thomas R. Cole Desegregation Papers, SC, UHL.
91. "The Strange Demise of Jim Crow: How Houston Desegregated Its Public Accommodations, 1960–63."
92. "Bob Dundas Diary 4/3/97," Box 3 Folder 3: Research and Consultants, 1993–1997, Thomas R. Cole Desegregation Papers. Courtesy of Houston History Archives, Special Collections, University of Houston Libraries.

93. "Downtown Sitdowners Reappear, Picket Store," *Houston Post*, March 24, 1960, 15. See also: "Bob Dundas Diary 4/3/97," Box 3 Folder 3: Research and Consultants, 1993–1997, Thomas R. Cole Desegregation Papers, SC, UHL.
94. "I Tell God About It: How Houston Integrated Its Public Accommodations, 1960–63," Box 2, Folder 1: Draft 1.1, 1993–1997, Thomas R. Cole Desegregation Papers, SC, UHL; Cole, *No Color Is My Kind*, 44.
95. "Sitdown Group Asks Study Committee: Panel Would End Picketing: No Bargain by City, Cutrer Says," *Houston Post*, March 27, 1960, 1.
96. Though rumored to be Jewish, Jaworski was in fact a Christian. See: "Bob Dundas Diary 4/3/97," Box 3, Folder 3: Research and Consultants, 1993–1997, Thomas R. Cole Desegregation Papers, SC, UHL.
97. "Cutrer Names 37 to Make Racial Study: Committee's Rule Will Be 'Strictly Advisory,'" *Houston Post*, April 7, 1960, 1. Other members included Bill Wallace, secretary-manager of the Retail Merchant Association; George E. Dentler, the president of the Houston Restaurant Association; and Jack Valenti, the mayor's press secretary.
98. "I Tell God About It: How Houston Integrated Its Public Accommodations, 1960–63," Box 2 Folder 1: Draft 1.1, 1993–1997, Thomas R. Cole Desegregation Papers, SC, UHL.
99. Tommy J. Domingue, "Memoir of Tommy J. Domingue" (unpublished memoir from Dorothy Domingue, March 6, 2014), Microsoft Word file.
100. Cole, *No Color Is My Kind*, 46–53.
101. "Mayor's Bi-Racial Group to Disband: Subcommittee Head Expresses Surprise Over Hamblen Move," *Houston Post*, June 10, 1960, 1.
102. "Cool Heads Kept Houston from Going Way of Selma in 1960, by Thomas Cole," File: H-Civil Rights, HMRC, HPL.
103. "12 Pickets March on City Stores," *Houston Post*, May 8, 1960, 2.
104. "12 Pickets March on City Stores."
105. "The Strange Demise of Jim Crow: How Houston Desegregated Its Public Accommodations, 1960–63," Box 2, Folder 4: Draft 2.0, 1993–1997, Thomas R. Cole Desegregation Papers, SC, UHL.
106. "12 Pickets March on City Stores." For more on the Harlem campaign in the 1930s, see: Cheryl Lynn Greenberg, *"Or Does it Explode?": Black Harlem in the Great Depression* (New York: Oxford University Press, 1991), 114–140.
107. "150 in Sitdowns; Lunch Counters are Shut Down," *Houston Post* (Houston, Texas), March 23, 1960 75th year Number 354.
108. "Documentary Proposal: 'The Strange Demise of Jim Crow' the Strange Demise of Jim Crow," Box 1, Folder 2: Fundraising Proposals (1 of 3), 1993–1997, Thomas R. Cole Desegregation Papers, SC, UHL; Jim Crow—Topical Interviews Segments (Eldrewey Stearns), Box 2

Folder 31: Transcript: Eldrewey Stearns, Thomas R. Cole Desegregation Papers, SC, UHL.

109. Jim Crow—Topical Interviews Segments (Eldrewey Stearns), Box 2, Folder 31: Transcript: Eldrewey Stearns, Thomas R. Cole Desegregation Papers, SC, UHL.

110. Jewish Federation of Greater Houston, *Golden Jubilee*, 24; "Bob Dundas Diary 4/3/97." Box 3, Folder 3: Research and Consultants, 1993–1997, Thomas R. Cole Desegregation Papers, SC, UHL; Letter, Lyndon Baines Johnson to Dr. Schachtel, 09/12/57," Sca-Schal," Senate Political Files, Box 165, LBJ Library.

111. "Lost in the Cause," p. 15, May 23–June 4, 1997 Houston Press Ethnic Groups-Civil Rights Vertical File, HMRC, HPL; "Weingarten's Lunch Counter Opens to All; Negro Cashiers Reported 'In Training,'" *Negro Labor News* (Houston), June 18, 1960, 1.

112. "Lost in the Cause."

113. Lisa Gray, "Gray: The Quiet Revolution to Open Segregation's Doors."

114. "Bob Dundas Diary 4/3/97," Box 3, Folder 3: Research and Consultants, 1993–1997, Thomas R. Cole Desegregation Papers, SC, UHL.

115. "Bob Dundas Diary 4/3/97"; Max Levine, Retired Chairman of the Board, Foley's of Houston, interviewed by Oral Business History Project Floyd S. Brandt, Direct of Interview Series Conducted by John F. Burnham, "A Venturing in Retailing Federated 'Foley's of Houston,'" University Business Oral History Records, DBCAH, The University of Texas at Austin [CAH], Box 3J246 Folder 7; "Integration in Houston": Marguerite Johnston Barnes Research Material for "Houston: The Unknown City, 1830–1946." MS 455, Box 10 Folder 13:1940's-Foley's, Woodson Research Center, Fondren Library, Rice University.

116. Max Levine, interviewed by Oral Business History Project Floyd S. Brandt, Direct of Interview Series Conducted by John F. Burnham, "A Venturing in Retailing Federated 'Foley's of Houston,'" Box 3J246, Folder 7, University Business Oral History Records, DBCAH, University of Texas at Austin [CAH]. See also: "Integration in Houston": Marguerite Johnston Barnes Research Material for "Houston: The Unknown City, 1830–1946." MS 455, Box 10, Folder 13:1940's-Foley's, WRC, Fondren Library, RU.

117. Alfred and Matt Kahn, interview by author.

118. "Rabbi Kahn, Integration Leader, Dies," *Houston Chronicle*, November 22, 2002, http://www.chron.com/news/houston-texas/article/Rabbi-Kahn-integration-leader-dies-2085638.php.

119. Rozelle Kahn, interview, Congregation Emanu El Houston, Texas. January 20, 1983, AJA.

120. Rozelle Kahn, interview; Lessons for Life, September 4, 1960, Box 4 Lessons for Life and Lectures, MS 853. Robert I Kahn Papers. American Jewish Archives, Cincinnati, Ohio.

121. Cole, *No Color Is My Kind*, 55; Bob Dundas Diary 4/3/97," Box 3 Folder 3: Research and Consultants, 1993–1997, Thomas R. Cole Desegregation Papers. Courtesy of Houston History Archives, Special Collections, University of Houston Libraries

122. "Integration in Houston," Marguerite Johnston Barnes Research Material for "Houston: The Unknown City, 1830–1946." MS 455, Box 10 Folder 13:1940's-Foley's, WRC, Fondren Library, RU. See also: Cole, *No Color Is My Kind*, 55; Bob Dundas Diary 4/3/97," Box 3, Folder 3: Research and Consultants, 1993–1997, Thomas R. Cole Desegregation Papers, SC, UHL.

123. "Integration in Houston."

124. Fred Zeidman, interview by author, Houston, April 14, 2014. See also: Cole, *No Color Is My Kind*, 55.

125. Quoted in Behnken, *Fighting Their Own Battles*, 77.

126. "ISJL-Texas Houston Encyclopedia."

127. "The News Blackout on Sit-Ins Was in Best Interest of Houston's Citizens," *Negro Labor News* (Houston, Texas), September 10, 1960, 1.

128. 1See: Jacoway, *Southern Businessmen and Desegregation*, Introduction, 92–97, 137–150; Rhiannon Saegert, "Waco Civil Rights Activist Who Fought for Integration Urges Next Generation to 'Keep Up the Fight," *Waco Tribune-Herald*, February 22, 2020.

129. "Houston Stores Drop Negro Ban," *New York Times*, August 26, 1960.

130. "The Press: Blackout in Houston," *Time Magazine*, September 12, 1960.

131. Barry Jagoda, ed., "The Teen Community," *JH-V*, March 16, 1961, 9.

132. "Bill" Lawson (Reverend), interview by Jane Ely.

133. Letter from Mrs. E. Pliny Shaw to Max Levine, August 16, 1961, Box 20, Folder 29: Integration—Letters Concerning Integration, 1963, Foley's Department Store Records, SC, UHL.

134. Cole, *No Color Is My Kind*, 69; Cora Johnson, interview by Adrienne Cain.

135. Letter from Dawn N. Miller, Box 21 Folder 32: Correspondence—Letters, Thanks & Invitation, Foley's Department Store Records, SC, UHL; Texas southern University Summer Workshop 1965, Box 23, Folder 5: Texas southern University Summer Workshop, 1965, Foley's Department Store Records, SC, UHL; "1969 N.A.A.C.P. of Houston Award Recipients," November 21, 1969, Box 27, Folder 6: Integration-NAACP Freedom Fund Dinner, 1969, Foley's Department Store Records, SC, UHL.

136. Weiner's later became a company that actually catered to minorities. Leon Weiner Obituary, *Houston Chronicle*, "Weiner's Stores, Inc.," History of Weiner's Stores, Inc.—*Funding Universe*, accessed October 20, 2016, http://www.fundinguniverse.com/company-histories/weiner-s-stores-inc-history/. September 15, 2013.

137. Advertisement, "May I Help You?," Judge Woodrow Seals Collection, MS 414, Box 2, Folder 6, HMRC, HPL; Letter from Mrs. E. Pliny

Shaw to Mr. Finger, Houston Council on Human Relations, RG E 64, Box 1, Folder 1: Correspondence 1959–1961, HMRC, HPL. Cvyia Wolff, interview by author, Houston, February 7, 2014.

138. Cvyia Wolff interview.

139. Art Gallaher, *The Negro and Employment Opportunities in the South: Houston: A Report Based Survey* (Houston, TX: Houston Council on Human Relations, 1961), 4–22.

140. "Fuehrer Rockwell Flits in Houston; Shoves Off," *JH-V* (Houston), March 15, 1962, 1.

141. "Fuehrer Rockwell Flits in Houston; Shoves Off."

142. Mease, *On Equal Footing*, 80–87, 100–101; Cole, *No Color Is My Kind*, 93; John F. Kennedy, "Moon Speech," *John F. Kennedy Moon Speech*, September 12, 1962, http://er.jsc.nasa.gov/she/ricetalk.htm; David Welling and Jack Valenti, *Cinema Houston: From Nickelodeon to Megaplex* (Austin, TX: University of Texas Press, 2011), 189.

143. Box 17 Folder 10: Transcript: Quentin Mease, Integrating the Proud Bayou City, Reels 1–4, Behind the Scenes transcript, 6-20-98 and 6-27-98, Box 17, Folder 10, Thomas R. Cole Desegregation Papers, SC, UHL.

144. Cole, *No Color Is My Kind*, 98; "Interview by Telephone with Dr. Sam Nabrit, By Tom Cole February 10, 1993," Cole, Tom, Voices from Houston (1 of 2), 1998–2001, Box 17, Folder 41, Thomas R. Cole Desegregation Papers, SC, UHL.

145. Box 17 Folder 41: Cole, Tom, Voices from Houston (1 of 2), 1998–2001, Thomas R. Cole Desegregation Papers. Courtesy of Houston History Archives, Special Collections, University of Houston Libraries.

146. Houston Council on Human Relations, "2 Questions" Box 17 Folder 5, Social Ethics Pamphlet Collection, Record Group No. 73, SC, Yale Divinity School Library.

147. Saul Friedman, "Houston, 'A Backwater of Revolt," *Texas Observer* (Houston), November 15, 1963, 8.

148. "Houston, 'The Backwater of Revolt," *The Informer* (Houston), December 7, 1963, 4.

149. Jewell McGowen, interview by Adrienne Cain, Gregory School Oral Histories, July 24, 2013, film, http://digital.houstonlibrary.net/oral-history/jewell-mcgowen_OHGS0066.php.

150. Bullard, *Invisible Houston*, 94–95; SoRelle, "Race Relations in "Heavenly Houston, 1919–45," 165; *This Is Our Home, It Is Not for Sale.*

151. "50 American Utility Firms Charged with Anti-Jewish Discrimination," *JTA* (New York), December 30, 1963. See also: "Four Houston Firms Listed by AJC As Biased in Employment of Jews," *JH-V* (Houston), January 2, 1964, 1.

Chapter Six

1. See: Jonathan Sarna, *American Jews and Church-State Relations: The Search for 'Equal Footing'* (New York: Institute of Human Relations of American Jewish Committee, 1989).
2. John Slawson, *The Realities of Jewish Integration* (New York: American Jewish Committee,1965), 19.
3. Roseman, "Six-Tenths of a Percent of Texas," 207; Wintz, "Blacks," 20; Sarna, *American Jews and Church-State Relations*, 33.
4. Extremism file, AJC Subject Files Collection, Memoranda and Minutes on Borderline Groups, Radical Right, and the Ultra-Conservative Movement (January-July 1961), "The American Jewish Committee April 10, 1961, From Fact-Finding to Dave Danzig Subject "Borderline Groups," AJC Online. See also: David Stricklin, "Fundamentalism," *Handbook of Texas Online*, accessed October 20, 2016, http://www.tshaonline.org/handbook/online/articles/itf01.
5. Dudziak, *Cold War Civil Rights*, 118–121; Carleton, *Red Scare!*, 296–297.
6. Allan Turner, "Ben Levy, Founder of Local ACLU made his Mark," *Houston Chronicle*, April 11, 2004, http://www.chron.com/news/houston-texas/article/Ben-Levy-founder-of-local-ACLU-made-his-mark-1962119.php.
7. Turner, "Ben Levy, Founder of Local ACLU made his Mark."
8. Turner, "Ben Levy, Founder of Local ACLU made his Mark."
9. Kellar, *Make Haste Slowly*, 149; Houston Independent School Board, "School Board Meeting 1959" (meetings, Houston Independent School Board, Houston, Texas, 1959); *Gertrude Barnstone: Home Movie*, directed by Jon Schwartz (Houston, Texas: Riverside Productions, 2015), DVD.
10. Kellar, *Make Haste Slowly*, 104, 124; Lede and Thompson, *Precious Memories of a Black Socialite*, 153.
11. Carter Wesley, "Ram's Horn," *Informer* (Houston), February 22, 1958.
12. "Ben C. Connally, 65, U.S. Judge in Texas" *New York Times*, December 4, 1975, 44; Behnken, *Fighting Their Own Battles*, 207; Kellar, *Make Haste Slowly*, 112–113.
13. "Houston Chapter AJC Announces January 20 Program on 'Desegregation in Our Schools,'" *JH-V* (Houston), January 13, 1955, 9; "Irving M. Engel to Address American Jewish Committee," *JH-V* (Houston), February 17, 1955, 1; "Public Relations Committee Meeting," June 4, 1956, American Jewish Congress records, 1–77, Box 104, Folder 2: Houston, Texas, 1955–1956, AJHS; Letter to Billy Goldberg, July 2, 1956, American Jewish Congress records, 1–77; Box 104, Folder 2:

Houston, Texas, 1955–1956, AJHS; Event for American Jewish Congress, November 11, 1957, American Jewish Congress records; 1–77, Box 104, Folder 3: Houston, Texas, 1956–1957, AJHS; Event for American Congress, June 21, 1957, American Jewish Congress records; 1–77, Box 104, Folder 3: Houston, Texas, 1956–1957, AJHS; "1957 Public Relations Committee," November 20, 1957, American Jewish Congress records, 1–77, Box 104, Folder 3: Houston, Texas, 1956–1957, AJHS.

14. "1957 Public Relations Committee," November 20, 1957, American Jewish Congress records, 1–77, Box 104, Folder 3: Houston, Texas, 1956–1957, AJHS.
15. Letter from Irwin Glatstein to Leo Pfeffer, December 8, 1955, American Jewish Congress records, I–77, Box 104, Folder 2: Houston, Texas, 1955–1956, AJHS.
16. David White, "Question of Hebrew in Our Schools," *JH-V* (Houston), October 8, 1959, 2. See also: "School Board Meeting 1959," (meetings, Houston Independent School Board, Houston, Texas, 1959).
17. White, "Question of Hebrew in Our Schools"; "School Board Meeting 1959," (meetings, Houston Independent School Board, Houston, Texas, 1959).
18. White, "Question of Hebrew in Our Schools."
19. "Bellaire, Westbury, Highschools Offer Course in Hebrew," *JH-V* (Houston), August 26, 1971, 2.
20. Ben C. Connally, interview by Louis Marchiafava, HMRC Oral History Interviews, April 2, 1975, audio, http://digital.houstonlibrary.net/oral-history/ben-conally.php. See also: Lede and Thompson, *Precious Memories*, 153, 154.
21. Kellar, *Make Haste Slowly*, 127; Salatheia Bryant, "Integration Did Not Come to HISD until 1984," *Houston Chronicle*, May 16, 2004, http://www.chron.com/news/houston-texas/article/Integration-did-not-come-to-HISD-until-1984-1512348.php.
22. Salatheia Bryant, "Integration Did Not Come." See also: Kellar, *Make Haste Slowly*, 127, 135, 136, 138, 155; Charles Allen, interview by Louis Marchiafava, HMRC Oral History Collection, August 27, 1975, audio, http://digital.houstonlibrary.net/oral-history/charles-allen_OH001.php.
23. "John F. Kennedy and Religion," John F. Kennedy Presidential Library and Museum, https://www.jfklibrary.org/JFK/JFK-in-History/JFK-and-Religion.aspx; Sean Savage, *JFK, LBJ, and the Democratic Party* (Albany, NY: State University of New York Press, 2004), 79; Michael W. McConnell, "Is There Still A 'Catholic Question' in America? Reflections of John F. Kennedy's Speech to The Houston Ministerial Association," *Notre Dame Law Review* 86, no. 4, (2011): 1636.

24. "John F. Kennedy and Religion," John F. Kennedy Presidential Library and Museum, https://www.jfklibrary.org/JFK/JFK-in-History/ JFK-and-Religion.aspx.

25. 25 Later, President Kennedy would still have trepidations about implementing any Civil Rights legislation because of the power of the conservative southern Democrats and their Republican allies, which could easily thwart such legislation. "John F. Kennedy and Religion"; "The Religious Issues in the Presidential Campaign by Robert I Kahn," October 7, 1960, Box 2, Folder SPG, MS 853, Robert I. Kahn Papers, AJA; Savage, *JFK, LBJ, and the Democratic Party*, 79; 1643; Dudziak, *Cold War Civil Rights*, 156; Shad Polier, "Kennedy's Impact on American Freedom," in *The Jewish 1960s: An American Sourcebook*, ed. Michael E. Staub (Waltham: Brandeis University Press, 2004), 37.

26. Ira Stoll, "Op-Ed: Jews Have Special Reasons to Remember JFK on 50th Anniversary of Assassination," *JTA* (New York), October 13, 2013.

27. Wendelin Nold (Bishop), interview by David Courtwright, HMRC Oral History Collection, August 20, 1975, audio, http://digital. houstonlibrary.net/oral-history/wendelin-nold_OH053.php.

28. Joseph Fiorenza (Archbishop), interview by David Goldstein, Houston Oral History Project, May 27, 2008, film, http://digital.houstonlibrary. net/oral-history/joseph-fiorenza.php; The Texas Catholic Herald, November 12, 1965, Archives of the Archdiocese of Galveston-Houston, Archdiocese of Galveston-Houston. Houston, Texas.

29. Judy King, *Except the Lord Build ... The Sesquicentennial History of First Presbyterian Church, Houston, Texas* 1839–1989 (Houston: First Presbyterian Church of Houston, 1989), 135, 147; Don McKee, "Southern Baptist Bar Race Plan," *Washington Post*, May 22, 1964, B8; David White, "What Problem Is Whose Problem?" *JH-V* (Houston), May 30, 1963, 2.

30. 30 Sarna, *American Jews*, 24–26; David White, "Time to Think of that Christmas in July," *JH-V* (Houston), July 30, 1959, 2; "Community Relations Committee Meeting," April 9, 1959; American Jewish Congress records, I–77; Box 104, Folder 4: Houston, Texas Chapter, 1958–1959, AJHS.

31. Aka Jaime Bloom, interview by author, Houston, February 28, 2014.

32. "Religion in the Schools," *JH-V* (Houston), January 14, 1960, 4; "Is There Religious Prejudice in the Public Schools," *JH-V* (Houston), November 2, 1961, 2; "Nat'l Lecturer to Discuss Intrusion of Religion in Public Schools March 23," *JH-V* (Houston), March 22, 1962, 2; "School Board Member at Minyanaire Event," *JH-V* (Houston), February 21, 1963, 4; "The Bible, the Constitution, and The Time

We Live In," *JH-V* (Houston), June 20, 1963, 2; "Prayers in Schools," *JH-V* (Houston), July 11, 1963, 1; "Two Guest Speakers at Adath Emeth Services," *JH-V* (Houston), December 19, 1963, 5.

33. David White, "Time To Think of Christmas in July," *JH-V* (Houston), July 28, 1966, 2.
34. 1980s, Kahn notes for TV Interview, Rabbi Kahn Papers, Congregation Emanu El Archives, Houston, TX.
35. "Festival of the Bible in the Arts to Be Held March 9–26," *JH-V* (Houston), March 16, 1961, 4; Dr. Robert Kahn, interview by Louis Marchiafava and David Courtwright, August 6, 1975, Texas Jewish Historical Society, Box 3A174, Folder 7, DBCAH, The University of Texas at Austin [CAH].
36. "Brotherhood and the Rights of Man," *Emanu El Bulletin* 18 (February 15, 1963): 3; Annette Levy Ratkin, "The History of the Temple Social Action/ Justice Committee," Temple Nashville, accessed October 20, 2016, https://www.Templenashville.org/_content/6_beit_tikkum_olam/social_action_programs/The%20History%20of%20Social%20Action.pdf.
37. Ratkin, "The History of the Temple Social Action/Justice Committee."
38. "Brotherhood and the Rights of Man," *Emanu El Bulletin* 18 (February 15, 1963): 3.
39. "School Board Member at Minyanaire Event," *JH-V* (Houston), February 21, 1963, 4.
40. "No. 63 Buzzes," *JH-V* (Houston), April 18, 1964, 11.
41. "Statement on Religion in the Public Schools," adopted by the Community Relations Committee January 17, 1963, MS 186, Box 2 Folder 28: Dr. Edgar, Robert Kahn Papers, HMRC, HPL.
42. David White, "Discussions Held as to Religious Practices in Houston Public Schools," *JH-V* (Houston), May 2, 1963, 1.
43. Melvin Steakley, "Jews Oppose Religion in School Here," *Houston Chronicle*, March 5, 1963, 1.
44. MS 186, Box 4 Folder 9: Ministerial Assn. of Greater Houston, Robert Kahn Papers, HMRC, HPL
45. Michael Cahana (Rabbi), interview by author, Portland, September 2, 2015.
46. Congregation Brith Shalom, "Rabbi Cahana Remembers," *Hineni*, November 2002, Pam Geyer Private Collection; Children's Crusade," *King Encyclopedia*, http://kingencyclopedia.stanford.edu/encyclopedia/encyclopedia/enc_childrens_crusade.1.html; Andre Ungar, "To Birmingham, and Back," *Conservative Judaism* 18, no. 1 (Fall 1963), 16.
47. Michael Cahana (Rabbi), interview.
48. Michael Cahana (Rabbi), interview.
49. David White, "There Are Some Who Remember," *JH-V* (Houston), May 16, 1963, 2.

50. Irving Pozmantier, interview by author, Houston, March 18, 2014.

51. "ISJL-Louisiana New Orleans Encyclopedia," *Institute of Southern Jewish Life*, 2014, accessed August 10, 2016, https://www.isjl.org/louisiana-new-orleans-encyclopedia.html.; "ISJL-Mississippi Jackson," *Institute of Southern Jewish Life*, 2014, accessed August 10, 2016; "ISJL-Tennessee Memphis."

52. Pozmantier, interview.

53. "Tribute to Jenard and Gail Gross and Jewish Women International," *Capitol Words*, May 2, 2000, accessed August 12, 2016, http://capitolwords.org/date/2000/05/02/H2379-2_tribute-to-jenard-and-gross-and-in-jewish-women-/.

54. Letter to Editor Jenard M. Gross to David White, *JH-V* (Houston) May 23, 1963, 2.

55. For more on the Nation of Islam in Houston, see Masjid Warithuddeen Mohammed, "Founded in the 1950s," 2015, http://masjidwdmohammed.com/history/.

56. David White, "What Problem Is Whose Problem?" *JH-V* (Houston), May 30, 1963, 2.

57. "Copy of Steering Committee Proceedings for Metropolitan Houston Conference on Religion and Race, May 24, 1963," Folder: Metropolitan Houston Conference on Religion and Race 1963, SC-2850, AJA; "Conference on Religion and Race," Folder: Metropolitan Houston Conference on Religion and Race 1963, SC-2850, AJA.

58. "Meeting May 30," Folder: Metropolitan Houston Conference on Religion and Race 1963, SC-2850, AJA.

59. "Conference on Religion and Race," Folder: Metropolitan Houston Conference on Religion and Race 1963, SC-2850, AJA. Other examples of the use of "non-negro" include: Letter from Martin Luther King to Mrs. E. Weidner, February 26, 1962, The King Center, http://www.thekingcenter.org/archive/document/letter-mlk-e-weidner; Ben A Franklin, "Non-Negro Units Hit March Chiefs: Charge They are Ignored and 'Abused' by Black," *New York Times*, May 26, 1968, 69.

60. "Conference on Religion and Race," Folder: Metropolitan Houston Conference on Religion and Race 1963, SC-2850, AJA.

61. "Conference on Religion and Race," Folder: Metropolitan Houston Conference on Religion and Race 1963, SC-2850, AJA.

62. "Conference on Religion and Race.

63. Letter from Mrs. Ruby Davis to Rabbi Moshe Cahana," June 25, 1963, Folder: Metropolitan Houston Conference on Religion and Race 1963, SC-2850, AJA.

64. Letter from Moshe Cahana to Mrs. Davis, July 1, 1963, Folder: Metropolitan Houston Conference on Religion and Race 1963, SC-2850, AJA.

65. Norton Shaw, ed., "Teen Community Jewish Community Center Youth Council," *JH-V* (Houston), November 14, 1963, 16.
66. Robin M. Williams, Daniel C. Thompson, and Oscar Cohen, *Social Action and the Social Scientist* (Houston: Public Affairs Research Center, 1964), 1; "Pre-Convention Committee Reports: June 11–14, 1966 Villa Capri Motel Austin, Texas, "Anti-Defamation League of Bnai Brith," Box 8, Folder: Pre-Convention Report 1968–1969, MS-180, B'nai B'rith District Grand Lodge No. & Records, AJA; Gordon, interview; "Twenty-Ninth Annual Concert Workmen's Circle—Auditorium Sunday," December 26, 1943, Workmen's Circle; RG 575, YIVO Institute for Jewish Research; "Workmen's Circle 51st Annual Picnic," June 26, 1966, Workmen's Circle; RG575, YIVO Institute for Jewish Research; Staub, *Torn at the Roots*, 45.
67. Jeff Woods, *Black Struggle, Red Scare*, 172–173; *Investigation of the Assassination of President John F. Kennedy* (Washington, DC.: US GPO, 1964), 645.
68. Gertrude Barnstone, interview by Jane Ely, HMRC Oral History Collection, March 25, 2008, film, http://digital.houstonlibrary.net/oral-history/gertrude-barnstone_OH008.php.
69. Raphael S. Schwartzman, "The Mosaic of Hate: With Our Rabbis," *JH-V* (Houston), December 26, 1963, 10.
70. "Memorial Services for the President," *Bellaire Texan* (Bellaire), November 27, 1963, 1,10; Robert I. Kahn, *May the Words of My Mouth* (Houston: Congregation Emanu El, 1984), 155–161.
71. Tennyson Whorton, "Clergymen Firmly For Rights Law," *Houston Post* (Houston, Texas), July 5, 1964, 1.
72. Whorton, "Clergymen Firmly For Rights Law."
73. Whorton, "Clergymen Firmly For Rights Law."
74. David White, "The Civil Rights Battle Has Just Begun," *JH-V* (Houston), June 25, 1964, 2.
75. Letter from Rabbi I. Kahn to FBI Houston, Texas, August 19, 1964, Box 2 Folder 42: Miscellaneous F, MS 186, Rabbi Robert Kahn Papers, HMRC, HPL.
76. "It Was a Long Journey," Box 1, Folder 20: "Sermons and Lecture Notes," MS 587, Gertrude Barnstone Papers, 1956–2015, WRC, Fondren Library, RU.
77. Barnstone, interview.
78. Barnstone, interview; "Mrs. Howard Barnstone to Speak to American Jewish Committee," *JH-V* (Houston), November 25, 1965, 5.
79. Asberry Butler, HMRC Oral History Collection, August 9, 1974, audio, http://digital.houstonlibrary.net/oral-history/asberry-butler_OH015.php.
80. "Downtown Lodge B'nai B'rith," *JH-V* (Houston), November 12, 1964, 8; "New Senior Adult Program at Center," *JH-V* (Houston),

January 19, 1967, 5; Barnstone, interview; Jennifer Radcliffe, "HISD Schools Get Extra Helping of Free Breakfast: HISD Begins Expanding Free Breakfast Program," *Houston Chronicle*, January 14, 2010, http://www.chron.com/news/houston-texas/article/HISD-schools-get-extra-helpings-of-free-breakfast-1715232.php.

81. Saul Friedman, "4 Houston Clergymen March with Negroes," *Houston Chronicle*, March 10,1965, 4. See also: "2 Protestant, Rabbi, 3 Houston Churchmen to March in Alabama," *Houston Post*, March 9, 1965, 5.
82. "The Houston Rabbinical Association Commends Rabbi Moshe Cahana," *JH-V* (Houston), March 18, 1965, 1.
83. "Rabbi Cahana to be Honored AT ZOA Dinner, Thursday, April 1st," *JH-V* (Houston), March 25, 1965, 1.
84. Balfour Brickner, "Projects Under Synagogue Auspices," *Religious Education* 59, no. 1 (January 1964), 77; "A Call to Conscience," Rabbi Kahn Papers, Congregation Emanu El Archives, Houston, Texas.
85. "A Call to Conscience," Rabbi Kahn Papers, Congregation Emanu El Archives, Houston, Texas.
86. Kellar, *Make Haste Slowly*, 155; "The Response Was Gratifying," *The Informer* (Houston), May 15, 1965, 4; Behnken, *Fighting Their Own Battles*, 154, 208; William 'Bill' Lawson (Reverend), interview by Veronica Perry, HMRC Oral History Collection, August 12, 1974, audio, http://digital.houstonlibrary.net/oral-history/william-lawson_OH100.php.
87. "Bill" Lawson (Reverend), interview by Jane Ely.
88. Quoted in Behnken, *Fighting Their Own Battles*, 208.
89. "The Response Was Gratifying," *The Informer* (Houston), May 15, 1965, 4; William 'Bill' Lawson (Reverend), interview by Veronica Perry; Kellar, *Make Haste Slowly*, 155.
90. Lesson for Life, May 22, 1965, Box 4 Lessons for Life and Lectures, MS-853, Robert I Kahn Papers, AJA.
91. See: Robert Kahn Papers, MS 186, Box 6, Folder 5: Teaching Religion in Public Schools, HMRC, HPL.
92. Letter from Rabbi Malev to Rabbi Kahn, July 6, 1965, Box 6, Folder 5: Teaching Religion in Public Schools, MS 186, Robert Kahn Papers, HMRC, HPL.
93. Hattie Mae White, interview.
94. "Letter from 'Houstonian'" to Mrs. Barnstone, Houston, TX., N.D., Box 1, Folder 2, Gertrude Barnstone Papers Small Collection HMRC, HPL.
95. "Our Sick Cities and How They Can Be Cured," *Look Magazine*, September 21, 1965, Box 1, Folder 2, Gertrude Barnstone Papers Small Collection, HMRC, HPL.

96. Ltr. Wm. H. Worrilow, Sec'y Treasurer Organized Minorities Association, to Editor Look article on Mrs. Barnstone, Box 1, Folder 2, Gertrude Barnstone Papers Small Collection, HMRC, HPL.

97. Ltr. 'Gentile' to Mrs. 'Jew Barnstone'; n.p., n.d. (Postmarked Houston, Texas, November 8, 1964), Box 1, Folder 2, Gertrude Barnstone Papers Small Collection, HMRC, HPL.

98. Jennifer Radcliffe, "Black History Month Profile: Elected Official Hattie Mae White," *Houston Chronicle*, February 14, 2011, http://www. chron.com/news/houston-texas/article/Black-History-Month-profile-Elected-official-1688202.php; Keller, *Make Haste Slowly*, 110.

99. Butler, interview.

100. "Board of Trustees Meeting July 27, 1964---4:00 P.M, Institute of Human Relations Presiding: Nathan Appleman," AJC Minutes, Board of Trustees, July-Dec. 1964, AJC Archives online, http://www.ajcarchives. org/ajcarchive/DigitalArchive.aspx.

101. Program for Action: 1966–1967, Museum of Fine Arts Houston, Houston Archives, MS 28, Frank and Eleanor Freed Papers, Box 1, Folder: American Jewish Committee, unprocessed.

102. "Newsletter Houston Chapter, American Jewish Committee, Vol 1. No. 1," n.d., Box E14, Folder 40, MS-780, AJC Records, AJA; Letter from Gene Burke to Chapter Member, Museum of Fine Arts, Houston Archives, MS 28, Frank and Eleanor Freed Collection, Box 1, Folder: American Jewish Committee; Behnken, *Fighting Their Own Battles*, 209.

103. Letter from James Hamilton, Chairman, Committee on Compliance and Enforcement, to Cooperating Organizations, December 15, 1966, Box E2, Folder 24, MS-780, AJC Records, AJA.

104. "The Houston School Desegregation Case," n.d., Box E2, Folder 24, MS-780, AJC Records, AJA.

105. Leslie Casmir and Lynwood Abram, "Activist Who Fought to Integrate HISD Dies at 81: Obituary Onesephor Peter Broussard Sought to Integrate HISD," *Houston Chronicle*, http://www.chron.com/news/houston-texas/ article/Activist-who-fought-to-integrate-HISD-dies-at-81-1630109. php; "The Houston School Desegregation Case," n.d., Box E2, Folder 24, MS-780, AJC Records, AJA; Steven Harmon Wilson, *The Rise of Judicial Management in the U.S. District, Southern District of Texas, 1955–2000* (Athens: University of Georgia Press, 2002), 209.

106. "The Houston School Desegregation Case," n.d., Box E2, Folder 24, MS-780, AJC Records, AJA.

107. Letter from Milton Feiner to Ed Lukas, November 23, 1966, Box E2, Folder 24, MS-780, AJC Records, AJA.

108. Letter from James Hamilton, Chairman, Committee on Compliance and Enforcement, to Cooperating Organizations, December 15, 1966, Box E2, Folder 24, MS-780, AJC Records, AJA; Southwest Region

American Jewish Committee, December 1966, Box E2, Folder 24, MS-780, AJC Records, AJA; Broussard v. Houston Independent School District School Desegregation Case, Folder: 016461-010-0378, Papers of the NAACP, Supplement to Part 23: Legal Department Case Files, 1960–1972, Series A: The South, Section III: Kentucky, Louisiana, Mississippi, Tennessee, and Texas, http://congressional.proquest. com/histvault?q=016461-010-0378.

109. Letter from Milton Feiner to Ed Lukas, March 6, 1967, Box E2, Folder 24, MS-780, AJC Records, AJA. See also: Letter from Milton Feiner to Sam Rabinove, August 7, 1967, Box E2, Folder 24. MS-780, AJC Records, AJA.

110. Letter from Irving M. Engels to Edwin J. Lukas, April 3, 1967, Box E2, Folder 24, MS-780, AJC Records, AJA.

111. Letter from Edwin J. Lukas to Irving M. Engels, April 5, 1967, Box E2, Folder 24, MS-780. AJC Records, AJA.

112. Wesley Phelps, *People's War on Poverty: Urban Politics, Grassroots Activists, and the Struggle for Democracy in Houston, 1964–1976* (Athens: University of Georgia Press, 2014), 17, 76; National Council for Jewish Women Collection, RG E 23, Box 1, Folder 9, 13; Box 5 Scrapbook, HMRC, HPL.

113. Rabbi Robert Kahn Papers, MS-186, Box 4, Folder 22: Operation Headstart, HMRC, HPL.

114. Joyce Gilbert, interview by author, Houston, April 21, 2014; Congregation Brith Shalom, "Brith Shalom History," *Your Jewish Journey Starts Here*, accessed October 20, 2016, http://www.brithshalom.org/about-us/brith-shalom-history; Operation Headstart, Box 4, Folder 22, MS 186, Robert I. Kahn Papers, HMRC, HPL; King, *Except the Lord Build*, 147.

Chapter Seven

1. Gay Block, "A Tribute to Spirit: The Beth Israel Experience," in *About Love: Gay Block, Photographs and Films 1973-2011* (Santa Fe, NM: Radius Books, 2011), DVD.

2. "Germany Asked for It—So We Marched," *JH-V* (Houston), January 21, 1965, 5; "Jews Picket German Consulate," Houston Zionist Organization Scrapbook, 1954–1965, Texas Jewish Historical Society, DBCAH, University of Texas at Austin [CAH], Box 3A185-3A186.

3. "Houston Jews Protest End of Nazi Trials" By Walt Mansell Houston Zionist Organization Scrapbook, 1954–1965, Texas Jewish Historical Society, DBCAH, University of Texas at Austin [CAH], Box 3A185-3A186.

4. "Israel Today," January 28, 1966, Box A1, Folder Sermons—1966 to June 1-1-67, MS 172, Rabbi Hyman Judah Schachtel Papers, HMRC, HPL.

5. Steven Windmueller, "The Jewish Contract with America" in *American Politics and the Jewish Community: The Jewish Role in American Life: An Annual Review of the Casden Institute for the Study of the Jewish Role in American Life*, eds. Bruce Zuckerman, Dan Schnur, and Lisa Ansell (West Lafayette, IN: Purdue University Press, 2013), 21; Carson, "The Politics of Relations," 139–140.

6. Jeanne Theoharis, "'Alabama on Avalon,' Rethinking the Watts Uprising and the Character of Black Protest in Los Angeles," in *The Black Power Movement: Rethinking the Civil Rights-Black Power Era*, ed. Peniel E. Joseph (London: Routledge, 2006), 30; Donna Murch, "The Many Meanings of Watts: Black Power, Wattstax, and the Carceral State," *OAH Magazine of History* 26, no. 1 (2012): doi: 10.1093/oahmag/oar062; William S. Clayson, *Freedom Is Not Enough: The War on Poverty and the civil rights movement in Texas* (Austin: University of Texas Press, 2010), 123.

7. Blair Justice, *Violence in the City* (Fort Worth, TX: Leo Potishman Fund, 1969), 1–2, 11.

8. The first Nation of Islam School did not open until the 1980s. Masjid Warithuddeen Mohammed, "Founded in the 1950s," 2015, http://masjidwdmohammed.com/history/; Matthias Gardell, *In the Name of Elijah Muhammad: Louis Farrakhan and the Nation of Islam* (Durham, NC: Duke University Press, 1996), 61.

9. "Some Predictions for 1966, January 7, 1966," Box A1, Folder: Sermons—1966 to June, MS 172, Rabbi Hyman Judah Schachtel Papers, HMRC, HPL.

10. Jerome Solomon, "Muhammad Ali and Houston, a Star-Crossed Pair," *Houston Chronicle*, June 16, 2016, http://www.chron.com/local/history/sports/article/Muhammad-Ali-and-Houston-a-star-crossed-pair-8272064.php; Steve Cady, "Clay Will Make His Home in Houston, Seeks 'Fabulous' $100,000 'Spread.,'" *New York Times*, February 5, 1967, S3; "C. Clay Attorney," KHOU-TV Film Collection, Box 6701 Reel 21, HMRC Film Archives, April 25, 1967, digital.houstonlibrary.net/film-archive/hmrc-film_6701-21.php.

11. Justice, *Violence in the City*, 43–45; Craig Hlavaty, "Looking Back at the Time Muhammad Ali Refused the Draft in Houston," *Houston Chronicle*, April 28, 2015, http://www.chron.com/news/houston-texas/article/48-years-ago-today-Muhammad-Ali-refused-the-5435356.php; Solomon, "Muhammad Ali and Houston."

12. Quoted in "Negro Group Breaks Up Racist Speech" by Donnie Smith (2-22-67)," RU Scrapbook Collection, 1907–1985, RU Archives, UA 230, Box 31, Folder 2, WRC, Fondren Library, RU.

13. Doug McNeal, "Stoner Stands for 'American Way,'" *The Rice Thresher* (Houston), February 23, 1967, 9.

14. Don Adams, "Negro Legislator Denies Texas Has Any Integration," March 23, 1967, Barbara Jordan Scrapbook: 1967 Session, January–May, book, 1967, from The Portal to Texas History, Barbara Jordan Archives, https://texashistory.unt.edu/ark:/67531/metapth616641/m1/114/.

15. Watson, *Race and the Houston Police Department*, 93–94; Justice, *Violence in the City*, 35–37; Benhnken, *Fighting Their Own Battles*, 157; Clayson, *Freedom Is Not Enough*, 124–125.

16. "Houston 101: An Earlier Time When Shots Rang Out at TSU," *Houston Press*, May 23, 2016, http://www.houstonpress.com/news/houston-101-an-earlier-time-when-shots-rang-out-at-tsu-6722963; Benhnken, *Fighting Their Own Battles*, 157; Watson, *Race and the Houston Police Department*, 94.

17. "Houston 101: An Earlier Time When Shots Rang Out at TSU," *Houston Press*, May 23, 2016, http://www.houstonpress.com/news/houston-101-an-earlier-time-when-shots-rang-out-at-tsu-6722963;

18. Ibid.; Watson, *Race and the Houston Police*, 94.

19. "Bill" Lawson (Reverend), interview by Jane Ely.

20. Quoted in Mimi Swartz,"The Louie File," *Texas Monthly*, October 1985, 248.

21. Behnken, *Fighting Their Own Battles*, 159–161.

22. Bill Lawson, "A Second Look at the 'TSU Riots,'" *Forward Times* (Houston), May 27, 1967.

23. "Peace and Justice: Houston Approaches a 50-year Memorial of Dr. King's Last Speech Here," *Houston Chronicle*, January 13, 2017, http://www.houstonchronicle.com/opinion/editorials/article/Peace-and-justice-10857140.php.

24. *Houston Legal Defense Fund Committee Public Rally Program*, July 30, 1967, text, from The Portal to Texas History, Barbara C. Jordan Archives, texashistory.unt.edu/ark:/67531/metapth595141/m1/1/?q=%22 Barbara%20Jordan%22; Watson, *Race and the Houston Police*, 96; Behnken, *Fighting Their Own Battles*, 161.

25. "Black Power and White Liberalism By Saul Friedman Delivered at the Eighth Annual Dinner Meeting of Houston Council on Human Relations Houston Room, University of Houston, November 6, 1967," Houston Council on Human Relations, RG E 64, Box 2, Folder 5: Annual Meeting 1967, HMRC, HPL.

26. Quoted in Swartz ,"The Louie File,"248.

27. David Berg, interview by author, Houston, February 17, 2014.

28. In 1969, Berg "represented some Black men arrested for being Black, like the young epileptic accused ... of assault on a police officer—the default criminal charge whenever a Negro sassed a cop." David Berg,

Run Brother Run, A Memoir of a Murder in My Family (New York: Scribner, 2013), 129–132.

29. Quoted in Swartz, "Louie File." See also: John D. Marquez, *Black-Brown Solidarity: Racial Politics in the New Gulf South* (Austin: University of Texas Press, 2014), 123.

30. Laurence Payne, interview by author, Houston, March 13, 2014. See also: Justice, *Violence in the City*, 14, 18.

31. Letter from MLK to Harry Belafonte, November 22, 1966, The King Center, http://www.thekingcenter.org/archive/document/letter-mlk-harry-bela-fonte; Letter from Adie Marks to Harry Belafonte, February 2, 1967, The King Center, http://www.thekingcenter.org/archive/document/jo-marks-writes-harry-belafonte-regarding-civil-rights-help#.

32. Jo Marks Writes Harry Belafonte Regarding Civil Rights Help, February 2, 1967, http://www.thekingcenter.org/archive/document/jo-marks-writes-harry-belafonte-regarding-civil-rights-help; Letter from Adie Marks to Harry Belafonte, February 2, 1967, The King Center, http://www.thekingcenter.org/archive/document/jo-marks-writes-harry-belafonte-regarding-civil-rights-help#; Jo Marks Writes Harry Belafonte Regarding Civil Rights Help, February 2, 1967, http://www.thekingcenter.org/archive/document/jo-marks-writes-harry-belafonte-regarding-civil-rights-help.

33. Allan Turner, "MLK Found Houston a City of Paradox during Last Visit," *Houston Chronicle*, January 19, 2014, http://www.houstonchronicle.com/news/houston-texas/houston/article/MLK-found-Houston-a-city-of-paradox-during-last-5158079.php.

34. Abbie Lipschutz, *Child of the 20th Century: Growing Up JEWISH in Holland, Belgium, Palestine, Israel, America, and Texas: A Memoir* (New York: Blue Thread Communication, 2011), 219. See also: Alwyn Barr, *Black Texans: A History of African Americans in Texas, 1528–1995*, 2nd ed. (Norman: University of Oklahoma Press, 1996), 192; Lee Otis Johnson Defense Fund, "Thirty Years is a Long Time," *The Rag* (Austin), November 25, 1968.

35. "Free Lee Otis Johnson Houston's Black Political Prisoner" (pamphlet), Fred and Laura Brode, MS 225, Box 4, Folder 9: Lee Otis Johnson Case, HMRC, HPL; Ellen R. Cohen, "A Houston History of the American Jewish Committee," *JH-V* (Houston), April 24, 1986; John Schwartz, "Lee Otis, Free," *Texas Monthly*, August 2002, http://www.texasmonthly.com/articles/lee-otis-free/.

36. Melvin Waxler, ed, "The Teen Community: Jewish Community Center Youth Council," *JH-V* (Houston), April 18, 1968, 11. See also: Ted Freedman, "Personally Yours," *JH-V* 60th Anniversary Passover Edition, April 11, 1968, 63; Rabbi Moshe Cahana, "King's Non-Violent Courageous Actions," *The Informer* (Houston), April 20, 1968, 2.

37. Rabbi William Malev Sermon, January 10, 1973, CD-6 to CD-8. Audio Collection, William Malev Sermons, 1972–1973 (DA-14 to DA-16), AJA; Houstonians March in King's Memory," The *Informer* (Houston), April 13, 1968, 1.

38. "Houston Jewish Center will be Open Saturday to Needy Negro Youth for Rest of Summer," *JTA* (New York), July 23, 1968.

39. Shape Community Center, "S.H.A.P.E. Community Center, Inc. Mission," *SHAPE*, 2017, accessed October 20, 2016, http://www.shape.org/about-us.

40. Jonathan Sarna and Nancy H. Klein, *The Jews of Cincinnati* (Cincinnati, OH: Center for Study of the American Jewish Experience, 1989), 174.

41. Quoted in Kellar, *Make Haste Slowly*, 153, 154.

42. Vic Samuels, interview by author, Houston, March 13, 2014; Felicia Coates et al., "Briar Patch," *Texas Monthly*, 2016, http://www.texasmonthly.com/articles/briar-patch-11/.

43. Letter from J. Victor Samuels, president to Houston teacher, Box 2, Folder 5: Citizens for Good Schools (CGS)-Literature, Publicity on Early Days of CGS, 1967–1968, MS 2, Eleanor Tinsley Papers, HMRC, HPL.

44. Citizens for Good Schools: Board of Directors Meetings, April 14, 1969, Box 1, Folder 3: Citizens for Good Schools (CGS)—Board of Directors 1969–1970, MS 2, Eleanor Tinsley Papers, HMRC, HPL.

45. "Goals for Citizens for Good Schools," Box 2 Folder 5: Citizens for Good Schools (CGS)-Literature, Publicity of Early Days of CGS, 1967–1968, MS 2, Eleanor Tinsley Papers, HMRC, HPL.

46. Letter from J. Victor Samuels to Dr. Regina Goff, April 27, 1969, Box 2, Folder 23: Citizens for Good Schools (CGS) Samuels, Victor; Correspondence, 1968–1970, MS 2, Eleanor Tinsley Papers, HMRC, HPL.

47. Samuels, interview.

48. Susan Septimus, email message to author, April 25, 2017.

49. Ibid.

50. Ernestine Mitchell Collection, MS 52, Box 1, Folder 7, African American Library at the Gregory School, HPL.

51. "The Crossover Teachers ... December 14, 1969 By Brenda Beust Smith," Ernestine Mitchell Collection, MS 52, Box 1, Folder 13, African American Library at the Gregory School, HPL.

52. Ibid.

53. "Howard Jefferson," interview by David Goldstein, Mayor Bill White Collection, Houston Oral History Project, May 15, 2008, film, http://digital.houstonlibrary.net/oral-history/howard-jefferson.php.

54. Samuels, interview.

55. Let's Finish the Job," *JH-V* (Houston), November 27, 1969, 6; "Wanted—A Good Educational System," *JH-V* (Houston), November 6, 1969, 6; "Once Again—The School Board," *JH-V* (Houston), November 12, 1969, 6.

56. Samuels, interview.

57. 57 Watson, *Race and the Houston Police Department*, 74; Roth, Kennedy, and Hunt, 222; "Andrew Jefferson," interview by Louis Marchiafava, HMRC Oral History Collection, December 23, 1974, audio, http://digital. houstonlibrary.net/oral-history/andrew-jefferson_OH081.php.

58. David White, "Those Who Would Destroy," *JH-V* (Houston), November 27, 1969, 6.

59. William Malev, *Living Creatively* (Houston, TX: D.H White Company, 1972), 18.

60. Edward S. Shapiro, *A Time of Healing*, vol. 5, Jewish People in America (Baltimore, MD: Johns Hopkins University Press, 1992), 201; Diner, *Jews of the United States*, 324–325; "Congressman Casey Speaks at Center Youth Council Sponsored Israel Emergency Meeting," *Jewish Herald- Voice* (Houston), June 15, 1967, 3; "Houston Answering Emergency Appeal ... Ask All to Participate in Work," *JH-V* (Houston), June 22, 1967, 1; "Houston Lagging," *JH-V* (Houston), June 29, 1967, 1; "Houston's Efforts Continue in Raising Full Quota for Israel," *JH-V* (Houston), July 6, 1967, 2.

61. Norman Baxter, "Texas Oil: Could It Come through Another Mideast Crisis?" *New York Times*, January 8, 1968, 80; Gregory Brew, "Is Opec's Reign Over? And Did It Ever Really Start? The Would-Be Cartel Has Always Been 'Dysfunctional, Divided and Discouraged,'" *Houston Chronicle*, June 6, 2016, http://www. houstonchronicle.com/local/gray-matters/article/Is-OPEC-s-rein-over-And-did-it-ever-really-start-7961819.php; Joe Feagin, *The New Urban Paradigm: Critical Perspectives on the City* (Lanham, MD: Rowman and Littlefield, 1998), 73–75.

62. "Hate Sheets Hits Jewish Homes Here," *JH-V* (Houston), November 30, 1967, 4. See also: "Houston Answering Emergency Appeal ... Ask All to Participate in Work," *JH-V* (Houston), June 22, 1967, 1.

63. "Hate Sheets Hits Jewish Homes Here"; Federal Bureau of Investigation, "National States Rights Party, Part I," FBI Records: The Vault, http://vault.fbi.gov/NationalStatesRightsParty/NationalStates RightsPartyPart1of1/view; "Negro Group, White Racists Draw Anti-Jewish Material from Same Arab Sources," *JTA* (New York), October 24, 1967.

64. "Houston Informer Editorial Takes SNCC to Task," *JH-V* (Houston), January 11, 1968, 2. See also: Katy Vine, "The Agitator," *Texas Monthly*, August 2015, http://www.texasmonthly.com/politics/the-agitator/.

65. Carson, *In Struggle*, 3; Dollinger, *Quest for Inclusion*, 192; Robert G. Weisbord and Richard Kazarian, *Israel in the Black American Perspective* (Westport, CT: Greenwood Press, 1985), 32.

66. "Negro and Jews Topic of Discussion at JCC," *JH-V* (Houston), November 14, 1968, 7.

67. "Graves Speaks on Negro and Jews," *The Informer* (Houston), November 16, 1968, 1. For another example of a discussion of Black anti-Semitism, see Ted Freedman, "Personally Yours," *JH-V* (Houston), November 21, 1968, 4.

68. See: Charles E. Jones, "Arm Yourself or Harm Yourself: People's Party II and the Black Panther Party in Houston, Texas," in *On the Ground: The Black Panther Party in Communities across America*, ed. J.L Jeffries (Jackson: University Press of Mississippi, 2010); 'Bill' Lawson (Reverend), interview by Jane Ely.

69. David White, "A New Approach Needed," *JH-V* (Houston), December 12, 1968, 2.

70. "Letter Writers Receive Hate Mail in Houston," *JH-V* (Houston), January 30, 1969, 1.

71. Ibid.

72. "The Letters of Hate Continue," *JH-V* (Houston), February 6, 1969, 2; "About," *Islamic Society of Greater Houston—Serving the Community since 1969*, accessed April 25, 2017, https://isgh.org/about/; Hoda Badr, "Al Noor Mosque: Strength Through Unity," in *Religion and the New Immigrants: Continuities and Adaptations in Immigrant Congregations*, eds. Janet Salzman Chafetz and Helen Rose Ebaugh (Walnut Creek, CA: AltaMira Press, 2000), chapter 11.

73. Letter from Rabbi Schachtel to Dr. Jacob Marcus, December 9, 1968, Box 1, Folder: Houston, TX-Congregation Beth Israel 1954, 1968 n.d., MS-132 Congregation Beth Israel (Houston) Records, AJA; Block, "A Tribute to Spirit."

74. "Houston to Join Many Communities in Protesting Iraq Action," *JH-V* (Houston), February 13, 1969, 1.

75. Jewish Federation of Greater Houston, *Golden Jubilee*, 30.

76. For more on the Bellaire incident, see: "Letters to Editor," *JH-V* (Houston), April 5, 1969, 10; "Community Relations Committee to Request Bellaire Graduation Change," *JH-V* (Houston), May 1, 1969, 10; "With Our Rabbis: 1969 Bellaire Commencement Exercises," *JH-V* (Houston), May 1, 1969, 11; "What Personally Yours By Ted Freedman," *JH-V* (Houston), May 29, 1969, 1; "Separation in Schools Subject on March 13 'Ladder' Panel," *JH-V* (Houston), March 9, 1972, 8.

77. Lesson for Life, September 4, 1960, Box 4: Lessons for Life and Lecturers, MS 853, Robert I Kahn Papers, AJA.

78. "We Can Do Anything," Rosh Hashanah 1969, Box 3, Folder: Sermons (after TAB), MS-853, Robert I. Kahn Papers, AJA.

79. Robert D. Bullard, "Environmentalism, Economic Blackmail, and Civil Rights: Competing Agendas Within the Black Community," in *Communities in Economic Crisis: Appalachia and the South*, eds. John Gaventa, Barbara Ellen Smith, and Alex Willingham (Philadelphia: Temple University Press, 1990), 196.

80. Vernon M. Briggs, Jr., and EEOC, *They Have the Power—We Have the People: The Status of Equal Employment Opportunity in Houston, Texas, 1970: An Equal Employment Opportunity Commission Report* (Washington, DC: US GPO, 1970), Introduction, 97–99, 8; Black Enterprise, "Houston," *Black Enterprise* (October 1970): 42–43.

81. Quoted in Briggs and EEOC, *They Have the Power*, 7, introduction, 99.

82. Letter from Milton Feiner to Lawrence Bloomgarden, October 30, 1967, Box E14, Folder 40, MS-780, AJC Records, AJA; Letter from Milton Feiner to Larry Bloomgarden, January 16, 1969, Box E14, Folder 40, MS 780, AJC Records, AJA; Letter from Milton Feiner to Lawrence Bloomgarden, December 16, 1968, Box E14, Folder 40, MS-780, AJC Records, AJA; Letter from Milton Feiner to Lawrence Bloomgarden, January 20, 1969, Box E14, Folder 40, MS-780, AJC Records, AJA.

83. Quoted in Maas, "The Jews of Houston," 186.

84. Quoted in Briggs and EEOC, *They Have the Power*, 27.

85. Ibid., 27; Guadalupe San Miguel, Jr., *Brown, Not White: School Integration and the Chicano Movement in Houston* (College Station: Texas A&M University Press, 2001), chapter 4.

86. Laurence Payne, interview by author, Houston, March 13, 2014.

87. Ibid.

88. "Houston," *Black Enterprise* (October 1970): 42–44.

89. Ibid., 43.

90. "Houston," *Black Enterprise* (October 1970): 43–45; Cecil E. Harrison and Alice K. Laine, "Operation Breadbasket in Houston, 1966–78," in *Black Dixie: Afro-Texan History and Culture in Houston*, eds. Howard Beeth and Cary D. Wintz (College Station: Texas A&M University Press, 1992), 223–236.

91. "KPFT Bombing," YouTube video, 8:44, posted by Houston Press in Brittanie Shey, "The Day the KKK Bombed KPFT," uploaded May 12, 2010, http://www.houstonpress.com/music/the-day-the-kkk-bombedkpft-6497751. See also: Brittanie Shey, "The Day the KKK Bombed KPFT," *Houston Press*, May 23, 2016, http://www. houstonpress.com/music/the-day-the-kkk-bombed-kpft-6497751.

92. "Houston," *Black Enterprise* (October 1970): 42; Jo Alessandro Marks, interview by Dena Marks, Houston Oral History Project,

October 4, 2010, http://digital.houstonlibrary.net/oral-history/jo-marks. php; Jones, "Arm Yourself or Harm Yourself," 15–23.

93. William Lawson, interview by Veronica Perry.

Chapter Eight

1. Samuel Karff (Rabbi), interview by David Goldstein, HMRC Oral History Collection, December 4, 2007, film, http://digital.houstonlibrary. org/oral-history/samuel-karff.php.

2. For more on Houston as an international center, see: Nat and Jill Levy, interview by Marjorie Hillman, HMRC Oral History Collection, July 22, 1982, http://digital.houstonlibrary.net/oral-history/nat-levy_OH411.php; Carolyn Elizabeth Whitsitt, "Caught in the Crossfire: Public Housing and Race in Houston" (master's thesis, Stephen Austin University, 2011), 21–22; Bullard, *Invisible Houston*, 7; McComb, *Houston: A History*, 143–144; Badr, "Al Noor Mosque," chapter 11; Zen T.C. Zheng, "A Texas Starting Place on Buddhism's Path," *Houston Chronicle*, July 30, 2009, http://www.chron.com/life/houston-belief/article/A-Texas-starting-place-on-Buddhism-s-path-1721691.php; Barbara Karkabi, "Hindu Learning Is the Focus of Sugar Land Temple: Chinmaya Mission Houston on a Quest to Educate the Faithful," *Houston Chronicle*, February 9, 2008, http://www.chron.com/life/houston-belief/article/Hindu-learning-is-the-focus-of-Sugar-Land-Temple-1756179.php; "A Finding Aid to Zoroastrian Association of Houston Oral History Interviews, 2014-2016," MS 632, WRC, Fondren Library, RU; John D. Harden, "How the 1970s and '80s Shaped Houston's Migrant Settlement Patterns," *Houston Chronicle*, September 2, 2015, http://www.houstonchronicle.com/local/themillion/article/Maps-reveal-density-of-immigrant-neighborhood-6390645.php; Rosemarie M. Esber, "Arab Americans in the Southern United States," *Baylor Institute for Oral History*, 2012–2013, http://www.baylor.edu/content/services/document.php/182127; Nestor Rodriguez, "Hispanic and Asian Immigration Waves in Houston," in *Religion and the New Immigrants: Continuities and Adaptations in Immigrant Congregations*, eds. Janet Salzman Chafetz and Helen Rose Ebaugh (Walnut Creek, CA: AltaMira Press, 2000), chapter 2; Mike Giglio, "The Burmese Come to Houston," *Houston Press*, April 2, 2016, http://www.houstonpress.com/news/the-burmese-come-to-houston-6573988; Fred R. von der Mehden, ed., *The Ethnic Groups of Houston* (Houston: Rice University Studies, 1984), 4.

3. Stephen L. Klineberg, *Houston Area Survey (1982–2002), Houston's Economic and Demographic Transformation: Findings from the Expanded 2002 Survey of Houston's Ethnic Communities* (Houston: Rice University, 2002), 11.

4. Roseman, "Six-Tenths of a Percent of Texas," 206.
5. Rosyln Barr, "Houston," in *The Jewish Traveler*, ed, Alan M. Tigay (Garden City, NJ: Doubleday &Company, 1987), 215.
6. Stephen L. Klineberg and Jie Wu, *Diversity and Transformation among Asians in Houston: Finding from the Kinder Institute's Houston Area Asian Survey (1995, 2002, 2011)* (Houston: Rice University, 2013).
7. Alvia J. Wardlaw, "John and Dominique de Menil and the Houston civil rights movement," in *Art and Activism: Projects of John and Dominique de Menil*, eds. Joseph Helfenstein, Laureen Schipsi, and Suzanne Deal Booth (New Haven, CT: Yale University Press, 2010), 111.
8. Michael Cahana (Rabbi), interview.
9. For information on Rothko Chapel, see: Susan Barnes, John De Menil, Dominique de Menil, Barnett Newman, Philip Johnson, *The Rothko Chapel: An Act of Faith* (Houston: Menil Foundation, 1989), 126; Pia Gottschaller, "The Rothko Chapel: Toward the Infinite," in *Art and Activism: Projects of John and Dominique de Menil*, eds. Josef Helfenstein and Laureen Schipsi (New Haven, CT: Yale University Press, 2010), 140; Annie Cohen-Solal, *Mark Rothko: Toward the Light in the Chapel* (New Haven, CT: Yale University Press, 2015); "For Immediate Release: Dr. King Honored in Houston: The Man and His Work Commemorated in Monumental Sculpture, August 25, 1969," Box 1, Folder 9, Rothko Chapel Collection, Menil Archives; "An Obelisk for Houston," August 27, 1969, Box 1, Folder 19, Susan Barnes Papers, Menil Archives.
10. "Address by Mrs. John de Menil, Friday—February 26, 1971 in the Rothko Chapel," Events at the Rothko Chapel, 1971–1986, Rothko Chapel Collection, Menil Archives.
11. The annual observance of Martin Luther King Jr.'s birthday began on January 15, 1979, seven years before its inception as a national holiday. "About," Rothko Chapel, accessed August 29, 2016, http://rothko-chapel.org/learn/about/.
12. "Special Seder Set for Sunday, April 4th, 1971," *The Message* 23 (April 1, 1971): 4. See also: Arthur Waskow, "Original 1969 Freedom Seder," *The Shalom Center*, June 24, 2005, http://theshalomcenter.org/content/original-1969-freedom-seder; Passover Haggadahs, Rabbi Segal Personal archive.
13. Congregation Beth Yeshurun, "Intermarriage, Black Jews, Christian Anti-Semitism, Akiba Institute Topics," *The Message* 23 (September 30, 1971): 5; Congregation Beth Yeshurun, Early Shabbat Prayers, *The Message* 5–7 (March 16, 1979); "Welcoming Synagogues," *Jewish Multiracial Network*, 2017, http://www.jewishmultiracialnetwork.org/resources-2/welcoming-synagogues/.

14. "Black Educators to Visit Israel," *JTA* (New York), October 21, 1971. See also: "Dr. Sawyer Travels to Israel," *Texas Southern Herald*, Nov. 5, 1971, Vol. 23, TSU Archives, SC, TSU Library.
15. Schulman, Gottlieb, and Sheinberg, *Jewish Community Council of Metropolitan Houston*, 28. See also: Justice, *Violence in the* City, 216–218; "River Oaks Old Money Mingles with Noveau Riche by Beverly Maurice," H-Subdivision—River Oaks, HMRC, HPL; Maas, "Jews of Houston," 82, 86, 179.
16. Maas, "Jews of Houston," 99–100; Albert Goldstein, interview by Florence Coleman, HMRC Oral History Collection, September 9, 1975, http://digital.houstonlibrary.net/oral-history/albert-goldstein_OH060.php.
17. Schulman, Gottlieb, and Sheinberg, *Jewish Community Council of Metropolitan Houston*, 1, x–xi, 60–64.
18. Schulman, Gottlieb, and Sheinberg, 63.
19. Block, "A Tribute to Spirit."
20. See: Marilyn Liddell, "The Creation of the Houston Community College: A Concept Become Reality," *The Houston Review*, 7, no. 2 (1985); Kellar, *Make Haste Slowly*, 155; Houston Independent School District, "Pupil Enrollment Data 1970–1984," Pupil Enrollment Division, 1984; Salatheia Bryant, "Integration Did Not Come."
21. Wright, "Easy Street"; Wintz, "Blacks," 37–38; Robert Fisher, "The Urban Sunbelt in Comparative Perspective Houston in Context," in *Essays on Sunbelt Cities and Recent Urban Americans*, eds. Robert B. Fairbanks and Kathleen Underwood (College Station: Texas A&M University Press, 1999), 46; Poinsett, "Special Report," 134; Curtis Lang, "A Depleted Legacy Public Housing," *Cite 33* (Fall 1995/Winter 1996), 15; "Public Affairs Forum to Present Panel on Gentlemen Agreement," *JH-V* (Houston), October 29, 1970, 12; Robert D. Bullard, "Housing Problems and Prospects in Contemporary Houston," in *Black Dixie: Afro-Texan History and Culture in Houston*, eds. Howard Beeth and Cary D. Wintz (College Station: Texas A&M University Press, 1992), 237.
22. Bruce J. Schulman, *The Seventies: The Great Shift in American Culture, Society, and Politics* (Cambridge, MA: Da Capo Press, 2001); Barr, *Black Texans*, 179; U. S. Congress House Office of History and Preservation, *Black Americans in Congress, 1870–2007* (Washington, DC.: US GPO, 2008), 240, 257; "Texas Redistricting," Texas Legislative Council, accessed October 30, 2016, https://tlc.texas.gov/redist/history/overview.html; Bullard, *Invisible Houston*, 133–137; Vine, "The Agitator"; Curtis Graves, interview by Adrienne Cain, HMRC Oral History Collection, January 23, 2015, film, http://digital.houstonlibrary.net/oral-history/

curtis-graves_OHGS0073.php; "Panel Approves Negro History Bill," *Odessa American* (Odessa, Texas), April 23, 1969, 13A; *Handbook of Texas Online*, Robinson, Shawna D. Williams, "Judson Wilbur Jr.," accessed October 20, 2016, http://www.tsaonline.org/handbook/online/articles/frobu; Jessica Faz; "Black History Month Profile: Activist Judson W. Robinson Jr.," *Houston Chronicle*, February 28, 2011, http://www.chron.com/news/houston-texas/article/Black-History-Month-profile-Activist-Judson-W-1685252.php; Judson Robinson, interview by Florence Coleman, HMRC Oral History Collection, September 3, 1974, audio, http://digital.houstonlibrary.net/oral-history/judson-robinson_OH154-1.php; U. S. Congress House Office of History and Preservation, *Black Americans in Congress*, 257.

23. Quoted in William Broyles, "The Making of Barbara Jordan," *Texas Monthly*, October 1976, http://www.texasmonthly.com/politics/the-making-of-barbara-jordan-2/.

24. Mary Beth Rogers, *Barbara Jordan: American Hero* (New York: Bantam Books, 1998), 189; *Handbook of Texas Online*, Mark Odintz, "Jordan, Barbara Charline," accessed October 20, 2016, http://www.tshaonline.org/handbook/online/articles/fjoas; Broyles, "The Making of Barbara Jordan."

25. Kevin Diaz, "In a Life of First, Barbara Jordan Won a Lasting Legacy: Houston Congresswoman Broke Down Barriers in Her Meteoric Political Career," *Houston Chronicle*, June 7, 2016, http:///www.chron.com/local/history/houston-legends/article/In-a-life-of-firsts-Barbara-Jordan-won-a-lasting-7966574.php.

26. Barbara Jordan, "Democratic National Convention Keynote Speech, 1976, part 1," YouTube video, 12:02, posted by "TSU Jordan Archives," September 5, 2012, https://www.youtube.com/watch?v=Bg7gLIx__-k.

27. "The Men Who Would Be Mayor," *Texas Monthly*, October 1975, 18.

28. Steve Gutow and Laurie Barker James, "Most Politics Is Local," in *Lone Star of David: The Jews of Texas*, eds. Hollace Ava Weiner and Kenneth Roseman (Lebanon, NH: University Press of New England, 2007), 212–225; Dick Gottlieb, interview by Louis J. Marchiafava, HMRC Oral History Collection, June 25, 1976, audio, http://digital.houstonlibrary.net/oral-history/dick-gottlieb_OH066.php.

29. Barbara C. Jordan, *Barbara Jordan: Joseph Prize for Human Rights Address, Anti-Defamation League of B'nai B'rith*, October 22, 1993, text, from the Portal to Texas History, Barbara C. Jordan Archives, texas-history.unt.edu/ark:/67531/metapth611227/m1/3/?q=%22Barbara%20Jordan%22%20%22jewish%22.

30. Letter from Mrs. J.H. Wilkenfeld to Rabbi Landman, November 16, 1971, Box 1, Folder 1: Local Organizational Materials 1971, P-927,

Dolores Wilkenfeld Papers, AJHS; Letter from Mrs. J.H. Wilkenfeld to Dr. Shannon, October 22, 1971, Box 1, Folder 1: Local Organizational Materials 1971, P-927, Dolores Wilkenfeld Papers, AJHS.

31. Congregation Beth Yeshurun, "Barbara Jordan to Address Soviet Jewry Convocation December 7th," *The Message* 14 (December 5, 1975).

32. "Barbara Jordan to Speak Here on Behalf of Soviet Jewry," *JH-V* (Houston), November 26, 1975, 1.

33. Photograph, *JH-V* (Houston), December 17, 1975, 29.

34. "Black Official Terms Black Convention Resolution on Israel and American Jewry," *JTA* (New York) May 23, 1972.

35. "Black Americans and Israel," *JH-V* (Houston), April 6, 1972, 6.

36. "Senator Jordan and Representative Curtis Graves Support Israel," *JH-V* (Houston), May 18, 1972.

37. "Martin Luther King, Jr 'Israel ... Is One of the Great Outpost of Democracy in the World," YouTube video, :12, posted by Israel SDM, January 15, 2012, https://www.youtube.com/watch?v=kvr2Cxuh2Wk. See also: "Dr. King's pro-Israel Legacy." YouTube video, 5:00, posted by "Institute for Black Solidarity with Israel," June 9, 2014, https://www.youtube.com/watch?v=0Dd7pIB0CP0.

38. Barbara C. Jordan, Barbara Jordan - Congregation Beth Israel, January 1992, text, from the Portal to Texas History, Barbara C. Jordan Archives, texashistory.unt.edu/ark:/67531/metapth611352/.

39. Houston Council on Human Relations et al., *The Houston Council on Human Relations: Black/Mexican American Project Report* (Houston, TX: Houston Council on Human Relations, 1972), 27.

40. Gregory Brew, "Is Opec's Reign Over? And Did it Ever Really Start? The Would-be Cartel Has Always Been 'Dysfunctional, Divided and Discouraged,'" *Houston Chronicle*, June 6, 2016, http://www.houstonchronicle.com/local/gray-matters/article/Is-OPEC-s-rein-over-And-did-it-ever-really-start-7961819.php; Hameed Al-Hajj, "The Middle East: Recriminations from Local Partisans Israelis 'Kill Civilians, Ignore UN,'" *Rice Thresher* (Houston), November 1, 1973, 3, from the Portal to Texas History, texashistory.unt.edu/ark:/67531/metapth245176/; Janice Rubin, "Arab 'Terrorize, Won't Negotiate," *Rice Thresher* (Houston), November 1, 1973, 3, from the Portal to Texas History, Rice University Woodson Center, texashistory.unt.edu/ark:/67531/metapth245176/; "The Cause of Peace is Served by American-Israeli Friendship" [pamphlet], Box 298, Folder Israel 1974, Congresswoman Barbara C. Jordan Papers, 1979BJA001, SC, TSU.

41. Letter from Richard Monell to Barbara Jordan, October 25, 1973, Box 343, Folder: Arab-Israeli Crisis, Congresswoman Barbara C. Jordan Papers, 1979BJA001, SC, TSU.

42. Letter from Richard Monell to Barbara Jordan, August 22, 1975, Box 343, Folder Israel 1975, Congresswoman Barbara C. Jordan Papers, 1979BJA001, SC, TSU. See also: Brew, "Is Opec's Reign Over?"

43. "JCC Community Relations Committee Meets with Congresswoman Barbara Jordan," *JH-V* (Houston), February 14, 1974, 21.

44. "Jewish Community Assists Wheatley in Goal to Play in Israeli Invitational Joseph H. Hiller Presents $1,000 Check to Coach Jackie Carr," *JH-V* (Houston), December 26, 1974, 1. See also: Erika Mellon, "Old Wheatley High School Demolished Thursday," *Houston Chronicle*, December 11, 2014, http://www.chron.com/news/education/article/Old-Wheatley-High-School-demolished-591166.php; McComb, *Houston: A History*, 154; Watson, *Race and the Houston Police Department*, 122.

45. "Jewish Community Assists Wheatley in Goal to Play in Israeli Invitational Joseph H. Hiller Presents $1,000 Check to Coach Jackie Carr," *JH-V* (Houston), December 26, 1974, 1.

46. "Black Group Supports Israel Denounces Arab Boycott Actions," *JTA* (New York), September 12, 1975; Robert Weisbord and Arthur Stein, *Bittersweet Encounter: The Afro-American and the American Jew* (Westport, CT: Negro Universities Press, 1970), 93.

47. Letter from Rabbi Moshe Cahana to Barbara Jordan, October 1, 1975, Box 343, Folder Israel 1975, Congresswoman Barbara C. Jordan Papers, 1979BJA001, SC, TSU.

48. "An Analysis By Rabbi Robert Kahn 'What's All This About Zionism and 'Racist'?," *JH-V* (Houston), 6.

49. "Zionism is Not Racism," *The Informer* (Houston), November 29, 1975, The Informer and Texas Freemen Newspaper 1975–76, October 4-December 25, DBCAH, University of Texas at Austin [CAH].

50. "Jordan Asks 'Sensible Race Relations'" by Terry Kliewer, Post Report, Houston Post, November 26, 1975, Scrapbook Vol. 13, E.A. 'Squatty' Lyons, MC001, Harris County Archives, Houston, Texas.

51. "Jordan Asks 'Sensible Race Relations."

52. "Barbara Jordan Denounces Boycott, Bigotry," *JH-V* (Houston, Texas), 32.

53. "Barbara Jordan Denounces Boycott, Bigotry."

54. "Barbara Jordan Denounces Boycott, Bigotry."

55. Anne Dingus, "Mickey Leland," *Texas Monthly*, November 1, 1999, http://www.texasmonthly.com/articles/mickey-leland/;"Leland, George Thomas (Mickey)," *History, Art, and Archives United States House of Representatives*, http://history.house.gov/People/Detail/16887; Deloyd Parker, "In Good Faith: Remembering John de Menil," in *Art and Activism: Projects of John and Dominique de Menil*, eds. John Helfenstein and Laureen Schipsi (New Haven, CT: Yale University Press, 2010), 114–115; Wardlaw, "John and Dominique de Menil," 110–111.

56. "Mickey Leland-Biography," University of Houston, Hobby School of Public Affairs, accessed February 27, 2017, http://www.uh.edu/class/hobby/interns/leland-fellows/bio-mickey-leland.php; Dingus, "Mickey Leland."

57. "Mickey Leland and Anthony Hall Were Asked to Support Israel," *JH-V* (Houston), June 1, 1978, 17.

58. Letter from Marie and Dan Moriarty, November 5, 1976, Box 343, Folder Israel 1975, Congresswoman Barbara C. Jordan Papers, 1979BJA001, SC, TSU.

59. Marcie Friedman, "Representative Mickey Leland—Israel's Policy a 'Covenant of Necessity,'" *JH-V* (Houston), November 10, 1977, 9.

60. Friedman, "Representative Mickey Leland—Israel's Policy a 'Covenant of Necessity.'"

61. Friedman, "Representative Mickey Leland—Israel's Policy a 'Covenant of Necessity'." See also: "Kahane: Defend Israel's Honor Against Insults from Black Hebrews," *JTA* (New York), October 14, 1971.

62. Friedman, "Representative Mickey Leland—Israel's Policy a 'Covenant of Necessity.'"

63. "Israel: History by the Inch," *JH-V* (Houston), August 9, 1979, 8.

64. Marcie Friedman, "Representative Mickey Leland—Israel's Policy a 'Covenant of Necessity.'"

65. 65 Diner, *Jews of The United States*, 332–333; Congregation Beth Yeshurun, "The Nazi Party in the United States and the Principle of Freedom of Speech," *The Message* 5, March 3, 1978.

66. Jack Segal, *Modern Problems, Some Jewish Solutions* (Houston: William S. Malev Schools for Religious Studies of Congregation Beth Yeshurun, 1981), 114.

67. "Nazi Bounty Offer Challenge Goes to Texas Supreme Court," *JH-V* (Houston, Texas), February 23, 1978, 1.

68. Joseph Samuels, "Zindler Stands Alone," *JH-V* (Houston, Texas), 2.

69. Samuels, "Zindler Stands Alone."

70. Congregation Beth Yeshurun, "The Nazi Party in the United States and the Principle of Freedom and Speech," *The Message* 5, March 3, 1978.

71. Rabbi Segal, "Rabbi Segal's Column: The High Holidays and The Houston Independent School District," *The Message 5* (September 15, 1978):1.

72. Joseph Samuels, "'Editorials' Mickey Leland, the Making of a Congressman," *JH-V* (Houston), April 6, 1978, 4; "To My Friends in the Jewish Community," *JH-V* (Houston), June 8, 1978, 32.

73. White House, "One America-Mickey Leland Kibbutzim Internship Foundation, Mickey Leland Kibbutzim Internship Foundation," accessed August 30, 2016, http://clinto4.nara.gov/Initiatives/OneAmerica/Practices/pp_19980804.4120.html; "Mickey Leland Kibbutzim Internship Program Celebrates 31st Year," *JH-V* (Houston), December 8, 2011,

http://jhvonline.com/mickey-leland-kibbutzim-internship-program-celebrates-st-year-p12198-111.htm; Lisa Klein, email message to author, September 9, 2016.

74. J. Kent Friedman, interview by author, Houston, February 26, 2014.
75. J. Kent Friedman, email message to author, May 13, 2014. See also: Six Weeks of Travel and Kibbutz Life: Student Leaders Prepare for Trip to Israel with Mickey Leland Kibbutz Internship Program," *JH-V* (Houston), June 19, 1980, 12.
76. Religious Action Center of Reform Judaism, prod., "Consultation on Conscience," C-SPAN, April 11, 1989; "14 Black Students in Israel for 17 Days to Study Lifestyles, Social Institutions," *JTA* (New York), August 20, 1970; "Leland Sends Inner-City Teens to Israel," the Mickey Leland Papers and Collections, "Intern J. Nalet"; see also: "14 Black Students in Israel for 17 Days to Study Lifestyles, Social Institutions," *JTA* (New York, New York), August 20, 1970.
77. "Six Weeks of Travel and Kibbutz Life: Student Leaders Prepare for Trip to Israel with Mickey Leland Kibbutz Internship Program," *JH-V* (Houston, Texas), June 19, 1980, 12.
78. "Six Weeks of Travel and Kibbutz Life: Student Leaders Prepare for Trip to Israel with Mickey Leland Kibbutz Internship Program."
79. "Foreign Affairs Israel Youth" (2015), Education, African Americans Repairs Education, African Amer. Racial Inequities (1981), *Series 11: Speeches, Articles, Trips and Meetings 1970–1984*, Box 49, Folder 8047, Paper 781, the Mickey Leland Papers and Collection Addendum, TSU.
80. White House, "One America"; Leticia Fehling, "Eisenhower High Student Selected for Mickey Leland Kibbutzim Internship," *Discover News, Information and More about Aldine HISDs Schools*, April 19, 2013, http://insideadeline.com/2013/04/eisenhower-high-student-selected-for-mickey-leland-kibbutzim-internship/;"Mickey Leland Kibbutzim Internship Program Celebrates 31st Year," *JH-V*, December 8, 2011, http://jhvonline.com/mickey-leland-kibbutzim-internship-program-celebrates-st-year-p12198-111.htm.
81. Religious Action Center of Reform Judaism, prod., "Consultation on Conscience."
82. "Foreign Affairs, Israel" (2015), Education, African Americans Repairs Education, African Amer. Racial Inequities (1988), *Series 11: Speeches, Articles, Trips and Meetings 1985–1989*, Box 188, Folder 9784, Paper 858, the Mickey Leland Papers & Collection Addendum, TSU.
83. White House, "One America"; "Endowment Fund Plans Tribute to Mickey Leland," *JH-V* (Houston), August 17, 1989, 4.
84. "Foreign Affairs, Israel Youth" (2015), the Mickey Leland Papers & Collection Addendum: Education, African American Repairs Education,

African Amer. Racial Inequities (1983). *Series 10: Public Relations 1973–1983*. Series 10, Box 75, Folder 13106, the Mickey Leland Papers & Collection Addendum, TSU.

85. *Jews and Hispanics in America: The Meeting of Two Historic Cultures: A Report of the Houston Conference on Hispanic-Jewish Relations* (New York: American Jewish Committee, Institute of Human Relations, 1982).

86. "A Statement Concerning the KKK March from the Houston Conference on Extremism, March 31, 1983," Houston Council on Human Relations, RG E 64, Box 44, Folder: Houston Conference on Extremism (Press Debriefing), HMRC, HPL.

87. "A Statement Concerning the KKK March from the Houston Conference on Extremism, March 31, 1983."

88. "Leland Sends Inner-City Teens to Israel." See also: "Photographs, 1944–1989," "Mickey Leland Kibbutz Foundation Summer Internship Summer 1989, featuring Jacqueline Nalett image from around Kibbutz, Israel, 274 images, 1 video oral history, 1 audio oral history taken 2013," Series 14: Audio Video Cabinet, USB49, the Mickey Leland Papers & Collection Addendum, TSU.

89. University of Houston, *Leland, Dr. Alison - Leland audio, 1 of 1*, March 5, 2014, Oral Histories from the Houston History Project, SC, UHL, http://digital.lib.uh.edu/collection/houhistory/item/1669/show/1667.

90. Dr. Alison Leland, interview.

91. Religious Action Center of Reform Judaism, prod., "Consultation on Conscience."

92. "Judge Ursula Hall for Judge Harris County 189th Civil District Court," *JHV* (Houston), February 25, 2010, 10 b.

93. See: Ors Mars, "The Effects of a Kibbutz Experience on the Lives of Inner-City Youth: A Study of the 'Operation Unity Israel Trip'" (Master's thesis, Hebrew Union College, 1995), 107–112; "Founders," Operation Understanding-Founders, accessed October 12, 2017, http://operationunderstanding.org/get-to-know-us/founders; "The International Kibbutz Program," Operation Unity Programs, accessed October 12, 2017, http://operationunity.org/programs.php.

94. Albert Goldstein, interview.

Conclusion

1. On Ethiopian Jews, see: Alemneh Dejene, *Environment, Famine, and Politics in Ethiopia: A View from the Village* (Boulder, CO: Lynne Rienner, 1990); Mitchell G. Bard, *From Tragedy to Triumph: The Politics Behind the Rescue of Ethiopian Jewry* (Westport, CT: Praeger, 2002), 113; William Recant, "A Friend of Beta Yisrael Is Lost," *JH-V* (Houston), August 17, 1989, 1.

2. J. Kent Friedman, "At Memorial Services on Aug. 14 Eulogy for Rep. Mickey Leland delivered by J. Kent Friedman," *JH-V* (Houston), August 17, 1989, 3. See also: Jacob N. Wagner, "The Legacy of Leland," *Houston History Magazine*, March 26, 2015, http//houstonhistorymagazine. org/2015/03/the-legacy-of-leland/.
3. Jerusalem Talmud, Tractate Sanhedrin 37a.
4. U.S. Congress, *Tribute to the Late Honorable Mickey Leland*, Congressional Record Daily Edition (Washington, DC: US GPO, 1989). See also: Jo-Carolyn Goode, "Remembering the 26th Anniversary of Congressman Mickey Leland's Death," *Houston Style Magazine*, August 7, 2015, http://stylemagazine.com/news/2015/aug/07/remembering-26th-anniversary-congressman-mickey-le/; HASJ Advisory Board; Records of the Houston Action for Soviet Jewry; I-500, Box 1, Folder 7: Advisory Board 1985-1987, AJHS.
5. J. Kent Friedman, interview by author, Houston, February 26, 2014.
6. "Honors Awards, Foreign Affairs, Israel" (2015), the Mickey Leland Papers & Collection Addendum: Education, African Americans Repairs Education, African Ameri. Racial Inequities (1987), Series 11: Speeches, Articles, Trips and Meetings 1985–1989, Series 11, Box 169, Folder 9397, Paper 477, TSU; "Jewish Community Mourns Two Friends as Congressman's Plane is Found Crashed," *JTA* (New York) August 14, 1989.
7. "Hunger, Youth" (2015), the Mickey Leland Papers & Collection Addendum: Education, African Americans Repairs Education, African Amer. Racial Inequities (1986), Series 11: Speeches, Articles, Trips and Meetings 1985–1989, Series 11, Box 149, Folder 9163. Paper 255, TSU.
8. "Black-Jewish Coalition Is a 'Two-Way Street,' Black Lawmaker Says," *JTA* (New York), April, 1986.
9. "Jewish Community Mourns Two Friends as Congressman's Plane Is Found Crashed," *JTA* (New York), August 14, 1989.
10. "Rabbi Roy Walter's Tribute to Rep. Mickey Leland," *JH-V* (Houston), August 17, 1989, 2.
11. J. Kent Friedman, "At Memorial Services on Aug. 14: Eulogy for Rep. Mickey Leland delivered by J. Kent Friedman," *JH-V* (Houston), August 17, 1989, 3.
12. "Endowment Fund Plans Tribute to Mickey Leland," *JH-V* (Houston), August 17, 1989, 4.
13. "Mickey Leland, a Man to Be Remembered," *JH-V* (Houston), August 17, 1989, 1. See also: "Max Goldfield," *JH-V* (Houston), August 17, 1989, 4; Ellen R. Cohen and David Mincberg, "AJC," *JH-V* (Houston), August 17, 1985, 5; "ADL," *JH-V* (Houston), August 17, 1989, 5.
14. "King Birthday Commemorated at D.C., New York Ceremonies," *JTA* (New York), January 16, 1960.

15. "Houston Councilman Out," *New York Times*, November 8, 1989, B10.

16. Aaron Howard, "Congressman Al Green on Black-Jewish Relations," *JH-V*, April 14, 2016, http://jhvonline.com/congressman-a-green-on-Blackjewish-relations-p20911-90.htm.

17. Alan Tigay, ed., Introduction to *The Jewish Traveler: Hadassah Magazine's Guide to the World's Jewish Communities and Sights* (Garden City, NJ: Doubleday & Company, 1987), x–xi.

18. Evans, *The Provincials*, 188.

19. William A. Henry III, "Beyond the Melting Pot," *Time Magazine*, April 9, 2009. See also: Ronald T. Takaki, *A Different Mirror: A History of Multicultural America* (New York: Back Bay Books/Little, Brown, and Co., 2008).

20. Barbara C. Jordan. Barbara Jordan - Congregation Beth Israel, January 1992, text, the Portal to Texas History, Barbara C. Jordan Archives, texashistory.unt.edu/ark:/67531/metapth611352/.

21. Quoted in Barbara C. Jordan. Barbara Jordan - Congregation Beth Israel.

22. Barbara C. Jordan. Barbara Jordan - Congregation Beth Israel.

23. "African American/Jewish Dialogue Two Informational Meetings," January 13, 1999, Pam Geyer Private Collection.

24. Rabbi Segal, "Let's Talk to Each Other," November 16, 1997, Rabbi Segal Personal Archives; Linda S. Wallace, "Cultural Coach: Good Exchange on Race, Religion Require Preparation: Culture Coach," *Houston Chronicle*, May 28, 2004, http://www.chron.com/life/article/Culture-Coach-Good-exchange-on-race-religion-1556998.php; Michael C. Duke, "'Zion' Radio Bridges to Christian Audience," *JH-V* (Houston), March 18, 2010, http://jhvonline.com/zion-radio-bridges-to-christian-audience-p8617.htm; Michael C. Duke, "Local Events Promote Hindu-Jewish Solidarity," *JH-V* (Houston), January 13, 2011, http://jhvonline.com/local-event-promotes-hindujewish-solidarity-p10396-96.htm; Michael C. Duke, "Holocaust Denier Hoodwinks Houston Critics," *JH-V* (Houston), October 22, 2009, http://jhvonline.com/holocaustdenier-hoodwinks-houston-critics-p7735-96.htm.

25. Michael C. Duke, "Houston Stands with Israel," *JH-V* (Houston), August 7, 2014, http://jhvonline.com/houston-stands-with-israel-p17663-294.htm; Michael C. Duke, "Illuminating Freedom, Friendships, Israel," *JH-V* (Houston), December 5, 2013, http://jhvonline.com/illuminating-freedom-friendships=and-israel=p16290-96.htm; *Next Steps in Israeli-Palestinian Peace Process: Hearing Before the Subcommittee on the Middle East and South Asia of the Committee on Foreign Affairs, House of Representatives, One Hundred Tenth Congress, First Session*, February 14, 2007 (Washington, DC: US GPO, 2007); "Mickey Leland Kibbutzim Internship Program Celebrates 31st Year," *JH-V* (Houston),

December 8, 2011, http://jhvonline.com/mickey-leland-kibbutzim-internship-program-celebrates-st-year-p12198-111.htm; Michael C. Duke, "Congressman Lauded for Protecting Equality," *JH-V* (Houston), February 21, 2013, http://jhvonline.com/congressman-lauded-for-protecting-equality-p14599-96.htm.

26. Aaron Howard, "Rabbi Samuel Karff Reflect on Religion and Social Justice," *JH-V*, December 8, 2016, http://jhvonline.com/rabbi-samuel-karff-reflects-on-religion-and-social-justice-p21982-89.htm.

27. Archbishop Joseph Fiorenza, Rabbi Sam Karff, and Bill Lawson, "Lawson, Fiorenza, and Karff: Our Shared Morals and Sense of Justice Demand Bail Reform: Current System Punishes the Most Vulnerable among Society," *Houston Chronicle*, July 16, 2016, http://www.houstonchronicle.com/opinion/outlook.article/Lawson-Fiorenza-and-karff-Our-shared-morals-and-8482349.php.

28. Jayme Fraser, "Trio Quietly Guides Houston's Conscience and Policy," *Houston Chronicle*, September 20, 2013, http://www./chronicle.com/news/houston-texas/houston/article/Trio-quietly-guides-Houston-s-conscience-and-4831317.php.

29. "Welcome to Truthhouston.org!" TRUTH: Traveling Revealing Understanding Truth-Hope, accessed August 30, 2016, http://truthhouston.org/default.html.

30. Arlene Nisson Lassin, "Taking Matters into His Own Hands," *Houston Chronicle*, November 5, 2009, http://www.chron.com/life/houston-belief/article/Taking-matters-into-his-own-hands-1726211.php.

31. Aaron Howard, "Congressman Al Green on Black-Jewish Relations," April 14, 2016, *JH-V*, http://jhvonline.com/congressman-al-green-on-Black jewish-relations-p20911-90.htm.

32. Roy Walter (Rabbi), interview with author, Houston, October 29, 2013.

33. "Black-Jewish Coalition Is a 'Two-Way Street,' Black Lawmaker Says," *JTA* (New York), April 9, 1986.

34. Aaron Howard, "Congressman Al Green on Black-Jewish Relations," *JH-V*, April 14, 2016, http://jhvonline.com/congressman-a-green-on-Black jewish-relations-p20911-90.htm.

Bibliography

Manuscript Collections

African American Library at the Gregory School, Houston Public Library
  Ernestine Mitchell Collection (MS.0052)
American Jewish Archives Cincinnati, Ohio
  Alan S. Green Papers (MS-724)
  Audio Collection. William Malev Sermons,1972–1973 (DA-14 to DA-16)
  American Jewish Committee Records (MS-780)
  B'nai Brith District Grand Lodge No. 7 Records, 1917–1976 (MS-180)
  Congregation Beth Israel (Houston) Records (MS-132)
  Colonel Mayfield's Weekly
  Hyman Judah Schachtel (Nearprint File)
  Joe Weingarten (Nearprint Biographies)
  Metropolitan Houston Conference on Religion and Race 1963 (SC-2850)
  Robert I. Kahn Papers (MS-853)
  Solomon Andhil Fineberg Papers (MS-149)
  Congregation Emanu El (Houston, Tex.) (Nearprint)
American Jewish Committee Online
  AJC Subject Files Collection
  AJC Minutes
  American Jewish Yearbook Vol. 20 (1918–1919)
  American Jewish Yearbook Vol. 43 (1941–1942)
American Jewish Historical Society, New York, NY
  American Jewish Congress (I-77)
  Dolores Wilkenfeld Papers (P-927)
  Houston Action for Soviet Jewry (I-500)
  Subject Files Collection, n.d., various dates (I-424)
Archives of the Archdiocese of Galveston-Houston
  Texas Catholic Herald
Congregation Emanu-El
  Emanu El Bulletin
  Robert I. Kahn Papers
Congregation Beth Israel
  Temple Bulletin
  Congregation Beth Israel Archives
Congregation Beth Yeshurun
  The Message

Dolph Briscoe Center for American History
 Colonel Mayfield's Weekly
 Ima Hogg Papers, 1924–1977
 State of Texas vs. NAACP Papers
 Texas Jewish Historical Society
 Christian American
 The Informer and Texas Freemen Newspaper, 1975–76, October 4-
  December 25
 Houston Vanguard
 University Business Oral History Records
Harris County Archives
 E.A. 'Squatty' Lyons (MC001)
Houston Metropolitan Research Center
 Anna Dupree Collection (MS110)
 Christia V. Adair (MS 109)
 Eleanor Tinsley Papers (MS 2)
 Eliza Johnson Home for Aged Negroes Collection (RG E 47)
 Ethnic Groups-Civil Rights Vertical File
 File: H-Civil Rights
 File: H-Subdivision—River Oaks
 Felix Tijerina Sr. Family Papers (MS 108)
 Fred and Laura Brode Collection (MS 225)
 Gertrude Barnstone Small Collection
 Dr. George Ebey Collection (MS 70)
 Houston Council for Human Relations (RG E 64)
 Judge Woodrow Seals (MS 414)
 League of Women Voters of Houston (RG. E.0013)
 Leopold Meyer Papers (MS 67)
 Maurice Nathan Dannenbaum Papers (MS 1120)
 National Council of Jewish Women Collection (RG E 23)
 Ray K. Daily Collection (MS 9)
 Ralph O'Leary (MS 40)
 Rabbi Robert Kahn Papers (MS 186)
 Rabbi Hyman Judah Schachtel Papers (MS 0172)
 Rev. Lee Haywood Simpson Papers (MS 0239)
 Sig Frucht Collection (MS 136)
Houston Independent School District, Pupil Enrollment Division
 Pupil Enrollment Data 1970–1984
 School Board Minutes.1955–1960
LBJ Presidential Library Archive
 Senate Political Files, 1949–1960.

The Menil Collection
Rothko Chapel Collection (MA 2002-002 ROCH.00.00)
Susan Barnes Papers (MA 2000-017 SCHO.15.000)
Museum of Fine Arts, Houston Archives
Frank and Eleanor Freed Papers (MS 28)
Papers of the NAACP
Broussard v. Houston Independent School District School Desegregation Case, Folder 016461-010-0378
Papers of the NAACP, Supplement to Part 23: Legal Department Case Files, 1960–1972, Series A: The South, Section III: Kentucky, Louisiana, Mississippi, Tennessee, and Texas.
NAACP 1940–55. *General Office File*. 1980. Frederick, MD: University Publications of America.
Pam Geyer Personal Collection
Rabbi Segal Personal Collection
Passover Haggadahs
Sermons
Schomburg Center for Research in Black Culture Manuscript, Archives, and Rare Book
Division, New York Public Library
Carnegie–Myrdal Study in Negro in America Research Memoranda Collection, 1935–1948 (SC Micro R-6534)
Texas Southern University
Congresswoman Barbara C. Jordan Papers 1936–2011 (197BJA001)
Mickey Leland Center on Hunger, Poverty and World Peace at Texas Southern University
Mickey Leland Papers & Collection Archives
Texas Southern University Archives
University of Houston
Foley's Department Store Records, 1845–2006 (ID: 07/2007-004)
This Is Our Home, It Is Not for Sale Film Collection, 1925–2011 (ID: 07/2010-020)
Thomas R. Cole Desegregation Papers,1963–2001 (ID: 07/2007-005)
Woodson Research Center
Zoroastrian Association of Houston Oral History Interviews, 2014–2016 (MS 632)
Gertrude Barnstone Papers, 1956–2015 (MS 587)
Marguerite Johnston Barnes Research Materials for Houston, The Unknown City, 1830–1946 (MS 455)
Rev. William Lawson Papers, 1955–2008 (MS 532)
Rice University Scrapbook Collection, 1907–1985 (UA 230)

Yale Divinity Library
    Social Ethics Pamphlet Collection, Record Group No. 73.
YIVO Institute for Jewish Research
    Workmen's Circle (RG 575)

Published Archival Sources

Central Conference of American Rabbis. "The Guiding Principles of Reform
    Judaism: 'The Columbus Platform'—1937." Platforms Adopted
    by the CCAR. October 27, 2004. http://ccarnet.org/rabbbis-speak/
    platforms/guiding-principles-reform-judaism/.
Conference of Reform Rabbis. "The Pittsburgh Platform (1885)." In *The
    Jews in the Modern World: A Documentary History,* 3rd ed., edited
    by Paul Mendes-Flohr and Jehuda Reinharz. 521–522. Durham,
    NC: Duke University Press, 2011.
"John F. Kennedy and Religion." *John F. Kennedy Presidential Library
    and Museum.* https://www.jfklibrary.org/JFK/JFK-in-History/JFK-
    and-Religion.aspx.
Kennedy, John F. "Moon Speech." *John F. Kennedy Moon Speech,*
    September 12, 1962. http://er.jsc.nasa.gov/she/ricetalk.htm.
Polier, Shad. "Kennedy's Impact on American Freedom." In *The Jewish
    1960s: An American Sourcebook,* edited by Michael E. Staub,
    37–39. Waltham, MA: Brandeis University Press, 2004.

Online Archives

Communist Party of the United States of America. Texas State Committee
    *Free Texas From Monopoly Control! Bring The New Deal to Texas!
    For Democracy, Security, Jobs, Peace.* Houston, TX, 1938.
    Communist Party of Texas 1940 State Platform. Houston, TX, 1940.
Houston Area Digital Archives
    KHOU-TV Film Collection (RG D 033)
King Center
    Letter from MLK to Mrs. E. Weidner, February 26, 1962
    Letter from MLK to Harry Belafonte, November 22, 1966
    Letter from Adie Marks to Harry Belafonte, February 2, 1967
    Jo Marks Writes Harry Belafonte Regarding Civil Rights Help,
    February 2, 1967
University of North Texas Archives on the Portal to Texas History
    Barbara Jordan Archives
    KXAS-NBC 5 News Collection
    Rice Thresher
    Recorded Texas Historic Landmark Files
    Texas Historian

Online Exhibits

African Americans and the Struggle for Justice. "The Church Awakens: African Americans and the Search for Justice." http://www.episcopalarchives. org/Afro-Anglican_history/exhibit/transitions/.

Golden, Harry. "The Vertical Negro Plan." *Race & Education in Charlotte.* http://speccollexhibit.omeka.net/items/show/74.

Patterson, Bettie M. "My Neighborhood in the 1950s and 1960s." University of Houston. http://www.uh.edu/honors/Programs-Minors/honors-and-the-schools/houston-teachers-institute/curriculum-units/pdfs/1999/the-history-economic-base-and-politics-of-houston/patterson-99-houston.pdf.

"To Bear Fruit for Our Race." University of Houston. http://classweb.uh.edu/cph/tobearfruit/story_1927-1954_section02.html.

Oral Histories

Abner Anderson. Interview by Adrienne Cain, Gregory School Oral Histories, August 22, 2013. Film. http://digital.houstonlibrary. org/cdm/singleitem/collection/gsinterview/id/59/rec/16.

Albert Goldstein. Interview by Florence Coleman, HMRC Oral History Collection, September 9, 1975. Audio. http://digital.houstonlibrary. net/oral-history/albert-goldstein_OH060.php.

Andrew Jefferson. Interview by Louis Marchiafava, HMRC Oral History Collection, December 23, 1974. Audio. http://digital.houstonlibrary. net/oral-history/andrew-jefferson_OH081.php.

Asberry Butler. HMRC Oral History Collection, August 9, 1974. Audio. http://digital.houstonlibrary.net/oral-history/asberry-butler_ OH015.php.

Barry Kaplan. HMRC Oral History Collection, April 29, 1979. Audio. http://digital.houstonlibrary.net/oral-history/barry-kaplan_ OHB27.php.

Ben C. Connally. Interview by Louis Marchiafava, HMRC Oral History Interviews, April 2, 1975. Audio. http://digital.houstonlibrary.net/ oral-history/ben-conally.php.

Benny Joseph. Interview by Cheri Wolfe, Institute of Texan Cultures, December 16, 1993. Transcript. http://digital.utsa.edu/cdm/ref/ collection/p15125coll4/id/1651.

"Bill" Lawson (Reverend). Interview by Jane Ely, Houston Oral History Project, March 14, 2008. Film.http://digital.houstonlibrary.net/ oral-history/bill-lawson.php.

Charles Allen. Interview by Louis Marchiafava, HMRC Oral History Collection, August 27, 1975. Audio. http://digital.houstonlibrary.net/ oral-history/charles-allen_OH001.php.

Christia V. Adair. HMRC Oral History Collection, October 22, 1977. Audio. http://digital.houstonlibrary.net/oral-history/christie-adair_OHC14.

Clifton Richardson Jr. Interview by Louis Marchiafava, HMRC Oral History Collection, June 9, 1975. Audio. http://digital.houstonlibrary.net/oral-history/cliff-richardson.php.

Cora Johnson. Interview by Adrienne Cain, HMRC Oral History Collection, April 16, 2013. Film. http://digital.houstonlibrary.net/oral-history/cora-johnson_OHGS0061.php.

Curtis Graves. Interview by Adrienne Cain, HMRC Oral History Collection, January 23, 2014. Film. http://digital.houstonlibrary.net/oral-history/curtis-graves_OHGS0073.php.

Debra Castleberry. Interview by Patricia Prather, Gregory School Oral Histories, March 22, 2011. Film. http://digital.houstonlibrary.net/oral-history/debra-castleberry_OHGS0030.php.

Dick Gottlieb. Interview by Louis J. Marchiafava, HMRC Oral History Collection, June 25, 1976. Audio. http://digital.houstonlibrary.net/oral-history/dick-gottlieb_OH066.php.

Doris Peavey. Interview by Nicholas Castellanos, Gregory School Oral Histories, February 26, 2010. Film. http://digital.houstonlibrary.net/oral-history/doris-peavey_OHGS_11.php.

Dr. Merline Pitre. HMRC Oral History Collection, 1980. Audio. http://digital.houstonlibrary.net/oral-history/merline-pitre_OHB45.php.

Dr. Tatcho Mindiola. Interview by David Goldstein, Houston Oral History Project, June 4, 2008. Film. http://digital.houstonlibrary.org/cdm/singleitem/collection/oralhistory/id/88/rec/1.

Eleanor Tinsley. Interview by Jane Ely, Houston Oral History Project, October 16, 2007. Film. http://digital.houstonlibrary.net/oral-history/eleanor-tinsley.php.

Ernest Equia. Interview by Thomas Kreneck, HMRC Oral History Collection, February 25, 1988. Audio. http://digital.houstonlibrary.net/oral-history/ernest-equia_OH369.php.

Evelyn Berkowitz. Interview by David Goldstein, Neighborhood Voices Oral Histories, April 12, 2008. Film. http://digital.houstonlibrary.net/oral-history/evelyn-berkowitz.php.

Gertrude Beatrice Scott Batiste. Interview by Maria Nora Olivares, Institute of Texan Cultures, February 8, 1995. Transcript. http://digital.utsa.edu/cdm/ref/collection/p15125coll4/id/587.

Geraldine Pittman Wooten. Interview by Adrienne Cain, Gregory School Oral Histories, February 5, 2013. Film. http://digital.houstonlibrary.net/oral-history/geraldine-wooten_OHGS0055.php.

Gertrude Barnstone. Interview by Jane Ely, HMRC Oral History Collection, March 25, 2008. Film. http://digital.houstonlibrary.net/oral-history/gertrude-barnstone_OH008.php.

Gloria Darrow. Interview by Vince Lee, Gregory School Oral Histories, December 8, 2010. Film. http://digital.houstonlibrary.net/oral-history/Gloria-Darrow_OHGS0023.php.

Harold Wiesenthal. Interview by David Goldstein, Houston Oral History Project, July 8, 2008. Film. http://digital.houstonlibrary.net/oral-history/harold-wiesenthal.php.

Hattie Mae White. Interview by Louis Marchiafava, Houston Oral History Project, August 9, 1974. Audio. http://digital.houstonlibrary.net/oral-history/hattie-mae-white_OH192a.php.

Howard Jefferson. Interview by David Goldstein, Mayor Bill White Collection; Houston Oral History Project, May 15, 2008. Film. http://digital.houstonlibrary.net/oral-history/howard-jefferson.php.

Hyman Judah Schachtel. Interview by Gay Block and Linda May, Congregation Beth Israel Digital Archival Oral Histories, October 27, 1975. Audio. http://www.beth-israel.org/learning-programs/library.

Isaac Bryant. Interview by Jacqueline Bartha, Gregory School Oral Histories, July 27, 2011. Film. http://digital.houstonlibrary.net/oral-history/isaac-bryant_OHGS0034.php.

Jewell McGowen. Interview by Adrienne Cain, Gregory School Oral Histories, July 24, 2013. Film.http://digital.houstonlibrary.net/oral-history/jewell-mcgowen_OHGS0066.php.

Jo Alessandro Marks. Interview by Dena Marks, HMRC Oral History Collection, October 4, 2010. Film. http://digital.houstonlibrary.net/oral-history/jo-marks.php.

Joseph Carper. Interview by Veronica Perry, HMRC Oral History Collection, May 29, 1975. Audio. http://digital.houstonlibrary.net/oral-history/joseph-carper_OH019.php.

Joseph Fiorenza (Archbishop). Interview by David Goldstein, Houston Oral History Project, May 27, 2008. Film. http://digital.houstonlibrary.net/oral-history/joseph-fiorenza.php.

Judson Robinson. Interview by Florence Coleman, HMRC Oral History Collection, September 3, 1974. Audio. http://digital.houstonlibrary.net/oral-history/judson-robinson_OH154-1.php.

Mary Jourdan Atkinson. Interview by Margaret Henson, HMRC Oral History Collection, October 1, 1974. Audio. http://digital.houstonlibrary.net/oral-history/mary-jourdan-atkinson_OH003.php.

Moses Leroy. Interview by Florence Coleman, HMRC Oral History Collection, October 30, 1974. Audio. http://digital.houstonlibrary.net/oral-history/moses-leroy_OH102.php.

Mrs. Gladys House and Mrs. Holly Hogrobrook. Interview by Gary Houston, The Institute of Texas Cultures Oral History Collection, January 21, 1994. Transcript. digital.utsa.edu/cdm/ref/collection/p15125coll4/id/1628.

Nat and Jill Levy. Interview by Marjorie Hillman, HMRC Oral History Collection, July 22, 1982. Audio. http://digital.houstonlibrary.net/oral-history/nat-levy_OH411.php.

O'neta "Pink" Cavitt. Interview by Nicolas Castellanos, Gregory School Oral Histories, May 22, 2010. Film. http://digital.houstonlibrary.net/oral-history/oneta-cavitt_OH_GS_0013.php.

Otis King. Interview by David Goldstein, Houston Oral History Project, August 6, 2008. Film.http://digital.houstonlibrary.org/cdm/singleitem/collection/oralhistory/id/78/rec/1.

Patricia Smith Prather. Interview by Gary Houston, The Institute of Texas Cultures Oral History Collection, January 21, 1994. Transcript. http://digital.utsa.edu/cdm/ref/collection/p15125coll4/id/1747.

Ray K. Daily. Interview by Don Carleton, HMRC Oral History Collection, December 10, 1974. Audio. http://digital.houstonlibrary.org/cdm/singleitem/collection/Interviews/id/343/rec/1.

Rozelle Kahn. Interview. Congregation Emanu El Houston, Texas. January 20, 1983. American Jewish Archives, Cincinnati, Ohio.

Samuel Karff (Rabbi). Interview by David Goldstein, HMRC Oral History Collection, December 4, 2007. Film. http://digital.houstonlibrary.org/oral-history/samuel-karff.php.

Serra Gordon. Interview by Josh Parshall, Goldring/Woldenberg Institute of Southern Jewish Life, July 14, 2011.

Thelma Scott Bryant. Interview by Patricia Smith Prather, Houston Oral History Project, August 3, 2007. Transcript. http://digital.houstonlibrary.net/oral-history/thelma-scott-bryant.php.

University of Houston, *Attwell, Ernie—Atwell transcript, 1of 1,* November 12, 2004, Oral Histories from the Houston History Project, Special Collections, University of Houston Libraries. http://digital.lib.uh.edu/collection/houhistory/item/570/show/569.

University of Houston, *Lawson, William Rev.-Lawson transcript, 1 of 1,* October 20, 2004. Oral Histories from the Houston History Project, Special Collections, University of Houston Libraries. http://digital.lib.uh.ed/collection/houhistory/item/500/show/499.

University of Houston, *Leland, Dr. Alison - Leland audio, 1 of 1,* March 5, 2014, Oral Histories from the Houston History Project, Special Collections, University of Houston Libraries, http://digital.lib.uh.edu/collection/houhistory/item/1669/show/1667.

University of Houston, *Williams, Beneva—Williams audio, 1 of 3,* July 13, 2006, Oral Histories from the Houston History Project, Special Collections, University of Houston Libraries. http://digital.lib.uh.edu/collection/houhistory/item/786/show/782.

Wendelin Nold (Bishop). Interview by David Courtwright, HMRC Oral History Collection, August 20, 1975. Audio. http://digital.houstonlibrary.net/oral-history/wendelin-nold_OH053.php.

William Lawson (Reverend). Interview by Veronica Perry, HMRC Oral History Collection, August 12, 1974. Audio. http://digital.houstonlibrary.net/oral-history/william-lawson_OH100.php.

Personal Interviews/Discussions

Alfred and Matt Kahn. Interview by author. Houston, February 1, 2014.
Alan Hurwitz. In discussion with author. Houston, June 14. 2014.
William Lawson (Reverend). Interview by author. Houston, April 9, 2014.
Carolyn Litowich. Interview by author. Houston, June 24, 2015.
Cary Wintz. Interview by author. Houston, May 27, 2014.
Cherry Steinwender. Interview by author. Houston, February 5, 2014.
Cyvia Wolff. Interview by author. Houston, February 7, 2014.
Dr. David Bell. In discussion with author. Houston, May 22, 2014.
David Berg. Interview by author. Houston, February 17, 2014.
David Eisenbaum. Interview by author. Houston, April 28, 2013.
Dena Marks. Interview by author. Houston, March 12, 2014.
*Diana Bloom. Interview by author. Chicago, March 26, 2014.
Ellen Trachtenberg. Interview by author. Houston, May 2, 2014.
Fred Zeidman. Interview by author. Houston, April 14, 2014.
Jeanne Samuels. Interview by author. Houston, June 19, 2014.
Garland Pohl. In discussion by author. Houston, November 11, 2013.
Gloria Ribnick. Interview by author. Houston, March 20, 2014.
Ira Bleiweiss. Interview by author. Houston, February 16, 17, 2014.
Irving Pozmantier. Interview by author. Houston, March 18, 2014.
Jack Segal (Rabbi). Interview by author. Houston, November 18, 2013.
*Julius Rosenblatt. Interview by author. Houston, April 21, 2014.
J. Kent Friedman. Interview by author. Houston, February 26, 2014.
*Jaime Bloom. Interview by author. Austin, February 28, 2014.
Joe Fiorenza (Archbishop). Interview by author. Houston, December 18, 2013.
Joyce Gilbert. Interview by author. Houston, April 21, 2014.
Judy Weidman. In discussion with author. Houston, November 5, 2013.
Laurence Payne. Interview by author. Houston, March 13, 2014.
Leon Mucasey. Interview by author. Houston, March 28, 2014.
Lionel Schooler. Interview by author. Houston, April 21, 2014.
Mallory Robinson. Interview by author. Houston, May 19, 2014.
Marilyn Hassid. Interview by author. Houston, January 28, 2014.
Maxine Reingold. In discussion with author. Houston, December 11, 2013.
Michael Cahana (Rabbi). Interview by author. Portland, September 2, 2015.
Monica Rose. In discussion with author. Houston, November 11, 2013.
Monica Woolf. In discussion with author. Houston, November 24, 2013.
Odette Comier. Interview by author. Houston, May 7, 2014.
Pam Geyer. Interview by author. Houston, February 25, 2014.
Pepi Nichols. Interview by author. Houston, May 21, 2014.

Rachel Davis. In discussion with author. Houston, March 24, 2014.
Renee Stern. In discussion with author. Houston, May 5, 2014.
Robert Jucker and Sigmund Jucker. Interview by author. Houston, June 11, 2014.
Roy Walter (Rabbi). Interview by author. Houston, October 29, 2013.
Sam Karff (Rabbi). Interview by author. Houston, February 17, 2014.
Sam Feldt. Interview by author. Houston, March 19, 2014.
Sandy Weiner. Interview by author. Houston, May 11, 2014.
Susan S. Septimus. Interview by author. Houston, April 28, 2014.
Tom Bass. Interview by author. Houston, March 11, 2014.
Vic Samuels. Interview by author. Houston, March 13, 2014.

*Not the person's real name

Email Correspondence

Alfred Kahn. Email to author. August 24, 2017.
David Eisenbaum. Email to author. May 9, 2013.
Gloria Ribnick. Email to author. March 10, 2014.
James SoRelle. Email to author. May 19, 2014.
Ira Bleiweiss. Email to author. August 6, 2016; January 31, 2017.
J. Kent Friedman. Email to author. May 13, 2014.
Lionel Schooler. Email to author. November 2, 2016.
Lisa Klein. Email to author. September 10, 2016.
Susan S. Septimus. Email to author. June 17, 2017.

Newspapers

Chicago Defender
Bellaire Citizens
Dallas Morning News
Forward Times
Houston Chronicle
Houston Post
Houston Press
Indianapolis Recorder
Jewish Herald-Voice
Jewish Post
JTA
National Jewish Post
Negro Labor News
New York Times
Rice Thresher

Southwestern Times
The Informer
The Rag
Waco Tribune-Herald
Washington Post

Primary Sources

Arsht, Marjorie Meyer. *All the Way from Yoakum: The Personal Journey of a Political Insider.* College Station: Texas A&M University Press, 2006.

Berg, David. *Run Brother Run: A Memoir of a Murder in My Family.* New York: Scribner, 2013.

Blair, Justice. *Violence in the City.* Fort Worth, TX: Leo Potishman Fund, 1969.

Block, Gay. "A Tribute to Spirit: The Beth Israel Experience." In *About Love: Gay Block, Photographs and Films* 1973–2011. Santa Fe: Radius Books, 2011, DVD.

Briggs, Vernon M. Jr., and EEOC. *They Have the Power—We Have the People: The Status of Equal Employment Opportunity in Houston, Texas, 1970: An Equal Employment Opportunity Commission Report.* Washington, DC: US GPO, 1970.

Bullock, Henry. *Pathways to the Negro Market.* Ann Arbor, MI: JW Edwards, 1957.

Carwan, Guy. *Nashville Sit-in Story: Songs & Scenes of Nashville Lunch Counter Desegregation.* Folkways, 1960. CD.

Central Conference of American Rabbis, "The Guiding Principles of Reform Judaism: 'The Columbus Platform'—1937," https://www.ccarnet.org/rabbinic-voice/platforms/article-guiding-principles-reform-judaism/.

Charr, Easurk Emsen. *The Golden Mountain: The Autobiography of a Korean Immigrant 1895–1960,* 2nd ed., edited by Wayne Patterson. Urbana: University of Illinois Press, 1961.

Cohen, Anne Nathan. *The Centenary History: Congregation Beth Israel of Houston, Texas, 1854–1954.* Houston, TX: n.p., 1954.

Congregation Beth Israel (Houston). Policy Formulation Committee. *A Handbook of True Facts Concerning the Basic Principles of Congregation Beth Israel, Houston, Texas (organized 1856) an American Reform Congregation.* Houston, TX, Congregation Beth Israel, 1943.

"Convention Not Houston." *The Living Church,* June 20, 1954.

Currlin, Alice Bruce. *Community Welfare Houston, Texas.* Houston: Community Chest and Council of Houston and Harris County, 1946.

Domingue, Tommy J. "Memoir of Tommy J. Domingue." Unpublished memoir from Dorothy Domingue, March 6, 2014. Microsoft Word file.

"Dr. King's pro-Israel Legacy." YouTube video, 5:00. Posted by "Institute for Black Solidarity with Israel," June 9, 2014. https://www.youtube. com/watch?v=0Dd7pIB0CP0.

Federal Bureau of Investigation. "Citizen Council Houston." *Citizen Council.* Accessed August 30, 2016. https://archive.org/details/ CitizensCouncilMovement.

Federal Bureau of Investigation. "National States Rights Party, Part I." *FBI Records: The Vault.* Accessed August 14, 2016. http://vault.fbi.gov/ NationalStatesRightsParty/NationalStatesRightsPartyPart1of1/view.

Forster, Arnold. *A Measure of Freedom: An Anti-Defamation League Report.* Garden City, NY: Doubleday, 1950.

Friedman, Saul. "Houston, 'A Backwater of Revolt,'" *Texas Observer* (Houston), November 15, 1963.

Gallaher, Art. *The Negro and Employment Opportunities in the South: Houston: A Report Based Survey.* Houston: Houston Council on Human Relations, 1961.

Gertrude Barnstone: Home Movie. Directed by John Schwartz. Houston, TX: Riverside Productions, 2015. DVD.

Glatstein, Irwin. "Letters to the Editor." *Conservative Judaism* 13, no. 1 (Fall 1958): 47–49.

Gold, H. Raphael, ed. *The Book of Redemption*, comp. Jewish National Fund Council of Texas. Houston: D.H. White Co., 1939.

Goldstein, Janice. "Jewish Neighborhoods in Transition." *Our Stake in the Urban Conditions: Pertinent Papers,* American Jewish Committee (AJC). October 1980. http://www.bjpa.org/Publications/details.cfm? PublicationID=13937.

Herberg, Will. *Protestant, Catholic, Jew: An Essay in American Religious Sociology.* Chicago: University of Chicago Press, 1960.

Houston Council on Human Relations, et al. *The Houston Council on Human Relations: Black/Mexican American Project Report.* Houston: Houston Council on Human Relations, 1972.

Investigation of the Assassination of President John F. Kennedy. Washington, DC: US GPO, 1964.

Jordan, Barbara. "Democratic National Convention Keynote Speech, 1976, part 1." YouTube video, 12:02. Posted by "TSU Jordan Archives," September 5, 2012. https://www.youtube.com/watch?v=Bg7gLIx__-k.

"KPFT Bombing," YouTube video, 8:44. Posted by Houston Press in Brittanie Shey, "The Day the KKK Bombed KPFT," May 12, 2010. http//www. houstonpress.com/music/the-day-the-kkbombedkpft-6497751.

Jewish Community Council of Metropolitan Houston. *A Six Year History of the Jewish Community Council of Metropolitan Houston: A Chronicle of Community Organization and Accomplishment.* Houston, TX: Jewish Community Council of Metropolitan Houston, 1943.

Jewish Federation of Greater Houston. *Golden Jubilee: A Half Century of the Houston Jewish Federation 1936–1986.* Houston: Jewish Federation of Greater Houston, 1986.

Jewish Federation of Greater Houston, Ira Sheskin, David Dutwin, Susan Sherr, and A.J Jennings. *The 2016 Jewish Federation of Greater Houston Population Study: A Portrait of the Houston Jewish Community.* Houston: Jewish Federation of Greater Houston, 2016.

Jews and Hispanics in America: The Meeting of a Two Historic Cultures: A Report of the Houston Conference on Hispanic-Jewish Relations. New York: American Jewish Committee, Institute of Human Relations, 1982.

Kahn, Robert I. *An Affirmative Answer to Communism: A Series of Four Sermons.* Houston, TX; Congregation Emanu El, 1952.

—————. *May the Words of My Mouth.* Houston: Congregation Emanu El, 1984.

Klineberg, Stephen L. *Houston Area Survey (1982–2002), Houston's Economic and Demographic Transformation: Findings from the Expanded 2002 Survey of Houston's Ethnic Communities.* Houston: Rice University, 2002.

Klineberg, Stephen L., and Jie Wu, *Diversity and Transformation among Asians in Houston: Finding from the Kinder Institute's Houston Area Asian Survey* (1995, 2002, 2011). Houston: Rice University, 2013.

Lipschutz, Abbie. *Child of the 20th Century: Growing Up JEWISH in Holland, Belgium, Palestine, Israel, America, and Texas: A Memoir.* New York: Blue Thread Communication, 2011.

Malev, William. "The Jew of the South in the Conflict of Segregation." *Conservative Judaism* 13, no. 4 (Summer 1959): 35–46.

—————. "Letters to the Editor." *Conservative Judaism* 13, no. 1 (Fall 1958): 49–51.

—————. Living Creatively. Houston: D.H White, 1972.

"Martin Luther King, Jr 'Israel … is one of the great outpost of democracy in the world.'" YouTube video, :12. Posted by "Israel SDM," January 15, 2012. https://www.youtube.com/watch?v=kvr2Cxuh2Wk.

Mease, Quentin. *On Equal Footing: A Memoir.* Austin, TX: Eakin Press, 2001.

Meyer, Leopold. *Days of My Years: Autobiographical Reflection.* Houston, TX: Privately published: 1975.

Meyerowitz, David. "Vos geven iz geven un nito." *Milken Archive of Jewish Music.* 1926. Accessed May 10, 2017. http://milkenarchive.org/music/volumes/view/great-songs-of-the-american-yiddish-stage/work/vos-geven-iz-geven-un-nito/.

Morris, Celia. *Finding Celia's Place.* College Station: Texas A&M University Press, 2000.

Myrdal, Gunnar. *An American Dilemma*. Vol. 1. New Brunswick, NJ: Transaction Publisher, 1996.

Next Steps in Israeli-Palestinian Peace Process: Hearing Before the Subcommittee on the Middle East and South Asia of the Committee on Foreign Affairs, House of Representatives, One Hundred Tenth Congress, First Session, February 14, 2007. Washington, DC: US GPO, 2007.

Park, Robert E. "Jews in the Gentile World, the Problem of Anti-Semitism." Review of *Jews in the Gentile World: The Problem of Anti-Semitism*, by Isacque Graeber and Steuart Henderson Britt. *American Sociological Review* 9, no. 6 (Dec., 1944): 710–711.

Piller, E. A. *Time Bomb: America's Sinister New Fascism Will It Explode on Schedule*. New York: Arco Publishing Company, 1945.

Ragsdale, C.S. *Living Longer than Hate: A Story of Survival and Success*. Houston: D. Armstrong Printing Co., Inc., 1997.

Ravitch, Diane, "My Ghetto and Yours," *Texas Observer* (Houston), August 20, 1965.

Rosenwald, Lessing. "Reply to Zionism: Why Many Americans of Jewish Faith Are Opposed to the Establishment of a Jewish State in Palestine," *Life Magazine*, July 28, 1943.

"Religion: Storm over Zion," *Time Magazine*, January 17, 1944.

Religious Action Center of Reform Judaism, pro. "Consultation on Conscience." C-SPAN. April 11, 1989.

Schachtel, Hyman. *The Life You Want to Live*. New York: E.P. Dutton & CO., Inc., 1956.

Schulman, Sam, David Gottlieb, Sheila Sheinberg, and the Jewish Community Council of Metropolitan Houston. *A Social and Demographic Survey of the Jewish Community of Houston, Texas*. Houston, TX: The Demographic Study Committee, 1976.

Segal, Jack. *Modern Problems, Some Jewish Solutions*. Houston: William S. Malev Schools for Religious Studies of Congregation Beth Yeshurun, 1981.

Slawson, John. *The Realities of Jewish Integration*. New York: American Jewish Committee, 1965.

"The House I Live In—with Frank Sinatra." YouTube video, 10:15. Posted by "KRT1934," November 10, 2008. https://www.youtube.com/watch?v=vhPwtnGviyg.

"The Press: Blackout in Houston." *Time Magazine*, September 12, 1960.

This Is Our Home, It Is Not for Sale. Directed by John Schwartz. 1987. Houston: Riverside Productions, 2007. DVD.

Ungar, Andre. "To Birmingham, and Back." *Conservative Judaism* 18, no. 1 (Fall 1963): 1–17.

U.S. Congress. Senate Committee on Banking, Housing, and Urban Affairs. *Club Membership Practices of Financial Institutions, Congressional Hearings, 1979–07–13*, 1979.

U. S. Congress. *In Recognition of an Interfaith Celebration of Thanksgiving.* Washington, DC: Congressional Record Daily Edition, 2003.

U.S. Congress. *Tribute to the Late Honorable Mickey Leland. Congressional Record Daily Edition.* Washington, DC: US GPO, 1989.

U. S. Congress House Office of History and Preservation. *Black Americans in Congress, 1870–2007.* Washington: US GPO, 2008.

Vorspan, Albert. "Blacks and Jews." In *Black Anti-Semitism and Jewish Racism,* by Nat Hentoff, James Baldwin, et al., 191–226. New York: Schocken Books, 1969.

————. *Negroes and Jews. Journal of Jewish Communal Service.* Jewish Communal Service Association of North America (JCSA), National Conference of Jewish Communal Service. Spring 1966: 239–242. http://www.bjpa.org/Publications/details.cfm? Publication ID=5031.

————. and Eugene Lipman. *Justice and Judaism: The Work of Social Action.* New York: Union of American Hebrew Congregations, 1956.

Wedlock, Lunabelle. "Comparison by Negro Publications of the Plight of the Jews in Germany with That of the Negro in America (1942)." In *Relations Between Blacks and Jews in the United States,* edited by Maurianne Adams and John Bracey, 427–443. Amherst: University of Massachusetts Press, 1999.

Who Killed the 4th Ward? Produced by James Blue. 1978. Film. https://www. uhd.edu/academics/humanities/news-community/filmfest/Pages/ Who-Killed-the-4th-Ward.aspx.

Williams, Robin M., Daniel C. Thompson, and Oscar Cohen. *Social Action and the Social Scientist.* Houston: Public Affairs Research Center, 1964.

Wise, Stephen S. "The Shame of Houston." *Opinion: A Journal of Jewish Life and Letter* 19, no. 4 (February 1944): 5.

Secondary Sources

Abram, Lynwood. "Minority Report: Dr. Ray K. Daily Battles the Houston School Board." In *Lone Star of David: The Jews of Texas,* edited by Hollace Ava Weiner and Kenneth D. Roseman, 227–232. Lebanon, NH: University Press of New England, 2007.

"About," BYDS.org, accessed October 7, 2017, http://byds.org/.

"About," *Islamic Society of Greater Houston—Serving the Community since 1969,* accessed April 25, 2017, https://isgh.org/about/.

"About," Rothko Chapel, accessed August 29, 2016, http://rothkochapel.org/ learn/about/.

Allen, Kerri. "A Digital Cotton Curtain? What Selma Means to Silicon Valley." *Public Relations Tactics* 22, no. 5 (May 2015): 9.

"Atlanta Jewish and Black Coalitions," *AJC*, September 25, 2017, accessed September25,2017,https://www.ajc.org/news/atlanta-Black-jewish-coalition.

Badr, Hoda. "Al Noor Mosque: Strength Through Unity." In *Religion and the New Immigrants: Continuities and Adaptations in Immigrant Congregations,* edited by Janet Salzman Chafetz and Helen Rose Ebaugh, 193–227. Walnut Creek, CA: AltaMira Press, 2000.

Bard, Mitchell. *The Politics Behind the Rescue of Ethiopian Jewry.* Westport, CT: Praeger, 2002.

Barnes, Susan, John de Menil, Dominique de Menil, Barnett Newman, and Philip Johnson. *The Rothko Chapel: An Act of Faith.* Houston: Menil Foundation, 1989.

Barr, Alwyn. *Black Texans: A History of African Americans in Texas, 1528–1995.* 2nd ed. Norman: University of Oklahoma Press, 1996.

Barr, Rosyln. "Houston." In *The Jewish Traveler,* edited by Alan M. Tigay, 151–160. Garden City, NJ: Doubleday &Company, 1987.

Bass, Jack. *The Transformation of Southern Politics: Social Change and Political Consequence Since 1945.* Athens: University of Georgia Press, 1995.

Bauman, Mark. Introduction to *The Quiet Voices: Southern Rabbis and Black Civil Rights, 1880s to 1990s,* edited by Mark K. Bauman and Berkley Kalin, 1–18. Tuscaloosa: University of Alabama Press, 1997.

―――. "Part V Identity." In *Dixie Diaspora: An Anthology of Southern Jewish History,* edited by Mark K. Bauman, 353–356. Tuscaloosa: University of Alabama Press, 2006.

Beeth, Howard, and Cary D. Wintz, eds. *Black Dixie: Afro-Texan History and Culture in Houston.* College Station: Texas A&M University Press, 1992.

Behnken, Brian D. *Fighting Their Own Battles: Mexican Americans, African Americans, and the Struggle for Civil Rights in Texas.* Chapel Hill: University of North Carolina Press, 2011.

Belluscio, Steven J. *To Be Suddenly White: Literary Realism and Racial Passing.* Columbia: University of Missouri Press, 2006.

Berger, Jenna T. "From the Ashes of Europe to The Opportunity City: Immigration and Resettlement of Holocaust Survivors in Houston." Master's thesis, University of Houston, 2005.

Bergoffen, Wendy H. "Taking Care of Our Own: Narratives of Jewish Giving and the Galveston Movement." *Shofar* 34, no. 2 (2016): 26–51.

Berman, Lila Corwin. "The Death and Life of Jewish Neighborhoods." *Sh'ma: A Journal of Jewish Ideas,* June 1, 2014. Accessed August 7, 2016. http://shma.com/2014/06/the-death-and-life-of-jewish-neighborhoods/.

Berman, Lila Corwin. "Jewish Urban Politics in the City and Beyond." *Journal of American History* 99, no. 2 (2012): 492–519.

Black Enterprise. "Houston." *Black Enterprise* (October 1970).

Botson, Michael R. *Labor, Civil Rights, and the Hughes Tool Company.* College Station: Texas A&M University Press, 2005.

Brady, Michael Kevin. "NASA Launches Houston into Orbit: The Political, Economic, and Social Impact of the Space Agency on Southeast Texas, 1961–1969." PhD diss., Baylor University, 2009.

Brickner, Balfour. "Projects Under Synagogue Auspices." *Religious Education* 59, no. 1 (January 1964): 76–80.

Brody, David, "American Jewry, The Refugees and Immigration Restriction (1932–1942)." In *America, American Jews, and the Holocaust,* edited by Jeffery S. Gurock, 181–209. Vol. 7. American Jewish History. New York: Routledge, 1998.

Brownstein, Bobby. "The Battle of the 'Basic Principles' Congregation Beth Israel and Anti-Zionist Revolt in American Reform Judaism." Master's thesis, University of Houston, 1991.

Broyles, William. "The Making of Barbara Jordan," *Texas Monthly,* October 1976.

Buhle, Paul, and Robin D.G. Kelley. "Allies of Different Sorts." In *Struggles in the Promised Land: Toward a History of Black-Jewish Relations in the United States,* edited by Jack Saltzman and Cornel West, 197–229. New York: Oxford University Press, 1997.

Bullard, Robert D. "Environmentalism, Economic Blackmail, and Civil Rights: Competing Agendas Within the Black Community." In *Communities in Economic Crisis: Appalachia and the South,* edited by John Gaventa, Barbara Ellen Smith, and Alex Willingham, 190–199. Philadelphia: Temple University Press, 1990.

Bullard, Robert D. "Housing Problems and Prospects in Contemporary Houston." In *Black Dixie: Afro-Texan History and Culture in Houston,* edited by Howard Beeth and Cary D. Wintz, 236–252. College Station: Texas A&M University Press, 1992.

————. *Invisible Houston: The Black Experience in Boom and Bust.* College Station: Texas A&M University Press, 1987.

Burrough, Bryan. *The Big Rich: The Rise and Fall of the Greatest Texas Oil Fortunes.* London: Penguin Group, 2009.

Carleton, Don E. "McCarthyism in Houston: The George Ebey Affair." *Southwestern Quarterly* 80, no. 2 (October 1976): 163–176.

————. *Red Scare! Right Wing Hysteria Fifties Fanaticism and Their Legacy in Texas.* Austin: Texas Monthly Press, 1985.

Carson, Clayborne. *In Struggle: SNCC and the Black Awakening of the 1960s.* Cambridge, MA: Harvard University Press, 1995.

Carson, Clayborne. "The Politics of Relations between African-Americans and Jews." In *Blacks and Jews: Alliances and Arguments,* edited by Paul Berman, 131–143. New York: Delacorte Press, 1994.

Ceplair, Larry. *Anti-Communism in Twentieth-Century America: A Critical History.* Santa Barbara, CA: Praeger, 2011.

Chapman, Betty Trapp. "A System of Government Where Business Rule." *Houston History Magazine* 8, no. 1 (July 12, 2011): 30–33.

"Children's Crusade." *King Encyclopedia.* Accessed October 20, 2016, http://kingencyclopedia.stanford.edu/encyclopedia/encyclopedia/enc_childrens_crusade.1.html

Clayson, William S. *Freedom Is Not Enough: The War on Poverty and the Civil Rights Movement in Texas.* Austin: University of Texas Press, 2010.

Coates, Felicia et al., "Briar Patch," *Texas Monthly,* 2016.

Cohen-Solal, Annie. *Mark Rothko: Toward the Light in the Chapel.* New Haven, CT: Yale University Press, 2015.

Cole, Thomas. *No Color Is My Kind: The Life of Eldrewey Stearns and the Integration of Houston.* Austin: University of Texas Press, 1997.

Cook, Alison, "Robert Sakowitz and His Fraying Empire: Why the Sakowitz Stores Went Bust," *Texas Monthly,* December 1985, 136.

Congregation Brith Shalom, "Brith Shalom History," *Your Jewish Journey Starts Here,* accessed October 20, 2016, http://www.brithshalom.org/about-us/brith-shalom-history

Davidson, Chandler. "Negro Politics and the Rise of the Civil Rights Movement in Houston, Texas." PhD diss., Princeton University, 1968.

Davis, Abraham., and Barbara Luck Graham. *The Supreme Court, Race, and Civil Rights: From Marshall to Rehnquist.* Thousand Oaks, CA: Sage, 1995.

DeBlasio, Donna B. "Architecture." In *Encyclopedia of African American History, 1619–1895: From the Colonial Period to the Age of Frederick Douglass,* edited by Paul Finkelman. 1st ed. Vol 1. New York: Oxford University Press, 2006.

Dejene, Alemneh. *Environment, Famine, and Politics in Ethiopia: A View from the Village.* Boulder, CO: Lynne Rienner, 1990.

Diner, Hasia. "If I Am Not for Myself/If I Am Only for Myself: Jews, the American South, and the Quandary of Self Interest." In *Jews and the State: Dangerous Alliances and the Perils of Privilege,* edited by Ezra Mendelsohn, 50–69. Vol. 19 of *Studies in Contemporary Jewry.* New York: Oxford University Press, 2003.

————. *The Jews of the United States 1654 to 2000.* Berkeley: University of California Press, 2004.

Dingus, Anne. "Mickey Leland," *Texas Monthly,* November 1, 1999.

Dinnerstein, Leonard. "A Neglected Aspect of Southern Jewish History." *American Jewish Historical Quarterly* 61, no. 1 (September 1971): 52–68.

————. "Southern Jewry and the Desegregation Crisis, 1954–1970." In *Anti-Semitism in America,* edited by Jeffery S. Gurock, 791–801. Vol. 6, pt. 2, of *American Jewish History.* New York: Routledge, 1998.

Dollinger, Marc. *Black Power, Jewish Politics: Reinventing the Alliance in the 1960s.* Waltham, MA: Brandeis University Press, 2018.

————. *Quest for Inclusion: Jews and Liberalism in Modern American.* Princeton, NJ: Princeton University Press, 2000.

Douglas, Susan J. *Listening In: Radio and the American Imagination.* Minneapolis: University of Minnesota Press, 2004.

Dressman, Fran. *Gus Wortham: A Portrait of a Leader.* College Station: Texas A&M University Press, 1994.

Dudziak, Mary L. *Cold War Civil Rights: Race and the Image of American Democracy.* Princeton, NJ: Princeton University Press, 2000.

Esber, Rosemarie M. "Arab Americans in the Southern United States." *Baylor Institute for Oral History,* 2012–2013. http://www.baylor.edu/content/services/document.php/182127.

Evans, Eli. *The Provincials: A Personal History of Jews in the South.* New York: Atheneum, 1973.

Fairbanks, Robert. *The War on the Slums in the Southwest: Public Housing and Slum Clearance in Texas, Arizona, and New Mexico, 1935–1965.* Philadelphia: Temple University Press, 2016.

Feagin, Joe. *The New Urban Paradigm: Critical Perspectives on the City.* Lanham, MD: Rowman and Littlefield, 1998.

Fehling, Leticia. "Eisenhower High Student Selected for Mickey Leland Kibbutzim Internship." *Discover News, Information and More about Aldine HISDs Schools,* April 19, 2013, http://insideadeline.com/2013/04/eisenhower-high-student-selected-for-mickey-leland-kibbutzim-internship/.

Fisher, Robert. "The Urban Sunbelt in Comparative Perspective: Houston in Context." In *Essays on Sunbelt Cities and Recent Urban Americans,* edited by Robert B. Fairbanks and Kathleen Underwood, 33–58. College Station: Texas A&M University Press, 1990.

Foner, Eric. *Forever Free: The Story of Emancipation and Reconstruction.* New York: Knopf Doubleday Publishing Group, 2013.

Friends of MacGregor, "Riverside Terrace," https://friendsofmacgregorpark.org/Riverside Terrace-terrace/."

Garcia, Maria Cristinia. Agents of Americanization: Rusk Settlement and the Houston Mexicano Community, 1907–1950." In *Mexican Americans in Texas History,* eds. Emilo Zamoro, Cynthia Orozco, and Rodolfo Rocha. Austin: Texas State Historical Association, 2000.

Gardell, Matthias. *In the Name of Elijah Muhammad: Louis Farrakhan and the Nation of Islam*. Durham, NC: Duke University Press, 1996.

Gibson, Gordon. "Looking Back," *UU World: Landmark Desegregation Ruling at Fifty*, accessed October 20, 2016, http://archive.uuworld. org/2004/03/lookingback.html.

Gilderbloom, John Igram. *Invisible City: Poverty, Housing, and New Urbanism*. Austin: University of Texas Press, 2008.

Giles, Robert C. *Changing Times: The Story of the Diocese of Galveston Houston in Commemoration of its Founding*. Houston: J.L. Morkovsky, 1972.

Glazer, Nathan. "The American Jewish Urban Experience." In *The Cambridge Companion to American Judaism*, edited by Dana Evan Kaplan, 271–282. New York: Cambridge University Press, 2005.

Goetschel, Willi. "Mendelssohn and the State," MLN 122, no. 3 (April 2007): 472–492.

Goldstein, Eric L. *The Price of Whiteness: Jews, Race, and American Identity*. Princeton, NJ: Princeton University Press, 2006.

Goode, Jo-Carolyn. "Remembering the 26th Anniversary of Congressman Mickey Leland's Death," *Houston Style Magazine*, August 7, 2015, http://stylemagazine.com/news/2015/aug/07/remembering-26th-anniversary-congressman-mickey-le/.

Gordon, Charles. "The Racial Barrier to American Citizenship," *University of Pennsylvania Law Review* 93, no. 3 (March 1945): 237–258.

Gordon, Melton J. ed. "National Conference for Community and Justice." *Encyclopedia of American Religions,* 7th ed. Detroit, MI: Gale Division of Cengage Learning Inc., 2003.

Gottschaller, Pia. "The Rothko Chapel: Toward the Infinite." In *Art and Activism: Projects of John and Dominique de Menil*, edited by Josef Helfenstein and Laureen Schipsi, 139–147. New Haven, CT: Yale University Press, 2010.

Govenar, Alan. *Lightnin' Hopkins: His Life and Blues*. Chicago, IL: Chicago Review Press, Inc., 2010.

Green, George. *The Establishment in Texas Politics: The Primitive Years, 1938–1957*. Norman: University of Oklahoma, 1979.

Greenberg, Cheryl Lynn. "Black-Jewish Relations in the United States." In *Encyclopaedia Judaica*, edited by Michael Berenbaum and Fred Skolnik. 2nd ed. Vol. 3. Detroit: Macmillan Reference USA, 2007.

————. *"Or Does It Explode?" Black Harlem in the Great Depression*. New York: Oxford University Press, 1991.

————. "The Southern Jewish Community and Struggle for Civil Rights." In *African Americans and Jews in Twentieth Century: Studies in Convergence and Conflict*, edited by V.P. Franklin, Nancy J. Grant, Harold M. Kletnick, and Genna Rae Meneil, 123–164. Columbia: University of Missouri Press, 1998.

Greenberg, Cheryl Lynn. *Troubling the Waters: Black-Jewish Relations in the American Century.* Princeton, NJ: Princeton University Press, 2006.

Greene, Casey. "Guardians Against Change: The Ku Klux Klan in Houston and Harris County, 1920–1925." *Houston History* 8, no. 1 (Fall 2010): 2–5.

Greenstein, Micah D., and Howard Greenstein. "'Then and Now': Southern Rabbis and Civil Rights." In *The Quiet Voices: Southern Rabbis and Black Civil Rights, 1880s to 1990s,* edited by Mark K. Bauman and Berkley Kalin, 325–337. Tuscaloosa: University of Alabama Press, 1997.

Greenstein, Howard R. *Turning Point: Zionism and Reform Judaism.* Vol. 12 of *Brown Judaic Studies.* Chico, CA: Scholar Press, 1981.

Gruber, Samuel D. "The Continuing Exodus: The Synagogue and Jewish Urban Migration." *Religion* 35 (2012): 14–19. http://surface.syr.edu/rel/35.

Guglielmo, Thomas A. "Fighting for Caucasian Rights: Mexicans, Mexican Americans, and the Transnational Struggle for Civil Rights in World War II Texas." *Journal of American History* 92, no. 4 (March 2006): 1212–1237.

———. "'Red Cross, Double Cross': Race and America's World War II-Era Blood Donor Service." *Journal of American History* 97, no 1 (June 2010): 63–90.

Gutow, Steve and Laurie Barker James. "Most Politics Is Local." In *Lone Star of David: The Jews of Texas,* edited by Hollace Ava Weiner and Kenneth D. Roseman, 212–225. Lebanon, NH: University Press of New England, 2007.

Handbook of Texas Online, Cary D. Wintz, "Texas Southern University," accessed May 17, 2017, http://www.tsaonline.org/handbook/online/articles/kct27.

———. Diana J. Kleiner, "Houston Informer and Texas Freeman," accessed May 27, 2017, http://www.tsaonline.org/handbook/online/articles/eeh11.

———. Diana J. Kleiner, "Fifth Ward, Houston," assessed October 16, 2016, https://tshaonline.org/handbook/online/articles/hpfhk.

———. Douglas Hales, "Nickerson, William N., Jr.," accessed July 04, 2017, http://www.tshaonline.org/handbook/online/articles/fnifp

———. David Stricklin, "Fundamentalism," accessed October 20, 2016, http://www.tshaonline.org/handbook/online/articles/itf01.

———. Mark Oditz and Mary Beth Rogers, "Jordan, Barbara Charline," accessed October 20, 2016, http://www.tshaonline.org/handbook/online/articles/fjoas

———. Nancy Baker Jones, "Dupree, Anna Johnson," *Handbook of Texas Online,* accessed May 17, 2017, http://www.tshaonline.org/handbook/online/articles/fdu39

Handbook of Texas Online, Cary D. Sanford N. Greenberg, "White Primary,"
accessed October 20, 2016, http://www.tshaonline.org/handbook/
online/articles/wdw01.
————. Shawna D. Williams, "Robinson, Judson Wilbur Jr," accessed
October 20, 2016, http://www.tsaonline.org/handbook/online/
articles/frobu
————. June Melby Benowitz, "Minute Women of the U.S.A.," accessed
September 12, 2016, http://www.tshaonline.org/handbook/online/
articles/pwm01.
Handbook of Texas Online, Virginia Bernhard, "Hogg, Ima," accessed
February 04, 2016, http://www.tshaonline.org/handbook/online/
articles/fho16.
————. William E. Montgomery, "African-American Churches," accessed
December 16, 2016, http://www.tshaonline.org/handbook/online/
articles/pkatz.
Harmon, Lawrence., and Hillel Levine. *Death of American Jewish Commu-
nity: A Tragedy of Good Intentions*. New York: Macmillan Interna-
tional, 1992.
Harrison, Cecile E., and Alice K. Laine, "Operation Breadbasket in Houston,
1966–78." In *Black Dixie: Afro-Texan History and Culture in
Houston*, edited by Howard Beeth and Cary D. Wintz, 223–236.
College Station: Texas A&M University Press, 1992.
Hartnett, Kimberly Marlowe. *Carolina Israelite: How Harry Golden Made
Us Care about Jews, the South, and Civil Rights*. Chapel Hill:
University of North Carolina Press, 2015.
Harwell, Debbi Z. "William S. Holland: A Mighty Loan at Yates High
School." *Houston History*, 8 no. 1 (December 20, 2010):9–13.
Haygood, Tamara Miner. "Use and Distribution of Slave Labor in Harris
County, Texas, 1836–60." In *Black Dixie: Afro-Texan History and
Culture in Houston*, edited by Howard Beeth and Cary D. Wintz,
32–53. College Station: Texas A&M University Press, 1992.
Haynes, Robert V. "Black Houstonians and the White Democratic Primary
1920–45." In *Black Dixie: Afro-Texan History and Culture in
Houston*, edited by Howard Beeth and Cary D. Wintz, 192–210.
College Station: Texas A&M University Press, 1992.
Hassid, Marilyn. "Jewish Community Center: An Arts and Culture for the
Houston Community." Unpublished Essay from Marilyn Hassid,
January 28, 2014. Microsoft Word File.
Helmreich, William B. "Research Report: Postwar Adaptation of Holocaust
Survivors in the United States." *Holocaust and Genocide Studies* 2,
no. 2 (1987): 307–315.
Henderson, Helene, ed. "Brotherhood/Sisterhood Week." In *Holidays, Festi-
vals, and Celebrations of the World Dictionary*, 3rd ed. Detroit:
Omnigraphics, 2005.

Henderson, Helene, ed. "Race Relations Sunday." In *Holidays, Festivals, and Celebrations of the World Dictionary*, 3rd ed. Detroit: Omnigraphics, 2005.

Henry III, William A. "Beyond the Melting Pot," *Time Magazine*, April 9, 2009.

Hero, Alfred O, Jr., "Southern Jews, Race Relations, and Foreign Policy." In *Anti-Semitism in America*, edited by Jeffrey S. Gurock, 803–825. Vol. 2 of *American Jewish History.* New York: Routledge, 1998.

Hecht, Esther. "Houston," *Hadassah Magazine*, October & November 2014, http://www.hadassahmagazine.org/2014/10/22/houston/.

Hine, Darlene Clark. "The Elusive Ballot: The Black Struggle Against the Texas Democratic White Primary, 1932–1945." In *The African American Experience in Texas: An Anthology,* edited by Bruce A. Glasrud and James M. Smallwood, 279–301. Lubbock: Texas Tech University Press, 2007.

"History," *Texas Southern University*, http://www.tsu.edu/about/history.php.

"History of HHA," *Housing Communities*, 2009, accessed August 8, 2016, http://www.housingforhouston.com/about-hha/history-of-hha.aspx.

History of Weiner's Stores, Inc.—*FundingUniverse*, accessed October 20, 2016, http://www.fundinguniverse.com/company-histories/weiner-s-stores-inc-history/.

Houston Jewish Federation. *A Half Century of the Houston Jewish Federation 1936–1986.* Houston: December 11, 1986.

Howard, Will. "Oil Industry Historical Markers of Harris County." *Harris County Historical Commission.* https://historicalcommission.harriscountytx.gov/Articles/ Oil Industry Historical Markers.pdf.

"ISJL-Alabama Birmingham" *Institute of Southern Jewish Life,* 2014, accessed August 10, 2016, https://www.isjl.org/alabama-birmingham-encyclopedia.html.

"————. Texas Houston Encyclopedia," *Institute of Southern Jewish Life,* 2014, accessed August 10, 2016, http://www.isjl.org/texas-houston-encyclopedia.html.

"————. Tennessee Memphis," *Institute of Southern Jewish Life,* 2014, accessed August 10, 2016, https://www.isjl.org/tennessee-memphis-encyclopedia.html.

"————. Louisiana New Orleans," *Institute of Southern Jewish Life,* 2014, accessed August 10, 2016, https://www.isjl.org/louisiana-new-orleans-encyclopedia.html.

"————. Mississippi Jackson," *Institute of Southern Jewish Life,* 2014, accessed August 10, 2016, https://www.isjl.org/mississippi-jackson-encyclopedia.html.

"It's Official: The Eldorado Ballroom Is Historic," *Houstonia,* April 29, 2014, http://www.houstoniamag.com/articles/2014/4/29/its-official-the-eldorado-ballroom-is-historic-april-2014.

Jacobus, Robert D. *Houston Cougars in the 1960s: Death Threats, the Veer Offense, and the Game of the Century.* College Station: Texas A&M University Press, 2015.

Jacoway, Elizabeth. *Southern Businessmen and Desegregation.* Baton Rouge: Louisiana State University Press, 1982.

Jackson, Larry J. "The Development of Black Business in Texas, 1919–1969: From Houston Perspective." Master's thesis, Texas Tech University, 1979.

Jensen, F. Kenneth. "The Houston Sit-In Movement of 1960–61." In *Black Dixie: Afro-Texan History and Culture in Houston,* edited by Howard Beeth and Cary D. Wintz, 211–222. College Station: Texas A&M University Press, 1992.

Johnpoll, Bernard K., ed. *A Documentary History of the Communist Party of the United States-Vol 2.* Westport, CT: Greenwood Press, 1994.

Johnson, Peniel E. Joseph. *Waiting 'Till the Midnight Hour: A Narrative History of Black Power in America.* New York: Henry Holt Company, 2006.

Johnston, Marguerite. *A Happy Worldly Abode: Christ Church Cathedral 1839–1964.* Houston: Cathedral Press, 1989.

Jones, Charles E. "Arm Yourself or Harm Yourself: People's Party II and the Black Panther Party in Houston, Texas." In *On the Ground: The Black Panther Party in Communities across America,* edited by J.L Jeffries, 3–40. Jackson: University Press of Mississippi, 2010.

Jones, Howard. *The Red Diary: A Chronological History of Black Americans in Houston and Some Neighboring Harris County Communities—122 Years Later.* Austin, TX: Nortex Press, 1991.

Jones, Jacqueline. *A Dreadful Deceit: The Myth of Race from the Colonial Era to Obama's America.* New York: Basic Books, 2015.

Jones, Yvette. "Seeds of Compassion." *Texas Historian* 37, no. 2 (November 1976): 18. https://texashistory.unt.edu/ark:/67531/metapth391307/m1/18/?q=%22anna%20dupree%22.

Kammen, Carol. *On Doing Local History.* Walnut Creek, CA: AltaMira Press, 2003.

Kaplan, Dana Evan. *American Reform Judaism: An Introduction.* Piscataway, NJ: Rutgers University Press, 2003.

Kaufman, Jonathan. "Blacks and Jews: The Struggle in the Cities." In *Struggles in the Promised Land: Toward a History of Black-Jewish Relations in the United States,* edited by Jack Salzman and Cornel West, 107–121. New York: Oxford University Press, 1997.

Kellar, William Henry. *Make Haste Slowly: Moderates, Conservatives, and School Desegregation in Houston.* College Station: Texas A&M University Press, 1999.

King, Judy. *Except the Lord Build ... The Sesquicentennial History of First Presbyterian Church, Houston, Texas 1839–1989*. Houston: First Presbyterian Church of Houston, 1989.

Kirk, John A. "The NAACP Campaign for Teachers' Salary Equalization: African American Women Educators and the Early Civil Rights Struggle." *Journal of African American History* 94, no. 4 (2009): 529–552.

Kirkland, Kate S. "For All Houston's Children: Ima Hogg and the Board of Education, 1943–1949." *Southwestern Historical Quarterly* 101, no. 4 (Apr., 1998): 460–495.

Kolsky, Thomas A. *Jews Against Zionism: The American Council for Judaism, 1942–1948*. Philadelphia, PA: Temple University Press, 1990.

Kossie-Chernyshev, Karen. "Houston Riot of 1917." In *The Jim Crow Encyclopedia*, eds. Nikki L.M. Brown and Barry M. Stentiford. Westport, CT: Greenwood Press, 2008.

Krause, Allen, "Rabbis and Negro Rights in the South, 1954–1967." In *Jews in the South,* edited by Leonard Dinnerstein and Mary Dale Palsson, 360–385. Baton Rouge: Louisiana State University Press, 1973.

Kraut, Benny. "Towards the Establishment of the National Conference of Christians and Jews: The Tenuous Road to Religious Goodwill in the 1920s." *American Jewish History* 77, no. 3 (March 1, 1988): 388–412.

Krochmal, Max. *Blue Texas: The Making of a Multiracial Democratic Coalition in the Civil Rights Era*. Chapel Hill: The University of North Carolina Press, 2016.

Lang, Curtis. "A Depleted Legacy Public Housing." *Cite: The Architecture + Design Review of Houston* 33 (Fall 1995/Winter 1996): 10–15.

Lede, Naomi W., and Constance Houston Thompson. *Precious Memories of a Black Socialite: A Narrative of the Life and Times of Constance Houston Thompson*. Houston: N.W. Lede, 1991.

"Leland, George Thomas (Mickey)." *History, Art, and Archives United States House of Representatives,* http://history.house.gov/People/Detail/16887.

Lewis, Herbert S. "The Passion of Franz Boas." *American Anthropologist* 103, no. 2 (June 2001): 447–467.

Liddell, Marilyn. "The Creation of the Houston Community College: A Concept Becomes Reality." *Houston Review* 7, no. 2 (1985): 69–77.

Lin, Jan. *The Power of Urban Ethnic Places: Cultural Heritage and Community Life*. New York: Routledge, 2011.

Litwak, Leon. "Jim Crow Blues." *OAH Magazine of History* 18, no. 2 (2004).

Lomax, John A. "History of the Society (June, 1966)," *Houston Folk Music*, http://www.houstonfolkmusic.org/audio_files/;

Lomax, John III. "John A. Lomax, Jr. (1907–1974): A Success in All He Did," *Cultural Equity*, http://www.culturalequity.org/alanlomax/ce_alanlomax_profile_johnlomaxjr.php.

"Looking Back," *UU World: Landmark Desegregation Ruling at Fifty*, accessed October 20, 2016, http://archive.uuworld.org/2004/03/lookingback.html.

Maas, Elaine. "Jews." In *The Ethnic Groups of Houston*, edited by Fred R. Von der Mehden, 135–156. Houston: Rice University Studies, 1984.

————. "The Jews of Houston: An Ethnographic Study." PhD diss., Rice University, 1973.

Malino, Sarah. "Southern Jewish Retailers (1840–2000)." In *Encyclopedia of American Jewish History*, edited by Stephen H. Norwood and Eunice G. Pollack, vol. 2. Santa Barbara: CA: ABC-CLIO, 2008.

Marquez, John D. *Black-Brown Solidarity: Racial Politics in the New Gulf South*. Austin: University of Texas Press, 2014.

Mars, Ors. "The Effects of a Kibbutz Experience on the Lives of Inner-City Youth: A Study of the 'Operation Unity Israel Trip'." Master's thesis, Hebrew Union College, 1995.

McComb, David G. *Houston: A History*. Austin: University of Texas Press, 1981.

McConnell, Michael W. "Is There Still a 'Catholic Question' in America? Reflections of John F. Kennedy's Speech to The Houston Ministerial Association." *Notre Dame Law Review* 86, no. 4 (2011): 1635–1653.

McWhorter, Thomas. "From Das Zweiter to El Segundo, A Brief History of Houston's Second Ward," *Houston History Magazine* 8, no. 1 (December 2010): 38–43.

Medoff, Rafael. *Jewish Americans and Political Participation: A Reference Handbook*. Santa Barbara, CA: ABC-CLIO, 2002.

Meltzer, Mildred Hubert. "Chapters in the Struggle for Negro Rights in Houston, 1944–1962." Master's thesis, University of Houston, August 1963.

Mohammed, Masjid Warithuddeen. "Founded in the 1950s," 2015, http://masjidwdmohammed.com/history/.

Moore, Deborah Dash. "Separate Paths: Blacks and Jews in the Twentieth-Century South." In *Struggles in the Promised Land: Toward a History of Black-Jewish Relations in the United States*, edited by Jack Salzman and Cornel West, 275–294. New York: Oxford University Press, 1997.

Murch, Donna. "The Many Meanings of Watts: Black Power, Wattstax, and the Carceral State." *OAH Magazine of History* 26, no. 1 (2012): doi: 10.1093/oahmag/oar062.

Nichter, Matt. "The Old Left and the Rise of the Civil Rights Movement, 1930–1965." Master's thesis, University of Wisconsin-Madison, 2005.

Novick, Peter. *The Holocaust in American Life.* Boston: Houghton Mifflin, 1999.

Olsen, Margaret Nunnelley. "Teaching Americanism: Ray K. Daily and the Persistence of Conservatism in Houston School Politics, 1943–1952." *Southwestern Historical Quarterly* 110, no. 2 (2006): 240–269.

Parfitt, Tudor. *Black Jews in Africa and the Americas.* Cambridge, MA: Harvard University Press, 2013.

Parker, Deloyd. "In Good Faith: Remembering John de Menil." In *Art and Activism: Projects of John and Dominique de Menil,* edited by John Helfenstein and Laureen Schipsi, 114–115. New Haven, CT: Yale University Press, 2010.

Parks, Douglas R., and Ruthe E. Pathe. "Gene Weltfish 1902–1980." *Plains Anthropologist* 30, no. 107 (February 1985): 59–64.

Phelps, Wesley G. *People's War on Poverty: Urban Politics and Grassroots Activists in Houston.* Athens: University of Georgia Press, 2014.

Pierce, Michael. "The Origins of Right-to-Work: Vance Muse, Anti-Semitism, and the Maintenance of Jim Crow Labor Relations." *LAWCHA,* January 12, 2017. https://www.lawcha.org/2017/01/12/origins-right-work-vance-muse-anti-semitism-maintenance-jim-crow-labor-relations/.

Pietila, Antero. *Not in My Neighborhood: How Bigotry Shaped a Great American City.* Chicago: Ivan Des, 2010.

Pitre, Merline. *In Struggle Against Jim Crow: Lulu B. White and the NAACP, 1900–1957.* College Station: Texas A&M University Press, 1999.

Plaut, W. Gunther. *The Growth of Reform Judaism; American and European Sources until 1948.* Philadelphia: Jewish Publication Society, 2015.

Pruitt, Bernadette. *The Other Great Migration: The Movement of Rural African Americans to Houston, 1900–1941.* College Station: Texas A&M University Press, 2013.

Raphael, Marc Lee, ed. *Columbia Anthology of Jews and Judaism in America.* New York: Columbia University Press, 2008.

Ratkin, Annette Levy. "The History of the Temple Social Action/Justice Committee," Temple Nashville, accessed October 20, 2016, https://www.Templenashville.org/_content/6_beit_tikkum_olam/social_action_programs/The%20History%20of%20Social%20Action.pdf.

Rockoff, Stuart. "Deep in the Heart of Palestine: Zionism in Early Texas." In *Lone Star of David: The Jews of Texas,* edited by Hollace Ava Weiner and Kenneth D. Roseman, 93–107. Lebanon, NH: University Press of New England, 2007.

Rodriguez, Nestor. "Hispanic and Asian Immigration Waves in Houston." In *Religion and the New Immigrants: Continuities and Adaptations in Immigrant Congregations,* edited by Janet Salzman Chafetz and Helen Rose Ebaugh, 29–42. Walnut Creek, CA: AltaMira Press, 2000.

Rogers, Mary Beth. *Barbara Jordan: American Hero.* New York: Bantam Books, 1998.

Rose, Chanelle Nyree. *The Struggle for Black Freedom in Miami: Civil Rights and America's Tourists Paradise, 1896–1968.* Baton Rouge: Louisiana State University Press, 2015.

Roseman, Kenneth D. "Six-Tenths of a Percent of Texas." In *Lone Stars of David: The Jews of Texas,* edited by Hollace Ava Weiner and Kenneth Roseman, 204–211. Lebanon, NH: University Press of New England, 2007.

Ross, Benjamin. *Dead End: Suburban Sprawl and the Rebirth of American Urbanism.* Oxford: Oxford University Press, 2014.

Roth, Michael P., Tom Kennedy, and Ray Hunt. *Houston Blue: The Story of the Houston Police Department.* Denton: University of North Texas Press, 2012.

Salzman, Gerald. "A History of Zionism in Houston 1897–1975." Master's thesis, University of Houston, 1976.

Salzman, Jack. "Introduction." In *Struggles in the Promised Land: Toward a History of Black-Jewish Relations in the United States,* edited by Jack Salzman and Cornel West, 1–19. New York: Oxford University Press, 1997.

San Miguel, Guadalupe. *Brown, Not White: School Integration and the Chicano Movement in Houston.* College Station: Texas A&M University Press, 2001.

Sarna, Jonathan. *American Jews and Church-State Relations: The Search for "Equal Footing."* New York: Institute of Human Relations of American Jewish Committee, 1989.

———. *American Judaism: A History.* New Haven, CT: Yale University Press, 2004.

———. and Jonathan Golden, "The American Jewish Experience through the Nineteenth Century: Immigration and Acculturation," *National Humanities Center,* 1999, accessed October 20, 2016, http://nationalhumanitiescenter.org/tserve/twenty/tkeyinfo/jewishexp.htm

———. "What's the Use of Local Jewish History?" *Rhode Island Jewish Historical Notes* 12, part B, no. 1 (November, 1995): 77–83.

Sarna, Jonathan, and Nancy H Klein. *The Jews of Cincinnati.* Cincinnati, OH: Center for Study of the American Jewish Experience, 1989.

Savage, Sean. *JFK, LBJ, and the Democratic Party.* Albany: State University of New York Press, 2004.

Savitch, Howard V., and John Clayton Thomas. *Big City Politics in Transition*. Newbury Park, CA: Sage Publications, 1992.

Schneier, Marc, and Martin Luther King III. *Shared Dreams: Martin Luther King. Jr. and The Jewish Community*. Woodstock, VT: Jewish Lights Publishing, 2009.

Schulman, Bruce J. *The Seventies: The Great Shift in American Culture, Society, and Politics*. Boston, MA: Da Capo Press, 2001.

Schwartz, John. "Lee Otis, Free," *Texas Monthly*, August 2002, http://www.texasmonthly.com/articles/lee-otis-free/.

Shabazz, Amicar. "Carter Wesley and the Making of Houston's Civic Culture Before the Second Reconstruction." *Houston Review of History and Culture* 1, no. 2 (Summer 2004): 8–13.

Shape Community Center, "S.H.A.P.E. Community Center, Inc. Mission," *SHAPE*, 2017, accessed October 20, 2016, http://www.shape.org/about-us.

Shapiro, Edward S. A Time of Healing: *American Jewry Since World War II*, Vol. 5, Jewish People in America. Baltimore, MD: Johns Hopkins University Press, 1992.

Shattuck, Gardiner H. *Episcopalians and Race Civil War to Civil Rights*. Lexington: University Press of Kentucky, 2015.

Slotboom, Erik. *Houston Freeways: A Historical and Visual Journey*. Cincinnati, OH: Oscar F. Slotboom; printed by C.J Krehbiel, 2003.

SoRelle, James. "The Darker Side of 'Heaven': The Black Community in Houston, Texas, 1917–1945." PhD diss., Kent State University, 1980.

SoRelle, James. "The Emergence of Black Business in Houston, Texas: A Study of Race and Ideology, 1919–45." In *Black Dixie: Afro-Texan History and Culture in Houston*, edited by Howard Beeth and Cary D. Wintz, 103–115. College Station: Texas A&M University Press, 1992.

————. "Race Relations in 'Heavenly Houston,' 1919–45." In *Black Dixie: Afro-Texan History and Culture in Houston,* edited by Howard Beeth and Cary D. Wintz, 175–191. College Station: Texas A&M University Press, 1992.

Stanton, Mary. *The Hand of Essau*. Montgomery, AL: River City Publication, 2006.

Staub, Michael. *Torn at The Roots: The Crisis of Jewish Liberalism in Postwar America*. New York: Columbia University Press, 2002.

Steptoe, Tyina. *Houston Bound: Culture and Color in a Jim Crow City*. Oakland: University of California Press, 2016.

Stone, Bryan. *The Chosen Folks: Jews on the Frontiers of Texas*. Austin: University of Texas Press, 2010.

Sundquist, Eric J. *Stranger in the Land: Blacks, Jews, Post-Holocaust America.* Cambridge, MA: Belknap Press of Harvard University Press, 2005.

Swartz, Mimi. "The Louie File." Texas Monthly, October 1985.

Svonkin, Stuart. *Jews Against Prejudice: American Jews and the Fight for Civil Liberties.* New York: Columbia University Press, 1997.

Takaki, Ronald T. *A Different Mirror: A History of Multicultural America.* New York: Back Bay Books/Little, Brown, and Co., 2008.

"Taylor, Hobart T. Sr." In *Encyclopedia of African American Business History*, edited by Juliet E.K. Walker, 555–556. Westport, CT: Greenwood Publishing Group, 1999.

Tehranian, John. "Compulsory Whiteness: Towards a Middle Eastern Legal Scholarship." *Indiana Law Journal* 82, no. 1: 2–47.

"Texas Redistricting." Texas Legislative Council, accessed October 30, 2016, https://tlc.texas.gov/redist/history/overview.html.

"The Men Who Would Be Mayor," *Texas Monthly,* October 1975.

Theoharis, Jeanne. "'Alabama on Avalon,' Rethinking the Watts Uprising and the Character of Black Protest in Los Angeles." In *The Black Power Movement: Rethinking the Civil Rights-Black Power Era*, edited by Peniel E. Joseph, 27–54. London: Routledge, 2006.

The Eugenics Crusade: What's Wrong with Perfect? Directed by Michelle Ferrari. 2018. Arlington, VA: PBS. DVD.

The City of Houston, "Emancipation Park," *The City of Houston Official Site for Houston, Texas*, accessed October 20, 2016, http://www.houstontx.gov/parks/parksites/emancipationpark.html.

The City of Houston, *Landmark Designation Report*, by Planning and Development Department, Houston, T.X.: 11L252, Archeological and Historical Commission, July 14, 2011, accessed August 25, 2016. http://www.houstontx.gov/planning/HistoricPres/HAHC_20110817/IId_3602_S_Mac_Gregor_Way_Hill-Perry_House.pdf.

Thompson, Laurence C. "Melville Jacob, 1902–1971." *American Anthropologist* 80, no. 3. (1978): 640–649.

Thurman, Howard. *Footprints of Dream: The Story of the Church for the Fellowship of All Peoples.* Eugene, OR: Wipft & Stock, 2009.

Tigay, Alan M., ed. *The Jewish Traveler: Hadassah Magazine's Guide to the World's Jewish Communities and Sights.* Garden City, NY: Doubleday, 1987.

Tobin, Gary A. *Jewish Perceptions of Anti-Semitism.* New York: Plenum Press, 1998.

"Tribute to Jenard and Gail Gross and Jewish Women International." *Capitol Words*, May 2, 2000, accessed August 12, 2016, http://capitolwords.org/date/2000/05/02/H2379-2_tribute-to-jenard-and-gross-and-in-jewish-women-/.

Tyson, Timothy B. *Radio Free Dixie: Robert Williams & Roots of Black Power.* Chapel Hill: University of North Carolina Press, 1999.

Urofsky, Melvin I. *A Voice That Spoke for Justice: The Life and Times of Stephen S. Wise.* Albany: State University of New York Press, 1982.

Vine, Katy. "The Agitator," *Texas Monthly,* August 2015.

Von Der Mehden, Fred R., ed. *The Ethnic Groups of Houston.* Houston: Rice University Studies, 1984.

Wagner, Jacob N. "The Legacy of Leland," *Houston History*, March 26, 2015.

Wardlaw, Alvia J. "John and Dominique de Menil and the Houston Civil Rights Movement." In *Art and Activism: Projects of John and Dominique de Menil*, edited by John Helfenstein and Laureen Schipsi, 103–113. New Haven, CT: Yale University Press, 2010.

Waskow, Arthur. "Original 1969 Freedom Seder," *The Shalom Center*, June 24, 2005, http://theshalomcenter.org/content/original-1969-freedom-seder.

Watson, Dwight. *Race and the Houston Police Department: 1930–1990: A Change Did Come.* College Station: Texas A&M University Press, 2005.

Webb, Clive. "A Tangled Web: Black-Jewish Relations in the Twentieth-Century South." In *Jewish Roots in Southern Soil: A New History*, edited by Marcie Cohen Ferris and Mark I. Greenberg, 192–209. Waltham, MA: Brandeis University Press, 2006.

————. "Closing Ranks: Montgomery Jews and Civil Rights, 1954–1960." In *Dixie Diaspora: An Anthology of Southern Jewish History*, edited by Mark K. Bauman, 331–350. Tuscaloosa: University of Alabama Press, 2006.

————. *Fight against Fear: Southern Jews and Black Civil Rights.* Athens: University of Georgia Press, 2001.

Weiner, Hollace Ava. *Jewish Stars in Texas: Rabbis and Their Works.* College Station: Texas A&M University Press, 1999.

Weisbord, Robert, and Arthur Stein. *Bittersweet Encounter: The Afro-American and the American Jew.* Westport, CT: Negro Universities Press, 1970.

Weisbord, Robert G., and Richard Kazarian. *Israel in the Black American Perspective.* Westport, CT: Greenwood Press, 1985.

Welcome to Truthhouston.org! TRUTH: Traveling Revealing Understanding Truth-Hope, accessed August 30, 2016, http://truthhouston.org/default.html.

Welling, David., and Jack Valenti. *Cinema Houston: From Nickelodeon to Megaplex.* Austin: University of Texas Press, 2011.

West, Richard. "Only the Strong Survive," *Texas Monthly,* February 1979, October 20, 2016.

White House. "One America-Mickey Leland Kibbutzim Internship Foundation, Mickey Leland KibbutzimInternship Foundation," accessed August 30, 2016, http://clinto4.nara.gov/Initiatives/OneAmerica/Practices/pp_19980804.4120.html.

Whitsitt, Carolyn Elizabeth. "Caught in the Crossfire: Public Housing and Race in Houston." Master's thesis, Stephen Austin University, 2011.

Wilson, Charles Reagan, ed., *Religion in the South: Essays.* Jackson: University Press of Mississippi, 1985.

Wilson, Ezell. "Third Ward, Steeped in Tradition of Self-Reliance and Achievement," *Houston History,* April 18, 2011, vol. 8, no. 2, pp. 31–35.

Wilson, Steven Harmon. *The Rise of Judicial Management in the U.S. District, Southern District of Texas, 1955–2000.* Athens: University of Georgia Press, 2002.

Windmueller, Steven. "The Jewish Contract with America." In *American Politics and the Jewish Community: The Jewish Role in American Life: An Annual Review of the Casden Institute for the Study of the Jewish Role in American Life,* edited by Bruce Zuckerman, Dan Schnur, and Lisa Ansell, 3–37. West Lafayette, IN: Purdue University Press, 2013.

Winegarten, Ruthe, Cathy Schechter, and Jimmy Kessler. *Deep in the Heart: The Lives and Legends of Texas Jews: A Photographic History.* Austin, TX: Eakin Press, 1990.

Wintz, Cary. "Blacks." In *The Ethnic Groups of Houston,* edited by Fred R. Von Der Mehden, 11–40. Houston: Rice University Studies, 1984.

Wood, Roger. *Down in Houston: Bayou City Blues.* Austin: University of Texas Press, 2003.

Woods, Jeff. *Black Struggle, Red Scare: Segregation and Anti-Communism in the South, 1948–1968.* Baton Rouge: Louisiana State University, 2004.

Zumoff, J.A. "The American Community Party and the 'Negro Question' from the Founding of the Party of the Fourth Congress of the Communist International." *Journal for the Study of Radicalism* 6, no. 2. (Fall 2012): 53–89.

Index

A

B

C

Fineberg, Solomon A., 78
Foner, Eric, 11, 298
Ford, James W., 43
Forster, Arnold, 80, 316
Freedman, Theodore, 112, 118, 191–192, 239, 249, 321
Freedmen's Town, 25
Freedom Seder, 261, 364, 405
Friends of SNCC, 235

G

Gentile, 9, 11–14, 20, 22, 24–25, 28, 38–39, 41–43, 49, 51, 53, 56–57, 63,
68–69, 71, 73, 75, 78–79, 89, 100, 103, 107, 118, 126, 128–130,
132–135, 142–143, 145–146, 149–150, 155, 157–159, 167, 169,
173, 175, 177, 188–189, 197, 206, 227–228, 230–231, 246, 258,
262–263, 285, 289–290, 313, 342, 354, 388
Gideon Bible, 201, 222
Goldberg, Edgar, 30
Graves, Curtis, 179, 247, 265, 365, 367, 380

H

Hadassah Magazine, 260, 288, 298, 373, 397, 404
Hampton, Carl, 255
Hannah, Mack, 165, 176
Hannay, Allen B., 226
Harris County Council of Organizations, 83, 104, 119, 182, 200, 220, 317, 321
Hebrew Immigrant Aid Society, 28
Henke & Pillot, 160, 175, 178
Hero, Alfred, 7
Holocaust Museum Houston, 2, 294
Hopkins, Lightin', 135, 162, 329, 360, 394, 403
House Committee on Un-American Activities, 46, 98
Houston Riot of 1917, 29, 303, 399
Houston School Board (HISD), 48, 95–96, 110, 113, 119, 195, 199, 202, 214,
244–245, 290, 309–310, 319, 389
Humanitarian Hour, 87, 318
Humble Oil, 252–253

I

In Re Ahmed Hassan, 67
Independent Jewish Press Service, 62, 312
Isserman, Fred, 62, 313

J

Jaworski, Leon, 182

Jeppesen Stadium, 185

Jewish Community Council of Metropolitan Houston, 10, 263, 298, 307, 310–311, 314, 327, 365, 386, 388

Jewish Community Relations Council (JCRC), 41, 47, 49, 56, 77, 84, 119, 185, 201, 208, 231, 250, 263, 268, 270, 314, 326

Jewish Herald-Voice (*JH-V*), 7–9, 14, 30, 60, 69, 75, 77–79, 82, 85, 90, 94–96, 104, 110, 120, 123–125, 129, 149, 163, 185, 190, 192, 206, 210, 213, 219, 239, 244, 247–249, 253, 267–268, 270–272, 275–277, 279, 281, 287, 294, 298, 301, 312, 314–320, 323–329, 332, 334–335, 337, 339–341, 345–353, 355, 358, 360–361, 365, 367–371, 384

Jewish Telegraphic Agency (JTA), 124; *JTA*, 124, 195, 239, 317, 327, 334, 346, 349, 359–360, 365, 367–370, 372, 374, 384

Jordan, Barbara, 7, 220, 256, 258–259, 265, 276–277, 288, 291, 317, 321, 357, 366–368, 373, 378, 391, 402

Johnson-Reed Act, 52–53, 67

Joske's, 178

Judge Roy Hofheinz, 104, 234

Judson W. Robinson, Jr. Community Center, 151

K

Kahn, Rabbi Robert, 8, 13, 56, 74, 87, 89, 100, 104, 115, 131, 138, 169, 188, 251, 321, 350, 352–353, 355, 368, 376

Kammen, Carol, 15, 299

Karff, Rabbi Samuel 230, 257–258, 293, 363, 374, 382

Kohler, Kaufmann, 55

Kollek,Teddy, 277

Kress, 167, 178, 184

Krochmal, Max, 21, 300

Kristallnacht, 56

L

Lawson, Reverend William, 120, 145, 220, 293

Leland, Mickey, 6, 14–15, 256, 258–259, 273, 277–281, 283–284, 286–288, 291–292, 294, 368–373, 377, 389, 392–394, 406

Leo Baeck School, 278

Lipscomb, Mance, 135

Loan Corporation, 35